D1333172

William Beckford

Other books by the author

Palladian Bridges
Cheltenham Betrayed
Elizabethan and Jacobean Style
Bristol: Last Age of the Merchant Princes
To Build the Second City: Architects and Craftsmen of Georgian
Bristol
Horace Walpole – The Great Outsider

Co-written with Adam Fergusson

The Sack of Bath and After

Co-written with Brian Earnshaw

John Wood: Architect of Obsession
Trumpet at a Distant Gate: The Lodge as Prelude to the Country
House
Architecture Without Kings: The rise of puritan classicism under
Cromwell

William Beckford

COMPOSING FOR MOZART

Timothy Mowl

John Murray
Albemarle Street, London

For Steven Parissien

Contents

Illustrations

Illustrations

The author and publishers would like to thank the following for their kind permission to reproduce illustrations:

Plate 1, The Worshipful Company of Ironmongers, London; 2, National Gallery of Art, Washington DC; 3 and 27, Wiltshire Archaeological & Natural History Society, Devizes Museum; 4, The Antique Fireplace Warehouse; 5, 6 and 7, The Hon. Alastair Morrison; 8, 11, 22, 23, 24, 25, 29, 30 and 31, Bristol University, Special Collections; 9, Private Collection: photograph Courtauld Institute of Art; 10, Board of Trustees of the National Museums and Galleries of Merseyside, Lady Lever Art Gallery, Port Sunlight; 19, The Royal Collection, Her Majesty The Queen; 20, City of Salford Art Gallery; 21, Bolton Museum and Art Gallery; 26, Partridge Fine Arts; 28, Victoria Art Gallery, Bath & North East Somerset Council. Plates 12, 13, 14, 15, 16, 17 and 18 are from the collection of the author.

Acknowledgements

It is to Helen Langley and Colin Harris, of the Modern Papers Reading Room, Department of Special Collections and Western Manuscripts at the Bodleian Library, Oxford, that I owe my first thanks. They answered my queries with courteous efficiency and allowed me to work with Dott. Laura Nuvoloni who translated Beckford's letters to his confidant Gregorio Franchi. Quotations from the Beckford Papers are made with the permission of the Bodleian Library, University of Oxford.

The Hon. Alastair Morrison gave me a fascinating and quite invaluable morning tramping around every grotto, cavern and garden building of the park at Fonthill. He tended to confirm my suspicion, later proved by documents, that all the surviving features on the east side of the lake were created by the Alderman, not his son.

The members of the international Beckford Society have shown a keen interest in the research, and I should like to make particular mention of Sidney Blackmore, Philip Hewat-Jaboor, Malcolm Jack and Jerry Nolan, who have been especially helpful and encouraging; the Society plans to hold a major Beckford exhibition in New York, probably in the autumn of 2000. Dr David Watkin has been a constant inspiration through his many writings on the Regency period.

Michael Briggs, Gillian Sladen, Lisa White, Vicky Harmer, Philippa Bishop, Sophie Scruton and Jesca Verdon-Smith of the Bath Preservation Trust and the Beckford Tower Trust have been very helpful over the Lansdown Tower, for which an appeal has been launched to restore the building and to reinstate some of Beckford's original interiors.

My thanks also to Michael Liversidge at Bristol University, for his insights into Beckford's connoisseurship, and to Michael Richardson and Nick Lee of the University Special Collections, who have made

Acknowledgements

every printed Beckford resource readily available. A former Bristol student, Adrian Craft, wrote a stimulating undergraduate thesis on the landscape at Fonthill which I had the pleasure of marking.

Pamela Colman was an enthusiastic guide to the Beckfordiana in her archive at Devizes Museum and Cedric Delforce was most helpful over William Courtenay and the Powderham background. Trevor Fawcett translated Beckford's idiosyncratic Portuguese for me, and discovered the important account of the 1797 fête at Fonthill in the *Bath Journal.*

There are many friends, scholars, curators and owners who have helped me over the past two years, but I should like particularly to mention the following: Brian Allen, Bruce A. Bailey, Reg and Maureen Barton, Geoffrey Beard, Anthony Beeson, Lord Courtenay, Luke Gasparo, Michael Hall, Edward Harley, John Harris, John Head, Jarl Kremeier, Alistair Laing, Haydn Mason, Robert Morris, Lucy Morton, Francesca Odell, James Oliver, Frank Partridge, John Phibbs, Martin Postle, Alexandre Pradère, Dorothy Presswell, Judy Sandling, Julian Self, Robin Simon, Susan Sloman, Nancy Stanfield, Patrick Taylor, Lucy Whetstone, Robert Wilson-North, Sarah Wimbush, Christopher Woodward.

Gordon Kelsey was meticulous in preparing many of the photographs for the book, and Douglas Matthews has compiled an exhaustive and illuminating index.

I have had the benefit of an enthusiastic and committed team at my publishers, John Murray, who have seen the book through to publication with calm assurance. I should like to thank Caroline Knox, Grant McIntyre and Gail Pirkis for shaping the typescript, and John R. Murray and Stephanie Allen for their vibrant promotion of the book. My agent, Sara Menguc, has always been a sympathetic mover behind the scenes.

I should like to thank my friend and usual co-author, Brian Earnshaw, for his help with many aspects of the research and for his constructive criticism at editing stage. Finally I must thank my wife, Sarah, for her constant support and encouragement as Beckford's character became at times unbearable, and computers contrived to frustrate me.

TIMOTHY MOWL, *Autumn 1997*

The price of a Romantic sensibility

There are two major traps in William Beckford studies. The first is unavoidable because Beckford prepared it himself: he forged his own life. He was a fluent and seductive liar who had ample funds to pay secretaries to rewrite letters, and ample time in an eighty-four-year life span to reconstruct the past. All his seven biographers have been aware of Beckford's unreliability; some have glossed over it. Many of the most revealing of his letters, often those through which whole sectors of his life have been interpreted, are not letters in the ordinary sense at all: they are revisions written in a secretary's hand, and their dates are uncertain. A large number may never have been sent in any form to their addressees; often, as in the case of several important letters supposedly to Alexander Cozens, Beckford's early guru, it is only speculation that it was to Cozens they were addressed, as they are fair copies in a secretary's hand with no name attached.

Hardly any sources are reliable. If we compare Beckford's two accounts, his *Journal* and his *Sketches*, of the year he spent in Spain and Portugal in 1787–8, they contradict each other on almost every page and clearly contain thumping if highly readable and enjoyable inventions – or, to return to the harsh fact, lies. One absolute staple of the whole Beckford legend is his enchanting account of the delayed celebrations for his twenty-first birthday held at Fonthill over Christmas 1781 – youth gathered together with lights, music, and vaguely forbidden pleasures. But we depend entirely on the description which Beckford wrote of it at some time in the 1830s – an old man's reminiscences fifty years later; and, as I point out in the

Portugal chapters, an account he wrote in 1787 of an evening party in Lisbon sounds suspiciously similar to the Fonthill revelry, with the same tone of quivering rapture, even the same light effects. At this point the ground shakes again under a biographer's feet: was the Lisbon passage itself written in 1787, or was it carefully revised years later? Certainly there were revisions from the original brief notes, but how soon after the events? Might both the Fonthill and the Lisbon passages be an ingenious old liar's roughly contemporaneous revisions? The earth gapes as wide as that crevice which swallowed up fifty children as a sacrifice to an evil Giaour in Beckford's Arabian novel *Vathek*. But then, those children did not really die: at the end of the book it is revealed that an angel magicked them all off to Paradise. So what, when Beckford is writing or speaking, can be believed? The answer must be: very little, as an absolute certainty; but something, if the texts are approached with positive caution.

The second trap is the one which biographers create for themselves: the 'if only' syndrome. No biographer has been able to resist this: Cyrus Redding in 1859, Lewis Melville in 1910, J.W. Oliver in 1932, Guy Chapman in 1937, H.A.N. Brockman in 1956, Boyd Alexander in 1962 and, most recently, Brian Fothergill in 1979 have all, to some degree or another, tried to air-brush over Beckford's sexual identity, to ignore, underplay or deplore his sexual love for young males. Redding, a journalist who knew Beckford personally and could be described as the authorised biographer, ignored his sexuality completely, a very Victorian response. Melville, the Edwardian, did the same but compensated by giving Beckford's relations with Louisa, the wife of his first cousin, good measure. Biographers writing after the 1914–18 war, when the unmentionable could be mentioned but was still morally unspeakable, were in more of a predicament. Chapman printed letters which proved a sexual involvement, but then drew back in desperate moral revulsion and insisted that Beckford's relations with 'Kitty' Courtenay of Powderham Castle were only 'sentimental sodomy'. In a final absurdity he declared that 'Beckford's life is completely sexless and it may be suggested that he was sexually rather subnormal than abnormal'. Yet during their brief marriage Beckford's wife bore him two daughters and suffered a miscarriage and a still-birth, all in the space of four years. Oliver had the same access as Chapman to his subject's letters, but drew the same mysterious veil over Beckford's 'sodomitical' associations.

In the more open post-1945 climate of opinion, Brockman, Boyd Alexander and Brian Fothergill had less excuse. Brockman, himself an architect, was more interested in Beckford's building ventures than his sexual predilections. In his two books on Beckford, Boyd Alexander made it clear that Beckford was in active pursuit of adolescents for most of his life, yet concluded, bewilderingly, that he 'wrote obsessively about sex because he was repressed and possibly impotent': anything, in fact, except actual fun in bed. Fothergill was the biographer Beckford would have most disliked, as he gives every sign of disliking Beckford, describing him as 'hysterical', 'insensitive', influenced by 'bizarre and aberrant tastes' and of a 'feminine nature'; when he was young he had a 'wayward, capricious and already at times morbid imagination', later he was distorted by 'a vicious mole of nature' and was guilty of 'complete selfishness' and the 'lack of any genuinely deep feelings'.

Far and away the most sensitive and satisfying study of Beckford was not a full-length biography but James Lees-Milne's short, lavishly illustrated *William Beckford*, published in 1976. Written with a detached, almost cynical sympathy for its subject, it avoided all the evasions and the confused moral reservations of earlier biographies.

A young American researcher, John Farrell, writing his D. Phil. thesis on Beckford in 1984, pointed out this long record of concealment and hypocrisy and then, in what I am tempted to describe as a typical late-twentieth-century determination that it should 'all hang out', demanded an analysis of Beckford which gave full and frank recognition of his homosexuality.

Here I have to insist upon the obvious: Beckford was not a homosexual, he was a confident, active, self-aware bisexual, and that is a much richer and more confusing condition. He had an emotional range which English society was not prepared to tolerate, as a result of which he faced moral choices, at first with a bewildered innocence, later with arrogant resentment. His importance stems from the fact that he channelled that resentment creatively, writing *Vathek* and his *Journal* and building Fonthill Abbey, his extraordinary mock-Gothic house in Wiltshire. As a man of enormous wealth in moral isolation, Beckford was directly confronted by huge possibilities, upon some of which he acted. This explains our continuing interest in his life long after his death, when in conventional terms of appraisal he appears to be remarkable only for that one short early novel, some letters of travel, and an Abbey which collapsed after a mere twenty-seven years.

Vathek is, however, a book of unique oddity. It may be short – a fast reader will absorb it in two or three hours – but moves from a light-hearted, elegant Arabian pastiche to a vision of Hell and eternity which makes Milton's equivalent descriptive passages seem to evoke no more than a scorched version of Vanbrugh's Blenheim Palace. John Keats is always praised for his 'negative capability', an unhelpful phrase intended to convey his ability to identify with the life of other living creatures. Beckford, writing thirty years before Keats, achieved in *Vathek* a moral 'negative capability' towards absolute evil and absolute good by adopting a stance of absolute neutrality to both extremes, contrived within a framework not of the Christian world but of an alien Mohammedan environment where, paradoxically, the values of Calvinistic Christianity were faithfully preserved. The most vicious behaviour is allowed to glitter engagingly in *Vathek* – mass murders are passed off as amusing trivia, the Devil is handsome and has good taste – yet the conclusion is an absolute and convincing condemnation of selfish folly. A monstrous personality like Carathis, the mother of Vathek, is allowed to indulge her theatrical sense of style until the very last moment, but is then cut down in terrible regret. It leaves the impression of a persuasively moral book which has explored evil with every sympathy. And its author was only twenty-two years old.

As for that short-lived house Beckford built, Fonthill Abbey, it was to have far more stylistic resonance than a contemporary structure, the Prince Regent's Brighton Pavilion, which has survived. Beckford was a pre-Romantic who during the eclipse of his reputation between 1784 and 1800 contrived to embrace Romanticism and then phase naturally into the Victorian, with his Abbey giving the nineteenth century a hefty push into that exhilarating collapse of taste and style which it has taken England another hundred years to absorb. Once the Abbey had become a legend, nothing was impossible; stylistically speaking, no holds were barred. While the Brighton Pavilion was a frivolous plaything, the Abbey was a serious proposal for the way ahead: when its frail tower of wood, stone and compo-cement went up, English historicism was put on the architectural agenda.

Of course Fonthill Abbey was a structural disaster. The temptation when writing about Beckford is to keep inventing ways in which he might have avoided his disasters, when in reality it is the disasters which have made him memorable: his bisexual predicament, his unpredictable aesthetic drive and his wildly eclectic range of taste.

Of course Beckford could have taken his mother's advice and not gone to Powderham Castle in 1784; of course he could have married Donna Henriqueta and settled down to dabble in Portuguese politics, or plant trees at Fonthill. Of course, with his money and his father's example, he could have given his energy to Westminster, and risen to Cabinet rank. If Pitt the Younger had not hated him, perhaps Beckford might have achieved a peace treaty with France in 1797. If he had not been in such desperate haste to raise Fonthill Abbey, its tower might have had proper foundations and the house might have survived to become a National Trust property open to visitors, with teas served in its cloister. But none of these things happened, and because disaster after disaster befell him as a result of his nature, his wealth, his Romantic sensibility and his contemporaries, he became an icon of Romanticism and a sexual and architectural Lucifer. It is wrong and foolish to wish that any of his disasters could have been avoided; they are of his essence and should be appreciated, not sympathetically, for sympathy is not needed, but merely with an open mind, the thought that This is how he was, This is why he is remembered.

My first chapter on 'the formidable and inaccessible Vathek' needs an explanation, if not quite an apology. It is not my original writing, only the result of my editing; consequently, it reads quite unlike subsequent chapters, more like the opening to a light historical novel than to a biographical study. It is taken, exactly in the sequence of its events and word for word where conversations are recorded, from a very slim volume, *Recollections of the Late William Beckford*, published in 1893. The author was a mediocre Bath artist, Henry Venn

Lansdown, who persuaded his way into Beckford's company for a few weeks when the old gentleman was living a ritualised retirement in the complex of two large houses which he had knocked together on a terrace high on Bath's northern hillside.

This book is, despite Beckford's notoriety, the only full first-hand account of what he was like as a person, of his manners and his speech patterns. There are no other revealing memoirs, because Beckford had no talent for friendship, and lust, after a first betrayal, seems never to have led him into love. Whether he avoided people of his own class or whether they avoided him is debatable; but when men like the poet Samuel Rogers did contrive to meet him, they were too absorbed in his building prodigies to offer telling details about his person. Venn Lansdown was the exception. He came consciously to meet and savour a legend. Himself a manipulative man, he was confronted by an arch manipulator, settled down to hero-worship, and took his ultimate brisk dismissal with equanimity. Where witnesses are concerned he was the most impartial, and I have deliberately left him to make the first impression.

CHAPTER ONE

To the formidable and inaccessible Vathek himself

It had taken several months. Henry Goodridge had made excuses, even offered grave warnings as to the kind of reception that might be expected. To a friend Mr Beckford could be 'all gentlemanly frankness and affability'; but Mr Venn Lansdown was not even an acquaintance, and to the world Beckford was 'retiring, reserved, distant, full of hauteur, cynical, impatient'. As a Bath resident, living near the Abbey in the Orange Grove, Venn Lansdown had heard much worse than that. Bath had Beckford marked down as not only its most celebrated citizen, but its most notorious: a sodomite whose workmen had once gone on strike in sturdy British protest against labouring for a 'bugger'. It was reported that he practised cabbalistic ceremonies and the black arts with a colony of ugly dwarves whom he lodged in a gallery-bridge that Mr Goodridge had designed for him. This bridge connected 20 Lansdown Crescent with 1 Lansdown Place West, on the other side of the mews road. When Beckford sold Number 1 he retained the bridge as an extension to Number 20, subsequently buying Number 19 and knocking the two adjacent houses into one. Being immensely rich and self-indulgent, he was said to often sit down to forty dishes at one dinner and to earn, by the labour of slaves on his Jamaica sugar plantations, a guinea a minute, or was it an hour? No one was quite sure, but the degree of his wealth was certainly immoral.

None of this troubled Henry Venn Lansdown. As a married man he could cope with old eccentrics of any moral persuasion. He had been around, travelled in Italy, visited Malta; and, what really mattered, he was an artist: Beckford's patronage of English painters was legendary. So he persisted and Goodridge, who as Beckford's jobbing architect and almost friend had been through it all before, eventually came back with a date and a precise time when this enthusiastic young artist would be given a tour of the Beckford art treasures by William Beckford in person.

Half an hour after twelve noon on 21 August 1838 the two Henrys, Goodridge soberly professional in his dress, Venn Lansdown consciously artistic with a silk cravat, knocked at the door of the Beckford establishment on the highest and most discreetly elegant of the city's several crescents. The new visitor had prepared carefully. He had re-read *Vathek*, and had not only read *Italy; with Sketches of Spain and Portugal*, Beckford's most recent publication, but had memorised a few passages from it to drop appreciatively into the conversation. It would take more than hauteur and cynicism to deflect him from his purpose, which was to charm and impress.

They were shown up to a large room which Venn Lansdown mistook for the library because it was littered with books – but so was every other room in the two houses. It had indeed once been the main library, but was now the ante-room to the flamboyantly draped 'Duchess of Hamilton's State Apartment', the Duchess being Beckford's younger daughter. It was as well that Goodridge had prepared Venn Lansdown for a cold reception, for when their host entered the only welcome they received was from his 'lovely spaniel', Elinor, which ran forward to lick their hands 'in the most affectionate and hospitable manner'. From Beckford himself there was only a curt nod, before he swung into his well-practised tour of the house. This may explain why Venn Lansdown opened his written account of the meeting with a rapturous delineation of 'the magnificent and palatial' scale of the room, its Persian carpets, the eight tall windows with their crimson curtains and the 'immense mirror' set on the end wall of the bridge gallery, but offered not a word of description of the owner himself. However, as an artist Venn Lansdown was curiously uninterested in the human form. He could manage tolerable ink and wash studies of local houses under lowering skies, but his human figures are only tokens, like his awful hump-backed, spindle-legged horses.

To the formidable and inaccessible Vathek himself

If he had troubled to observe his unwelcoming host he would have recorded a small, slender seventy-eight-year-old, very agile and quick moving, as ready to leap over a stool as to step around it. Because all his teeth had fallen out he had an old man's head on that youthful body, the hooked beak of his nose coming very close to his chin, but the small grey eyes were aggressively alert and assessing. He wore his hair short and powdered in the eighteenth-century fashion and his clothes were those of a modest country gentleman, buffs and greens predominating. As he talked he gesticulated freely, but when examining one of his paintings he put both his heavily freckled hands over his mouth as if in self-restraint. The light easy flow of his English was peppered with French phrases, pronounced always in the accent of the old pre-Revolutionary Court.

Now, quick to assert himself in the presence of an artist, Beckford turned to a Rembrandt self-portrait to deliver the shock statement:

> What a glorious fellow the Dutchman was, without grace or beauty. He threw his light like another sun – what strength he had – the very Samson of art! – but his native dykes and dams stagnating all. How unfortunate that the nature he copied partook of his mental constitution – he revelled in Dutch grossness!

Goodridge was silent. He had heard all this before. Registering that here was a shrewd critical intelligence, Venn Lansdown held his fire, agreeing that, while trying to look dignified by holding his head back, Rembrandt had spoilt the effect by the 'sly humour' of his eyes.

When their host moved on to his superb Bronzino of Cosimo de Medici, however, the visitor was ready with a little one-upmanship: 'The works of that master are rare,' he accepted deferentially, 'but a friend of mine, Mr Day, had a noble one at his rooms in Piccadilly, St John in the Wilderness. The conception of the figure and poetical expression of the face always seemed to me astonishingly fine. Pray, Sir, do you know that picture?' Interrupted in mid flight and constitutionally unable to confess ignorance, Beckford was thrown. 'Perfectly,' he snapped back, 'it partakes of the sublime and is amazingly fine.' But before he could get another word in, the visitor had launched into a well-informed discursion on the Medici family's fratricidal and parricidal activities. Trapped into a conventionally banal

9

moral argument, the old gentleman had to admit lamely that 'we have the consolation of knowing that two broods of vipers were destroyed.'

He turned quickly to the next picture, a Titian of the Constable Montmorency, only to have his knowledgeable visitor riposte perfectly with Henri Quatre's *bon mot*, *'Avec un Connétable qui ne sait pas écrire, et un Chancelier qui ne sait pas le Latin, j'ai réussi dans toutes mes entreprises'*, then immediately deflect the discussion to another painting, one by Lawrence not in Beckford's collection at all but apparently relevant to Titian's technique of poetic deception. At that point only two courses were open to Beckford: he could, in one of his famous rages, show this impertinent puppy the door, or he could admit the presence of an art fancier every bit as glib as himself. To his credit he laughed heartily at the Lawrence comparison, and the tour continued as between two equals. Venn Lansdown's next contribution was unfortunate. He commented that a beautiful Velásquez portrait of an unknown man was 'amazingly like Lord Byron'; Beckford, who disliked Byron intensely and with good reason, snapped back, 'But much more handsome.'

Any rogue can talk impressively about paintings, but Venn Lansdown was fluent in that particular nineteenth-century style of art criticism that may seem naïve now but has always the merit of being limpidly accessible to the understanding. He found the *'tout ensemble'* of Benjamin West's portrait of Beckford's mother 'as dry and hard as if painted by a Chinese novice'. As this was no more than the truth, Beckford took it like a lamb. An oil sketch by Veronese had 'great sweetness and juiciness', while the star of the collection, Raphael's *St Catherine*, combined 'all the refined elegance of the Venus de Medici, in form, contour, and flowing lines, with an astonishing delicacy of colour, and masterly yet softened execution'. Delighted to hear such acceptable jargon poured out over one of his treasures, Beckford responded with a joke. Some French visitors had found his Raphael insipid. '"*C'est un assez joli tableau*," say they, "*mais le tête manque de l'expression; si elle avait plus d'esprit, plus de vivacité! Mais Raphael, il n'avait jamais passé les Alpes.*"' '*Le pauvre Raphael*,' his visitor interposed swiftly, '*quel dommage, de ne savoir rien du grand Monarque! ni de la grande nation.*'

To the formidable and inaccessible Vathek himself

There was more laughter. Nothing draws the English closer together than jokes about the French (unless it is jokes about the Germans). The atmosphere became so genial that when Venn Lansdown offered the opinion that the English artist Stotherd was Raphael's equal, Beckford, who had patronised Stotherd at Fonthill, agreed readily. Indeed, a feature of the remainder of the tour was the time the two men spent discussing British painters, contemporaries for the most part, though they were surrounded by European Old Masters. Howard's representation of *The Planets* was, they agreed, 'a wonderful picture', Martin, Danby and Turner were all much praised in their absence, while 'some of the rarest specimens by G. Poussin, Wouvermans, Berghem, Van Huysum, Polemberg, and others' were passed without comment, though all actually hanging on the walls. Beckford did not show any of the three Turners he had retained from the original six of Fonthill because they were 'too poetical, too ideal … Turner took such liberties with it that he entirely destroyed the portraiture, the locality of the spot.'

Venn Lansdown had heard that the architect John Buonarotti Papworth was considering a project to rebuild the Abbey. Beckford dismissed the idea as impossible, 'unless it were to be made a national affair'. But the mention of Fonthill seemed to stir his conscience – or perhaps he saw a way of getting back at Goodridge, who had upset him as they were climbing the stairs by mention of a new book which claimed that his father, Alderman Beckford, had never really made the celebrated speech to George III on which his political reputation largely rested. 'I assure you I had no idea of parting with Fonthill,' he insisted, 'till Farquhar made me the offer. I wished to purge it … but as to the building itself I had no more notion of selling it than you have (turning to his architect) of parting with anything, with' – at that point he paused slyly for effect, and Venn Lansdown faithfully registered the pause in his written account by a dash – 'with the clothes you have on.'

Given Beckford's reputation, it was an uneasy moment. Back in 1817, when Fonthill was still a closed and guarded estate, work on the Abbey was proceeding at a hectic pace. Was Henry Goodridge, son of a Bath builder and then only only a twenty-year-old apprentice, allowed to make a water-colour of the unfinished Abbey? One of his sketches of this period is of a pinnacled Gothic mansion. Beckford admitted freely to his biographer Cyrus Redding: 'I like to be among workmen. I never had less than one hundred employed at Fonthill. Sometimes I had three hundred.' He also bathed regularly each morning in Bitham Lake, just below the Abbey. Was that when he first met the talented young draughtsman–labourer? Did he find him reluctant to strip off and join him in the water, but still encourage his skills, even paying for that surprising trip to France which Goodridge is known to have made before 1818? It would explain why, when Beckford settled in Bath in 1822, he immediately chose Goodridge, a young and virtually untried architect, to join with him in designing Beckford's Tower up on Lansdown, one of the most innovative and remarkable structures of its time.

Without further comment the trio turned to study a precious Japanese vase protected under a glass dome. There followed an incident which William Hazlitt would have relished. In the *London Magazine* of 1823 the journalist had published an attack on Beckford's collecting mania, scornfully dismissing his celebrated art objects as 'nothing more than obtrusive proofs of the wealth of the immediate possessor', deployed 'to excite the wondering curiosity of the stranger, who is permitted to see (as a choice privilege and favour), even to touch, baubles so dazzling and of such exquisite nicety of execution that, if broken or defaced, would be next to impossible to replace.' That was precisely what Beckford, having embarrassed Goodridge, proceeded to do with this new 'stranger'. Taking off the glass dome, he desired Venn Lansdown to carry the vase to the window for closer study. 'I really am afraid to touch it,' he protested, but Beckford 'forced it into my hands.' On this occasion nothing was 'broken or defaced'. What had looked heavy 'proved as light as a feather', but Venn Lansdown was clearly excited by the enforced 'choice privilege'.

As the tour proceeded the visitor, impressed despite himself, went out of his way to flatter the 'Master' about his decorative devices and demonstrate an admiring familiarity with his published works. Noticing in the hall of number 19 'a singular and harmonious light ... produced by crimson silks strained over the fanlight of the outer door', he declared, 'This place puts me in mind of the Hall of Eblis.'

To the formidable and inaccessible Vathek himself

'You are quite right,' Beckford replied, much gratified, 'this is unquestionably the Hall of Eblis. Then you have read "Vathek". How do you like it?' 'Vastly,' declared Venn Lansdown. 'I read it in English many years ago, but never in French.' That was not a perfectly tactful response. The English version had in fact been written by the Revd Samuel Henley, Beckford having been too airily refined to translate his original French version into his native language. 'Then read it in French,' he urged sharply. 'The French edition is much finer than the English.'

To make amends for this error Venn Lansdown, on being shown a Gaspar de Crayer of Philip II of Spain, 'almost involuntarily ejaculated "Pale slave of Eblis",' claiming disingenuously that 'Just then my head was too full of the Hall of Eblis, of "Vathek" and its associations, for mere ordinary admiration of even one of the finest portraits painted.' He ingratiated himself with his host even further in the new drawing room suites which Beckford had recently created in the union of the two adjacent houses. Seeing 'the magnificent effect produced by a scarlet drapery, whose ample folds covered the whole side of the room opposite the three windows from the ceiling to the floor,' he quoted from Beckford's *Sketches* his very words on 'the powers of drapery ... Nothing produces so grand and at the same time so comfortable an effect.' He continued, 'I was never so convinced of the truth of your observations as at the present moment. What a charming and comfortable effect does that splendid drapery produce!' Beckford accepted the compliment graciously, only remarking that the drapery was 'nothing to what I had at Fonthill in the great octagon. There were purple curtains fifty feet long.'

In the same room was a silver-gilt lamp that had hung in the Oratory of St Anthony at Fonthill Abbey. Its shape and proportions were very elegant, 'and no wonder,' the by now uninhibitedly oleaginous Venn Lansdown added, 'it was designed by the author of "Italy" himself.' Mercifully the tour was nearing its close, reaching a climax with a Greek vase ten inches high carved from a single block of chalcedonian onyx which revealed more of Beckford's collecting spirit than perhaps anything else in the house. Its attraction for him was 'the number of diamonds it must have taken to make any impression on such a hard substance' and the fact that, as a perfect collector's conjuring trick, like a rabbit from a hat he could produce an engraving from a drawing which the great Rubens had made of that self-same vase when it was in pawn two hundred years earlier.

The two visitors hoped they had not outstayed their welcome, and were told that it was a pleasure to show the collections to those who really appreciated them, 'for I assure you,' Beckford added, 'I find very few who do.' Learning that Venn Lansdown had not visited the Tower, he insisted, 'Then you must come up again.' Goodridge was favoured with a handshake, Venn Lansdown only with a bow. The tour had, after all, taken on at times the nature of an intellectual battle. But then, as if recalling the recent shower of compliments, Beckford, 'stepping back, held out his hand in the kindest manner, repeating the words "Come up again". We found we had spent three hours in his company.' Even at the age of seventy-eight Beckford, aided by wealth, possessions, a ruthless confidence in his own judgement and a threatening charm, had been able to recruit a new admirer. After those three hours of crimson half-light Venn Lansdown was avid to see the Tower, 'that extraordinary structure, but still more to see again the wonderful individual to whom it belonged.'

In the event, the trip a few weeks later to the Tower was a disappointment. Once more in Goodridge's company, Venn Lansdown was left in an ante-room of number 20 crammed with golden vessels, then shown up the newly planted nature trail to the Tower by a servant. Beckford, accompanied by his old gardener Vincent, met them outside the Tower and pointed out a few choice trees and shrubs which Vincent had persuaded to grow on that windswept hilltop, but he did not accompany them on their tour inside the building. Clouds had dimmed the sun, the views were less than perfect, but the plate glass in the windows was considered a prodigy, and to be admired there was, as always, a great vase of flowers, picked and arranged by the Master.

More impressive than any of the Tower's treasures was the sight of Mr Beckford leaving in mid morning to ride down to Lansdown Crescent for his breakfast 'with two servants standing respectfully and uncovered at the door, whilst two more held the horses'. Venn Lansdown wound himself up for what he appears at the time to have believed would be a last glimpse of his new hero. The scene, 'whilst this extraordinary man mounted his horse', had 'a poetical feeling'; he was 'reminded most forcibly of similar scenes in Scott's novels. In particular the ancient Tower of Tillietudleni was presented to my mind's eye.' He had a 'melancholy foreboding' that this would be a last glimpse and experienced 'an elevation of feeling ... impossible to describe'. Such moments, he insisted, 'are worth whole years of everyday existence'. Lost for words, he quoted lines of Petrarch taken from Beckford's *Sketches*:

> *O ora, o giorno, o ultimo momento,*
> *O stelle conjurate ad impoverime.*

Despite this turgid farewell Venn Lansdown was soon back at the Tower, obviously hoping for a chance encounter. None occurred, and once again it was the colour symphonies of the rooms that impressed him, rather than the collections. He noticed reverently that 'the walls are covered with scarlet cloth; the curtains on each side of the window being a deep purple produce a striking contrast; the colouring of the ceiling, crimson, purple and gold, is admirable.' In that rich, outrageously confident evocation of Eblis, Venn Lansdown was hailing and enjoying an anticipation of the visuals of Victorian interior decoration, a foreshadowing of countless rooms of heavily bright paint and Turkey carpeting.

Over the next month the would-be acolyte did manage to contrive four more meetings with the great man, and on each occasion Beckford went shamelessly to work creating his own image by a mixture of lies, half-lies and name-dropping. He knew, for instance, that a large section of a Michelangelo currently for sale had been repainted by Benjamin West, because the American artist had told him so, personally. Lord Byron had been desperate to read Beckford's unpublished 'Episodes of Vathek', calling once with *Vathek* in his pocket and proclaiming it his 'gospel'; Venn Lansdown was even allowed a privileged glimpse of that text. Another Beckford 'triumph' had been to write a book in a French so perfect (he was speaking of *Vathek* again) that for years everyone believed a Frenchman must have been the author; it had in fact been heavily edited and corrected by a Frenchman before publication, but that was not mentioned.

Inevitably, by the third meeting, the Mozart legend had surfaced. 'How poor dear Mozart would be frightened' (moralised Mr Beckford) 'could he hear some of our modern music!' The usual story followed. Mozart had been eight, Beckford only six: 'it was rather ludicrous one child being the pupil of another'. That, however, was what had happened, and then Mozart went to Vienna, obtained 'vast celebrity', but still had the generosity to write to Beckford, saying: 'Do you remember that march you composed which I kept so long? Well, I have just composed a new opera and I have introduced your air.' The opera was the *Nozze di Figaro*. 'Is it possible, sir!' exclaimed Venn Lansdown. 'And which then is your air?' 'You shall hear it,' Beckford replied eagerly. Then, as so often before in a long lifetime, he sat down to the piano and sang, in his high, almost castrato tenor, to a captive audience. The piano was one of a pair – the two largest ever made, or so Beckford claimed. The air was '*Non piu andrai*'. It was not only one of Mozart's most celebrated but also, and this was Beckford's cleverness, one which, with its simple repetitive marching step, could just conceivably have been composed, in its basic notes, by a very precocious six-year-old. Even now, while few believe the story, no one can put hand on heart and confidently swear that Beckford could not possibly have been the original composer. A legend was in projection.

'He struck the notes with energy and force, he sang a few words' and, so his listener reported, 'his eyes sparkled, and his countenance assumed an expression which I had never noticed before.' It could easily have been one of delighted mischief. When Venn Lansdown came to write Beckford's obituary for the *Bath Herald* he stated as a fact that 'many justly admired airs were originally his composition, and improved on by Mozart and other great composers of the time'.

On that penultimate meeting Beckford was in high fantasy-form. He claimed shamelessly that when he was in Portugal, 'I had as much influence and power as if I had been the King'. One lie led naturally to another; the Prince Regent of Portugal had acknowledged him in public as his relation, 'which indeed,' Beckford added, 'I was.' The reality had been an eight-year struggle merely to be presented at the Portuguese Court by a furtive back-door route. But, he continued nonchalantly, 'I had the privilege of an entrance at all times, and could visit the Royal Family in ordinary dress. Of course,' he added, 'on grand occasions I wore Court costume.'

Once launched on this orbit there was no stopping him. In Germany he had been treated as a grandee of the first rank, while his younger daughter was not only Duchess of Hamilton in Great Britain but accepted as 'Duchess de Châtelerault' by the restored Bourbon Kings of France and allowed to sit in the Royal presence when all others stood. To cap his visit and as a reward for his muscular gullibility, Venn Lansdown was permitted to read the first sentences of Beckford's ultimate literary mystery, the 'Episodes of Vathek', and memorise *Mes malheurs, O Caliphe, sont encore plus grands que les vôtres, aussi bien que mes crimes*. Beckford was withholding the 'Episodes' from publication until a thousand pounds was on offer (the money never came). Intoxicated by these confidences, Venn Lansdown deliberately left his umbrella behind as an excuse for a return visit. His friend Goodridge was not optimistic about the success of this device. Mr Beckford's famous fits of fury had been moderating as he grew older, but 'for my part,' Goodridge warned, 'I am always looking out for squalls.'

After a fortnight of hesitation Venn Lansdown went back, found his umbrella exactly where he had left it, and asked the porter to announce his name to the Master. A few minutes later 'the author of "Vathek"' entered 'beaming with good nature and affability'. Sensing the perfect moment, Venn Lansdown proposed the tactless and ill-conceived scheme that had been at the back of his mind throughout their meetings: would Beckford come to his house, he asked, as it would give him 'the greatest possible pleasure' to show him some copies of pictures that were once in Beckford's possession but which he had sold. To suggest that such a fastidious collector might want to view copies of paintings which he had sold because he was tired of them was a crass error of judgement. If Venn Lansdown had made the copies himself it was even worse, as he was a notably third-rate artist. Even so, Beckford let him down gently: 'I shall be delighted to see them,' was his reply, 'but for some days I am rather busy; I will come next week.'

Of course, he never did: this was their last meeting. He turned swiftly to one of his favourite topics, 'the awful state the country is in', to explain that 'one', meaning himself, 'has scarcely time to think about poetry or painting'. With 'our stupid, imbecile Government' permitting assemblies of as many as 150,000 of 'the common people' to agitate and, which was worse, even pray together, there would soon be no security for works of art. 'The ground we stand on is trembling,' he declared, 'and gives signs of an approaching earthquake.'

Poor Venn Lansdown had still not got the message. He ventured to argue that 'whatever political changes might happen, property was perfectly secure'. 'Have you time to go through the rooms with me?' Beckford asked, beginning to steer his visitor towards the front door, and following up more pointedly with, 'But perhaps you are going somewhere?' Venn Lansdown was indeed going somewhere: he was going out, despite a protest that he was 'perfectly disengaged'. Along the landing they walked, past a severe portrait of Alderman Beckford. 'If my father's advice had been taken we should not now be in danger of starvation'. Beckford was in apocalyptic mood as he ushered Venn Lansdown through the library with its concealed doorway. This time there were to be no exchanges of opinion on Old Masters, no handling of Japanese vases. Only one subject still preyed on Beckford's mind. As they paused in the entrance hall he turned to his uninvited guest to report, apropos of nothing except his own abiding obsession: 'I have been to Fonthill since I saw you. I don't think much of what Papworth [the architect] has done there. I rode thirty-eight miles in one day without getting out of the saddle. That was pretty well, eh?'

And that was the last Venn Lansdown ever heard directly from Beckford's own lips: from a man still anxious for admiration and receiving it, a man still deeply concerned over every development in that loved and lost Wiltshire Elysium. The door was closed.

William Beckford died on 2 May 1844, politely refusing the consolations of religion, ordering his favourite dog to be removed from his bedroom where it had always slept and its blanket burnt: a consistent denial of normal human emotional weakness.

If Venn Lansdown attended the funeral – and the majority of

To the formidable and inaccessible Vathek himself

Bath's citizens, some 20,000, did line the streets to see the procession pass – then he left no record of it. Instead, on 28 October in the same year, with an unnamed companion, male and possibly Goodridge, he set off to visit Fonthill in a personal act of homage to the hero who had so firmly rejected him.

They took the Salisbury stage-coach as far as Warminster and walked the remaining twelve miles over the downs, hiring a 'clown-ish bumpkin' to carry their carpet-bag. While they were still nine miles away from Fonthill the 'gigantic remains' of the ruined Abbey, the East Transept, 'a point, pinnacle and round tower', were visible on 'a blue hill of singular form'. At Hindon a new lad took over the carpet-bag and led them through the tunnel under the Terrace to skirt the 'Barrier', a seven-mile wall, pass Fonthill Gifford's 'purely Italian' church and arrive at the Beckford Arms.

There they were shown into 'a lovely parlour that savoured of the refined taste that once reigned in this happy solitude'. In its bow window were stained-glass shields with the arms of Alderman Beckford, his wife and 'their eccentric son'. An hour of hazy autumn sunshine remaining, they determined to penetrate 'the sacred enclosure that once prevented all intrusion to this mysterious solitude'. It is evident that the guarded privacy of Beckford's Fonthill, the seven-mile wall as much as the Abbey itself, is the staple of the gathering Romantic legend, Coleridge's 'Xanadu' in 'twice five miles' of wall, Poe's gloomy 'Domain of Arnheim'. Through a gate and up a steep winding road arched over with trees they came to what was once the 'gem and wonder of the earth'. There, suddenly revealed, with 'oct-angular' turrets a hundred and twenty feet high, arched windows sixty feet high, was the East Transept, never perfectly completed and now roofless 'as Glastonbury Abbey'. 'If you wish for a sight of all that is melancholy, all that is desolate,' Venn Lansdown wrote that evening, 'visit a modern ruin.'

They pressed on through briars and brambles into the great octagon and looked up. Only two sides of it to the north remained standing, two arches and above them two windows of the four 'Nunneries' or guest bedrooms, then higher still two round windows that once lit the domed vault. But 'the noble organ screen, designed by "Vathek" himself' – Beckford's real identity lost within his literary creation – survived, 'its gilded lattices ... yet glitter in the last rays of the setting sun'. The western transept was a mere roofless shell, its thirty-foot doors gaping, but a statue of St Anthony still held out its right hand 'as if to protect the sylvan and mute inhabitants of these groves ... from the cruel gun and still more cruel dog'.

There was time only for a quick tour of the long south wing. In the Brown Parlour, fifty-two feet long, were eight windows each with four gigantic plate-glass lights, painted 'in the midst of red, purple, lilac, and yellow ornaments ... with four elegant figures, designed by the artist Hamilton, of kings and knights, from whom Mr Beckford was descended ... thirty-two figures drawn most correctly'. In this room at least Venn Lansdown's imagination could still work upon a substantial base: 'in this very room dined frequently the magnificent "Vathek" on solid gold, and there, where stood his table, covered with every delicacy to tempt the palate, is now a pool of water, for the roof is insecure, and the rain streams through in torrents'. He could, he believed, still smell 'odiferous perfume' in the Cedar Boudoir next door.

Out in the Fountain Court the marble basin was dry, but Venn Lansdown was in the mood for poetry and quoted, from Byron's *Giaour*, another fountain's music:

> 'Twas sweet of yore to hear it play
> And chase the sultriness of day,
> As springing high the silver dew
> In whirls fantastically flew
> And flung luxurious coolness round
> The air, and verdure o'er the ground.
> 'Twas sweet, when cloudless stars were bright,
> To view the wave of watery light
> And hear its melody by night.

They made their way back through the gloomy wood, or in the writer's Latinate diction 'an umbrageous covert', to the Beckford Arms, anticipating a closer inspection of the half-ruined Abbey in the morning.

Next day they woke to sunshine, breakfasted, and at the Barrier Gate met an old woman, picturesque enough in her dress to have served Gainsborough or Venn Lansdown's old teacher Benjamin Barker as a model. Lansdown decided to quiz her. Did she know Mr Beckford? 'I have seen him, sir, many, many times; but he is gone, and I trust – I do trust – to rest. He was a good man to the poor, never was there a better.' With perhaps a touch of personal feeling, Venn Lansdown expressed astonishment. He had heard that Beckford never gave anything away. But this released a flow of angry defence: 'Who could have invented such lies? There never was a kinder friend to the poor, and when he left they lost a friend indeed … in the winter when snow was on the ground and firing dear, he used to send wagons and wagons for coal to Warminster, and make them cut through the snow to fetch it, and gave the poor souls plenty of firing, besides money, blankets and clothing, too, and as for me,' she continued, 'I can answer for three half-sovereigns he gave me himself at different times with his own hand.' She had met him as she was carrying her baby daughter, 'and I was shuffling along to get out of his way, when he called out, "What a beautiful little babe, let me look at it," and then he smiled and made as though he would shake hands with the child, and bless you, he slipped half-a-sovereign into my hand.'

Venn Lansdown was not only delighted by this anecdote, he was amazed. He confessed that he had expected at Fonthill to hear curses from the peasants, not praise. The image of the demon king was well established in Bath, but the old woman's story lends substance to a claim which Beckford once made to his biographer Cyrus Redding, that his one real regret at leaving Fonthill was that he could no longer protect the poor of the parish. He read books of sermons as well as books of travel, and wrote in one of them: 'The Voice which calls us to look into ourselves and prepare for Judgement is too piercing, too powerful to be resisted; and we attempt, for worldly and sensual considerations, to shut our ears in vain.'

In Bath Beckford never allowed his name to be put down to charitable subscriptions; but this does not mean that he never subscribed, and there are several accounts of him emptying his pockets of gold and silver when he met cripples who were not even attempting to beg. Beckford was Victorian not only in his taste in interior decoration but in his impulses towards charitable giving and his feeling for the duties of the upper class. There was also the story that St Anthony, Beckford's patron saint, once preached on the text 'Where your treasure is, there shall your heart be also', and next day they found an old miser dead with his withered heart locked in his money-box.

After some delay at the stables a key was found for a door into the northern arm of the Abbey, and soon the pilgrims were bounding up the 210 steps of the great circular staircase, a flight six feet broad around a newel three feet in diameter. This brought them out onto the roof leads, with a wide view of hanging woods and luxuriant plantations, the dark waters of the Bittern (or Bitham, originally simply 'Bottom') Lake almost buried among groves of pine and beech. The Beacon Terrace led south to a high hill 'where the Alderman began, but never finished, a triangular tower', and to the west was the mile-long reach of the Western Avenue.

The high point of the visit came in what had been St Anthony's Oratory at the end of the north wing. After King Edward's Gallery, with a ceiling of dark oak 'as fresh as if just painted' and a cornice of three gilded mouldings, came three more compartments with gilded oak roofs but all their carved ornaments vandalised. Only the ceiling of the last apartment still kept its original Beckford splendour: 'It gleams as freshly with purple, scarlet, and gold [the same colour scheme as the Lansdown Tower] as if painted yesterday. Five slender columns expand into and support a gilded reticulation on a dark crimson ground', and there, in the centre of the ceiling, was still dangling a dark crimson cord, severed roughly at the end. Six years earlier at Lansdown Crescent the writer had seen the elegant silver lamp, designed by Beckford himself, which had originally hung from that cord over John Charles Felix Rossi's statue of St Anthony. There could be no closer link with the hand of 'the great "Vathek" himself'.

They made their way back, often precariously balanced on exposed beams over gaping voids, past book recesses empty of books but still furnished with sliding shelves, to a tall door covered in 'a crimson list', a felt border to exclude the draughts that must have beset that cathedral-home. The door yielded to firm pressure and they came out on a balcony of the Octagon. Above them were those windows which had 'once lighted the highest bedrooms in the world', below was the floor of St Michael's Gallery which had once been 'covered in a crimson carpet, thickly strewn with white roses'. Beckford's boast that from the balcony where they now stood had hung draperies fifty feet long was recalled; above them had once soared a dome lit by eight gilded windows.

Venn Lansdown closed the crimson door, 'not without a feeling of sadness'. After a brief exploration of the Lancaster Tower they made for Bitham Lake, 'so buried in wood', then as now, 'that it was not without some difficulty we found it'. Autumn was at its peak of turning leaves. The mirror of the lake reflected not only the trees but the ruined building: 'its lofty towers trembled on the crystal waves as if they were really rocking and about to share the fate of the giant Tower that was once here reflected'. In 1844 the planting of the American Garden, on which Beckford had spent so much care, was reaching a ravaged maturity with 'a labyrinth of exotic plants, a maze of rhododendrons, azaleas and the productions of warmer climes, growing as if indigenous' among native oak, beech and fir. The writer climbed up to a seat and declared that what he had seen and admired so much on Lansdown was here carried to its utmost perfection: 'I mean the representation of a southern wilderness. In this spot the formality of gardening is absolutely lost.'

And there, after a typically Venn Lansdown speculation that beneath the waters of Bitham Lake lay 'the fairy palace of the Naiads, the guardians of this terrestrial Paradise', the narrative ends, abruptly, as if the author could not bear to think about a return walk across the dreary downs with carpet-bag and 'ignorant bumpkin' porter. But the pilgrimage had been made, the first after Beckford's death of many such by questing aesthetes half repelled, half fascinated by the scale of the man's life, the scandals, the wrecked achievements and the carefully woven fabric of lies.

While it may seem perverse to have begun a life of Beckford only six years before his death, Venn Lansdown's preciously pompous narrative serves a purpose. Where this complex and elusive man is concerned there is the problem not only of Beckford himself, but of the Beckford admirers. The reader's mind needs to be fixed on both, as the Beckford cult is rather more impenetrable than Beckford's own nature. He had little of Byron's Romantic charisma and a far smaller literary output, while Portugal was in no need of liberation from the Turks.

Venn Lansdown suggests some of the answers. Beckford has served as a patron saint to the better-class antique dealers of life, those who appreciate provenance and craftsmanship as much as beauty: nineteenth-century Sèvres porcelain, eighteenth-century buhl furniture. He has become an icon for men hovering nervously but knowingly, always very knowingly, on the edge of their own identities. Show the Venn Lansdowns of this world the door and they will admire the gesture. Be arrogant and thoughtless, but stylish, and they will relish every detail of subsequent scandal and fall. But Beckford has a wider, more generous significance. He is everyone who has the sensibility to enjoy a perfect creation but not the genius to achieve it. After *Vathek*, nothing quite worked. Fonthill Abbey, as he was the first to admit, was flawed in composition as well as construction. His parks with garden flowers planted around the roots of native trees were unnatural. The flowers reverted; the briars and nettles invaded after three years. But he kept trying. That was his near-greatness. He was the eager amateur in pursuit of the Sublime. To leave Venn Lansdown in that ruined autumn garden is the way to approach the beginning of Beckford's life – made wary by an understanding of what it was to be like at the end.

CHAPTER TWO

Aesthetic education and a second Emile

When Beckford was a little boy he kept rabbits: the Beckford Papers and source books are crammed with such helpful snippets. Of course he kept rabbits. A man who believed that when he walked in a wood flights of finches gathered near him, drawn by a mysterious affinity, was likely to have kept rabbits, later to have built a seven-mile wall round his park to protect hares, and to have prepared a tasteful tombstone for a favourite black and brown spaniel, not when the dog died, but a full year before the anticipated bereavement. There is a pattern here, and if William Beckford had not endured an intense childhood and isolated adolescence he would never have touched briefly upon creative genius or lived such a remarkable life. The shaping forces of those first twenty-one years are of the greatest interest. The tensions of his life were the usual ones between nature and nurture, between the genes of his excitingly piratical ancestors and life in a heavily landscaped Wiltshire valley with a strict, Methodistical mother and his dead father's subversive library.

There can be no question about the genes. Beckford's great-great-grandfather was a London tradesman who went out to grow sugar in Jamaica shortly after Cromwell snatched the island from the Spaniards. His great-grandfather was a bullying autocrat who became Governor of Jamaica and died of a fall downstairs during a brawl in the Assembly House in which his son, Speaker Peter Beckford, was held down at swords' point in the Speaker's Chair. Speaker Peter survived to own twenty-two plantations and twelve hundred slaves when the island was at the peak of its prosperity, and he had the reputation of being the richest subject of the British Crown. His temper was terrible. He murdered Jamaica's Deputy Judge-Advocate, but escaped the consequences and left his huge fortune to be divided among nine legitimate children. The second eldest son was William, always referred to as 'Alderman' Beckford or 'the Great Alderman'. Sent to Westminster School in England in 1723 when he was fourteen, he moved on to Balliol College, Oxford and inherited money and property not only from his father but from his elder brother Peter, who died in 1737. Prospering mightily by the processing and selling of sugar as well as by producing it, he became an MP in order to safeguard his sugar interests at a time when France and England fought wars every few years to increase their commercial empires. He was thus a natural and valued supporter of the great war minister, Pitt the Elder, Earl of Chatham.

With Alderman Beckford, William's father, the genetic inheritance takes a distinctly Vathek-like, *Arabian Nights* turn. As a young man he fell in love with a pretty Dutch girl, and when his family opposed the marriage, he brought her over to England and settled her in a handsome establishment. Trouble at the plantations called him back to Jamaica for a year, and when he returned to London he found her pregnant by her sixteen-year-old mulatto servant. She was paid off, more in sorrow than anger as he was apparently an affectionate lover, and sent back to Holland. It cannot be claimed that the incident persuaded him to concentrate on politics rather than domesticity, as he subsequently had two other mistresses by whom he fathered seven bastard children: Richard, Barbara, Nathaniel, John, Rose (who was a boy), Thomas and Susannah. He was a good father and left them all well provided for in a complex will which later involved his legal wife in years of costly litigation. Richard, the eldest, was much closer to him than his legitimate son William ever had time to become. Until the Alderman's marriage Richard lived with his father, worked with him in commerce, visited Jamaica, and acquired a knowledge of the Beckford interests which William Beckford would never attain, nor wish to.

The Alderman's town house in Soho Square is long gone, but by a happy chance the London home of his younger brother Richard, only a few doors away at the corner of the Square and Greek Street, survives intact, preserving the decor of the colonial Beckfords and William's earliest years. Outwardly his uncle's house is an austerely geometrical brick box, but the front door opens into a cavernously grand stair and entrance hall occupying almost half the building's cubic space and intended instantly to overawe. Rich but coarsely moulded rococo plasterwork cascades down the side wall above an elegant wrought-iron stair rail. In two of the first-floor rooms the same rough garlands of conventional flowers riot around the ceilings and chimney-pieces while cherubs and blowzy nymphs dance against stylised clouds. The atmosphere of unrefined merchant ostentation is still heavy in the air, suggesting that those Beckford brothers may have been a rather vulgar set.

Even by eighteenth-century standards Alderman Beckford was a forceful character. His fiery speeches often reduced the House of Commons to laughter at his impetuously fragmented grammar delivered in an accent now usually associated with the Notting Hill Carnival. But as a landowner he controlled three pocket boroughs and he was a powerful influence in the City of London, so he was a political force to be feared as well as mocked. In 1745, still unmarried, he bought Fonthill House and some 3,000 acres on the Wiltshire–Dorset border from Francis Cottington, a Jacobite and a Roman Catholic. The house, an enormous lumbering pile of five wings, recently classicized in sub-James Gibbsian manner, needed no additions. But the Alderman had an income that fluctuated between £30,000 and £100,000 a year in ready money, anything from £600,000 to £2,000,000 in current value, varying with the fortunes of war and the accidents of the hurricane season in the West Indies. This was far more than most British dukes enjoyed, and he set about spending it on the park, preparing the nursery and environment which was to shape and inspire the imagination of his only legitimate child, William, as yet unborn.

The house stood near a medieval church and the village of Fonthill Gifford on the west bank of a small, ruler-straight, canalised stream running due north–south in a shallow, fertile valley between wooded hills. Fonthill was not a part of the barren Wiltshire Downs, though it was very close to them. The hill east of the stream, which later became young William's 'Satyr's Range' and his favourite resort, was an outlier of the fine-quality Chilmark limestone that had been used to build Salisbury Cathedral. This hillside was promptly opened up by the Alderman to supply stone for the first and most enduring of his park buildings, the arched gate-lodge which still stands north of the house over the public road from Fonthill Bishop. By the late 1740s the Palladian style was coming to be gently modified by rococo influences, and the new lodge reflects that change. Its outline is confidently Palladian, as Inigo Jones might have designed it if he had ever worked to such a scale, but the detail – the scowling key-stone masks and the dramatically vermiculated rustication – lend it a sensuous rococo enrichment that suggests the designing hand of John Vardy, one of Lord Burlington's protégés. Vardy's interest in Inigo Jones can be dated to 1744 and the publication of his volume of engravings, *Some Designs of Mr. Inigo Jones and Mr. William Kent*; the 'grand gate-way' was in existence and recorded by Dr Richard Pococke in the summer of 1754. At a stroke the new owner of the Fonthill estate had committed himself to the scale and *nouveau-riche* over-emphasis of the new house that was to rise later.

In the meantime, the old church was pulled down and the village was rebuilt out of sight, in another valley beyond the hill to the west of the house. A new Classical church, described by Pococke as 'on the plan of Covent garden' (another Inigo Jones link), was built some distance down the valley, inconveniently remote from both the house and the new village. Its cupola, however, offered a park feature to be glimpsed from the south-facing garden front of the house. Half-way up the western hillside a large open-fronted Classical temple was raised, and a Chinese pagoda was built on the top of the hill where the kitchen gardens and orchard were sited, out of the valley frosts. To secure greater privacy for his house the Alderman dammed the stream a mile to the south to create a typical rococo garden feature, a sinuous, smooth-sided 'serpentine river', and the public road was re-routed to run along its east bank, away from the house. That left its old course, under the arched gate-lodge, as a private gravel drive to the mansion. To bring the road back to its old route on the west bank downstream, a five-arched stone bridge with a balustrade was thrown across the serpentine water, providing another attractive park feature.

Then in 1755 Fonthill House burnt down. This was probably a genuine accident, because the Alderman lost most of his paintings in the blaze. When the news was brought to him in London, he made a famous gesture to establish business confidence: opening a drawer crammed with bonds, he pointed to them and calmly ordered a new house. 'Fonthill Splendens', designed by a City builder named Hoare, was begun on a site slightly to the south of the gutted remains of the old house, and was to be a structure of ducal grandeur. To provide stone the new quarry was opened up further, exposing a cliff face of raw rock. At the same time the Alderman decided to get a legitimate heir, and in 1756 he persuaded Maria Marsh, the widow of another London merchant and fellow Jamaican, Francis Marsh, to marry him.

It was an unexpected match and with his income he could probably have aimed higher: one of his brothers married a daughter of the Duke of Ancaster and a sister married the Earl of Effingham. Maria Marsh, though already the mother of an eight-year-old daughter, Elizabeth, was fifteen years younger than her second husband, 32 to his 47, and an attractive, imperious woman, a devout Protestant with the Calvinistic inclinations of her Scots breeding. Though strong-willed, she was socially unpretentious and opposed to airs and graces. This would have suited her new husband, as the Alderman made a point of never fitting comfortably into the English class system or acquiring the title which could have been his for the asking if he had hidden his contempt for the aristocracy and kept a lower profile in Parliament. Mrs Marsh had been born Maria Hamilton, the daughter of an MP for Wells and a granddaughter of the Earl of Abercorn, hence her son's later close links with the Scottish aristocracy, and the Hamilton connection through which he contrived to trace his ancestry back to the kings of England and Scotland. By the failure of the direct line Mrs Beckford's brother-in-law, Lord Archibald Hamilton, later became 9th Duke of Hamilton. Despite these aristocratic connections Mrs Beckford settled easily into what must have been a complex family of legitimate and illegitimate relations. Richard no longer lived with his father, and she struck up a close friendship with her sister-in-law Lady Effingham, who shared her low church pietism, and had access to Royal circles through her husband.

William, the only child, was born at Fonthill four years into the marriage on 29 September 1760. His father had only another nine years to live, but they were to be the years of his greatest fame, when his fearless, tactless oratory in Parliament made the name of Beckford synonymous with that of constitutional liberty. During that short time he also served an unusual two terms as Lord Mayor of London. A few months before his death he defied Royal protocol by haranguing King George III to his face on the rights of the people, rudely urging him to get rid of the corrupt ministers he had chosen. Next day the speech, or a polished version of it, was on sale in the bookshops. The Alderman, 'the Great Beckford', with his craggy looks, his furious glance and his Jamaican malapropisms, was on the way to becoming a national institution. Add the factor of his enormous wealth, and it became apparent to the Government that a serious error had been made in not elevating him to an earldom at the very least, thereby removing him to the calming atmosphere of the House of Lords.

A few months after that famous encounter, the Alderman was dead of rheumatic fever, brought on by the exhaustion of work and of travel between London and Fonthill. He acquired by death some of the aura of martyrdom – the lost hero in the cause of liberty – a formidable reputation to pass down to his young son. William was still not quite ten years old, and in those years his life and his father's had touched only intermittently. Sons were no novelty to the Alderman, though in his rough, shrewd way he had noticed that his wife was rearing a precocious imp, reasonably schooled in French at the age of four, foolishly proud of his royal ancestry from the Hamilton side of the family but easily teased by a reminder that the earliest known Beckford had been a shoemaker. Both parents were given to towering rages, and William had already picked up the same emotional self-indulgence. The one warm charmer in his limited social world was Elizabeth, his half-sister, twelve years his senior and in that sense almost a young mother-figure. Fluent in French and Italian, soon to become a popular Romantic novelist, Elizabeth read stories to him and introduced him to foreign literature. If anyone led him to the copy of the *Arabian Nights Entertainments* in his father's library it must have been Elizabeth. Antoine Galland's *Mille et Une*

Nuits, translated from an Arab manuscript, came out in twelve volumes between 1704 and 1717 and English translations from his French were being published as early as 1715, such was the attraction for English readers of a world ruthless, poetic and entirely amoral.

The impact of such a book on a rich, impressionable young boy may be judged from just one of its stories, that of Schahzenan, King of Grand Tartary. Schahzenan had cut to pieces his unfaithful wife and her lover in the bed where he found them fornicating. To ease his grief he visited the palace of his friend, Schariar, King of the Indies, but when he looked out one night from his bedroom window he saw Schariar's Queen and her ladies joining in an orgy with their black slaves. 'This amorous company continued together till mid-night, and having bathed together in a great pond, which was one of the chief ornaments of the garden, they dressed themselves, and re-entered the palace.' The escape from Christian morality is absolute: it could explain much of Beckford's later carefree sexuality, and the elegantly vicious behaviour of his Caliph Vathek. Cross this Arabic literature with his mother's Christian Calvinism, and much of Beckford's subsequent history becomes explicable.

There was also, to confirm the child in his taste for the epicene East, his father's remarkable 'Turkish Room' down in the vaulted darkness of the ground floor or 'rustic' of the new Splendens. With its low divans and silken and velvet furnishings it made a perfect playground for a small child. To pass from the gloom of the vaulted 'Egyptian Hall' to an over-decorated chamber of mirrors, soft colours and painted flowers would itself have been a transformation and an adventure. This sybaritic apartment indicates that the Alderman was as fascinated by the Islamic East as his son was to become, not only by its literature but by its fabrics and its sensuous style. In such a room the young Beckford could play out Galland's corrupting narratives. It was the Alderman, not Alexander Cozens, that painter of dim, idealised European landscapes, who fired the child's imagination.

Those nine years were formative. There was London in the winter, Fonthill in the summer – the marble luxury of the great house, artist's scaffolding always cluttering the spaces as Andrea Casali's scandalous frescos of antique lewdness actually grew before the child's eyes.

Music lessons and dancing lessons were given regularly to a boy who was a natural extrovert and performer. To share the dancing with him and admire his growing facility on the piano there was Elizabeth, the sophisticated story-teller, drawing him on into judgements on music, literature and painting that were more mature than was natural for his age. In the background, something of a shared joke yet feared, was 'Mam', Mrs Beckford, devout, firm and forthright, the person who made the decisions and solved all problems. When her son was seven she brought in as his tutor Robert Drysdale, a naïve young Scot whom everyone else, including his charge, looked upon as an uncouth northerner. Mrs Beckford had intended that Drysdale should introduce masculine airs and sound Scottish moral standards, but he was ill-chosen and probably came much too late. Occasionally the Alderman himself would appear, an admired monster, just a little scornful of that women's world surrounding his son. The one presence notably lacking was that of another young boy as playmate. Boys were the missing characters and the real exotics. Rabbits, dogs and horses had to serve as their substitutes in William's emotional world.

What the Alderman did provide which influenced his son in his absence was Fonthill Park. Fifteen years had passed since the start of the first, rococo phase of gardening; now Capability Brown was setting a fashion for natural-looking lakes and relaxed landscapes of clumped trees. With true Beckfordian impetuosity, a characteristic his son inherited to the full, the Alderman decided to raise his dam, spreading the 'serpentine' out to make natural inlets and irregular banks and thus create a sheet of water worthy of the overblown (and, to be honest, faintly dated) Palladian palace of Splendens. He did not employ Brown for the landscaping; instead, it seems likely that he was advised by Richard Woods, a landscape gardener of the same school who was working from 1764 to 1768 on Lord Arundell's park at Wardour, only a few miles away from Fonthill. One favourite device of Woods's was the creation, not of a lake but of the impression of a long reach of a sizeable river, like the Thames, and that certainly is the effect of the new water which took the place of the old 'serpentine': Beckford never referred to it as the 'lake', always as 'the river'.

One consequence of this new 'river' was that the five-arched bridge and the new road on the east bank were both flooded. Public traffic returned to the west bank, running again on its way to Tisbury through the arched lodge and very close to the windows of Splendens. The wide new lake made the micro-climate of the valley unhealthily damp, a breeding ground for sinus troubles; the new quarry-face spoilt the view from the garden front; and the public road bisected the park, cutting the house off from the pleasures of the lake. But for a man like the Alderman a problem only meant the satisfaction of finding a solution. Although London was his power base and Westminster his arena, he was beginning to take his country duties seriously. He had armed and equipped a troop of local yeomanry with a brass band, and made a point of exercising them as their commanding officer every summer. Several of his bastards lived locally and one daughter had married the rector of East Knoyle, but through his Hamilton wife there were now grander gentry to entertain, and with his usual vigour he set about making his new river not merely an ornament to be viewed from the house, but the picturesque route to an entirely new sector of the park on the east bank.

This was to be a minor Cythera of bejewelled and flowery grottoes, an Island of Venus as imagined by the painter Watteau, a place worth sailing to, poetic, faintly erotic but also subterranean. The late 1750s had seen another shift in garden and landscape aesthetics. Edmund Burke had published his *Philosophical Enquiry into the Origin of our Ideas on the Sublime and Beautiful* in 1757, and as a result garden fanciers questing after the 'Sublime' began to move from the 'Arcadian Picturesque' of the Alderman's earlier, templed landscape to the 'Savage Picturesque' of a wilder, rocky nature. Fortunately, at this point the Alderman discovered a local quarryman, Joseph Lane from Tisbury, who proved to be a genius at rock-vaulted grotto work. Eventually Fonthill Park had no fewer than four grottoes by the Lanes – Joseph, who died in 1784, and Josiah, his son, who retained the old quarry workings at the top of the east hill as a workshop until at least 1791. The Revd Richard Warner, in his 1801 *Excursions from Bath*, states firmly that Lane 'exhibited the earliest specimen of his talents in the construction of a grotto at Fonthill'. It must, therefore, have been at Fonthill that the Hon. Charles Hamilton talent-spotted the local genius on one of his visits to his cousin, Mrs Beckford, and lured Lane away to create in 1761 a much larger and more famous grotto on the island of his pleasure grounds at Painshill in Surrey. Thereafter, Lane and his son Josiah were much in demand as grotto builders and continued to work at Fonthill and elsewhere in the south-west. Their speciality was a grotto which looked from the outside like a natural rocky feature but opened up, down a dark passage, into a glittering wonderland of minerals, fossils and the effects of falling water.

Two routes were devised at Fonthill to reach that Cythera on the east bank. If a long voyage was required the travellers would set sail from a 'boathouse', so-called. This was actually a temple, landing stage, cold bath and nymph's grotto combined, a place of subtle architectural beauty set at the northern, islanded extension of the lake. John Vardy is again the likely architect for one of the century's most evocative garden buildings. Those who knew it in romantic decay, groaning under tree roots and choked with rocks, should gain permission to visit it again, now it has been cleared of debris. The trees and the romance have gone; instead there is an expensive, Aldermanic structure, triple-aisled, of crisp masonry, the arches set in deep water, the cold bath a space of shadows and changing lights.

For a shorter crossing with more Gothic events, Joseph Lane dug 'a dark Passage' under the road. This was a long winding tunnel vaulted with small 'tumbler' stones and lit at intervals from round spy-holes. It led the visitor out into a deep wooded dell where the two dark arches of a Hermitage lowered threateningly from under a ferociously rocky, artificial cliff. Inside the Hermitage on the right was a fireplace for Gothic picnics, and in the centre an altar with the reclining figure of a river god holding a sceptre and framed in an ogee arch of flints. To the left was the figure of a hermit (or Merlin), bent over his studies. All the figures can still be traced in shallow relief, though vandals have hacked away the detail. Nothing remains of the original enrichment to the walls except the outlines of arches in flints and traces of coloured decoration on the stones in the high concaves of the vault.

An oak tree grew from the roof of the Hermitage, and immediately behind it was a rough Gothic tower with steps to an upper room looking out across the lake to Cythera. By 1823, when Rutter and Britton were writing about the park, this tower had fallen into such shapeless ruin that it was described, wrongly, as a 'Cromlech', which it in no way resembled.

Down a steep slope from the tower was a landing place only a minute's boat ride across to the grand 'New Landing Place', a quay set with stone spheres copied from those on the arched gate-lodge and poised on pedestals. After these Palladian pomps came a level walk along the lakeside to the Lanes' next three grottoes. In the 1790s Beckford described all three in accurate detail in the second volume of his *Modern Novel Writing, or the Elegant Enthusiast*. In the lakeside grotto the hero, Lord Charles Oakley, and 'his dear friend Henry Lambert would sometimes smoke a comfortable pipe'. This and the Cold Bath grotto above it, stripped now of their original corals, spars, shells, fossils and flower vases, survive in atmospheric ruin among the great trees which have overwhelmed them; but the third grotto, the highest, with its petrifying spring, was never roofed over and is now nothing more than a heap of boulders overgrown with box and yew.

This east bank is now strictly private, the trees are mature and the woodland is very dark, but it is still a remarkable experience to come down the hill with flashes of sunlit water gleaming occasionally between the tree trunks and to find yourself facing into the gloomy mouth of a grotto, the passage bending away into the shadows. It is easy to understand how Beckford, in his adolescent mystic stage, saw these grottoes as symbols of initiation: dark caverns down which the Brahmin sage Moisasour could lead a trusting acolyte to cleansing, or to a revelation of light and calm water.

But for his father, the genially lecherous Alderman, these were places to entertain visitors with the surprise of sudden luxury after rocky gloom. In his maturity, his son used them in exactly the same way. The lowest, lakeside grotto was for picnics, and still has the remains of rustic seats under its impending Lane vault. It is approached from either side by dark winding passages leading to the sudden visual surprise which *Modern Novel Writing* recalls: 'A broken arch opened to your view the broad clear expanse of the lake, covered with numerous aquatic fowl, and weeping willows adorning its banks.' That is quite unchanged, and the lake water still laps to within an inch of the grotto floor while the stream from the Cold Bath higher up the hill still seeps through.

The Alderman apparently commissioned Lane to decorate the Cold Bath grotto very lavishly; Beckford's novel mentions that 'One of the grottoes was destined for a bath, and ornamented with branches of coral, brilliant spars and curious shells. A lucid spring filled a marble basin in the centre, and then losing itself for a moment under ground, came dashing and sparkling forth at the extremity of the cave to the lake below.' Its vault has fallen now, but the smooth oval of its polished Chilmark stone basin is just visible under the rocks. Why another cold bath should have been built so far from the house is a puzzle, privacy the only explanation. The one in the boathouse is much deeper and more accessible, and from it a bather could swim out into the lake; the bath in the Grotto was only a plunge pool, but the water from the 'font-hill' would be pure. In the mystic pilgrimage of 'The Centrical History', written in 1777, Beckford described how his guides through the caves stripped him, and 'instantly divesting me of my garments poured over me a balsamic oil'. After 1800, when he began to live in the new Abbey on its hilltop site to the west, he bathed regularly every day from spring to November in Bitham Lake, a small fishpond in the woods to the west of Splendens; before that, from Splendens, he had bathed on summer evenings in the 'river'.

In a typical Beckford gesture, if the description in his novel is to be believed, he was accustomed, when the violets and the lilies-of-the-valley were blown, to substitute 'tuberoses, jessamine and orange trees. The pots were concealed in the earth and appeared natives of the cave' – an exotic and perfumed cheat in that dim, crystal-lined retreat: Beckford always valued flowers more for their scent than for their colour. This is more likely to be an account of standard practice in the park than a mere wish-dream of fiction: Henri Meister, a French visitor to Fonthill who in 1799 published a description of his tour, relates how his party was welcomed in one 'enchanted cave' by 'a table covered with pine apples, grapes, and other refreshments, in gold and china vases'.

Further up the hill from the lakeside Grotto and the Cold Bath was the quarry where the Lanes had their workshops for rockifying. Here are twin caves, connected at the back by a narrow passage – a dark, exciting transit for a young boy. One cavern contains the detritus of the Alderman's garden: the wreck of an artificial stone statue of a naked god, much larger than life-size, and two broken nymphs. Meister, after rhapsodising over the Boat House, mentions a temple 'dedicated to Hercules' and 'a temple of the Naiad, the guardian of this beautiful valley ... in a secret cavern, ornamented in the Etruscan taste, on the banks of a river with whose stream she waters it'. The two caves of the Hermitage by 'the remains of an ancient tower' had, according to Meister, a dual function: one for the worship of Bacchus (that would be the reclining figure with the staff or thyrsus); the other, containing the Hermit with his books, was 'to celebrate the sublimest mysteries of the institutions and wisdom of fairy land'.

Twentieth-century garden historians, dazzled by his son's reputation, have not generally realised that much of what survives today in the park at Fonthill is of the Alderman's time. When he died in 1770, the park was just maturing into a fantastic, multi-caverned playground for a boy. William never, as an adult, claimed the east side of the park as his own creation. As he told his first biographer Cyrus Redding, 'the east bank [of the lake] was ornamented with rocks, caverns, baths and grottoes in the taste of the earlier part of the [eighteenth] century'. His tone was faintly scornful, as by the 1830s he had become a committed 'Green', a tree planter and earnest ecologist; but his youthful aesthetic conditioning had been his father's rococo–Gothick park, crossed with the bizarre Eastern mysticism he picked up from his father's library. The park and the atmosphere of Splendens, together with an enormous fortune, were his father's influential triple legacy: a rococo legacy, a cultural hang-over from those years (the 1730s and 1740s) when the Prince of Wales was the francophile Frederick Louis, and French rococo fashions were infiltrating the forms of English Palladianism.

Despite his wealth, the Alderman's death left Mrs Beckford in a worrying situation. By the terms of the will, if her son died all the money and the estates would go not to her, nor even to the Alderman's brothers, but to Richard, the eldest bastard. Her young son had to be kept alive at all costs. Mistrusting the health record of public schools, she resolved to keep William at home, educated by private tutors. Apart from this, the will was an obscure and complex document. Two executors, Lord Bruce and Henry Hoare, were honest but soon retired in despair, while the remaining three did everything possible to favour the Alderman's bastard children, Richard especially, rather than William, the legal heir. Because these three were still technically William's guardians, Mrs Beckford could only circumvent them by having her son declared a Ward in Chancery, after which she was able to decide on his education, aided by a committee of three of the Alderman's old political friends – William's godfather, the great Pitt himself, now Earl of Chatham, Lord Lyttelton and Lord Camden.

In 1771 Robert Drysdale was dismissed and a generally under-estimated figure, a true father-substitute, was brought into William's life, the Revd John Lettice, a Fellow of Sidney Sussex College, Cambridge who had been tutoring the daughter of Britain's ambassador in Copenhagen. Because Fanny Burney once described him as 'a good sort of half stupid man', perhaps also because of his unfortunate surname, Lettice is rarely given much attention. Yet on his arrival Mrs Beckford installed him in her dead husband's bedroom suite at Fonthill, so he was quite literally a father-figure in the house. He should by rights have become detested by his wilful, intelligent charge, because he was obliged to administer an intolerable curriculum of work drawn up by the gout-ridden and crotchety Lord Chatham. Lettice played a clever game, writing soothing and probably deceitful letters to Chatham to keep him quiet, handling the widow Beckford discreetly, and sensibly encouraging a boy who already loved knowledge and read avidly.

On the much-quoted occasion when Beckford was made to burn some treasured Oriental papers, probably mildly pornographic, Lettice presided over the bonfire of vanities but he could easily have laid the blame on Chatham, who had ordered their destruction as a moral rather than aesthetic gesture. It is to Lettice's credit that while Mrs Beckford and Chatham supposed he was preparing the next Prime Minister but three, he was encouraging his pupil to write experimentally in a variety of styles – a pompous, aureate English, light comic wit, direct simple reportage, quivering Romantic emotional, and pastiche Arabian. Once a budding author achieves a first publication, literary ambition knows no limits, and it was Lettice who single-handedly brought Beckford's precocious *Biographical Memoirs of Extraordinary Painters* to the admiring attention of Cambridge academics, and eventually to publication in 1780.

There can be no doubt that Lettice, who accompanied Beckford three times to the Continent and once around England, knew every nuance of his emotional range, accepted the consequences, respected his creativity, and tried wherever possible to shield him from the results of his actions. Paid to educate a high-spirited, emotionally indeterminate boy, he did not condemn but if anything condoned his fancies and inclinations. Not many educators could claim as much. Many years later Beckford appointed him tutor to his own two daughters, and the friendship between the two men endured into old age, when they still wrote and met to discuss poetry and style.

Although Beckford had small talent for drawing, he had been literally surrounded by the art of Casali's creation in his infant years, so he must have had a lively interest in painting and it was natural that in his fourteenth year he should be given a fashionable drawing master. Alexander Cozens, who was also working part-time at Eton, was unfortunately never able to teach him to draw – only to flaunt artistic theories. He was an experimental artist of modest talent who trained his pupil to look for general visual effects – sunsets, areas of shadow and the like – rather than particular detail, resulting in the long, actively boring passages in Beckford's travel book *Dreams, Waking Thoughts, and Incidents.* What a boy largely isolated from other children and normal society needed was not a landscape processor but a Hogarth, to train him to look at people. Significantly, Beckford and Cozens dropped each other in the last two years of Cozens's life (he died in 1786). No single letter from Cozens to Beckford survives, and there is no evidence that most of Beckford's interesting letters to Cozens were ever sent, or even written during the artist's lifetime. Stylised letters were one of Beckford's ways of exploring his own consciousness, rather than of communicating with a friend.

'Poor old Cozens', as Beckford once described him, must have been a sympathetic listener, and from his childhood in Russia and his extensive travels in Europe must have had a fund of anecdotes about the Tsar's half-barbaric court and the glories of Italy. But he was physically dwarfish and slow-moving, certainly not the sexual seducer or practitioner of black magic sometimes suggested, and it is hard to equate him with the ideal companion addressed in the fair copies of those letters supposedly sent to him in the period between 1775 and 1781. In these ideal reveries he accompanies Beckford on long rambles through the woods, takes wholesome breakfasts in a peasant's cottage, and is to share with him in the future a poetic, adventurous existence, sometimes feasting in an Arthurian tower, sometimes exploring the grasslands and forests of America.

As a boy Beckford never made real friends of his own age, but throughout his life he related warmly to much older men like Cozens and Lettice. Later there would be Dr Verdeil, the Marquis of Marialva, the Abbade, the Prior of Aviz and the Abbé Macquin, all foreigners to whom he could respond without the confinements of the English class system but with respect for their age and their religious background. Meanwhile, in default of young friends he had his imagination; and he grew up, more by accident than by design, enjoying the same pattern of education and nurture as Rousseau's Emile: but a child not so much of Nature as of an Arcadian park and a French translation of a lewd epic of Eastern lust and arbitrary power.

CHAPTER THREE

The dangerous facility of a teenage author

It was this valley of the mingled Arcadin and Savage Picturesque at Fonthill which gave Beckford, at that time very little travelled, the images for his juvenilia *L'Esplendente* (1776) and 'The Centrical History' (1777–8): a park of temples for the gods, lonely cold baths deep in woodland, hermits' dens, a pagoda, and grottoes hidden under mounds of fallen rock. A third work, *Biographical Memoirs of Extraordinary Painters* (also 1777–8), contains a number of references to grottoes but owes more to the contents of Splendens than to the structures of the park, and reads as though written by a completely different person – hence the 'dangerous facility'. Already there was not one Beckford, but many.

L'Esplendente is a deeply introverted piece of writing offering an irresistible mine for amateur psychologists to quarry. When Beckford was writing it Alexander Cozens was still influential and his pupil was hoping to become an artist rather than the politician his mother and her advisers were planning. A distinct ambivalence emerges from the text on the subject of Beckford's dead father, the great patriot and politician.

The hero is a young Mohammedan, Mehemed, living with his family in the remote Andalusian countryside soon after the Christian reconquest of Granada. He has a dual identity: to protect him from Christian persecution he has been christened Ferdinand, but his father Abdouerahmen (who has three wives – an Aldermanic touch) is a devout worshipper of Allah. When his son is mature enough Abdouerahmen takes him to a secret hidden valley only approach-

41

able by an underground tunnel. There in a chasm, behind fragrant trees, is a little mosque. In the mosque is a copy of the Koran, which the two study together. Afterwards Mehemed runs wildly around the vale 'looking into every fissure and [leaving] no thicket unexplored'. For no apparent reason his father abandons him there for several days. 'Lulled by the rippling of the water he dropped asleep. The forms of Eblis and of Harnt were in his dreams' – the first mention of Eblis, the beautiful and youthful Lord of Evil, in Beckford's writings. When Mehemed wakes he tries to escape the 'mounds of rock that rose perpendicularly on all sides'. Trying to scale the cliffs he falls down into a bush: this sounds like a real memory of juvenile misadventure. His loneliness becomes unbearable; 'had I but a Companion, said he, I should be contented – one human being to whom I might communicate my thoughts.' To pass the time he takes a pencil and draws 'the visionary groups which had enlivened his slumbers', Eblis the Lord of Evil included.

When his father returns to take him home he is enraged by these drawings, 'idolatrous recreations' of the human form. 'He furiously snatched up the leaves which were scattered about and, tearing them asunder, committed them to the winds and to the torrent.' Mehemed 'sobbed not daring to reply ... but the loss affected him more than can be imagined'.

With Methodism, Chatham and his Alderman father all evoked and exorcised by that act of writing, Beckford brings in his saviour, a kindly white-haired, white-bearded old Jew named Ben Jacoub, presumably modelled on Cozens. The old man, staying with his parents, is very 'struck by the blooming aspect of Mehemed'. (William himself was a more than presentable young man at this time, of medium height, with wide hips and an agile pouncing gait, his face handsome and confident with a searching, even slightly predatory expression.) Ben Jacoub teaches him to despise Islamic superstitions about art and talks of the pleasures of Seville (London), 'where agreeable symphonies echoed every evening in the streets'. He takes the boy to a 'magazine' (a technical term for a large grotto), shows him 'some manuscripts beautifully illuminated and glittering with gold and azure' and promises to teach him to draw. When Mehemed returns home his mother quizzes him about the Jew: is he 'employed in magical Researches?' Mehemed sets her mind at rest, and his parents allow him to study with Ben Jacoub. He vows to draw 'strange castles, and deserts scattered over with tents, priests ministering at altars, and the antient King of China with his long nails, surveying his golden fountain'.

The 'Kubla Khan' elements in this exotic list may have been drawn from Beckford's reading of travel books in his father's rich library; what is less easily explained is the inclusion of 'priests ministering at altars'. One of the most obstinately individual traits in Beckford's character was his delight in and apparent familiarity with the rituals of the Roman Catholic church, despite having been brought up by a 'methody-body' mother in an England still violently anti-Catholic, as the Gordon Riots of 1780 were to demonstrate. In his next piece of writing, the *Biographical Memoirs*, Beckford revealed a detailed though not yet sympathetic knowledge of St Anthony of Padua, who was to become his patron saint and an intermediary between him and any too oppressively close contact with God.

There is a likely if unprovable explanation for this delight in liturgical pomps. Within three miles of Fonthill and between 1771 and 1776, the years of Beckford's impressionable adolescence, the most splendid Roman Catholic place of worship to be built in Britain since the Reformation was going up: a structure that a Jesuit priest in Rome could describe as a 'basilica' – the chapel, a tall, five-bay vaulted nave with fluted Corinthian pilasters and apses at each end, pure Catholic triumphalism, which James Paine had designed for the 8th Baron Arundell of Wardour at Wardour Castle, just south of Tisbury.

This remarkable building was inaugurated on 1 November, All Saints' Day, in 1776, the year *L'Esplendente* was being written. The opening ceremony, conducted by Bishop Walmesley, was the first Solemn High Mass to be held outside London and the various embassy chapels since the Reformation. Lord Arundell's two resident Jesuit chaplains and a flock of other priests assisted, the fifteenth-century Westminster chasuble enriched with Tudor roses and pomegranates and two other superb mediaeval vestments were worn. The high altar, designed by Giacomo Quarenghi, had been brought from Italy at a cost of 600 guineas. The columned tabernacle which topped it had a cupola of porphyry supported on columns of jasper with capitals of silver gilt – exactly the kind of artefact to delight a youthful Beckford. Ornate silver sanctuary lamps by Luigi Valadier hung on either side. An industrious Jesuit based in Rome, Father John Thorpe, had supplied relics of St Ignatius and Edmund Campion, also a 'Giorgione' of Luther's patron, the Duke of Saxony, and 'a fine box in which Alexander the Great kept the *Iliad* of Homer'. The religious relevance of these last two eighteenth-century 'collectibles' is obscure.

The Arundells had remained faithful Catholics, despite having enriched themselves with confiscated monastic property at the Dissolution, and the Tisbury area held half the Papist population of Wiltshire. Until the Alderman bought Fonthill there had always been Benedictine chaplains in the house, serving the Cottingtons and the villagers of Fonthill Gifford, and a Catholic census of the 1780s revealed at least six practising Catholic servants working for the Beckfords. So, despite his mother's firm Protestantism, it is possible to describe Beckford as having been brought up in a Catholic environment. Could a curious and self-willed adolescent have resisted the allure of the fumes of incense and that Quarenghi high altar? Did Father Forrester, actually a young French Jesuit, M. Fleury, resident at Wardour from February 1775 onwards, ever get into conversation with Beckford? While there can be no answers, these questions need to be considered, as Beckford remained ambivalently semi-Catholic for the rest of his life – at the same time as being (and this is a quintessentially Beckford paradox) closely involved with Freemasonry, a movement deeply hostile to the Catholic Church. Both the Freemasons and the Catholic Church offered, of course, the pleasures of solemn ritual.

L'Esplendente peters out with Mehemed taking up his alternative personality as Ferdinand, going to Seville and becoming a famous artist, cleverly deceiving the Christians as to his true identity (Beckford himself would always enjoy playing a double game). But there the train of Beckford's imagination collided violently with harsh reality. Ben Jacoub–Cozens did not manage to teach him to become even a mediocre artist; his few surviving drawings are wholly untalented. Beckford's true facility was to write well in a number of styles. Art was a distraction from this. With Cozens he had fallen in with a second-rate artist determined to apply neo-Classical theories of the Ideal to landscape. Such theories might work with the human form, but when it came to ideal landscapes there was no equivalent method, there were no antique or Raphaelesque landscapes from which to draw inspiration. Cozens's solution was to teach his students to make wet splodges of ink on one piece of paper, then press them onto another sheet and model a landscape around the resultant blots. This explains his contemporary nickname of 'Mr Dingy Digit', and was guaranteed to produce original visions and compositions: it could hardly produce anything else. More seriously, it harmed and limited Beckford's 'seeing eye' for the next ten years.

Exactly contemporary with *L'Esplendente* is a series of letters written by Beckford to a friend, Lord Morton, who was at Eton. These correct any impression that Beckford at this time lived in total rural isolation with no companions of his own age. He had been enjoying the London opera season and was already an active critic of performances, having booed a female singer for 'the consummate vulgarity of an English recitative'. A link which Beckford had in common with his Scottish cousins was that they were all being given tuition by Alexander Cozens, referred to as 'the Persian'. Beckford, Morton and a cousin on the Hamilton side, Lord Strathavon, were going through that schoolboy stage of disastrous experiments with alcohol and playing cards for money, which may in part explain why Mrs Beckford did not send her son on to Oxford but to what she hoped was a sober, Calvinistic Geneva.

In tone these letters are both manipulative and vulnerable. Beckford was plainly anxious for more contact with Morton, who was about to put on a puppet play at Eton. He suggested various twists in the plot, how a knight could be devoured by a giant oyster, and what scenery would be appropriate. To coax Morton into a rather longer reply than the 'nicest, smallest, minnikinest' two lines he had just received, Beckford taunted him, saying that Strathavon 'swore point blank' he would not get a letter. In an attempt to join in the fun of the school activities from which he was inevitably excluded, he wrote out a full-length script for a puppet play. Very macabre, it featured skeleton puppets which abuse each other roundly and repetitively from the gallows on which they hang, and live in terror of marauding crows picking at their last scraps of flesh and skin. Eventually they all fall down, 'legs, ribs, arms and shins scattered pell mell, higledly pigledy all over the Stage', and are left appealing pathetically to be sorted out and put together again by the Keeper of the Skeletons.

Beckford included, for good measure, an example of schoolboy wit, more Shakespearean in its word play than Johnsonian:

Question. Why is a gardener the most extraordinary person in the world?

Answer. Because he has more business than any other man upon *Earth.* He commands his *Thyme*, he is Master of the *Mint.* He meets with more *boughs* than a Minister of State and makes more *beds* than the French King. He is sure to raise his *selery* every year. Distemper fatal to others never affects him as he thrives in a *Consumption.*

The play of the skeleton puppets was never staged at Eton.

In another carefully measured and controlled exercise in contact with children of his own age, Beckford was allowed to stay on several occasions at Burton Pynsent, the Somerset house of his godfather, Lord Chatham. (In mid twentieth-century terms, this was the equivalent of staying with Winston Churchill at Chartwell.) If Mrs Beckford was hoping to direct her son on a political path, this should have worked perfectly: the second Pitt son, William, was the same age as Beckford, and was to become Prime Minister at the age of only 24, and Beckford was initially a great favourite at Burton. Lord Chatham praised his declamation of a passage of Thucydides, and on one occasion the entire household, William Pitt included, signed a testimonial to 'the graces of his Reason', expressing the hope of a return visit. Indeed, it is clear from a study of the handwriting that it was William Pitt himself who wrote out the highly flattering text for the rest to sign. What happened to divide the two Williams so sharply is not known, but this early affection and familiarity must have added a personal bitterness to their later quarrels. William Pitt never married.

In these teen years of golden promise and precocity Beckford continued to scribble away. Cozens may not have been able to turn him into an artist, but he had certainly turned him into an art critic of malicious wit and sharply defined tastes. If Lettice, Beckford's half-sister Elizabeth, and Beckford himself as recorded by Cyrus Redding are to be believed, Beckford wrote his earliest published book, *Biographical Memoirs of Extraordinary Painters*, during the first half of 1777, when he was only sixteen and before he left for Geneva. He continued to be so pleased with it (not unreasonably, as it still makes fascinating reading) that he arranged for it to be republished in 1824 and again in 1834. Internal evidence – the obvious dislike of Antwerp and the Low Countries and a familiarity with the Roman Campagna – indicates that in claiming it had been written quite so early he was 'composing for Mozart'. There was probably some rewriting up to 1779, when Lettice showed it around the Sidney Sussex Common Room. While reasonably well informed about European art, it expresses a strong prejudice against painting too closely from life. That would be Cozens's influence: the neo-Classical determination to paint the Ideal rather than the real, theorising which resulted in Beckford travelling around the Continent on his 1779–80 Grand Tour with his eyes half-closed, gaining impressions of cloudscapes, storms and mountain masses silhouetted against vivid effects of light, but ignoring most of those human contacts and misadventures that make a journey interesting to an average reader. These neo-Classical convictions and a delight in mocking mischief led him in the *Biographical Memoirs* to invent the lives of six fictional artists, all closely modelled on real painters who were, in Beckford's opinion, artistic disasters because they observed the actual too closely. All of them except 'Blunderbussiana' had some Flemish connection, Flanders being seen as a source of this aesthetic corruption. The most impressive of the six studies was an ingenious character assassination of Gérard Dou, under the name of Jeremy Watersouchy. Beckford was parodying the serious tone of J.B. Descamps' *Vie des Peintres Flamands*, and the obscurity of his humour explains the puzzled reactions of some contemporary reviewers.

Watersouchy, born in Amsterdam, had been taken up by an artist with a genius for painting 'eatables, old women and other pieces of still life'. Moving to Antwerp, he achieved fame by painting a banker's counting-house with the gold just coming out of the vaults.

His success assured by this, he went on to paint 'a cheese in a china dish with mites in it for a venerable old lady', a hanging wart on the nose of Burgomaster Van Gulph, Adam and Eve, 'so exquisitely finished that every ligament on their fig leaves was visible', and another patron's favourite dormouse. After spending three months 'painting a flea', he died. Beckford's dislike not just of Gérard Dou but of the Flemish bourgeoisie who patronised him brims over in a description of the banker's reception, with 'well dressed people passing and repassing each other with many courteous bows and salutations, whilst two sets of chimes in the spires above them fills the air with sober psalmody'.

Apart from the foolish nomenclature – Count Zigazagi and Prince Henry Suckingbottle – the book is often rewarding, with inventions like Blunderbussiana, son of a Croatian bandit, born in an immense grotto or 'magazine', who as an artist specialised in 'vast perspective caverns red with the light of fires, round which banditti were carousing, or else dark valleys between shaggy rocks strewed with the spoils of murdered travellers. If he represented waters, they were dark and troubled, if trees, deformed and withered.' The obvious and squarely hit target is Salvator Rosa. Another invention, Og of Basan, a Pomeranian, seeks inspiration by living several years in a cave system, to emerge as an expert in studies of rocks.

Overall, what emerges rather surprisingly from his satire – or, as the *Quarterly Review* described it, his 'sarcasms at once deep and delicate' – is not so much a genuinely venomous dislike of the schools he pillories as a detached appreciation of them all, a knowing superiority which hints more at a future art dealer than at an art lover. The Cozens-inspired disapproval would pass, and an informed connoisseur survive.

His next piece of writing, never given a proper title, Beckford called 'my Centrical History'. It also lacks a conclusion, and is the last of Beckford's adolescent trilogy of experimental writing, dating from the last half of 1777 and early 1778. Twentieth-century editors have published it as *The Long Story*, or *The Vision*. It shares with his other two works the obsessively underground and grotto-rich background of Fonthill park, although it was written in Geneva. In mood, subject matter and emotional stance it is, however, in a different world. As a result of his contacts and experiences in Switzerland he had moved from the eighteenth century of the Enlightenment – urbane, informed and critical – to the Romanticism of the nineteenth century – confused, mystic and rebellious. Consideration of *The Long Story* has, therefore, to be postponed to the next chapter, in spite of the tight chronological sequence of the three books.

Lying under his hand in his father's library was Galland's *Arabian Nights*, eventually to inspire him with its psychopathic sultans, sudden death, absolute authority and lust veiled in poetic periphrasis. He was interested in Eastern art and he already knew the book well, but in 1777 he was not prepared, sexually or emotionally, to take it in, to see his own life in its terms, or to write *Vathek*.

But it was waiting for him. He had the power: his wealth; he had the repression: his mother; he had the bisexual instinct ready to set him excitingly free from ordinary morality. He had also the essential background for any future Caliph or Sultan – a palace – because he had been born in one. With so much surviving today of the Alderman's garden and so little, mere grassy mounds, of the Alderman's house, there is always a danger of underestimating the conditioning role which Splendens itself, a house of fleshly affluence and arrogant display, must have played in the formation of Beckford's character.

Splendens was in many ways an architectural disaster: an outdated Palladian design, its interior decorated in an even more old-fashioned baroque style by Andrea Casali. The lewd animal passions of Zeus splashed brightly over the walls would have amused the Alderman, but must have been a permanent embarrassment to his devout widow. More seriously, the ground plan with its nine-bay central block and the servants and offices banished to two pavilions at the ends of long colonnaded quadrant arms might have been designed to isolate a young man from the realities of life. It is hard to imagine him, his possessive widowed mother, the amiable Mr Lettice and Elizabeth, the much-loved and admired older half-sister, rattling about in those 'Grand Apartments' on the first floor. These had been fifteen years in the decorating and were only completed in the year of the Alderman's death: so the purpose of the place had gone just as the artists and decorators were paid off. There were some visitors during the widow's eleven years of control – the two aunts, the Alderman's sister Lady Effingham and Mrs Beckford's sister, Mme Elizabeth de Fay; Lady Euphemia Stewart, who was Mrs Beckford's particular friend and moral adviser; a Wiltshire neighbour, the Earl of Pembroke; Lord Thurlow, the Lord Chancellor, who had been a political ally of the Alderman and always took a kindly interest in the orphaned boy; some Hamilton relations – but not the swirl of house parties and political intrigue for which it had been designed.

There must have been a certain poetry in living isolated not simply in an enchanted park but in that outrageously formal, almost vulgar, palace. In a normal house the ground floor would have been alive with the clatter of servants, but Splendens had an empty, echoing Egyptian Hall. It was not 'Egyptian' in Palladio's concept of a lofty two-storey central space but, as Beckford recalled it, a place of darkness, 'as if hewn out of the living rock. The line of apartments being infinite were all vaulted – a gloomy staircase, which appeared, and which was in fact, of enormous height, led to suites of stately apartments gleaming with marble and pavements.' These first-floor apartments ran in the usual Palladian sequence around a central 'Organ Hall', or 'Grecian Hall', a thirty-six-foot cube. There was a Dining Room, forty-two feet by twenty-four, with a marble fountain representing the Four Elements. There was a Bedchamber, eighteen feet by twenty-six, with hangings of crimson and silver, and a State Bed so grand that the Herberts borrowed it when King George and Queen Caroline stayed at Wilton in 1777. Apparently it was too magnificent even for monarchs, and the Royal pair insisted on using their portable camp bed. Beckford later commissioned another State Bed from the architect John Soane, with a fanfare of tasselled draperies and a top modelled on the Lysicratic Monument in Athens.

The 'Turkish' or 'Tartarean Chamber' down on the ground floor was an Aldermanic fantasy, 'as splendid and sumptuous', according to the antiquary John Britton, 'as those magical recesses of enchanted palaces in the Arabian Nights entertainments'. It was from this room, its golden ceiling painted by François Boileau with interlaced designs and flowers, that Beckford acquired his taste for mirrored extensions to the true dimensions of a space. As visitors entered they faced their reflections in a floor-to-ceiling mirror, and all the window shutters were mirrored, producing confusions between interior and exterior perspectives. Orange and gold curtains and ottomans caught up the gilding of the ceiling to create a union of the sensuous and the affluent, a banker's bordello of exotic charm. It is not recorded how this room was intended to function, but it made its impact on Beckford, and in Venice and Madrid he responded with immediate interest to the presence of real Turks.

The 'Organ Hall' greatly impressed Beckford's first tutor, Robert Drysdale. He noted: 'Apollo and the Muses are finely painted on the ceiling by Casali and a group of Cupids seem to hold the chain which supports the lanthorn. There are eight basso-relievos over the doors by the same hand, also over the chimneypiece a picture of Io transformed into a white cow. Argus lulled asleep by Mercury's pipe.' Seeing this improbable episode of Zeus's animal passions every day must have sunk into Beckford's mind: when he contrived his first seduction of a young boy, he compared himself to Mercury with his pipe and the school matron to Argus.

It was a home of many resonances. In Beckford's childhood only music can have filled those vaults and high spaces. This may explain his abiding passion, not simply for hearing music, but for performing it himself, an abstract and introverted joy, a substitute for real feeling and a source of easy tears. In those empty rooms and flattering acoustics he tried out that counter-tenor voice of which he was so unselfconsciously proud and which was to create predictable sexual *frissons* in the minds of many English listeners.

One feature which must be given its place in this survey of conditioning factors and adolescent responses is the 'Tower'. When the Alderman died one structure of his picturesque park composition, the one most needed, was incomplete, was indeed barely begun, and that was a tower from which to view it all. A large, triangular edifice with round bastions to rival Alfred's Tower at nearby Stourhead park was under construction on Stop Beacon, the highest point in the estate, but only ten feet of its walls had been raised when the widow cut back on all park expenditure. That ten-foot stump among the trees, a memento of a great project unfinished, remained to obsess the Alderman's son, to inspire the writing of *Vathek* and be one of the seeds from which Fonthill Abbey eventually grew. In his 'Red Book', in the Beckford Papers, is a long letter, one of many supposedly written to Cozens, but not sent. It contains a passage often quoted:

> Sometimes when our minds are exalted by the sublime reveries of philosophy we will ascend a lofty hill which till lately was a Mountain in my eyes. There I hope to erect a Tower dedicated to meditation on whose summit we will take our station and survey the vast range of countries beneath, extending to the very sands of the Ocean ... When we inhabit the Tower, think with what pleasure we shall return to our elevated apartments after conversing with Nature in the groves. The freshness of the Evening will invite us to linger some moments on the grass plot before the Tower from whence our sight will be directed towards the woods ... Whilst we are investigating the cause of musick the painted windows of a Hall high above in the Tower will gleam with the light of many tapers and summon us to our evening's repast. We will ascend the hundred steps that lead to the spacious Hall wainscoted with Cedar, whose arched roof will be strangely sculptured with gothic devices ... The pavement is ruddy marble and the seats are painted with achievements, the tall windows are crowded with gorgeous figures coloured in ancient times. Here are Knights and Sovereigns clad in rich mosaic, Saints distinguished by their glories ... above is a broad and ample Gallery enclosed with gilt lattices and supported by thin waisted pillars fretted with scrupulous dexterity,

and so on. And the reader naturally thinks, as Beckford intended: 'What prescience! What purpose and continuity of aim! How similar it all is to that atmospheric ruin in which Venn Lansdown clambered around that October day in 1844. This is very nearly Fonthill Abbey as Beckford eventually achieved it, and all this was confided to that good old artist, Alexander Cozens, as early as ...' But here again the uncertainty sets in. Guy Chapman, who of all Beckford's biographers was most suspicious of the old fraudster, accepted these writings as letters to Cozens of perhaps 1780. But not one of them is safely dated, and many are copies in a secretary's refreshingly legible hand. They could as easily have been dictated and written in the 1830s, long after the penultimate 'Tower' had fallen. On the other hand, the structure described is very close to the drawing of a Belém-like tower which the artist Joseph Farington illustrated in his diary for July 1796 as an early design by James Wyatt for Beckford's park. Cozens was dead when Beckford first saw the Belem tower in Lisbon, so what is the date of his letter, and who was the addressee? Was Beckford composing again for Mozart, pretending to a continuity of aesthetic purpose and a life of noble dedication to high ideals? The whole Arthurian concept of Knights and Sovereigns, the arched roof and gilt lattices, sound more like a nineteenth-century memory of Fonthill Abbey than an eighteenth-century anticipation of it.

Beckford claimed, in one of his 'Cozens' transcripts, to have kept all his old art master's letters in a special blue box, yet not one survives. While there is no doubt that Cozens, 'the Persian', was a real man who had real contacts with Beckford over roughly a nine-year period, there has to be a possibility that much later in life Beckford reconstituted the dead teacher into an ideal companion and inspiration of his idyllic youth. That possibility becomes even more relevant to Beckford's time at Geneva: there are numerous long 'Cozens letters', all of them transcripts, describing his Swiss expeditions.

CHAPTER FOUR

The sorrows of an English Goethe

There is a book called the Sorrows of Werther, read it and tell me if every line is not resplendent with Genius.

William Beckford, Fonthill, 3 December 1779

Goethe's 1774 masterpiece of adolescent despair, *Die Leiden des jungen Werthers*, hit Beckford's generation like an emotional typhoon. As popular fiction it was the book of the century; the youth of Germany, France and Britain were all swept away by it. Beckford will have read the book in Aubry's French translation, *Les Passions du jeune Werther* of 1777, when it was the scandal and delight of Geneva's *jeunesse dorée*. Daniel Malthus's fine English translation, *The Sorrows of Young Werther*, came out in 1779; the book went through twenty-six English editions before the end of the century, and was blamed for any number of suicides. Werther, an appealing creation of vulnerability and honour, commits suicide because he has fallen in love with Charlotte, the wife of his best friend, there being no other proper response to frustrated love in the intense canons of Romantic integrity. Once again, as in the time of the Troubadours, Love was worth dying for. As Werther mused to himself:

Everything passes away; but a whole eternity could not extinguish the flame which was yesterday kindled by your lips, the flame I feel within me – She loves me! These arms have encircled her waist, these lips have trembled upon hers; she is mine. – Yes, Charlotte! You are mine forever!

It may seem turgid stuff, but the book is still very readable, its sixty-two short letters tracing the whole affair from first meeting to bloody end.

Beckford might have survived his isolated early life and education and still ended as an English gentleman at ease in English society if he had been allowed to go to Oxford or Cambridge. It was that year in Switzerland, with two short stays in Paris on the way there and back, which turned him into a sophisticated expatriate, an ardent Francophile with the sensibility of a German Romantic and virtually no conventional patriotic instincts. Mrs Beckford must have known that successful parliamentary politicians need a whole network of friends and contacts, and that an English university was the place where such friends could be made. That she still decided on Geneva indicates not so much her suspicion of Oxbridge society as her lack of confidence in her son's maturity and judgement. By 1777 she had probably realised that she had reared a brilliant, wilful isolate who needed a far more intellectually stimulating environment than he would have been likely to find if he had gone, like his father, to Balliol College, Oxford or followed the young William Pitt to Pembroke College, Cambridge. So when her half-Swiss cousin, a middle-aged bachelor, Colonel Edward Hamilton, who had served in the army of the East India Company and now lived with a spinster sister in Geneva, offered to look after her son while Geneva academics nurtured his mind, she agreed, provided John Lettice went along to supervise. Mrs Beckford's confidence in the ability of the benignly permissive Lettice to control her wilful son is evidence that she was no judge of character.

Beckford and his party went down to Geneva via Paris. It is most unlikely that they were following Mrs Beckford's approved route, but he must have spent some days in the city because in a letter to his half-sister Elizabeth written later from Geneva he analysed the church of the Invalides knowledgeably. The first letter home which he allowed to survive for posterity to read, in an eight-page copy in a beautiful secretarial hand, was not to his sister or his mother, but to his aunt Lady Effingham, and carefully crafted to manipulate the tough old lady who virtually controlled his parent. It was dated 22 August, two months almost to the day after his arrival in Geneva, the city of Calvin and Protestant propriety. It had been planned that he should follow intensive courses in Civil Law, Philosophy and Natural Sciences from an impressive group of academics; and he had to explain why he had instead been living the high life for several weeks at Evian-les-Bains, a small spa town on the shores of Lake Geneva in Savoy, a province of the oddly named Kingdom of Sardinia (capital, Turin). Evian was a Catholic town, while Geneva had been chosen to complete Beckford's education expressly for its safe Protestant connections.

Word may also have got back to the family that on his way to Dover and the Continent he had called at Canterbury Cathedral to pay his respects to 'my tutelary Saint Thomas à Becket', who he had chosen to believe was a remote ancestor from the similarity of their surnames. This would explain why the letter to Aunt Effingham was long and flattering. In an England still neurotic about the threat of Catholicism to decent God-fearing Protestants, it would have been difficult for the Beckford family to appreciate that William was not in any real danger of 'going over to Rome'. He was, in the broadest and most intelligent sense of the word, 'superstitious'; he loved, that is, to lose himself in a mystery. His favourite study was comparative religions, Hindu, Buddhist, Islamic, Zoroastrian. These had been his background reading at Fonthill, and continued to be his real interest at Geneva when his newly appointed lecturers bored him. If a religious faith could also offer him aesthetically exciting ritual, as in the Catholic Mass and the Protestant Masonic ceremonies, so much the better; but then he would flit on to the next experience, preferably to a fine musical accompaniment of choirs and organs. Though it is hard to accept, with so much distraction from architecture, sexuality and socialising, Beckford was a man obsessed throughout his life by the nature of the Divinity and inclined, in this obsession, to pessimism. If superstition is 'the workings of that religion natural to the human heart', then Beckford's natural workings were open-minded but apprehensive.

All this was hidden from Aunt Effingham, classed by Beckford as a 'Methodistical Dowager' along with his mother and Lady Euphemia Stewart (who was not technically a dowager at all, but a spinster and a moral activist). He had a considerable snobbish respect for Aunt Effingham, however, because as a Lady of the Bedchamber she was 'a prime favourite ... dining very often with the K & Q – when few ladies & fewer Lords ever enjoyed that distinction'. Hence his letter, a minor masterpiece of personal trumpet-blowing and tactful grovelling. 'Dear Aunt,' it began, 'as you have always very kindly interested yourself in what concerns me, I find it impossible to refrain from troubling you with these lines ... I should be very happy could I transport myself for a moment to Stoke to find you amongst your shrubberies ... could I but send you, as indeed a far more valuable present, a little portion of our warm sunshine and serene weather, your Magnolia would be covered with far more blossoms than it had last year.'

Beckford had apparently persuaded his obliging colonel-cousin to settle for the season in Evian – a town, he hastily assured his aunt, 'in the style of Tonbridge'. At Evian it was the custom for all the quality to take the waters at seven in the morning, then dance for an hour in 'a long mall or alley of noble trees' to 'very simple but harmonious music', which does not sound like Tunbridge Wells at all: this was before breakfast. One of Beckford's many engaging qualities was a delight in 'the simple life', a life, that is, conducted in a fastidious peasant mood of open-air activities, with buffets of brown bread, fresh cream and eggs, grilled river trout and mounds of ripe fruit. Salamon Gessner of Zurich had popularised such Arcadian pleasures in his *Idylls*, rococo versions of Theocritan Eclogues, widely translated and enjoyed in England since the 1760s. Their idealisation of shepherd life and loves appealed naturally to a young man who had been reared in an Arcadian park landscape. Now Beckford had come to the Alps, and found life there very nearly as Gessner had described it, with a peasant gentry in full frolic.

Anxious that his aunt should get the correct impression, he stressed in his letter the high class of the company, 'so good and agreeable', and he accorded all the initiative in his most recent social enterprise, most improbably, to his elderly cousin: after decades of peaceful bachelor existence 'Colonel H.' (Beckford insisted) 'was resolved to give a fête in the woods of Blonay'. The money to find it, of course, came from the sixteen-year-old manipulator.

The fête began at three in the afternoon. 'Col. H. and myself had arrived long before and had the pleasure of seeing the whole company clambering a natural terrace which forms a steep bank almost thirty feet perpendicular, covered with herbage, continually grazed by Goats and Sheep.' With sunshine, 'a cold collation' and country dancing to an orchestra hidden among pine trees, it was an *Idyll* realised, pure Gessner. Later in life Beckford always valued occasions when people were happy together and he was the impresario; now, with the eye of a born producer, he relished the symmetrical whirl of white veils as the ladies turned in the unison of the dance figures. His partner was Madame la baronne de Montailleur, 'the beauty and heroine of the King of Sardinia's dominions'; but from the tone of his writing, he resented every minute away from the music when she insisted on a flirtatious stroll, arm in arm with him, up into the wood.

In the dancing after supper he demonstrated literal panache by inserting a long green fern into his partner's head-dress. All the other men, gentry and uniformed officers, followed suit, and so they danced on by moonlight and lanterns before a gathering crowd of peasantry. Finally the boats pulled in for the voyage back to Evian, and even Aunt Effingham could hardly fail to be charmed by her nephew's description of the moonlight, as 'That luminary shortly moved to the mid heaven above the mouldering Towers of the Castle of Blonay, and in a few minutes cast a track of silver which quivered like the scales of a China fish on the waters.' He had contrived to dump the over-enthusiastic 'beauty and heroine' for a Neapolitan lady with a more polite eye for the Picturesque: she compared 'the Castle of Blonay to the Palace of Tiberius or some other antique villa which decorated those classic shores', and it must indeed have resembled a scene from a Claude painting, perfectly re-created. Beckford reminded his aunt of Alexander Cozens's tuition by noting that 'the firelight and the lustre of the full moon occasioned some noble effects of the Chiara Oscura'.

It was a very precious letter, one that Beckford intended should impress not only his aunt but also posterity, hence the fair copy. However, before the impressions conveyed by this careful writing and courtly behaviour have quite faded, it will provide a corrective note of realism to turn to a quick scribble written in Beckford's own ugly hand on the back of a trial page of a letter which he was preparing, two weeks later, to send to his half-sister. It reads: 'Bologna sausages are filthy things because the ogres shite them which accounts for the composition being so nicely mingled.' At this stage Elizabeth was still his soul-mate. He had not yet realised that she faithfully reported his every revelation to 'my dear mother', who must have been having second thoughts as to the wisdom of the Geneva enterprise. Where, in all that dancing, had Mr Lettice been?

In Geneva, when Evian's summer season was ended, a new urban society closed pleasantly around Beckford. Colonel Hamilton's first cousin by his Genevan mother was the artist Jean Huber, a self-assured eccentric, a Freemason, and an influential member of the city's ruling Council of the Hundred. Beckford, always whimsically inclined, was delighted to be taken up by Huber who, a passionate falconer, was actually training his birds to pull a balloon with a man in a basket beneath. A competent painter and a silhouettist, Huber had portrayed his friend and fellow Freemason Voltaire with a shoe dangling coyly from one absent-minded foot; Voltaire, by this time very old and infirm, was living just outside Geneva's city boundary, at Ferney. Huber had three sons, all talented. There was François, 'Huber *des abeilles*', who though blind had written a book on bees, Pierre, 'Huber *des fournis*', an authority on ants; and Jean-Daniel, 'Huber *le Jeune*', six years older than Beckford and soon to become a role model, a substitute for the elder brother he lacked.

In the manuscript of his biography Redding wrote that 'at times it was difficult to detach young Beckford from this amiable family and get him back to his studies'. In addition to their town house the Hubers had, as did Colonel Hamilton, a country villa. But whereas the Colonel's lay east of the old city near the brooding cliffs of the Salève, the Huber villa was at Cologny on the lake shore, a place where Beckford could swim and row boats, just as he had done at Fonthill.

It was Jean-Daniel who became, to quote Redding again, 'an intimate friend of Mr Beckford and resembled him much in the liveliness of his imagination and his humorous satirical turn'. Through him, Beckford joined an amateur dramatic society of young Genevans who met every week and divided into groups; each group was given a proverb or folk-saying and would then have to write and perform a play to illustrate the allotted theme. Fifty years later Beckford still proudly treasured the script of one he had written. It has not been preserved, but we know the cast was made up of an old attorney, a young captain, a widow and a lackey; Beckford played the young captain. At the time it was written, Beckford was seventeen; Jean-Daniel was twenty-three, and had been married for three years – the result of a romantic adventure in Rome where he had eloped with Isabella Ludovisi, a rich young heiress, a novice in a convent: hardly the ideal friend Mrs Beckford had been hoping for when she sent her son abroad to avoid the temptations of Oxford.

In his *England's Wealthiest Son* Boyd Alexander noticed that Beckford fell in love with a young man in Geneva, but dismissed it as 'a crush' and did not realise that the young man can only have been Jean-Daniel. The affair remained Platonic and, with Isabella in the equation, perfectly respectable: but it was far from being a mere 'crush'. Jean-Daniel went on to become a well-known artist of rural Switzerland, '*le Peintre de l'Oberland*'. Whereas Salamon Gessner and Rousseau idealised the peasant life into a rococo-style idyll, Jean-Daniel painted it as it really was, picturesque but mired in cow-dung, the chalets battered and untidy, the peasants themselves sometimes in rags. Beckford was a natural idealiser, an escapist, given to elegant rural frolics like that at Blonay, but in week-long expeditions into the mountains with Jean-Daniel he came to appreciate the hard lot of the average countryman. This, as much as anything, may have gone into the making of the caring and responsible landlord at Fonthill whose depature in 1822 was still regretted twenty years later, as Venn Lansdown discovered, by the cottagers. Jean-Daniel Huber's influence on Beckford has not been appreciated, simply because Beckford wrote up only one of their expeditions, and even in that he failed to name Jean-Daniel as his companion.

In contrast, his close relationship with Jean Huber, the father, is always noted, because Beckford left an affectionate and witty pen-portrait of him, rather in the style of a *Times* obituary. There is a strong possibility that the elder Huber, in league with Colonel Hamilton, persuaded Beckford to become initiated into a local lodge of the Geneva Freemasons at this time. Beckford's great-uncle on his mother's side was James Hamilton, 7th Earl of Abercorn, in 1726 the Eighth Grand Master of the first Grand Lodge of England. Freemasonry in its eighteenth-century revival moved out from Scotland to England, and then to the Continent. Between 1723 and 1726 a John Hamilton introduced Freemasonry to Geneva, at a time when Abercorn had become a member of the Lodge of St Thomas in Paris. Another Hamilton, George, was later a Provincial Grand Master in Geneva. It seems probable, therefore, that Colonel Hamilton, himself a second-generation Geneva resident, was also a Freemason. Certainly Dr Verdeil, whom Beckford chose a few years later as his physician—companion, was a prominent Mason and political activist who eventually rose to the rank of Grand Maître du Grand Orient National Helvétique Roman.

An experience such as initiation into Freemasonry would explain the obscure and mystic slant of the 'Centrical History', which Beckford began to write as soon as he was settled in Geneva. It was a 'Centrical History' because it describes a journey to the centre of the earth, and it includes a series of initiation ceremonies with experiences of nudity, baths, anointings and trials of fire, ice and mental concentration. Some 25,000 words long, this of all Beckford's literary projects was the most oddly misconceived. When he was surrounded by glorious Alpine scenery, it was perverse to begin a story in which all the events took place underground. He was still so fascinated by the grottoes and quarries of Fonthill that for his interminable descriptive passages he relied upon his memories of Joseph Lane's decorative devices and his imagination, rather than the cliffs of the Salève and the snows of Mont Blanc. The book has no real plot, only a chain of improbable obstacles that have to be overcome in order to reach a mystery which is never explained, as the narrative was never completed. The moral character of the work is too benign and improving, giving no scope for Beckford's worldly cynicism or his delight in villainy. But if his interest in comparative religions was leading him through the Hindu and Buddhist faiths at the time and he had just been through a Masonic initiation ceremony, he would have been full of those vague, high-minded aspirations which suffuse the writing: purification, forgiveness, understanding and fidelity.

The story opens with Beckford wandering alone at night on a

Swiss mountain, but then reverts, disappointingly, to Fonthill, with a grove, a house and a lake. There is 'a gloomy dell skirted with huge masses of rock' penetrated by 'grottoes'. Beckford can distinguish 'the awful mouth of a cavern' and a stream 'that trickled and oozed from the porous stone'. Two strange beings confront him, one a good old man, an Indian priest, Moisasour. (It is hard to find a bad old man in Beckford's writings: for him, old age and goodness were virtually one and the same. It is significant that he made Eblis, the Lord of Evil in *Vathek*, youthful and good-looking.) The other figure is a lovely woman, Nouronihar, and together they lead a willing but nervous Beckford through endless 'lustrations' and torrents and over vertiginous gulfs. The story has no structure, only subterranean vignettes: 'light illumined the concave vault above ... crystals of every colour, minerals and ores of the most vivid hues [a Joseph Lane speciality] were studded on the craggy arches which irregularly bent over our passage'. There is 'an iron grated door by which I was brought in', and he marvels at 'two ranges of colossal statues' (both iron gratings and colossal statues still feature in the Lanes' quarry grottoes at Fonthill). Then, as they lead him ever deeper into the underworld, Beckford enters 'another grot, small in comparison with the former for it was not 50 paces long': suddenly 'two wide arches at one extremity [the Hermitage, perhaps, in its dell] admitted the view of a little lawn blooming with wild flowers'. So the image of an underworld is not sustained, but has become a park. Then he returns to the cave motif:

> the sides, the roof and part of the pavement of the grot were covered with an incrustation of greyish spar, very pleasing to the eye [this could be that lost grotto of the petrifying spring] and several shells were fixed to the rock at irregular distances, which contained a variety of flowers [flower vases decorated the Fonthill grottoes] ... At the end opposite the arches, a basin scooped out of the same spar as the rest of the cave [polished Chilmark limestone?] received the current of the stream and afforded a very commodious bath.

Eventually Moisasour reveals that he is the controlling angelic spirit of the Earth, a fallen angel who has worked his way back into the Almighty's favour by a series of virtuous reincarnations

climaxing with him as a Brahmin priest: Moisasour was Eblis/
Lucifer, but arrived at a happier fate. According to Arab legend Eblis,
also the controlling angel of the Earth, rebelled against Allah when
Allah created Man and told Eblis to obey his new creation; refusing,
Eblis became the Lord of Evil, in permanent rebellion against the
Almighty. Like Milton before him, Beckford was inclined to sympathise with rebellious evil; indeed, there was obviously some question
in his mind as to what really was evil, and what good. God could
forgive the Devil, if Moisasour was to be believed. One object of the
interminable cave quest was to visit 'The Eternal Records of Truth',
where Beckford found lists of 'a numerous tribe of philosophers
without wisdom, of learned men without knowledge, of good ones
without virtue'. This might be a standard adolescent exercise in cynicism about worldly values, or it could be a sign of a permanent
detachment from conventional morality.

Finally, after reaching a hollow land in the earth's core,
Nouronihar promises Beckford the secrets to a great mystery. She
seats him in yet another grotto and then, in a musical equivalent of
sexual congress – which at this stage in his life Beckford had clearly
not experienced, only imagined – 'she breathed a strain of fire which
wrapped me in such enthusiastic ecstasies that I seemed to behold
the spirits of the stars of which she sang'. The musical climax was
reached and Nouronihar, more satisfied than Beckford, 'consumed
by the fervour of her sensations, languidly sank on the carpet of
flowers'. As she then opens the book of mysteries, the 'Centrical
History' ends abruptly. Had Beckford realised that he had no mysteries to unfold? Or was sexual intercourse the mystery, and one that
had already been delivered, in the form of a musical abstraction?

In truth, the 'Centrical History' is tedious adolescent nonsense in
which Beckford was practising one of his many 'voices', a mode of
aureate gushing prose, Blakeian in its numinous abstractions and
high-flown terminology. Much later in life he attended one of
William Blake's London exhibitions, and in those awesome, long-
night-gowned Gods whom Blake repetitively illustrated may perhaps
have recognised Moisasour, his own Indian sage.

Blake took his gods from Emmanuel Swedenborg (1688–1772), his
century's equivalent of today's distinguished scientist who in late

middle age sees a flying saucer and dedicates his last years to tracking down UFOs – hence the attraction of Swedenborg's voluminous ramblings for the more esoteric modern scholar. He was a purveyor of theology and science for the self-educated and credulous, men like William Blake, but Beckford owned a copy of his *Heaven and Hell,* and doubtless found his anthropomorphic vision of God and the Hereafter encouraging. Academically the book rates no higher than Tolkien's *Lord of the Rings,* and in its time had much the same influence.

Whether Beckford ever became a Swiss Freemason must remain a speculation. What is certain is that his mood in the autumn of 1777 was both Gothic and Goethean. It is unlikely that he spent any more time than was absolutely necessary to his studies in Colonel Hamilton's confined town house, where he had only a bedroom. As usual he had travelled from England with a considerable retinue, not only Lettice but several body-servants, and he seems to have spent as much time as possible writing his 'Centrical History' in the Colonel's villa at the foot of what was to become his magic mountain, the Salève. 'Our house is not large', he wrote to Elizabeth, 'but it has thick walls and odd windows that give it an antique air I am fond of. Besides, every piece of furniture glistens with cleanliness – sunflowers and jasmine in the garden, two rivulets and a wood … a meadow dropping down from the Salève.'

Almost at once Beckford began to seek Romantic refuge from those courses in civil law and natural sciences. They bored him to tears, but helpfully convinced him that his true bent was artistic. He escaped by going up the Salève, a long ridge of cliffs, two thousand feet high, that level off into a rolling green plateau. A Catholic curé of one of the hill villages took paying guests, and Beckford revelled in the peasant simplicity of the experience, describing the curé as 'a meagre figure in a black robe who seemed nearly related to Merlin'. In the presbytery he was given a room with a plain board floor and a bed with tattered curtains hanging from the bed-posts; the roughness of it all charmed him. Considering that he was one of the richest subjects of the British Crown, his feeling for peasant simplicities and homely living was remarkably individual and assured.

Taken by his host for a long moonlight walk, he decided to play a role, one possibly practised already at Wardour Castle, certainly one he was to play again in Portugal:

> The old Bigot imagining he had a most zealous Catholic for his guest began a long conversation about the perverse heretical disposition of my country.... I began a pathetic harangue upon the separation of England from the Mother Church ... not to mention Thomas à Becket and fifty more sufferers on the like occasion.

Queen Elizabeth's soul, the Curé assured him, 'was taken away in a black cloud after her death'.

As they stood on the brink of the Salève's terrifying cliffs admiring 'the precipices that caught additional horrors from the glimpses of the moon', the priest pointed to a ruined tower and began a very long ghost story about the Prince of Nemours, imprisoned in the tower by the wicked Count de la Roche. Beckford included the entire story in a lengthy letter to sister Elizabeth, and here the whole episode becomes suspect. Elizabeth had just sent him a copy of her novel *Louisa, or The Recollection of an Affectionate Daughter*. Was the ever-competitive half-brother replying in kind? On their return walk to the village, the Curé allegedly related a personal experience of seeing the spectral figure of a giant in armour clanking among the rocks: was this the Curé's own story, or had Beckford recently been reading Horace Walpole's *The Castle of Otranto*, with its similar giant armoured ghost?

The letter turns to self-mockery at all these 'delicious superstitions', 'the wan Spectres and the prowling Curé and all the fa fa fummical narrations I dulled you with a page or two ago'. Realising that these were not impressive enough, Beckford casually dropped the detail that Madame Crasner Dillon had invited him to dinner to meet Voltaire, 'but being seized with an attack of fissick the old sinner did not choose to be unkenelled'. Voltaire's niece had come in his place, dressed 'strikingly like a smart frenchified Commode both in shape and hue'. With her was a marquis, 'a nice, slim, sweet thing between the Rt. Hon. Humphrey Morrice and an Italian greyhound, as perfumed and as full of Epigrams and pretty Conceits as a quilted Ladies' portfeuille'. The letter is an early example of Beckford's wit and indicates the tone – light, spiteful and camp – which he and his

half-sister must have practised together in their long Fonthill togetherness. By September he was, he told Elizabeth, sending chapters of
his 'Centrical History' to Cozens, 'in numbers would not, I fancy,
meet with your applause'. At all costs, truth included, Elizabeth had
to be impressed. She was a successful authoress with two novels to
her credit and recently married to an army officer, Colonel Thomas
Hervey, a grandson of the Earl of Bristol.

Beckford recalls affectionately how she used to hold him fascinated for hours 'when I was a very small Animal' by her translations
of Ariosto. At the mere memory, his prose suddenly brims with
images:

> ... thro' all the wild excursions of his enchanting poetry, thro' Forests
> of Oaks in Caledonia and thro' Woods of Citron and myrtle in the
> groves of India, now stalking across the Mountains of Spain. One
> moment descending into the cells of enchantment and at another
> diving into the very depths of the Ocean, wandering amongst corra-
> lines and sporting amidst all the treasures which the Sea has swallowed.

At the same age, Thomas Chatterton wrote with the same eclectic
brilliance, and Beckford had Coleridge's range of literary images and
the same Gothic drive to fantasy. All that was needed was direction,
and a wise friend. Most of the 'letters' from these Swiss months of
excited experimental writing which survive in transcript appear to
have been intended for Alexander Cozens; they are just as likely to
be reveries, exercises in dramatic self-analysis inspired by the episto-
lary form of Goethe's *The Sorrows of Werther* and written with an eye
to eventual publication, the record of a lively adolescent mind in self-
induced turmoil. The letters addressed and actually sent to his half-
sister, as she moved around the Low Countries following her new
husband in his military postings, are quite different in tone, relaxed
and amusing, full of reminiscence and advice, while the 'reverie' or
Cozens letters vary in mood according to Beckford's literary model
on the day he was writing. Geneva was not so much the place where
Beckford was educated by distinguished academics as one where he
educated himself as an experimental stylist and *pasticheur*.

On 12 September Sterne was his model, so the style was colloquial
and whimsical:

Let us hasten forward or we shall miss the Sunset from the promontories we ogled from Thun. What an abominable Bridge! Never in my Life did I behold so crazy a composition. We must unlight and lead our Horses. Hark, what a rambling amongst the planks echoed by the cove! The trotting of my poor sober Mare becomes as stately as the paces of three managed Horses moderately speaking. A very good Mountain Bridge!

In another letter, dated 21 November, Beckford had turned himself into a haunted figure from Macpherson's Ossianic *Fragments*, fake Celtic twilight of 1760–5, but still high fashion in 1777 because Goethe's Werther had written that 'Ossian has taken the place of Homer in my heart and imagination. To what a world does the illustrious bard take me! To wander in the heaths and wilds, surrounded by impetuous whirlwinds in which, by the feeble light of the moon, we discover the spirits of our ancestors!' Accordingly, Beckford too had to wander by feeble moonlight on a Celtic ghost-hunt.

The Duchess of Queensberry, a relative on his mother's side, had recently died. A formidable old lady, she had made Beckford read the Bible when he was paying her a visit as a small boy: she would provide a convenient ancestral spirit. He wrote, with many Ossianic rows of dots:

I call ... but the bellowing of the tide deadens my Voice. I am alone on the Shore ... dread is my situation ... The blasts increase and wistle dismally in my ears. I shudder ... What shriek was that? – no Bird is on the wing! ... I must hasten home. I tremble, and of what am I afraid? – ah! Too well I know what means those shades, for surely I beheld something flit before me pale as the Ashes of an Altar. Something roze on a Wave and sighed. See it rears itself again and moans – it moans. – O How am I deceived or that shade wears the resemblance of one that is no more and was most dear to me ... cruel illusion.

Perhaps it was cruel to drop the old Duchess into Lake Geneva on a stormy night, but it was competent Macpherson pastiche.

Even more mischievously, out to imitate the innocent pastoral mood of Gessner's *Idylls*, Beckford proposed in a letter dated 24

November to take his idealised Cozens figure on a camping expedition into the savannahs of South America. The real Cozens was old, very slow, and so small that Beckford once jokingly suggested making cat-flaps for him to get through doors; but for the ideal Cozens,

> Yes that time may arrive when we may seek the green solitudes and roam about foreign Mountains, when we may sit together in such a Valley as I have described and gaze at the last gleams of departing Day. How should I delight to wander with you thro' remote Forests and pitch our tents by Moonlight in a Wilderness. Then would we observe the Deer bounding over the Lawn and the Goats frisking on the margin of a Stream without a wish to disturb their happiness. Neither the Gun, the Arrow or the Net should be in our hands. We would cultivate some pastures and in the season gather ripe Corn sown by ourselves. Every week we would vary our abode and sleep upon Hills in the twilights of Midsummer, there to catch the Dream of inspiration from whence to presage the events of future Times.

This is wonderful nonsense, but just the beginning of a wilder fantasy. Not only would old Cozens have to pitch his tent in the wilderness, but when they met 'Savages' he would have to 'take up [his] Lute and make sweet harmony, an harmony breathing benevolence understood even by the rude Tribes'. If Beckford was thinking of the Jesuit missions in Paraguay, he carried his imaginings much further: 'Next would succeed the dance, the clang of instruments and universal joy. Our hearts would be dilated and we should join in the wildest expressions of our feelings' – by which time the notion of taking Cozens with him to these noble savages was becoming a little too improbable. 'But to whom am I expressing these romantic Ideas of living in Tents?' he asks himself. 'Am I addressing myself to a Spirit that catches fire at my own Enthusiasm?' It is apparent that he is either addressing himself, his own best and most satisfying company, or fantasising ever more ambitious expeditions on the lines of the rambles which he and Jean-Daniel Huber had been making in the hills behind Evian. A few lines later the expedition is off to the North Pole for a snatch of 'sublime horror', even to 'the Country of Odin', where they will see 'thro' the Mist of Blood that fills the Horizon, his

Ministers, the Gigantic *Valkyriur* shooting along with the Souls of
the Brave to his *Valhalla*'.

The 1770s were a stimulating time to be alive and reading in a
well-stocked library. There was Macpherson, Thomas Gray's poetry,
Mallet's *Northern Antiquities* and, as the great Southern Ocean was
explored, travel books published in Spain, Portugal, France and
Britain. In his usual airy style, Beckford claimed to be absorbing new
languages almost in his sleep. Portuguese was allegedly one of his
acquisitions, though when he arrived in Lisbon ten years later he had
to start learning it from scratch: all his knowledge of Portuguese
travels in the Far East came in reality from the notes to Mickle's
English translation of Camoens's *Lusiades*.

The 'Gothic' castle of Prangins, where Beckford had to spend
several weekends following a course of lectures by the Chevalier
d'Espinasse on natural science, illustrates perfectly the way his mind
was working. Set on a hillside overlooking the lake north of Geneva,
the château is a four-square classical building with a pediment and
corner pavilions. It was designed and built for the Baron Prangins by
Abraham Le Coultre between 1732 and 1739, and has not a single
Gothic feature in its fabric. But Beckford, while pretending to an
indifferent contempt for him, always had one eye on Horace
Walpole: Walpole had written in *Otranto* of a Gothic castle in which
comical servants had amusing adventures, so the château de Prangins
had to be transformed. 'What I would not give', Beckford wrote to
Elizabeth, 'for you to see this strange edifice, especially at Night when
its vast Halls and winding passages are just visible by the light of
expiring fires. It is then that I frequently pace along the deserted
apartments, listen to the murmurs of the Lake and mark the Owls
shreiking from the battlements of the gateway.' With the scene set,
it was time for a touch of noble melancholy: 'It is at these moments
I recollect all that has happened to me, lament those Friends that are
no more and cast a trembling look towards Futurity.'

'Futurity' was Beckford's 'in' word. He had picked it up, *futurité*,
from French translations of Goethe's *Werther*, along with Werther's
habit of fluent emotional introspection. Prangins was given 'tall
windows painted with every colour you can imagine ... the history
of Saints and Dragons and the adventures of Heroes long since

forgotten'. There is not a shred of truth in these descriptions or that of a hall with 'Gothic Arches', but they made an ideal setting for an episode of Otrantine comic relief, complete with foolish servitor:

> I am always obliged to pass thro' this Hall at Midnight to get to my bedchamber and I assure you Norman has more than once wished to be excused following of me, for it happened of a Moonlight Night, last week, just as he had got by three of the painted windows, a very reverend owl who had taken possession of the fourth saluted him with such a hoop as made him believe all the swiss Devils (as he terms them) were bouncing out of the Casement, so down dropped a snug warming pan he was conveying to poor shivering Mr Lettice's bed.

In the two novels he wrote in the mid 1790s in rivalry with 'my dear sister', Beckford's humour seldom rose above this elementary level. Elegant alienation was his true forte, and for that he required the detachment from normal Christian values to be found in the casual ruthlessness and instant amorality of the *Arabian Nights*. Throughout these richly active writing months in Geneva he was moving in the Muslim direction and *Vathek*, supposedly written in a white heat of inspiration in 1782, had begun to take shape in experimental drafts before he returned to England in the autumn of 1778.

In the more interesting and constructive passages Beckford wrote as he attempted to conclude the 'Centrical History', the religious background shifted from Hinduism to Persia and Islam. But first he had to write Nouronihar out of his system, and this he did by having her make passionate sexual love all night in the tomb house of her semi-divine ancestors. This time he took no refuge in mere musical ecstasies: her lover was the full-blooded Prince Humaison. To begin with, Nouronihar resisted his advances, but 'at length after an infinity of struggles which served but to foment my desires, all agitated – all enamoured, I threw myself in his arms and there, without reflecting on the sanctity of the place, impiously compleated my felicity. O deified Brama why didst thou withdraw thy sacred influence and abandon thy wretched descendent?'

This, the only description of heterosexual intercourse in any of Beckford's writings, is followed by agonies of remorse: 'I believed the cold hand of my ancestors was upon me – I screamed – the Prince awoke and flew to my assistance ... in one instant the whole transaction rushed into his mind, he exclaimed – "O Nouronihar what have we done?" – I answered alone by tears.' Unable to cope with the situation and apparently rather disgusted by his own imagination, Beckford broke off in mid sentence: 'After several moments of the saddest silence ...'

With Nouronihar, for all her earlier spirituality, now beyond the pale, Beckford wrote the idyll of Hylas and Hercules. In this a band of lustful Naiads pull Hercules' beautiful young boyfriend into their pool as he is drawing water for his lover. Young girls are seen as the sex-crazed enemies of a lovely male friendship, and in one strange little scribble among his papers Beckford admitted, 'Whenever I see a bubble rising from the water I think someone like Hylas is concealed by the Naiads below.' He seems to have been delighted by this elegantly written venture into homo-eroticism, as he had several fair copies made and as late as 1834 was still hoping to publish it.

After 'Hylas' Beckford returned to the East for inspiration, and found in Herbelot's *Bibliothèque Orientale* the strange legend of the seventy-two 'Ante Adamite' Solimans who had ruled the earth and controlled the Dives and Genii before the creation of Man. Fanoun was their royal capital, and their burial place a great cavern under the Mountain of Caf. Also in Herbelot was Aherman, the evil opposite in Persian mythology of Ormozd, the Lord of Light. Beckford's first vision of the dead had a dreadful grandeur. In a stately tomb house under the mountain,

> Let me behold the forms of antient & venerable personages, their brows bound with regal diadems, extended on beds of state – this their last abode – Let me survey these chambers of perpetual sleep in silent reverence – Let me undisturbed gaze at the solemn roof arching above my head, the succession of strange and stupendous columns ranged on either side – the austere coutches in the intervals between – the faded forms stretched upon them. And as I muse may some plaintive and solitary voice fill the space with holy melody.

It was a chamber such as he was to describe again in the last brilliant chapter of *Vathek*.

But in his next vision, still set in a cavern under Caf, he expressed the most lasting obsession of his whole life, one with which he was still struggling in 1843, a year before his death. This was the horror of the living dead. Now, in the cavern, all the wicked 'Magicians & pretended Sages whose lives have been spent in the service of Aherman & in the exercise of unlawful power' were lying in a terrible un-death. Horrid spectres in the form of noxious birds and toads guarded the living corpses. 'I have been told,' Beckford scribbled in fascinated horror,

> and tremble to repeat it, that these wretches, tho' seeming sunk in the repose of death & exhibiting to all appearances the most loathsome images of corruption, still retain a sense of life & are conscious to all the horrors which surround them. Nay, those who have been permitted to view this melancholy place pretend to have perceived a languid motion in their eyes, to have noticed, ever & anon, a convulsive start, even to have heard a feeble moan spring from coffers of incorruptible cedar.

This is committed writing, and when Beckford wonders 'what term Alla has placed to their affliction', the answer, straight from the Methodistical lips of Aunt Effingham, is pitiless: 'When these rocks, these mountains, and even Caf itself will pass away like the clouds of the morning, when the last Earthquake arrives, Aherman may claim them for his own & awake them to keener torments.' From this second account of Caf it seems that the optimistic view of Judgement Day expressed in the 'Centrical History', where even a fallen angel like Moisasour could, after doing penance, be forgiven, has altered to one featuring Alla, the permanently vengeful.

These writings, together with his regular courses in law and the sciences, carried Beckford through to May 1778. Then, in a mood of nervous religiosity, he persuaded Lettice, his faithful and obliging tutor, to accompany him on a 'pilgrimage' – that was the actual, Catholic term he used – to the mother-house of the Carthusian order, the Grande Chartreuse, founded by St Bruno in 1084 in a remote mountain valley south of Chambéry. Here, yet again, he was copying Horace Walpole, who had made the same 'pilgrimage', though in no religious spirit, with his friend Thomas Gray on their journey to Italy in 1739. Beckford claimed that Gray, not Walpole, was his inspiration, and encouraged Lettice to write a poem to set down alongside Gray's offering in the monastery's visitors' book.

In their general determination to believe that Alexander Cozens was the sinister controlling influence behind the adolescent Beckford, biographers ignore the evidence that it was John Lettice who presided benignly over all these jaunts, wrote poetry to order, maintained a detached balancing act between the suspicious dowagers and the errant son, and allowed his charge to do exactly as he pleased while encouraging a flow of experimental writing. It helps to put the relationship between the two into perspective to know that Beckford signed his letters to Lettice 'affc yrs Zizzi'. For good or ill, Beckford was virtually Lettice's creation.

The whole Chartreuse episode was written up as a set-piece of Continental travel and published, once in the suppressed *Dreams, Waking Thoughts and Incidents* of 1783, then again in Beckford's *Italy; with Sketches of Spain and Portugal* of 1834, where it has no natural place. Perhaps the original impetus which led to the pilgrimage was sincere, but it is not easy to sympathise with Beckford's posturings in the text. On his way he brooded by torrents, finding that they 'answered my ideas of those dismal abodes, where, according to the druidical mythology, the ghosts of conquered warriors were bound'. Then, as he approached the Chartreuse, he felt 'a thousand sensations I despair of describing and stood before the gate of the convent with as much awe as some novice or candidate newly arriv'd to start the holy retirement of the order'.

Walpole endured only one vegetarian meal at the Chartreuse before he retreated back to humanity. Beckford, always for moral reasons a semi-vegetarian, loved the regime, stayed three days with the hospitable monks, and gave them the impression, as he had with that village curé, that he was all but a Catholic convert. He insisted one evening on having the great gate opened to allow him to walk the woods in romantic moonlight, believing that St Bruno would have done the same. When it rained he pored over a life of the Saint and found, as usual, what he wanted to find: an account of a funeral at which the corpse suddenly uttered the dreadful warning, 'I stand before the tribunal and I am condemned by the justice of God'. When he left, the monks, who seem to have been enchanted by his whimsical enthusiasms, assured him that if ever he found life too burdensome he would be very welcome to return. Could it have been then, in a mood of self-indulgent melancholy, that he first conceived the outrageous scheme of retiring, not to the Grande Chartreuse, but to an equally magnificent home-made monastery, where he himself would be the Abbot?

By mid June they were back in Geneva and Beckford was penning for one of his guardians, Lord Thurlow, a suave and essentially mean-ingless account of the tuition he had received over the past year, an end-of-term report designed to secure another rewarding year for him in Geneva; but he was to be disappointed. Boyd Alexander believed that Mrs Beckford had become alarmed by her son's homo-erotic vapourings, which he quoted. But these were private writings, 'reveries' which it is most unlikely she can have read; what is more probable is that the pilgrimage to the Grande Chartreuse had stirred up the family's fears of a Catholic conversion.

Beckford ignored the orders to come home as he was enjoying manly excursions in the high Alpine pastures with Jean-Daniel, and an undated letter to his sister from Féternes, if it was ever passed on to their mother, might explain some of Mrs Beckford's concern about her son's welfare. As usual Beckford had been hunting caves, in this case a Grotte des Fées with stalactites on a cliff high up above the Dranse. After a stiff climb it could be reached only by using an iron ladder which a peasant guide provided for them, and even Beckford seems to have been astonished at the daring of his own actions: 'I began ascending and hung for a second or two between the craggs above and the Woods and Valley below. Had I dropped I should have fallen plump into the clear winding Rivulet whose appearance now for the first time began to alarm me.'

When he had reached the cave, 'this pleasure was rather damped by the ideas of another aerial expedition and another adventure on the River below'. Wordsworth later wrote about the same kind of perilous situation in the *Prelude*:

> Oh! When I have hung
> Above the raven's nest, by knots of grass
> And half-inch fissures in the slippery rock,

but carried it off with more pantheistic aplomb:

> While on the perilous ridge I hung alone,
> With what strange utterance did the loud dry wind
> Blow through my ears! The sky seem'd not a sky
> Of earth – and with what motion moved the clouds!

There is all the difference here, in two decades of maturing sensibilities, between a Romantic poet and a pre-Romantic prose writer; and Beckford, of course, would never have collected birds' eggs; the sight of a trout gasping for air in a fisherman's catch was enough to upset him for a whole day. At no point in his letter, though it is clear from the pronouns that he has a companion in addition to the guide, does he name that companion.

This glimpse of Beckford, not tripping country dances with a baroness or yearning soulfully around a saint's shrine but clinging nervously to a rock face, wearing rough clothes and collapsing exhausted on the grass beside a friend, is a reminder of a masculine, physical side to his nature which is easily forgotten. Later in life he staged hugely popular football matches at Fonthill and encouraged rural sports, rode twenty miles a day, bathed regularly in cold lakes as late in the year as November, and took pride in his fitness well into his late seventies, as Venn Lansdown recorded. However wild his imagination, Beckford was never physically effete, and his mother would have been aware of his fondness for risks and dangerous scrambles: one slip on that iron ladder, and the whole of the Alderman's fortune would have been inherited by Richard, the eldest bastard son.

Rough details of Beckford's other jaunts with Jean-Daniel, often little more than ungrammatical notes, are contained in a small green-backed pocket-book which he used exclusively and very irregularly over a ten-year period to record expeditions. One such account gives a rare glimpse of Jean-Daniel at work: 'Huber took up his abode in the hollow of a colourful chestnut and fell a drawing everything within his reach, cows, peasants, alps, boats, woods and vapours.' Cyrus Redding mentions that Beckford sketched extensively while he was in Switzerland, and regretted that he did not persevere. Jean-Daniel must have been responsible for that resurgence of interest.

Their major 1778 expedition began on 5 July. Hitherto Beckford's mountain attentions had been directed, naturally enough, towards Mont Blanc, often visible from the Salève. Jean-Daniel now persuaded him towards his own favoured peasant-country, the Bernese Oberland. After a tremendous rapture over a storm on the lake, viewed from the top of a Gothic tower at St-Prex near Lausanne, the pocket-book account becomes broken and episodic, as Beckford clearly began to find the going not merely rough, but horrifying. Here he, like Horace Walpole before him, was failing at a Romantic hurdle: Walpole had found the wild massif around the Chartreuse inspiring, but the real Alps at the Mont Cenis an ugly chaos of rock. In the same way, Beckford recoiled when Jean-Daniel took him up the zig-zag path that scales the sheer two-thousand-foot precipice behind Leukerbad and leads to the Gemmi Pass. His notes run:

> July 1778. The Mont Gemmi, a terrifying path Bulwarks of Rock, misshapen masses. After we had mountain 3 leagues, we began to discern the glaciers of Savoy & the Valais, shooting up their white spires into the deep blue sky. We quit the frightful edge of the precipice & enter a savage desert, the summit of the Mount. Beds of Snow, ramparts of ice & rugged rocks slewed all over in the wildest confusion – a full torrent rolls from one of the cliffs and, tumbling over the crags with a hoarse murmur, joins the little blue lake surrounded by shelving steeps & framed in by a smooth green margin, whose flowers & daisies (Antirrhina alpenium) invited us to repose ourselves in their herbage.
>
> We enjoyed wonderfully the green spot which the desolate & savage airs of its environs rendered still more lively – Whilst we were collecting plants, a young peasant wound along the steeps with her goat & offering some milk, we were inclined to stop & accept it, Spread in our Bread on the turf, perfumed with the arromatic herbs we made a chearful meal.

This is no precious prose of noble 'Chiara Oscura' to impress an aunt, and Beckford's relief at reaching a humane landscape and an acceptably picturesque peasant girl is palpable. The lake is the Daubensee, and the Gemmi meadows are still famous for their June flowering.

There is no more about this expedition, and the brevity of his notes may have prevented Beckford from writing an attractive account of it. But the experience cannot have been all fear and exhaustion, for Jean-Daniel took Beckford and his new wife exploring the mountains on their honeymoon in 1783 and he was with Beckford again in 1786, after Lady Margaret's death, on a gruelling horse-back expedition into the Alps around Martigny, where the savagery of the rocks seemed to reflect the ruin of Beckford's own life. As for any homo-erotic passion between the two young men, the words Beckford used in 1778 to describe the emotion are suspect:

> He seemed to hang on to my words, whose eyes drank eager draughts of pleasure from my sight, whose inmost soul was dissolved in tenderness when by chance he touched me, whose countenance was flushed with conscious blushes, who feared to own the passion that stole every vein and poisoned the serenity of his mind … he but pined in solitude and consumed his hours in vain lamentations.

This reads like a wishful and elaborate description of a complete non-event, but the details are pure *Werther*. When Werther broods on his love for Charlotte, now married to Albert and therefore forever beyond his honourable reach, he writes:

> How my heart beats, and my blood boils in my veins, when by accident I touch her finger! – when my feet meet hers under the table. I draw them back with precipitation as if from a furnace; but a secret power again presses me forward and disorders all my senses.

He would not have been Beckford if he had not been even more emotionally vulnerable and verbally ebullient than the fictional Werther. As Werther loved the simple life – flowers, dancing and children – so did Beckford. There was just the one important difference: Werther loved only women. Beckford ignored this, and wrote as if the identification were complete. For him, as for Werther, love excused every verbal excess and emotional gesture. Jean-Daniel probably laughed off any such *longueurs*, if he ever noticed them, and there would be no pining in solitude or vain lamentations for him. For Beckford the danger, more precisely the disaster, was the style, the tempting precedent of an outpouring in letters, uninhibited and unreserved. From Werther on the subject of Charlotte it was captivating; from Beckford to a boy six years his junior it would be ruinous when the letters fell into the hands of a malicious relative.

Beckford came home, chaperoned by his mother, who went out to enforce his return. But now he was warmed by the memory of his first close friendship with another young man. They had sketched together, shared mountain dangers together, picked flowers together. In England he still recalled Jean-Daniel's voice, 'whose thrilling accents sunk with such pleasing, such melancholy tenderness, into the inmost recesses of my existence'. He could only be waiting to repeat the experience, but playing the older role himself and, following Goethe, playing it with a most un-English lack of inhibition.

CHAPTER FIVE

A paedophile as literary hero

Beckford returned from Switzerland determined to frustrate his mother's ambition for him to make a career in politics. Geneva might be part of the Swiss union, but it was culturally French, a city of the French Enlightenment, and there, influenced by the genial, intelligent Hubers, Beckford had become, as he was to remain all his life, a European first and an Englishman only second. In 1778 the first British Empire was falling apart. The American colonists were winning victories; in February France had joined the war on their side; Spain would follow in 1779, and soon the combined fleets of the two Catholic powers would be bottling up the British Navy in Plymouth. In the last war Lord Chatham, then still plain Mr Pitt, had fought back successfully against the odds, and Beckford had been brought up to admire and follow Chatham; now should have been the time to strike defiant attitudes. Instead, in one of his self-indulgent reveries that December, he wrote:

> I scarce ever reflect at present on the state of affairs either in England or America. If I did, what should I encounter but Disgust and Indignation?

In what amounted to a 'Manifesto for Life', written in the spring of 1779, he opted for Art and introversion:

> I will seclude myself if possible from the World and converse many hours every day with you Moisasour and Nouronihar. I am determined to enjoy my dreams and my phantasies and all my singularity, however irksome and discordant to the Worldings around. In spite of them I will be happy.

As a symbol of his independence he chose to identify with the rooks flying noisily about the Fonthill elms. 'How great would be my exultations', he enthused, 'when I found myself returning in a still Evening like this, with innumerable friends all cheerfully conversing together, all smoothly waving Wings and vying with each other in the ease and rapidity of our motions.' But at that point what could so easily have become a sensitive and original evocation of wild life stumbled backwards from the Romantic to the pre-Romantic as his birds were tricked out in Gothick whimsicalities:

> those hollow Cavities beneath in the tree, are they not regarded by your Poets as aweful Caverns where many adventures have happened to Rooks of yore. Perhaps ye have also your superstitious Fears and when warmly established in your nests relate what Spectres have haunted the Beech-roots so far below and croak forth the prophecies your ancestors heard issuing from bowers of Ivy.

The writing is so close to Coleridge's 'ancestral voices prophesying war' and Keats's 'pale mouthed prophets dreaming', yet it ends by being no more than a possible opening to a charming tale for children – 'Rooks of Yore' – that was never told. At this point in his life Beckford had all the instincts for poetry, but not the voice: some time at an English university might have changed him, as it had changed his literary hero, Thomas Gray. A year later, Beckford's instinctive response to Evensong at York Minster, to architectural beauty and the hidden voice of music, was latently as poetic as Wordsworth's response to Westminster Bridge and the sleeping city of London. So it is legitimate to express regret that the scholarly John Lettice, the one man in a position to influence his writing as opposed to his art appreciation, was such a satisfied practitioner of the old-style heroic couplet. Beckford did send his 'Rook Reverie' for Lettice to read, but his tutor was too busy preparing the precocious trivialities of the *Biographical Memoirs* for publication to do more than discuss it in the Senior Common Room of Sidney Sussex College and dismiss it with faint praise. It probably took at least two critical and committed souls to launch one Romantic poet into fame. Gray had Horace Walpole, Wordsworth had Dorothy; Beckford had only John Lettice.

In that spring season Beckford did try his hand at a prose-poem,

'Satyr's Range', a Fonthill version of those *Idylls* by Salamon Gessner so admired, in their French translations, in Geneva. Gessner's artfully simple prose-poems, the literary equivalents of John Flaxman's linear drawings, 'Athenian' Stuart's Greek illustrations and Henry Holland's colonnades, had been coming out in English translations in books and magazines from 1762 onwards. *Rural Poems* and *Select Poems from Mr G...'s Pastorals* both appeared in 1762, *Daphnis* in 1768 and *New Idylles* in 1776; this last was so popular that one or more of its twenty-one separate 'Idylles' was reprinted in seventeen different British periodicals during that year alone. Beckford took the *New Idylles* with him on his Grand Tour in 1780, the only book mentioned by name in his journal. Their translator was William Hooper, whose faithful versions of the Swiss–German originals achieved a neo-Classical simplicity of style that English readers and critics found refreshing after the turgid predictabilities of earlier Augustan translations or derivations from the Classics. Gessner was still alive; he died in 1788, holder of the appropriately Arcadian post of Warden of the Sihlwald, a forest on the road from Zurich to Zug. His artist heroes and models in the *Idylls* were the two Poussins and Claude Lorraine, and their influence is apparent in Hooper's rendering of 'Lycas', which Beckford seems to have taken as his inspiration for 'Satyr's Range'. Lycas and his friend are making a journey to seek the Gods:

> We soon increased our pace when we saw before us, even on the border of our path, some high and spreading trees. There shade was dark as night. Seized with religious awe we entered the grove, and there inhaled a most refreshing breeze. This delicious place at once afforded all that could regale each sense. The tufted trees enclosed a verdant spot, watered by a pure and most refreshing stream. The branches of the trees, bending with golden fruit, hung o'er the bason, and the wild rose, jessamine and mulberry twined in rich clusters round their trunks. A bubbling spring rose from the foot of a monument, surrounded by honeysuckles, the sickly willow and the creeping ivy – O Gods! I cried, how inchanting is this place!

In his own pilgrimage to seek 'the Universal Pan' Beckford, so recently a devout pilgrim at St Bruno's shrine, left Splendens very early, and alone:

I hasten to my skiff, sheltered by a narrow creek and traverse the river between fleets of aquatic birds ... surely they know it is all my care to protect their peaceful reign. Never are they alarmed with Guns, scared with stones or pursued by malicious dogs and their more cruel Masters ... Nor tho' I rest on my oars & listen attentively can I hear anything but those cries of Birds and the lowing of cattle afar off. Happy I am, thrice happy, for no human voice echoes in all the range of prospect.

Having set the scene, he indulged those dreams, fantasies and 'all my singularity' which he found so infinitely preferable to the real life of eighteenth-century politicking. First came the nymphs of Fonthill lake:

Methought new purple was added to the waving flag flowers & a fresher bloom to the Lilly amongst which the eye of my fancy descried a circle of Naiads hand in hand, rising from their caerulean abode to caress the Swans I admire.

'So, willing to be deceived by this sweet illusion', he rowed towards them, 'but a low murmur runs along the shore, the waters foam ... and my intrusion has driven them to their secure cool grottoes.' He determined instead to land on the opposite side of the lake, that 'Satyr's Range', as he called it, which his father had conjured up out of bare quarries and grassy slopes, to 'experience whether the sylvan deities are not more propitious, for surely those thickets, those deep retirements are not unpossessed of Divinity'. Climbing up 'its steeps amongst fern and broom in Blossom' he rested briefly under a lofty pine to 'gather the mushrooms scattered about its roots. These are the food of fauns & whilst I eat them esteem myself one of their number.'

There follows a remarkably beautiful 'phantasy' where, ignoring a path leading to 'glades where Dryads slumber ... or listen to the songs of the Golden Age', Beckford 'ran lightly along the alley where spreading boughs cast a chequered shade' and, applying to his lips 'the horn a Satyr gave me in the groves of Savoy',

Blew an inspiring air that Dale & thicket rang
The Hunters' call to Fame & Dryad known

> The oak-crowned sisters & their chaste eyed Queen,
> Satyrs & sylvan Boys were seen
> Peeping from forth their alleys green.

'O ye rural powers', he continued, in possibly his most sincere declaration of faith in a life of equivocations, 'Deities I have worshipped from my earliest youth – on whose altars I have often heaped produce of a garden I cultivated with my infant hands.' But then an interruption – Pan pipes responded, 'the strain repeated by a 1000 echoes', and he followed this 'more than mortal melody' to a cluster of seven wooden huts. These, the dens of his childhood mentioned in one 'Cozens' letter, had now become the abode of the Gods. In one was a bowl of milk and chestnuts: 'let me pour the milk and offer the chestnuts on a mound of those turfs raised no doubt as an altar to Universal Pan', whom 'prostrate on the turf' he then adored, and wove a garland of woodbines.

In a dream within a dream he falls asleep in the first hut, and then the Gods come down in person. 'The woods are still – Divinity is at hand for hark I hear inumerable feet tripping along the paths & the sound I heard in the Range approaches each instant nearer & nearer – what wild ecstatic flute – what melody – I am calm – I am happy without fear or dread, for never did I offend the power which delights in wilds and mountains. I see them descend that woody slope. What antick forms – & what benignant smiles.' Or, as Keats put it, later, 'What pipes and timbrels? What wild ecstasy?' The same neo-Classical vision is at the heart of English Romanticism; it is the message of Wordsworth's *Tintern Abbey*.

> Knowing that Nature never did betray
> The heart that loved her; 'tis her privilege,
> Through all the years of this our life, to lead
> From joy to joy.

Wordsworth hears it from an inner voice; Beckford prefers to hear it from the God's own lips: 'We have heard thy call & led thee with inviting sounds to this our peaceful & solitary abode. We preserve the herds from the bane of malignant eyes & we will ever defend thee from those who are thine enemies. They end & retire to the . . .' And there, in his accustomed casual manner, Beckford broke off a piece of writing which, if published, would have established him as a pre-Romantic. It remains unpublished to the present day.

If Mrs Beckford ever saw 'Satyr's Range', her Methodistical sensibilities would have been shaken; and if Beckford behaved true to form, he probably read it to her on the evening it was completed. Nervous by now not only of Continental influences but of the predatory presences in her own park, she decided to postpone her son's Grand Tour for a year and instead introduce him to hard economic facts and potential political allies by a tour of England under Lettice's guidance. If she had been able to foresee the result, she would have packed him straight off to Italy.

Setting out in June 1779, they first made a show of patriotic solidarity with the British Navy at Plymouth. Unfortunately, pupil and tutor were both arrested as spies for taking notes of the shipping and had to be bailed out by the Governor, a family friend – exactly the kind of incident calculated to make Beckford defensive and neurotic about the Establishment, and militarism. Their next move should have been harmless enough: a tour of great houses in the south-west, to establish ties of political solidarity. One of their first stops was at Powderham Castle, south of Exeter, the Gothicized seat of the wealthy and indolent 2nd Viscount Courtenay, descended from a family of lineage so ancient and noble that Gibbon spent a whole page of his *Decline and Fall of the Roman Empire* celebrating it. But this Viscount had done nothing more memorable than marry a pretty barmaid in his undergraduate days and raise a family of twelve daughters and one son – William, eleven in 1779.

As Beckford and Lettice went up the Castle drive it was evening, and Beckford caught his first glimpse of little William, playing in the park among the deer: a good-looking child but in no way angelic – black, shoulder-length hair, a long straight nose, and an air of confident superiority engendered by respectful sisters. He was at Westminster School, and from the ease with which he and Beckford, who was only nineteen, hit it off together, may already have been accustomed to admiring 'crushes' from the older boys. It appears to have been, on both sides, love at first sight. The fact that it was a forbidden love, like Werther's for Charlotte, will have made it all the more exciting for Beckford. Now he could play out Werther's doomed love himself, wrong in the eyes of convention, right by the standards of Goethe's seductive adolescent outpourings.

A second attraction at Powderham was the triangular viewing tower on the hill behind the Castle, completed by the Viscount in 1773 as a retreat from his children. An upper room with attractive plaster-work commanded fine views of the Exe estuary. Redding writes that the 'young Beckford was quite enchanted' with the 'lofty tower', and it must have reminded him of his father's unfinished triangular tower on Stop Beacon.

In the course of a three-day visit, Beckford became completely smitten with little William. In a long rapturous reverie written in Exeter the first night after leaving Powderham, he projected his parting from William in the same terms Goethe had used for Werther's parting from Charlotte. Werther lamented:

> She went down the walk: I stood and followed her with my eyes, then threw myself on the ground in a passion of tears; I got up again and ran to the terrace, and there I still saw, under the shade of the lime trees, her white gown waving near the garden gate. I stretched out my arms, and she was gone.

Beckford wrote:

> Why did we experience this sudden love for each other? Did it not increase each hour and when I quitted his native castle – what expressive melancholy looks were cast after one down the long avenue – the solemnity of which was increased by the dusk – for it was dusk – when I parted from all my soul doted on. During the whole journey that evening no other object filled my soul.

The end of his 'Centrical History' left Beckford uneasily seated in a grotto with Nouronihar, drinking coconut milk. Now, in his Exeter hotel bedroom, he dreamed or fantasised himself back into 'a dreary cave across which ran several bubbling streams': it was the lakeside grotto at Fonthill again, but this cave had 'heaps of coco-nuts' piled so high 'that Whole nations I think could never have consumed them'. Into this odd realm of darkness, 'sunk deep in the centre of the Earth', an 'Angelic Shadow issued suddenly ... leading in its hand the one I love – he flew to me. I sprang forward to catch him in my arms. "Rest happy" said a thrilling voice – "no one shall disturb you for ages".'

The bargain which the voice, 'the great power-source of all felicity', then arranged was that the two Williams might live forever together, eating coconuts, provided that they 'freely renounce the lustre of the Sun for each other'. This deeply unattractive condition was immediately agreed to in the dream, but then Beckford awoke, 'just as I stretched out my hand for a nut – and behold no C was near'. What is so strange about Beckford's cave image, quite apart from the unfortunate nuts, is that the cavern seems to be associated in his mind with both the ghoul-haunted tomb of the living dead and this safe refuge of love eternal. Symbolically it only makes sense if love and death were equally disagreeable or equally attractive to him.

If Beckford is to be believed, the face of his 'dear C' obsessed him throughout his English tour. Without hesitation or self-questioning he adapted his child lover to all the standard poses of Romantic infatuation:

> I ventured to pour forth my complaints and have many times told my story to the lake at Keswick as I walked on its banks ... Every morning I discovered some new recess in the rocks – some rude neglected spot where I might indulge my reveries and think undisturbed on my dear C... his engaging looks and unaffected partiality for me ... I wept – I sighed and growing intolerably restless – mounted the cliff – and look'd towards London.

At no point is there the slighest sign of guilt: this is a pure Love, and such a Love excuses everything and calls for no concealment. When the tour ended at London, 'the most supreme joy awaited me for my C was almost the first person that came out to receive me. A few minutes ...' But written words could no longer contain Beckford's joy, and there he broke off. Cleverly – perhaps 'cunningly' would be more apt – he saw that in Courtenay's crowded female household Aunt Charlotte Courtenay was the one who made the decisions. Charlotte was approaching thirty, an old maid by the standards of the day, and vulnerable, so Beckford cultivated her as a friend.

Mrs Beckford was never under any illusions about the sexual antics of her emotional son. In his absence she had been preparing counter-measures, and had invited a couple of well-bred women, one of them unmarried, to stay at Fonthill. As usual her plans went dreadfully wrong. The two were sisters, daughters of Lord Rivers of Stratfield Saye in Hampshire, and it was Louisa, the married one, a walking disaster-area of emotional frustration, who attracted the ever susceptible Beckford and who fell desperately in love with him.

If art is to be the only consideration, Louisa was precisely what Beckford needed at this juncture: a flattering soul-mate to encourage him in every emotional self-indulgence. She was married to his cousin Peter Beckford of Iwerne Stepleton, a village eighteen miles from Fonthill, over the Dorset border. Her husband, an admirably civilised countryman, was writing a book, *Thoughts upon Hare and Fox Hunting* (1781), which has remained a classic. They had one young son but had grown apart, as Louisa despised fox hunting and the hunting fraternity that thronged her house. In Beckford, a committed animal lover, she found a fellow spirit. Where humans were concerned, however, she was without moral scruples: she subsequently offered to murder her husband and give her only child to Beckford as a rival catamite to 'my dear C', anything to hold his attention. He, to be fair, showed not the slightest interest in either proposal, but used her shamelessly, as confidante and emotional prop, whenever his relatives pressured him to behave more conventionally. Some allowance must be made for her as from the very start of her involvement with Beckford she was in decline with tuberculosis and desperate for any and every experience before the tomb opened.

In all her turgid outpourings of need and love to Beckford, Louisa never refers to any explicit incident of a sexual nature occurring between them, and she was so deeply involved emotionally that if there had been any physical relations, it seems likely she would have dredged them up time and again. All their acquaintance, however, seem to have believed that they were lovers, with the result that Peter Beckford became angry and jealous. It may well be that Beckford encouraged such suspicions, as a cover for his pursuit of Courtenay. In the portrait of Louisa which Beckford commissioned from Sir Joshua Reynolds, the artist's dislike of the woman can be sensed in her spiteful lips, weak chin and malicious eyes. Most authorities describe her as sacrificing to Hebe the goddess of health and eternal youth, but in fact Reynolds has painted Louisa as the goddess herself, going about her duty of handing out nectar and ambrosia to the gods during their feasts. Louisa–Hebe holds aloft the sacred ewer containing the divine draught to fill their goblets. Less easily explained is the sacrificial brazier around which two ugly serpents are entwined. Louisa posed to Beckford as something of an adept in black magic: the painting prompts one to wonder whether she confided any of this to Reynolds. In Greek legend, Hebe exposed herself indecently as a result of a fall, lost her job, and was replaced by Ganymede, a beautiful boy whom Zeus, disguised as an eagle, carried off to Olympus on his back. Such ironic symbolism must have delighted Beckford. The picture has a horrid, commanding beauty, and the image is anything but one of health.

As his first experience of womanly love, Louisa goes far to explain his eventual homosexual identity. She, not poor Mrs Beckford, was the model for the appalling Carathis in *Vathek*: a witch, a murderess, and an ingenious plotter. Beckford's devout and strictly moral mother would never have dreamed of 'stripping herself to her inmost garment', as Carathis does on Vathek's tower, or of burning rhinoceros horns and mummies on a bonfire – but that is exactly the sort of pseudo-evil charade Louisa would have delighted in, and very much what she appears to be doing in the Reynolds portrait, which was being painted as the first chapters of *Vathek* were being written. When at the end of the book the Caliph has a few hours of magic power left to him before he faces damnation, he uses that power to have Carathis brought to Hell on the back of an Afrit so that she too will be damned: whereupon even Eblis gives up, and retires behind a curtain. This appears, in literary form, to express very faithfully Beckford's opinion of Louisa at the time.

If Beckford was behaving as he was writing during that spring of 1780, his mother must have been concerned for his sanity. On occasions whimsicality can topple over the edge, and Beckford, always highly strung, was deeply frustrated in his pursuit of a Westminster schoolboy. 'Those I love are absent,' he moaned, 'thus desolate and abandoned I seek refuge in aerial conversation and talk with Spirits whose voices are murmuring in the Gales. They sing of departed

Seers and Heroes who bring me indian intelligence.' ('Indian' was a term he often used when writing; it meant nothing more than 'intuitive'.) A few months later, half crazed by his solitary condition, he was rambling on in a 'letter' to Cozens about the 'ancient and venerable Spirits who reside in Vases ranged mysteriously around the Cell' – his Fonthill study. Some disturbed adolescents take to their teddy bears: Beckford had Japanese jars.

Mrs Beckford seems now to have concluded that her eccentric son would after all be safer on the war-torn Continent than mooning around Wiltshire. After Presentation at Court to establish his status, he and Lettice were to leave for Italy; but even that plan went wrong. First, Beckford had arrived in London to find it torn apart by mob rule in the anti-Catholic Gordon Riots. These, despite his Catholic sympathies, he found very exciting; the flames, the violence and the smashed windows made a most memorable event. Then, at St James's Palace, when Aunt Effingham's second husband, Sir George Howard, was presenting him to His Majesty, the King, already some way down the paths of eccentricity, had nothing more to say to the elegantly dressed and bowing young man than an abrupt 'Well, I suppose all your chickens are dead?' before passing on down the line. Hearing long before, when Fonthill Splendens was being built, that it was to be roofed in copper, Prince George (as he then was) had prophesied that everyone in the house would die of verdigris poisoning. In the obscurity of the Royal mind, the young man before him became confused with the memory of the Alderman who had once confronted him so rudely. From that time onwards Beckford never liked the Hanoverians and, in his later building ventures, always kept a competitive eye on Windsor Castle. Anything the Royals could do, he would do better.

It was in London at this time that Beckford became a confirmed melomaniac, enchanted by the virtuoso singing, the unpredictable improvisions and inhuman voice range of Gasparo Pacchierotti, who had succeeded Farinelli as Europe's most celebrated castrato opera star. On an impulse, Beckford decided to arrange his Grand Tour, not around the usual trail of galleries, palaces and churches, but around Pacchierotti's seasons of opera in various Italian cities. For him music worked like a drug and, as ever, John Lettice was in smiling accord.

CHAPTER SIX

Italy, with castrati

The escape from Louisa's embarrassing endearments and from his own obsession with a boy acted like a bracing tonic on Beckford. Once again he became a rich and cultivated 'milord'. He landed, sneering, at Ostend and continued to sneer, at squalling children, 'paralytic monks' and the 'gigantic coarseness' of Rubens's paintings, for the rest of his time in Flanders. Only the soaring steeple of Antwerp cathedral impressed him. As he made copious notes, for a travel book which was to be a tribute to the taste and judgement of Alexander Cozens, his writing took on a tone of supercilious criticism with only the occasional self-indulgent whimper about a hidden sorrow and absent loved ones. Holland – neat, clean and prosperous – disturbed Beckford's sense of romantic chaos: there were no impoverished peasants or beggars to minister to his self-esteem. For a young idealist to find a society in no need of reforms was unsettling, and he was glad to cross again from that bourgeois paradise back into the Empire, and the corrupt aristocratic disorder of an unreformed Europe where he could feel superior again.

Entering Spa one evening at the height of its social season, he rejected all invitations to attend routs and receptions and instead raced out alone into the wooded rocks of the Ardennes, claiming, when he wrote up the episode next day, that he had been searching for Merlin's Fountain of Hatred, a drink from which would 'free illustrious knights and damsels from the torments of rejected love'. No explanation for this quest was offered in the text which followed, nor could it have been, since the 'rejected love' involved a twelve-year-old boy whose parents were becoming suspicious. Either Beckford was immune at this period to any straight talking about the harsh realities of life, or he had neither relative, friend nor tutor willing to give such direct advice on the dangers of his emotional state. Louisa, more than anyone, must bear any blame for Beckford's isolation from common sense, as her letters prove that she actively encouraged him in the Courtenay idolatry. But then, the whole essence of *Vathek* is that the will or the whim of the Caliph is the law: Carathis never discourages Vathek from folly, or rebukes him for hurling fifty pretty young boys into an abyss where an ugly demon is waiting to devour them. *Vathek* was Beckford's sardonic depiction of his own lack of wisdom, and his own lack of good counsel. The moral issue of the Courtenay affair was confused in these early stages by the fact that it was still a pure, innocent affection. The implicit element of lust had yet to be acknowledged, and Beckford was able for a time to feel genuinely misunderstood and persecuted. For all his artistic sophistication he was still amazingly unworldly, a true figure out of Rousseau, brought up in a careful isolation from moral complexities. Goethe's Werther, Rousseau's Emile and Voltaire's Candide were all disastrously yet rewardingly compounded in his personality.

Dreams, Waking Thoughts, and Incidents, the book which emerged for publication in 1783 from his careful jottings at this time, was written to a formula, the formula imbibed from Alexander Cozens, the absent guru. As the heavy coach rolled on through Germany and over the Alps it came to a halt at suitable intervals, before a cathedral, a garden vista, or a mountain view. So did the narrative. Like an artist setting up his easel, Beckford would take his notebook and rough out the scene, in words rather than water-colours but usually with a dab of crimson for contrast, as in a real painting. The shades, textures and detail were later adjusted and finally, like a varnish, an emotional response was brushed in.

The resulting word pictures were, in the beginning, as conventional and commonplace as the Cozens 'blot' paintings which had inspired them. Only in Italy, away from too-obvious mountain sunsets and falling, rather late in the day, under Lettice's influence, did Beckford begin to relate to architecture, and to anticipate, by his feeling for an eclectic entanglement of styles, Ruskin's aesthetic writings of the middle nineteenth century. In critical terms it was a tragedy that when *Dreams, Waking Thoughts, and Incidents* was printed in 1783 in a lavish large format edition of 500 copies, the Beckford family stepped in and banned it. Whether it was his emotional indiscretion or his obvious sympathy with Roman Catholic religious practices which alarmed them was never stated, but mother, aunts and family lawyer united, and Beckford gave way. Of those 500 copies, only five survived. The rest were destroyed to avoid any damage to his political career. Perhaps the most surprising aspect of the affair was Beckford's own weakness. The book, for all its priggish arrogance and perverse humours, was a labour of love. Had it been published as intended in 1783, instead of as late as 1834 in a revised version under the title *Italy; with Sketches of Spain and Portugal,* it would have been hailed as an ice-breaker, preparing the way for the nineteenth century's stylistic eclecticism.

One of Beckford's best passages was written in response to the Campo Santo at Pisa, which John Lettice visited while Beckford was indulging his mania for opera at Lucca. On his return Lettice insisted that Beckford too should go to Pisa. This was the result:

> I seated myself on a fair slab of *giallo antico,* that looked a little cleaner than its neighbours (which I only mention to identify the precise point of view) and looking through the fillagreed covering of the arches, observed the domes of the cathedral, cupola of the baptistery and roof of the leaning tower, rising above the leads, and forming the strangest assemblage of pinnacles, perhaps, in Europe. The place is neither sad, nor solemn; the arches are airy; the pillars light; and there is so much caprice, such an exotic look in the whole scene, that without any effort of imagination, one might imagine oneself in fairy land. Every object is new; every ornament original: the mixture of antique sarcophagi, with gothic sepulchres, compleats the vagaries of the prospect, to which, one day or other, I think of returning [he did, a day later] to act a visionary part, hear visionary music, and [the inevitable touch of whimsical varnish, the applied emotional response] commune with sprites.

Here, facing one of Ruskin's and Dante Gabriel Rossetti's favourite buildings, Beckford anticipated their responses. All the passage lacks is Ruskin's persuasive high seriousness and the golden flow of his long period sentences. By 1787, writing in Portugal, Beckford would have mastered even that stylistic voice, though never with quite Ruskin's quivering intensity.

It was when Beckford's party reached Italy that his Grand Tour began to liven up and supply him with emotional experiences. Two Welsh women – or, to be accurate, one Welsh and one Welsh-Italian – took him in hand. The pure Welsh lady, Pembrokeshire born and Swansea reared, was his cousin by marriage, Catherine, Lady Hamilton; the other lady, eminently impure, was the Contessa Giustiniana Wynne d'Orsini-Rosenberg. Fortunately for Beckford's sexual education, it was the Contessa who got her hands on him first. She was an adventuress who prowled the decadent casinos and salons of Venice looking for vulnerable young men from whom she might squeeze money to service her gambling debts. She sang, wrote poetry, and slept with anyone wealthy enough to afford her; but she was forty-odd, and thus outside Beckford's range of preferences. He owed his introduction to her to old Jean Huber, who may have mischievously decided that a determined and experienced woman was needed to initiate William into heterosexual normality.

Certainly the Contessa did her best. As well as humouring Beckford's fixation with music and opera, she introduced him to gilded youth: in particular, two sisters and a brother of the Cornaro family. Predictably contrary, Beckford fell heavily for the brother, a young man of his own age with 'amazing eyes'; the sisters, however, one of whom was married, threw themselves at Beckford, or so he maintained when boasting about the affair fifty-eight years later. He even claimed, in one of his Mozartian moods, that the married sister poisoned herself by mistake when she was trying to poison her husband in order to leave the field clear for himself. This invention may have been inspired by Louisa's offer to do the same to her husband Peter. Both proposals fit perfectly into the strain of casual and amusing butchery which runs through *Vathek* – dwarves pinched to death by negresses and loyal subjects burnt on a fire to achieve magical spells, and so on.

Under the allure of the Cornaro family, little Courtenay was temporarily forgotten. When another handsome well-bred youth came his way, Beckford was in love all over again. As he was leaving Venice he persuaded the Cornaros to sail with him up the canalised river almost to the gates of Padua, only parting from them in a storm of emotion and night music. When Marietta Cornaro sang '*Pur nel sonno almen talora*' from Gluck's *Orfeo*, Beckford claimed he and his male lover 'suffered a strange delirium which had nearly proved fatal'. For the remainder of his Italian tour suicide was to be in the air. Hence Beckford's prostration next day at the shrine of St Anthony in penance for a mortal sin. 'Delirium' was Beckford's code word for sexual play.

The Contessa accompanied her profitable charge a little longer, arranging a literary pilgrimage to Petrarch's house at Arqua, but it was her secretary–companion, a wonderfully seedy old rogue, Count Benincasa, who became Beckford's confidant in the Cornaro affair. Beckford believed in wringing the utmost emotional despair from any separation, and bombarded Benincasa with letters for the next few months, demanding sympathetic replies – and getting them: he intended a return visit to Venice in the winter for a second Pacchierotti session, so there were still good profits in view for the Contessa, and a chance of some polite blackmail, provided the letters could be kept flowing.

In Florence, where he passed some time waiting for his real enthusiasm, Pacchierotti's opera season in Lucca, Beckford was more impressed by the sculpture and the bronzes than the paintings. Morpheus was now his persistent fixation, and in his notebooks various representations of the God of Sleep in the Pitti galleries were compared with each other. Sleep brought release from pain and could lead to death, and while Beckford had not the slighest intention of imitating Werther and committing suicide, the idea of it as a gesture was thrilling. The only two gallery paintings he mentions are a Polemburg of Dante viewing the torments of Hell and a Leonardo of the Medusa's head with snakes exuding from her eyes and toads crawling around her neck. At this stage art had to be 'horrid' in order to please.

When Pacchierotti finally opened his season in October, Beckford was in high spirits. He attended ten performances of Bertoni's opera *Quinto Fabio* simply to hear what new coloratura improvisations

Gasparo Pacchierotti would invent each time he took the stage after the Grand March in Act 2. Such complex warbling worked on him like cocaine: having had his fix, he wrote that appreciation of the Campo Santo, then galloped up to Valombrosa to see if the autumn leaves really did strew the brooks there, as Milton had claimed in *Paradise Lost*. When Rome was finally declared free of summer's prestilent airs the Beckford party moved south. Forty years earlier, Horace Walpole had experienced eerie presentiments in the half-ruined hunting lodge at Radicofani on the road to Rome. Beckford made a point of spending a night there, and of having a far more Gothick experience, with wild cats, which he wrote up superbly. His competitive instincts were thus creatively satisfied.

Rome lived up to its reputation. 'I met the Holy Father in all his pomp, returning from Vespers. Trumpets flourishing, and a legion of guards drawn out upon Ponte St Angelo.' 'The beautiful symmetry' of St Peter's pleased him and, in his habitual mood of the egotistical sublime, he day-dreamed of building a little house on top of its façade with another pavilion to balance it where Cozens, or any friend of the moment, could live. Suicide might be the emotion of the month but in reality life was good.

Intoxicated with whimsies and eager to inspect that ultimate in grottoes, the one at Posilippo which Virgil was supposed to have created by magic arts, Beckford gave Rome only three days and headed down to Naples, arriving in a violent thunderstorm. Next morning he awoke to find his ideal parents, but rather too late for them to be effective influences on his character. Sir William Hamilton was an awesomely perfect all-rounder: the finest dancer in the Neapolitan court, healthy and hyperactive, a vulcanologist and a connoisseur of ancient art, a hunting, shooting and fishing man and an influential friend of the foolish, happy King Ferdinand. He had been envoy at Naples since 1764, and had another twenty years in post ahead of him. Shrewdly he perceived that his odd relative would relate better to his wife, and beyond arranging expeditions for Beckford he left the two to get on together.

They made a precious pair. Lady Hamilton was composing a musical accompaniment to Homer's *Iliad* on the piano, which she played, Beckford marvelled, 'as if she had thrown her own essence into the music'. She had a 'sweetly soft' touch on the keys, while Beckford strummed and hammered away dramatically: two music bores, blissfully happy with their art. Her other forte, one most appropriate in a mother-figure, was morality, in which she had a very Welsh interest. As she was sympathetic and gentle, Beckford told her everything about the Cornaro boy in Venice, while keeping little William to himself – apparently because the William attachment did not yet count as vice, while Cornaro did. Lady Hamilton was impressively horrified, and preached penitence and regeneration to an eagerly listening but unconvinced sinner.

When they were not strumming their instruments or discussing vice, Beckford explored the usual sights, Vesuvius and Pompeii, and was presented at Court. Because King Ferdinand was openly childish, Beckford thoroughly approved of him. Childishness forever was one of his own avowed aims. Sir William gave him 'a savage' to guide him around the grottoes and together the pair rooted about the volcanic features of the Bay. Here, surprisingly, Beckford was disappointed, and his disappointment explains some of the future directions in his life.

If he had any enduring religion, apart from touching base with St Anthony when things were going wrong, it was Pantheism, but a Pantheism approached via the Classics. His shadowy deities were 'Pan and good old Sylvanus', and he had expected to find both at home down there in the ruins of Roman civilisation. In the event, he found Italy too dry. His ideal scenery was moist, 'western, green and fern-filled': Fonthill park and south-west England, in fact. Later, as he travelled home, he wrote to Alexander Cozens: 'I cannot help sighing after my native hills and copses: which look (I know not how it happens) more like the haunts of Pan, than any I have seen in Italy.' He was homesick: Italy was not lush enough. Browning's 'Oh to be in England now that April's here' and 'The Englishman in Italy' catch the same mood.

Before this, on 16 November, Beckford had written another Cozens transcript brimming with nostalgia for Fonthill, 'the peaceful palace' and its park. He promised himself a return to all those grotto features created by the Alderman which had been the playground of his childhood and the shaping influences upon his adult fantasies. After a declaration for 'that heartfelt satisfaction which comes from innocence and tranquillity' (so much for those suspicions of Cozens and black magic that most of Beckford's biographers harbour) he 'resolved to be a Child for ever'. Next summer he would be lying in the park 'under my beeches on the Hill of Pan', the hill immediately west of the house, or running on 'the Satyr's Range' east of the lake, where he had set his early Idyll. When Cozens joined him, 'sometimes we shall inhabit our Huts on the borders of the Lake, and sometimes our vast range of solemn subterraneous Chambers, visible by the glow of Lamps and filled with Cabalistic Images.' The quarries with their broken statues, the 'Cabalistic images', still exist to prove the very earliest origins of those Halls of Eblis that haunt Beckford's writing. For variety Beckford intended to go out, as in the past, on Salisbury Plain, 'the green Desert' as he called it, and drink coffee in open tents, 'dreaming ourselves in Yomen' (the Yemen). 'Next day perhaps we shall repair to the stone of power [Stonehenge] where, to speak the language of Fingal, "Spirits descend by night in dark red streams of Fire".'

This one letter quite contradicts the sketch of Beckford's childhood offered in Redding's *Life*. In place of a carefully controlled round of studies it suggests a lively open-air life with adventures based imaginatively on his reading of Macpherson's Ossian and *Fingal*: dark deeds from the Dark Ages, with boy-scout-style camping by the lake and the grottoes used as dens. Beckford assured Cozens that Lady Hamilton was 'perfectly in our way', another romantic dreamer, and drew a delightful picture of how he and she played strange dreams upon the pianoforte and talked in a melancholy visionary style 'which would recall your ancient ideas and fill you with pleasing sadness'. At such times Beckford was more of a flower-child or a New Age enthusiast than a disciple of Eblis. The Hamilton villa was his happy valley, and Lady Hamilton his mother of innocence.

All good things come to an end. The Beckford interests in Jamaica and London were entirely in the control of Thomas Wildman, the family lawyer, and at this point he sent a peremptory summons to Naples: Richard, the Alderman's eldest bastard, was laying siege by lawsuit to the Jamaica sugar plantations, and Beckford would have to come home to fight his corner if he wanted to retain his wealth. Grumbling pitifully, Beckford began his return journey, but determined to put off the evil day of legal responsibilities by stopping in Venice again, for another season of Pacchierotti's operatic warblings. Lady Hamilton was deeply distressed. Venice meant the Cornaro boy, and the Cornaro boy meant Sin. Her earnest entreaties followed Beckford up Italy. If her emotional diatribes are read in their correct strong Welsh accent, they come to life and the whole correspondence becomes like a comic episode from *Under Milk Wood*:

> . . . if you fall – Gracious Heaven forbid it! – You will be as imminent [*sic*] for your vices as you may be for your talents and virtues. The eagle who soars so high falls with greater force than other birds.

To provoke her to satisfyingly caring responses, Beckford loaded his own letters with accounts of the terrible temptations to which he was subject. He had indeed returned to Venice, and his beloved idol Pacchierotti was in full voice. 'But I almost fear attending to it,' he wrote. 'Such Musick – O Heaven, it breathes the very soul of voluptuous effeminacy.' He mentioned 'those fascinating eyes you have too often heard me rave about', but whether the pair had given way to 'a soft but criminal delight' was left unclear. 'What I would not give', the hypocritical young man declared, 'for you to hear this dangerous melody and steel me against its influence.'

Lady Hamilton took the bait like some minister preaching against 'Demon Drink':

> Take courage, My dear Friend, you have taken the first step. Continue to resist, and every day you will find the struggle less – the important struggle! What is it for? No less than *honour, reputation* and all that an honest and noble Soul holds most dear, while Infamy, eternal Infamy (my soul freezes while I write the word) attends the giving way to the soft alluring of a criminal passion.

There was much more of the same kind. She had heard that Mrs Beckford was pining for her son, 'that she existed only for you, and said such things of her affection for you that would have melted a heart of Adamant', so Beckford should hurry home. His mother had been concealing a serious illness from him, and soon it might be too late.

Quite unmoved, Beckford reported from Germany that 'The gulf into which I was upon the point of being precipitated has disappeared', and that no sooner had he abandoned his fatal connection 'than my spirits seemed to flow with redoubled activity'. The result was music, 'strange exotic tunes' which from his descriptions sound like Grieg's *Peer Gynt* suite, but were probably quite different. 'Did you ever read', he asked Lady Hamilton, 'in some Lapland history of certain gnomes who lurk in mines and chasms of tremendous mountains? The music I have been just now composing was exactly such, I should imagine, as elves and pigmies dance to – brisk and humming – moody and subterraneous.' Lady Hamilton's reply shows how little she understood '*My Child*', and how much she deserved him and all his effervescent nonsense:

> Thanks to all Gracious Heaven you are escaped. I begin to take breath, for I have been in an agony about you. My poor Dear Friend! Your letter has drawn tears of joy and sorrow from my eyes; of joy at your escape, at the noble efforts you have made, an effort worthy of '*My Child*'; and of sorrow at your present sufferings, which I hope in God will every day become brighter ... Take courage, My Dear William, don't talk of wishing for death.

So William had been playing the suicide card again. Not to be outdone, she too had been composing,

> a dead march upon the Pianoforte to accompany the body of Hector (who is my hero) into Troy. It begins with the Morning dawn and Cassandra's spying the procession from the Walls and as it goes on is intermix'd with the Screams and Laments of the people – in short I put my own Nerves in such an agitation and made an honest plain man that was present cry so much that I was obliged to leave off.

These letters are valuable because they appear, more than most, to catch the actual speech patterns of the writers: Lady Hamilton earnest and intense, Beckford high, reedy and affected.

The nearer Beckford got to England, lawyer Wildman and family business, the gloomier he became: 'Whilst I write my hand trembles like that of a paralytic Chinese. Strange colours swim before my eyes and sounds keep ringing in my ears for which I can hardly account.' A natural hypochondriac, in later life he always travelled with a personal physician to administer purges. This time there was Paris to revive him – though officially England and France were at war – and he was soon writing competitively back, true to form:

> I cannot describe how much I sympathise with your ideas of the *Iliad*. That aweful march you have composed vibrates in my ears. Perhaps, if I am not too presumptuous, I have been playing this very evening a composition which greatly resembles it. I shall remain contentedly at Paris a month or six weeks longer.

'Contentedly' was his choice of word: 'hubristically' would have been more apposite. His Grand Tour had been a great success. He had the makings of a new book under his belt; he had found a true soul-mate in Naples; Pacchierotti was lined up for a coming-of-age ceremony that would astonish all Wiltshire; Lettice had behaved with perfect discretion; and Beckford had enjoyed not only a decadent love affair in Venice, but the even greater moral luxury of abstaining from a second round of the same wicked dalliance on his return journey.

Now, in Paris, he cavorted about the city with two young women, the confusingly titled Duchess of Berwick, who was Austrian by birth and married to a Spaniard, and the far from respectable Georgina Seymour, who was desperate to marry him and thought well of her chances. But with England not far away Beckford's enthusiasm for little William was reviving, and Louisa had a role to play in that plot. He wrote to her that he was 'absorbed in Musick, bent over my instrument and dissolved in tears' – because he had just received a letter from William, 'my dearest friend'. Would William ever, he speculated, 'lose that amiable childishness we doat upon? No – I flatter myself he will not – his Letters breathe its genuine spirit and are tinted with our own beloved melancholy.' Beckford had recently run up against a wall of disapproval from the Courtenay family. Viscount Courtenay was not replying to his letters and Beckford could see that Louisa might make a useful *poste restante* in the future. She, for her part, was besotted enough to put up with anything to keep some kind of contact with Beckford, who never attempted to deceive her about his priorities.

Ambassadors' wives tend to be well informed on international gossip and Lady Hamilton did not like what she was hearing from

Paris. She wrote two firm letters. The first, on 2 March, was full of her own 'rheumatick aches': like Louisa, she was actually dying gently of tuberculosis. But she was still composing her threnody for Hector, which 'if well conducted might form one of the most particular and most glorious pieces of musick ever composed'. She ended by urging 'my Dear Beckford' to 'shut every portal against the remembrance of what you have escaped' and telling him to return to 'a Mother who adores you and who will absolutely die without you.'

The second letter was much firmer:

> Is it possible My Friend, that you are still lingering at Paris! Awake, for Heaven's sake awake, and let a Mother's Sorrows touch your heart. Oh, Beckford, she has wrote me such a letter, so full of passionate tenderness and anxiety about you that, was you to see it, every instant would appear to you an age till you could by your presence cheer her drooping spirits.

On 19 March Beckford wrote to her, confiding that 'I fear I shall never be half so sapient, nor good for anything in this world, but composing airs, building towers, forming gardens, collecting old Japan, and writing a journey to China or the moon' – all true prophecies, and much quoted in Beckford studies. On 14 April he landed in England, possibly with the view of cheering his passionately tender mother's 'drooping spirits', possibly not.

One other letter he wrote from Paris, in February, was to ensure that his future would include not only towers, gardens and old Japan, but a resounding scandal. He had learned something on his Grand Tour about vice and goodness, but not enough about how other people's minds worked. Confident, emotional and, in his own way, innocent, he wrote to little William's Aunt Charlotte appealing, in outrageously tactless terms, for her support in his attempts to contact her nephew. Charlotte was soon to marry the Chief Justice of Common Pleas, Lord Loughborough, and in his hands this letter alone (it is many pages long) would ensure Beckford's exile from Britain and inability to mount a libel case against attacks in the newspapers. In essence it was a frantic appeal that she should put in a word on his behalf with her brother, William's father. As a mark of Beckford's friendship for her, which he stressed shamelessly, would she testify to his pure morality and to the justness of his claim to be William's closest friend? A few excerpts will give the flavour of folly:

> Surely he will never find any other Being so formed by nature for his companion as myself ... There would be more luxury in dying for him than living for the rest of the Universe. Good God – were he to receive me with coolness and indifference I should desire to close my eyes for ever! ... My chief treasure, my consolation, my last refuge is centred in Wms friendship.... He is the first object which enters my mind when I awake and the last which quits me when I fall asleep. Even my dreams are full of his image ... How often has my sleep been disturbed by his imaginary cries? ... All those who live and move and have their being in his company are more fortunate according to my ideas than St Peter and all his Saints in the conception of a Catholic ... When we die let us be laid side by side in the same dark tomb. If anything could reconcile me to death twould be the promise of mingling our last breaths together and sharing the same grave.

The letter containing these hopelessly unwise statements was written on 22 February 1781, at the same time as Beckford was being bombarded by Lady Hamilton's good advice. The Courtenay family, influenced apparently by Charlotte, would continue to allow a relatively friendly relationship between Beckford and William until October 1784. But Mrs Beckford always maintained that Charlotte, by then Lady Loughborough, was the prime mover in the action to disgrace her son. In the light of this letter it has to be said that Beckford gave Charlotte every assistance by the wild hubristic innocence of his confessions that February.

CHAPTER SEVEN

A soft but criminal delight

By the end of April 1782, a year after his return from the Continent, Beckford had finished his *Dreams, Waking Thoughts, and Incidents* and was at least half-way through a first version of *Vathek*. So this, the year including his twenty-first birthday and double celebrations, was his first creative peak. There was another much later, in the 1830s, when with time on his hands and an eye to his future reputation Beckford set about rewriting letters he half remembered and devising reveries and memoir notes to guide subsequent biographers in directions which would enhance his image and create a personal legend.

In this he was completely successful. In particular, from Cyrus Redding onwards Beckfordists have concentrated on one or both of the two birthday celebrations which Beckford staged in 1781. The first, a three-day affair from 28 to 30 September, was the official party for relatives, local gentry and a host of tenantry; the second was a private Christmas-week party for a select group of young friends with a scattering of older people, including two clergymen, to keep it respectable. Beckford's two seductively-written accounts of this Christmas party vary considerably in points of detail, which seems to indicate that he spent some time perfecting them, heightening the poetic mystery and intoxicating atmosphere. Neither mentions the presence of the clergy and a number of quite young children, but in the second Beckford expressly claims:

No wonder such scenery inspired the description of the Halls of Eblis. I composed *Vathek* immediately upon my return to town, thoroughly embued with all that passed at Fonthill during this voluptuous festival.

This is ingenious nonsense, but the passages are so brilliantly written and describe English country house life in so much the terms that twentieth-century readers and disciples of the Heritage Industry want it to have been lived that his clever image-building has been generally accepted, and certainly quoted at length.

In reality the Halls of Eblis had been gestating in Beckford's mind for at least the past five years and had their origins, not in the Egyptian Hall, the ground floor of Fonthill Splendens, but in the quarries up on the hill east of Fonthill lake. Nor does the description of them in *Vathek* have any of the perfumed charm, laughter and gaiety of that 1830s retrospective. Beckford went straight back to town, not to begin *Vathek* but to write a very inferior Gothick tale which one of the two clergymen had told him he must add to his travel book *Dreams, Waking Thoughts, and Incidents* to spice it up a little. These retrospective accounts of that Christmas party are so well written that they have to be given a place in any telling of the Beckford legend, but he had used the same phrases, the same lilting, mellifluous prose of youth, music at night and intoxicated happiness, to describe a successful evening party at a house in Lisbon, fifty years before the inventions of the 1830s.

For the genuinely significant events in this year of Beckford's maturity, it is necessary to look in directions other than those he indicated in his manipulative old age. It was in 1781 that he lost his moral and sexual innocence, became an actual rather than a potential paedophile, and thereby acquired the necessary sense of doom, guilt and experience to write the terrible ending to *Vathek* which gives the book that feeling for unguarded but threatened innocence which is one of its most telling features – innocence as a foil to evil.

On his return to London from the Continent, Beckford found himself invited everywhere; he was the rich, handsome catch of the season. Louisa wrote in full, plaintive cry from the various spas her long-suffering husband took her to in the vain quest for a cure, while the ruthlessly persistent Georgina Seymour had crossed the Channel to press her suit with a gift of a knitted purse and coy yet threatening reminders of the confidences he had shared with her about his Venetian antics with the Cornaro 'children':

> ... had I been Empress of the whole world I wou'd have given it to have kept you with me – but alas happiness is not for me. I do nothing but think of your children. Were they *not wicked* and did they not love you with the affection that I do – I shou'd like to go and end my days with them.

Understandably, Beckford kept his distance and took refuge in Fonthill for the summer. Even there he was not secure. 'How happy I should be', Louisa wrote in August, 'to ramble with you in the woods where far from the prying eyes of our torrments [*sic*] we might without fear say and do whatever we chose.' She later became even more intense: 'Your love is become absolutely necessary to my existence. Every fresh proof I receive of it binds me more strongly to you.' But when she eventually made her way to Fonthill, the house was beginning to fill in preparation for the great twenty-first birthday gathering. Among so many guests, who included Pacchierotti, the pianist John Burton and Alexander Cozens, Louisa had few opportunities for intimate rambles. In any case, Mrs Beckford was keeping a watchful eye on the intrigues. She and her gossip, Lady Euphemia Stewart, had decided to impel William into marriage as soon as possible, and among the favoured house guests invited for that late September weekend of birthday celebrations was the ideal match: Lady Margaret Gordon was Scottish, the nineteen-year-old daughter of the Earl of Aboyne and a niece of Lady Euphemia. While she had no fortune, she was a blonde beauty, with a high colouring and large eyes, simple and trusting. It was arranged that William should lead her out in the first cotillion of the Friday night ball, in what by the social code of the day would amount to an open acknowledgement of an attachment between the young couple.

Friday was the first and the formal public day of the celebrations. In perfect still autumn weather two hundred guests, including the furture Lord Chancellor Thurlow, were gathered in the house, and, such was the Beckford wealth, no fewer than ten thousand more, tenants and country people from miles around, thronged three grand tents set up on the north lawn, between Splendens and an illuminated triumphal arch. Oxen were roasted whole, meat and suet puddings were washed down with beer. When darkness fell the house guests came out under the portico. Three great bonfires were lit on the surrounding hills and the crowds parted to allow Beckford and his entourage to pass under the triumphal arch and climb the hill to a classical temple lit 'by a continuous glow of saffron-coloured flame'. Looking down Beckford thought 'the throng assembled before me looked dark and devilish by contrast ... I could not believe myself at Fonthill. I rubbed my eyes and thought the whole a dream.' The evening's entertainment ended with a burst of fireworks, Catherine wheels whirling on wooden frames and a barrage of rockets soaring up from the river bank.

There is no mention of William Courtenay's presence at these events, though his father and his Aunt Charlotte were present among the guests. One undated letter, written apparently by Courtenay to Lady Margaret sometime after her marriage to Beckford, seems to suggest the young woman and the boy were on good terms. As the only Courtenay letter to escape Beckford's thorough purge of such reminders of the past, it seems to deserve to be quoted in full, as his is otherwise the silent voice in the relationship.

> My dear lady,
> I am sorry I should have managed mother so badly, but you desired to know what time all plagues will be out of the way, and as that will be the only day I mentioned it to you. I hope you will persuade William to come with you. But I am sorry to say Lord and Lady Loughborough dine here that day, if you dont think that will hinder you I hope you will come. I shall expect you both.
> I remain yours affectionately
W. Courtenay.
>
> My love to W and hope he will come.

It is a simple yet sensitive letter, courteous, easy, as one conspiratorial friend to another. It handles the regrettable presence of relatives, the Loughboroughs, as a shared burden, and while it reads like a young boy's writing – that PS, for instance – it is that of an intelligent boy, confident in the relationship. As a letter from Beckford's lover to Beckford's wife, it would go some way to explain why Lady

Margaret remained loyal to her husband when the slanders, libels and suggestions of sodomy were made. In discussions of the affair William Courtenay tends to be dismissed not so much as a helpless victim, but as 'that wretched boy'. Here he seems, if anything, to be in control, friendly and assured of his place in everyone's affections, and anything but a victim.

This is hardly surprising, as the letter is a forgery, convincing in style but factually impossible. Courtenay's mother died on 5 April 1782; Lord Loughborough did not marry Charlotte until 12 September in the same year. So Courtenay could not have been mismanaging his mother at a time when Lord and Lady Loughborough were coming to dine. Dictating the 'letter' fifty years later, Beckford may have grown hazy over details while remaining a creative and intelligent liar, eager to readjust reality to his own advantage. If his wife and young Courtenay had been in friendly, even conspiratorial contact, then what could have been amiss with the relationship? There is no proof that Beckford faked this 'letter' himself. It is not, of course, in his own hand but in a plausible, rounded and legible schoolboy style. But it lies among his other papers in the Bodleian Library (MSS. Beckford c. 28, folio 103), and who else would have taken the trouble to reshape the past, to invent an innocent friendliness and fabricate evidence for a trial of morality which could only be staged when the accused and all the witnesses were long dead? It proves that Beckford still cared, yet cared only to deceive.

Not many people these days strike attitudes about homosexuals, but paedophilia remains another thing – an area grey to the point of sooty blackness. The relationship between the two Williams was soon to become actively and physically paedophiliac. They slept together as lovers, and that was to lead to Beckford's social disaster of 1784; but since it also made him a sensitive writer and a great builder, it would be hypocritical to sound conventionally disapproving about the affair. It was conducted with affection on both sides. All through his life, Beckford's sexuality was bound up with his writing: to understand his books, its complex nature needs to be faced.

One person who understood exactly what was going on at this stage was Beckford's mother. In bringing the castrati Pacchierotti and

Giusto Tenducci together at Fonthill on the second day of the birth-day celebrations to perform in Rauzzini's pastoral cantata *Il Tributo*, Beckford achieved the contemporary equivalent of a modern Three Tenors concert in Hyde Park. But the words of the cantata, suppos-edly by Girolamo Tonioli, must have been written by Mrs Beckford herself, specifically as a warning to her son to be carolled, fortunately for his blushes, in the Italian and not the published English version, to a crowded audience of gentry and friends in the Organ Hall of Splendens. The great Pacchierotti, in the part of the shepherd, Philenus, sang:

> ... and often have I heard, from his earliest Days, the Mother thus instruct her excellent Son: Suffer me, my dear Son, to point out to you your chief Good. In every Stage of Life let your Father's bright Example be your Guide. First, reflect, that in vain does Man pretend to conceal his Actions from the Eye of Heaven. Next, that to your Country and to your King, the strictest loyalty is due. But, rather than any Circumstances should induce you to commit one base Action, Die, first my Son, and your Death will be a Subject of Envy.

This was remarkably strong language for a supposedly happy occa-sion. As up to that point Beckford's mother had been paying for the celebrations, it seems more than likely that she insisted on a castrato's warning to a son all too prone to project himself in public as an hon-orary castrato. What the listening audience thought of the pro-ceedings it is hard to say. Castrati were the pop stars of the upper classes, but not usually their intimate friends.

After a short Cornish holiday with Pacchierotti, Beckford moved to his London town house in Wimpole Street, where in term time he could entertain Courtenay at weekends. The draft of a letter dated 11 November, possibly to Lady Hamilton, has a moving beauty of expression and suggests the physical intensity of his feeling for the boy:

> The myrtle is still alive we brought from Powderham & Wm. every Saturday religiously clips its branches – I never loved Winter before – don't you know how much I used to hate it & shiver when ever the north wind blew. At present I love its murmurs, even the dark fog that consumes vegetation.

Never shall I see my breath exhale in a nippy frost without thinking of the little blue vapour that comes from Wm. and that I used to
attempt appropriating with such avidity. Don't talk to me of Spring.
I dread its approach & no wonder since with it come the whole family
to town & there will be an end to my felicity, t'other day I went to
West End [the Beckford dower house in Hampstead] and saw Nature
almost retired to sleep for the Winter with satisfaction. Lie still said
I, & if possible forget you are to wake this ten months.

Another draft, this time in French and dated 8 December, indicates that within a month of writing the letter above Beckford had
gone very much further than inhaling a boy's breath on a cold winter
morning. Boyd Alexander, who of all Beckford's biographers has
come closest to accepting the truth about his subject's paedophilia,
left the draft in its original French and consigned it to a special
appendix. It should be central:

From the theatre I carry him to my bed. Nature, Morality and Fame
are all forgotten, confused and swept away. Oh God! I wish I could
die in these embraces and my soul dive down with his into eternal
bliss or eternal punishment. Do I have to live on in the fear of a time
when we will be parted again? Don't be surprised that I should seek
death so eagerly. Make haste! Prepare some sweet potion which will
make all three of us drowsy, which will close our eyes without pain,
free our souls and carry them gently away to the flowery pastures of
another existence.

An unconvincing description of the washed-out joys of Paradise
follows, very like those allotted to Gulchenrouz, the child hero in
Vathek. They were to be shared by three souls, not one, so presumably the letter was intended for Louisa. The talk of triple suicide
means nothing: Beckford had been wallowing in that emotional
cliché ever since Venice, and confusing love with death and the tomb
all his life. But that factual evocation of a visit to the theatre, then
bed and passion, does not read like a mere fantasy. William
Courtenay was thirteen years old at this time of rapture, no more
than that.

A few days later Beckford, Courtenay and Cozens travelled down
together from London to Fonthill for the private birthday celebra-

tions. For some reason he never made clear, it was a journey of peculiar significance to Beckford. As they were crossing the Thames at Staines there was an unusually beautiful sunset, which all three appreciated with some intensity. Beckford reminded Cozens of that golden moment in at least three subsequent letters, as if it were Heaven's blessing on a relationship. The week-long revelry at Splendens which followed offered a house party's usual opportunities for philandering, but it was a house party, nothing more. Beckford's much later accounts coloured it up, rather as the celebrated impresario Philippe Jacques de Loutherbourg coloured it up at the time by passing painted lenses and fabrics across powerful lanterns strategically sited around the stony halls and corridors of that huge house. These created sunrise and sunset effects, volcanic eruptions and moonlit glades. This was primitive cinema, a device soon to be popular in London under the title of an 'Eidophusikon'. Inevitably, given Beckford's delight in perfumes, there were incense burners and braziers of scented coals. All combined to create, in Beckford's hectic account, 'that strange, necromantic light ... a realm of Fairy, or rather perhaps, a Demon Temple deep beneath the earth set apart for tremendous mysteries'.

With the castrati again in attendance, their singing rising unexpectedly from unseen sources, the effect must have been magical:

Sometimes a chaunt was heard – issuing no one could divine from whence – innocent effecting sounds – that stole into the heart with a bewitching langour and melted the most beloved the most susceptible of my fair companions into tears. Delightful indeed were these romantic wanderings – delightful the straying about this little interior world of exclusive happiness surrounded by lovely beings, in all the freshness of their early bloom, so fitted to enjoy it ... Whilst the wretched world without lay dark and bleak and howling, whilst the storm was raging against our massive walls and the snow drifting in clouds, the very air of summer seemed playing around us; the choir of low-toned melodious voices continued to soothe our ear; and, that every sense might in turn receive its blandishment, tables covered with delicious viands and fragrant flowers glided forth by the aid of mechanism at stated intervals, from the richly draped and amply curtained recesses of the enchanted precincts... It was, in short, the realisation of romance in its most extravagant intensity.

But it was never magical in the black-magical sense that Louisa tried to imply in her increasingly frantic letters of the next months as she hailed Beckford as 'my lovely infernal', 'a descendant of the great Lucifer', offering to lure victims into his snares – 'and you shall find them at your return panting on your altars' – her own small son as one of the prospectives. Quite apart from the obvious fact that Beckford, squeamish to a fault, could never possibly have sacrificed anything, Louisa completely misjudged his nature. For all his wealth, his later ostentation and vast building schemes, he was personally moderate in his drinking, eating, gambling and sexuality. Multiple partners would have been a vulgarity to him. One young boy romantically adored for five years was his line at this stage in his emotional development. He was fastidious; he still believed in Love. When he married in 1793 his wife Margaret was possibly the first woman he had ever slept with; he was immediately happy with her, and faithful, except that (and he might not have seen the illogicality of it) he still made love to Courtenay when the opportunity arose. The ordinary world simply would not see it as he saw it.

With de Loutherbourg's fancy light effects as a backdrop, he took his chances that weekend. Writing months later to Louisa from Italy, he asked her about 'Kitty', the name they used as a concealment for Courtenay. Was 'she' in good spirits?

> But above all does she yet love to talk of the hour when, seizing her delicate hand, I led her, bounding like a kid to my chamber? Will she be faithful, will I ever again be happy? Can her cursed relations separate us for ever? Is she not mine? Did she not swear she belonged to me? I faint Louisa, support me. Tell her what I endure for her sake.

Aside from the necessary comment that these are the self-indulgent writings of a barely socialised psychopath (which is what, quite often, Beckford was), what is relevant is that the letter was dated 30 June 1782 – when, as far as it is possible to be precise, Beckford had just manoeuvred the Caliph Vathek and his bride Nouronihar out of the ruins of Persepolis and down into the Halls of Eblis and eternal damnation. He had come, by his own experience, to sense that psychopaths tend to perish with a flame eating out the place where their hearts should be, yet he wrote that ridiculous letter and revelled coarsely in the memory of a seduction. At the same time, he gave the innocent young boy of his book, Gulchenrouz, in the very last lines, 'whole ages in undisturbed tranquillity, and in the pure happiness of childhood'. This is the creative tension of interests which makes *Vathek* such a vibrant and elusive book. Could Beckford have written an amusing and elegantly turned study of the nature of evil if he had not, at the time of writing, been wilfully enjoying his own limited version of evil?

CHAPTER EIGHT

A quest for the talismans of Solomon

The most significant event of that Christmas-week house party at Splendens was not some romp in a bedroom, as the initial seduction had already taken place a few weeks earlier. Nor was it those *son et lumière* experiments by de Loutherbourg, which were only trial runs for his later spectacular Eidophusikon presentations in London. What really influenced Beckford, causing him to strike out in a new literary line which led directly to *Vathek*, was his meeting with the Revd Samuel Henley.

Henley had joined the party as tutor-chaperon to Beckford's young Hamilton cousins, Alexander (later 10th Duke of Hamilton, and Beckford's son-in-law), and his younger brother Archie. These two had been invited as companions for William Courtenay – which says something for the tone of a supposedly corrupt and even infamous house party. Some months afterwards, indeed, the boys' father, Lord Archibald Hamilton, wrote to Beckford congratulating him on the good influence he was having on Alexander and Archie. So any impression of decadence and darkness created by Beckford in his much later accounts of that Christmas party is simply journalistic over-writing.

Henley, a scholar, had been forced out of a good academic post at William and Mary College in Virginia by the American wars. He and Beckford struck up an immediate rapport as they were both keen orientalists, and both enjoyed frolicking around in hearty children's games. 'I wish I had Archie or a lap dog,' Beckford confided to Henley a few months later, 'or something or other to fondle and play the fool with.' He was to write an interestingly similar parallel between boys and dogs, commenting on his new friend Franchi in his Portuguese *Journal* of 1787: 'As I have renounced dogs this long while, I enjoyed being welcomed home by the gambols of Franchi, whom I have reason to think a very faithful animal strenuously attached to me.' Horseplay and demonstrative affection were the pathways to Beckford's deeper emotional relationships, part of the eternal schoolboy in his nature.

Once he had established a sympathetic relationship with this rich young man and possible patron, Henley moved in quickly to oust both Lettice and Cozens from their roles as Beckford's literary advisors. His influence was immediate, and on the whole positive. Up to this time, for all his experimentations, Beckford had not found the exact register in which to express his own quicksilver personality. Cozens had steered him to imitate writers of the Picturesque like William Gilpin and Richard Payne Knight, artists *manqués*, forever asserting an assumed aesthetic superiority through their ability to analyse a landscape. Left to himself, Beckford had been in danger of turning into a whimsical poseur, a Madame O'Carty of the wild woods, as evidenced by one of his reveries of the preceding summer:

> And so far has my imagination sometimes roamed into antiquity that as night approached, I began to grow alarmed, looked around me with suspicion, fancied I heard the howl of Wolves or saw in some aged Oak the form of the Giant whom Corineus destroyed – my heart began to beat, I deserted my haunt with precipitation, fled trembling across the Forest, caught flying glimpses of faint forms amongst the trees, gladly left them behind, swiftly ran along the shores of a little lake that lurks amongst the Hills, seemed to hear voices calling across it, and running speedily along a succession of meadows which lay beyond, arrived breathless at home, chilled with fear.

There was no future for that kind of airy nonsense unless, as Wordsworth was to demonstrate in *The Prelude* a decade later, in his account of a poaching expedition –

> and when the deed was done
> I heard among the solitary hills
> Low breathings coming after me, and sounds

Of undistinguishable motion, steps
Almost as silent as the turf they trod

– it could be refined into blank verse. Henley was, for all his wide
reading, a populist. He waded through the precious descriptive passages of the *Dreams, Waking Thoughts, and Incidents* manuscript and
offered ruthless editorial advice – liven it up with a melodramatic
Gothic episode but keep it moral, and give it more political weight
with a survey of contemporary European politics – an ideal preparation for a prospective Member of Parliament.

Within weeks Beckford was obediently scribbling out the turgid
rubbish of 'The Guilty Lovers', to be included in *Dreams, Waking
Thoughts, and Incidents* as Letter XXIII, a nonsense of poisoning and
suicide set among those cliffs and grottoes around Portici which
Beckford had explored with his Italian 'savage'. This new writing
experience thrilled him: 'I have given way to fancies and inspira-
tions,' he wrote proudly to Henley; and, a little later, 'not a nerve in
my frame but vibrates like an aspen'. But he also found time to write
the long Letter XXVII, 'Reflections on the Economy, Politics and
Fine Arts of Several European Nations', a remarkably shrewd survey
and an accurate prophecy of the coming war with France.

In that Christmas week Beckford must also have shown Henley
his unfinished 'Centrical History', and all his Arabian fragments and
beginnings. Later he would suggest that he wrote the entire manuscript of *Vathek* in the course of three days: six months was probably
more accurate, and an unedited version was complete by the end of
July. But Beckford was hopeless at structuring a plot: perhaps the
truth behind the 'three days' is that in the course of them, with
Henley's help, he roughed out the simple, effective plot-line of a
Faustian compact. Vathek, Caliph of the Faithful and leader of the
Muslim world, is a complete hedonist, his mother Carathis is a Greek
witch who practises magic at the top of a very tall tower. When a
Giaour, an evil goblin, promises him the key to a magic talisman and
huge treasures in the Halls of Eblis if he will deny God and sacrifice
fifty beautiful boys, Vathek agrees. Abjuring God and throwing the
boys into a chasm, he sets off to Istakhar (Persepolis), a ruin which
guards the entrance to the subterranean palace of Eblis. On the way

he falls in love with Nouronihar, the daughter of a devout Emir, and takes her off with him even though she is promised to Gulchenrouz, an innocent young boy. Mocking religion and scorning angels, he arrives at the Halls of Eblis only to discover that, after a few days of enjoyment, his heart and Nouronihar's will burst into eternal flame. Before this happens he makes sure that Carathis is brought to suffer the same fate.

Influenced by the story-within-a-story structure of the *Arabian Nights*, at the very end of *Vathek* Beckford introduced a group of wicked princes waiting to have their hearts incinerated, whose stories he proposed to tell in a series of 'Episodes' to be included with *Vathek*. This was to result in most unfortunate delays to the book's publication.

As events turned out, *Vathek* became a reflection, a fictional diary, of his own joys, follies and gloom in London and in Italy over the next six months. But it was based on a character and a disastrous fictional life which also allowed Beckford to explore and even regret his own feelings of guilt over the recent seduction of Courtenay's innocence.

The first half of *Vathek*, set in the Caliph's capital of Samarah, was written over February, March and April and was essentially a detached commentary on the pleasures Beckford enjoyed and the public spectacle he made of himself during the London Season of 1782. He was, it seems, an uninhibited success in fashionable drawing rooms, as virtuoso counter-tenor, bravura pianist and exhibition dancer. Drunk on his own notoriety he claimed, almost certainly quite accurately, that when he stepped out onto the dance floor people jumped up onto the tables to get a good view of the performance. Contemporary minuets and country dances could, apparently, be extemporised extravagantly. Sir Christopher Hatton was known as Queen Elizabeth I's 'dancing Lord Chancellor', but no one is ever recorded as having stood on the furniture to observe him. Beckford's performance sounds closer to that demonstrated by John Travolta in a New York dance hall in the 1970s film *Saturday Night Fever*. 'All London, notwithstanding ten thousand malevolent insinuations, is at my feet,' Beckford boasted in a letter, and all the Misses in array whenever I show myself ... if I promise to sing at such and such a place on such and such a night the rage and intriguing to be one of the party is truly ridiculous. Our holy Aunt saw me at the zenith of this sort of glory last Saturday at Marlborough House – where I contrived to dance, and by song and by frolic to produce a vivid sensation.

It was all great fun, but desperately undignified. Horace Walpole made no acid comments, but his friend George Selwyn reported:

He is a perfect master of music but has a voice, either natural or feigned, of an eunuch. He speaks several languages with uncommon facility, but he has such a mercurial turn that I think he may finish his days *aux petites maisons* [in a madhouse]: his person and figure are agreeable. I did not come till late, and till he had tired himself with all kinds of mimicry and performances.

Georgina Seymour ended one of her letters to Beckford with the sour report that 'I heard you called one of the greatest coxcombs that exist – which I could not bear to hear'. But nothing could reduce his high spirits. The actor, the vaudeville artist, had at last a stage on which to perform. What he had not reckoned with, or if he had was perhaps prepared to weather the consequences, was an Englishman's instinctive mistrust of counter-tenors. Today, when a natural counter-tenor makes a reputation singing castrato roles in revived Handel operas, pointed references are usually made to his respectable married status and the testimony of his children. In an age when castrati were literally so, George Selwyn's reaction and Beckford's own mention of 'ten thousand malevolent insinuations' are pointers to his growing reputation for sexual oddity.

The text of *Vathek* perfectly shadowed Beckford's moods. As he made a fool of himself in the great town houses of London, so his Caliph Vathek indulged himself in front of his subjects in Samarah, burning old mens' beards off and playing football with the rolled-up body of a Giaour. In February Beckford wrote gleefully in a Cozens 'letter' that he had evaded Courtenay's female guardian and 'the mystic Argus slumbered last Saturday while I enjoyed the prize and revelled till ten in the morning'. His Caliph was promised the talismans of Solomon and the treasures of the Pre-Adamite Sultans if he sacrificed fifty beautiful boys to the hideous Giaour. Pretending to stage competitive games he gathered the children together near the Giaour's chasm. 'The fifty competitors were soon stripped and presented to the admiration of the spectators the suppleness and grace of their delicate limbs.' During the prize-giving 'the Caliph undressed himself by degrees', then pushed the children into the pit. At this point, however, Beckford the connoisseur of innocence takes over the plotting from Beckford the expert in evil: the fifty lovely boys are rescued by a good Genius and taken to join that other brainless innocent, Gulchenrouz, in a refuge above the clouds 'remote from the inquietudes of the world, the impertinence of harems, the brutality of eunuchs and the inconstancy of women'. Beckford was hedging his moral bets and passing a knowing commentary on his own folly and vice, but the symbolism of a naked man pushing naked children into an abyss requires no exegesis.

Beckford's last exploit of that London season was not as an actor but as an impresario, and it can reasonably be described as a triumph of innocence. Deploying a large cast of well-born children (an echo certainly of that sacrifice to the Giaour) and sparing no expense in costumes, scenery, musicians and professional singers to back the amateurs, he staged an operetta, 'Pastoral', written by a new friend, Lady Craven, and set to his own music.

Beckford admitted that Lady Craven's libretto was 'lackadaisycal trumpery', while Lady Clarges' summing up of his score was 'Thank God! – at least you have made a good end', but what mattered was that it was a tremendous success socially. It was performed in a temporary theatre at the back of the Duke of Queensberry's town house; the Archbishop of York and Lord Thurlow were present, and half the aristocracy turned up to see their children perform. For a young man in his first social season, it was a remarkable coup. To have achieved it in happy concert with the notorious Lady Craven was, however, yet another blow to his reputation. She had been found in bed with the French Ambassador, after which her husband left her to her own sexual courses. She and Beckford recognised one another for what they really were, amoral extroverts. Untroubled by any thought of physical relations, they were to remain warily friendly for life. In her *Memoirs* Lady Craven conveys better than any other contemporary

Beckford's spontaneous charm and talent. While she was talking to him one evening he spied his adviser, Lord Thurlow, chatting flirtatiously with a young woman on the other side of the room. Beckford promptly sat down at the piano and composed a comic duet, singing both voices himself, between the future Lord Chancellor and the lady of his intentions. This was what George Selwyn meant by 'all kinds of mimicry and performances'.

With 'Pastoral' as a last fine gesture, Beckford prepared for another and far more lavish visit to Italy and to the Hamiltons at Naples. At the same time he wrote his Caliph into an even more spendthrift expedition, from Samarah to Persepolis. The book was already plotted in draft but then, in one of those prophetic anticipations that seemed to occur throughout Beckford's life, giving it a grandiose resonance, reality followed fiction. This second Italian journey turned out to be almost as disastrous as Vathek's quest for the talismans of Solomon.

The Beckford fortunes were no longer healthy. Lawsuits in Jamaica were eating into reserves, as were election expenses in England. While he was indifferent to politics he had inherited three rotten boroughs from his father and at every election felt obliged to feast and bribe the limited electorates of villages like Hindon next to Fonthill to vote for his candidates. The Wildman brothers – Thomas the solicitor, James the agent in Jamaica and Henry the London banker – were quietly embezzling huge tranches of sugar profits. One of their specialities was to lend Beckford his own money, at high interest rates. He never tried seriously to master the intricacies of commerce and banking, merely expressed dismay and anger at any notion of cutting back on his profligate expenditure. Now he insisted on travelling, like Vathek, in state, not with twenty thousand lances but with three coaches and outriders. He and Lettice occupied the first; his tame artist, Alexander Cozens's son John Robert, and his captive musician, John Burton, the second; lesser servants were piled into the third. According to Beckford, this cavalcade was often mistaken in Italy for that of the Emperor Joseph, travelling incognito to see the Pope. When Beckford arrived in Naples he fell seriously ill with a fever; Burton was similarly stricken and died, raving and cursing his employer for bringing him to such a pass. In parallel, Vathek's 'little pages, famished with hunger, exerted their dying voices in bitter reproach on the Caliph, who now, for the first time, heard the language of truth'. Beckford quarrelled with the young Cozens for not painting hard enough and, as a final blow, Lady Hamilton, his personal Good Genius, died of tuberculosis.

Such was the setting of unlimited depression in which Beckford, very pale and frail, finished his first version of *Vathek*, consigning Carathis, Nouronihar and Vathek himself not to anything so crude as an eternal bonfire, but to the simple horror of an everlasting flame burning in their hearts while they were surrounded by the arched magnificence of an underworld they could never enjoy. This completed an autobiographical allegory of a time that began with the December seduction of Courtenay and ended in September 1782 when Beckford and Lettice quietly took ship from Naples to Leghorn to begin a chastened return journey to England.

In a folly typical of this creative year, Beckford had written his tale in French, which he prided himself, quite falsely, on speaking like a native. His written French was in fact full of errors, and he often translated English idioms, word for word, directly into French; but that was the kind of harsh truth he was too rich ever to need to absorb. As they sailed home, he set Lettice to making a translation: Beckford never translated his own French but instead corrected his translator's English. Lettice only began the chore. At Christmas he would be superseded, when Henley took over the task of translating, editing, and adding voluminous footnotes about as long as the original text. So the *Vathek* which was to achieve such celebrity was not, in the strict sense of the phrase, Beckford's own work: its pace, its lightness, its pastiche of Eastern poetry were all Henley's rendering of Beckford's French.

The only explanation for this retreat into a foreign language is that most of Beckford's reading of Oriental stories had been in French texts, and perhaps he found writing in French stylistically liberating. But it has to be added that the three 'Episodes' of Vathek, which were written in French over a four or five year period and neither published nor translated until this century, are distinctly inferior to *Vathek*, which brims with mordant humour:

the portal of the subterranean palace will shut in thy face with such force as shall shake thee asunder: thy body shall be spit upon, and bats will nestle in thy belly,

and also frequent touches of beautiful yet self-mocking imagery:

Here the nightingale sang the birth of the rose, her well-beloved, and at the same time lamented its short lived beauty: whilst the dove deplored the loss of more substantial pleasures; and the wakeful lark hailed the rising light that reanimates the whole creation.

The relative dullness of the 'Episodes' could be explained by the fact that Henley never got his editorial hands on them.

In the last fatal weeks at the Hamilton villa, writing possibly to the command of the dying Catherine, Beckford produced a moral mirror-image to *Vathek*. Possibly because innocence never has the same commercial appeal as wickedness, this story, also written in French, has never been translated, or published in this country; but to do justice to the workings of Beckford's mind it needs to be noticed.

'Darianoc, Jeune Homme du Pays de Gou-gou' is about a country in the central highlands of Africa where the entire population is naturally virtuous and kind. The people believe firmly in God, whom they call '*le Grand*', but they have no creed, no rites and no priesthood: '*leurs temples sont dans leurs coeurs*'. In Gou-gou, Beckford even controlled the problem of death. When a Gou-gouan dies the body is carried to a great cavern where the corpse never decays and '*Les peuples simples*' – the relatives – '*croyent qu'ils dorment au murmure des eaux qui déroulent des roches*': yet another deployment of the grottoes of Fonthill, this time a kindly one with no horrors, only peaceful sleep.

Everyone in Gou-gou is a vegetarian and the idea of killing an animal is inexpressibly shocking, though it is usual for a Gou-gouan family to keep rabbits, possibly for their wool. Into one unlucky family is born a child who kicks and fights and upsets his parents. When he grows up he falls in love with Dhulkianous, a conventionally virtuous girl, but distresses her terribly by catching some butterflies and bringing them to her as a present. One of the insect's wings is broken and this is seen as an ultimate offence. From that point onwards Darianoc must be reformed, and after many adventures with pygmies, on the green sea and in the house of smoke, he is finally made regenerate by Love and brought to complete Gougouan virtue.

Obviously the story is naïve, but it has a direct charm and an inventive narrative. If Beckford had pulled its episodes firmly together and had it published, it would have done his reputation nothing but good. He treats virtue as a positive force, convincingly and not cloyingly, and Darianoc could easily have become the English Candide.

On his way home Beckford spent some time with the Hubers in Geneva hoping to persuade Jean-Daniel to draw illustrations for *Vathek*, but these were never used and have been lost. England was not warmly welcoming. A letter from Louisa announced dramatically that she was near death and that her mother was taking her to the South of France in the hope that she might benefit from the warmer climate, though there was little chance of improvement. 'I soothe myself', she ended threateningly, 'with the idea that when I am no more, my soul may still be permitted to hover round you.' She tried to arrange a meeting but Beckford, neither then nor later one for easing the last days of the dying, contrived to avoid any poignant farewell scene, even though in his letters he had many times professed to love her dearly.

Over Christmas he and Henley worked hard at the text of *Vathek*. An old Mohammedan, Zemir, whom Beckford had picked up in Paris as a teacher of Arabic, was present to help on scholarly detail, though like most Oriental pasticheurs they relied heavily on Herbelot's massive *Bibliothèque Orientale*, published as long ago as 1697. It was an entry in Herbelot which gave them the original grain of the idea for a doomed and superstitious Caliph:

> Vathek. *C'est le nom du neuvième Khaliphe de la Race des Abbassides ... petit fils de Haroun Al Raschid ... Sa mère qui se nommait, Carathis, etiot Greque de nation ...* He was particularly addicted to Astrology and his teachers in that science, having drawn upon his Horoscope, promised him a fifty-year life span. He had, however, scarcely passed ten days from that prediction when he dropped dead of hydropsy in the thirty-sixth year of his life.

There should have been nothing to prevent *Vathek*'s publication simultaneously in English and French versions early in 1783. But Beckford delayed publication until those needless 'Episodes' were complete. Meanwhile *Dreams, Waking Thoughts, and Incidents* was printed in a lavish, large-format edition of 500 copies – and then banned by his family. For the last two years the 'dowagers', his aunt, Lady Euphemia Stewart and his mother, had been becoming increasingly alarmed by rumours picked up in the polite parlours of Bath about Beckford's moral standing. Louisa, though her supposed relationship with Beckford was scandalous enough in itself, had at least been a good cover for his love affair with Courtenay, but she was out of England; and Charlotte Courtenay, now married to Lord Loughborough, could no longer be considered responsible for her nephew and so had no further reason to protect Beckford from suspicion.

In 1783 Loughborough's great rival and Beckford's only reliable friend and protector in government, Lord Thurlow, became Lord Chancellor. Loughborough, a mere Chief Justice of Common Pleas, was ambitious for the Woolsack (which he eventually attained ten years later). He was both ruthless and militantly moral – unlike Thurlow, who was one of Lady Craven's several admirers. By February 1773 Loughborough had made it clear to his nephew by marriage, William Courtenay, that his relationship with Beckford was a scandal and should end. The dowagers, 'Scrag and Phemy', as Beckford called Lady Effingham and Lady Euphemia Stewart, had made the dangerous move of warning William Courtenay's father to be on his guard. 'I fall lower and lower in the World's opinion,' Beckford wrote to the distant Louisa. 'C's ruin is joined with my own. There is but one remedy for that – Good God how violent!' Werther's suicide was still on his mind. Yet if at that stage Beckford had taken his own advice and ended the Courtenay affair, he could still have saved himself.

Marriage was now considered by the controlling family committee of dowagers to be essential if his reputation was to be saved. Lady Margaret Gordon, the partner of that first cotillion of his birthday celebrations, had been around long enough to know exactly what she would be taking on – a very rich, very charming, wholly unreliable young man – and on 5 May 1783 they were married, quietly and by special licence, at Aunt Phemy's London town house.

Both parties sensibly made the best of the situation. Writing a Cozens letter or 'reflection' on the morning after the couple's first night together in Tunbridge, Beckford spoke of 'the sweet smiles of Lady M's countenance. She looks happy [he went on], and that sight gives me more joy than Sunshine ever imparted.' He had a gift for overstatement which he could use to convince himself of anything he wanted to believe, and it served him well that day. But the sunset seen the previous evening had revived 'the recollections of a certain journey to Fonthill', so he was still brooding over that mystic experience at Staines in December 1781. As a true bisexual, Beckford saw nothing illogical in continuing a long-standing male love affair now that he had a wife.

There followed an uncreative year and a half of fairly happy marriage. The honeymoon was lengthy, from that May until the following March. Much of the time they were in Geneva, staying sometimes with the Hubers, sometimes in rented houses. In August they held, in memory of times past, a splendid fête in the woods at Blonay with all the trees turned into giant candelabra by long tapers tied to their branches, but for all the expense it never achieved the casual bucolic charm of that earlier occasion. Beckford went riding through the Bernese Oberland with Jean-Daniel Huber, and Lady Margaret accompanied him on another expedition, guided by Dr Michel Paccard, up into the glaciers around Mont Blanc. She proved herself more confident than her husband among the treacherous crevasses, and he began to appreciate her engaging tomboy nature.

Louisa, unfortunately, with the aid of a telescope, could see Mont Blanc from where she was staying, and this proximity made her frantic with jealousy. In a stream of long, passionate letters (which Beckford, with cat-like cruelty, sometimes encouraged and sometimes ignored) she pestered him for a meeting at Lyons, which never happened, then proposed a *ménage à trois* in which she would act as a nursemaid to possible little Beckfords. In his replies he sometimes taunted her with the novel success of his love life with his wife. 'My attachment to her', he teased, 'has been of so terrestrial a nature ...' 'Never William', she replied, 'shall I be reconciled to the idea of your being in the arms of another. Tis like a bar of iron dropped between me and happiness.' If he had been wiser, Beckford would have extricated himself from Louisa's emotional coils. She was becoming a woman whose only resource was an ability to harm.

In late September Lady Margaret suffered a miscarriage, which left her, so he carefully informed Louisa, prettier than ever: 'the colour which glowed so rudely in her cheeks is softened with a bloom, like the innermost leaves of a blush rose; the more she pines the lovelier she looks.' It is now accepted that a husband can be deeply involved in the traumas of a wife's pregnancy. Beckford had always been highly strung, liable to react with nervous wildness to any setback, and he had, as he often readily admitted, a feminine streak to his own nature. The loss of his child, the interruption of the mental process of coming to terms with his new role as a father, threw him even further off mental balance. It had never been a part of his nature to act with wise moderation, but for the next year his folly was extreme.

All this time he and 'Kitty' had been exchanging letters. Courtenay had sent him a fragrant lemon leaf, and in an escapist fantasy Beckford wrote that he would keep it in 'a Japan cabinet with golden galleries & scented drawers'. If only they were both tiny they could 'creep into this neatly varnished Palace, live upon Cachous & slide along the smooth lacquer like Laplanders upon Ice. Lady M. [his wife] would watch over us whilst we slept, and keep the Devil and Loving at a distance' – a strange conclusion which seems to suggest that some kind of accommodation had been achieved between the three of them.

The young couple moved to Paris. Lady Margaret was soon pregnant again but became ill, and Beckford's mother was brought across the Channel to look after her. By his own account of this time, written in the 1830s, Beckford became half-demented. He trolled about Paris with two inappropriate woman companions, picked fights, deliberately spilled water into the lap of Madame Necker (who had corrected his manners). Whether he entered a lioness's den and charmed the beast, as he claimed, is doubtful, but his account of semi-magical experiences in a sanctum of Freemasonry, to which the architect Claude Nicolas Ledoux had taken him, may contain a grain of truth. He claimed that Ledoux took him one night in his carriage to an underground Masonic Temple in the Paris suburbs, which appears to confirm that he was already an initiate of the Order. But with his description of a wizard-like figure and a room of bronze vases, the narrative becomes nonsensical. Vases were always an obsession with him, of spiritual significance. In certain moods, he even believed that they spoke to him.

More dangerously, Beckford had begun to use old Cozens as a *poste restante* for letters to and from Courtenay, not appreciating that Courtenay had become a neurotic adolescent who was beginning to relate quite closely to his new uncle, Lord Loughborough. Beckford persuaded his wife to write Courtenay friendly letters, and began to set up a hare-brained scheme whereby Samuel Henley, newly inducted as Vicar of Rendlesham in Suffolk, should take Courtenay to stay in his vicarage, tutor him there and make him readily available for Beckford's amorous attentions. The level of his infatuation can be judged from one 'letter' to Cozens in which Beckford can only be described as courting disaster: 'I hear a voice whose tone pierces my very Soul and throws me into delirium, against the influence of which I cannot steel myself. The attraction is too powerful, it is in vain for me to think of resistance.' When Beckford and his wife returned to England in March, he pressed ahead with the Rendlesham scheme, even enlisting a neighbour of the Courtenays, Sir George Yonge, the Secretary at War, to support this unlikely project for reform. After appearing for a time to play along with the scheme, Viscount Courtenay suddenly backed out and appointed a tutor named Taylor.

In May 1784 Lady Margaret was delivered of a dead boy child, an incident which must have disturbed Beckford intensely. Hitherto he had always been able to preserve an airy detachment from reality. Now the conventional respectability of fatherhood had been snatched away from him twice: marriage was not delivering what it had offered. He had taken a seat in the Commons as MP for Wells, but found the experience distasteful: his boyhood friend William Pitt was Prime Minister, while he was a mere unregarded newcomer, with a high-pitched voice ill-adapted to debate. Using Lord Thurlow's influence he applied to be given a barony – in the style of Lord Beckford of Fonthill – which would move him up into the politer world of the Lords.

In July he travelled to Scotland with Lady Margaret to visit relatives. Once again she was pregnant. Then they received an invitation to stay at Powderham Castle. Beckford's mother, well aware of what was being said about her son's relations with William Courtenay, advised him to decline it. Beckford rejected her advice, and went down with Lady Margaret to spend a fortnight at the Castle. They were back at Fonthill by 13 October.

It is not known exactly what Beckford got up to with Courtenay at Powderham during his visit; nor is it known for certain who spread the rumours of sodomy between the two men, or how those rumours of sodomy got into the papers during November. But it was these which made Beckford's social position in England intolerable for someone of his intense and sensitive nature. When the *Morning Herald* for 8 December 1784 could publish 'If anything could heighten the detestable scene lately acted in *Wiltshire*, by a pair of fashionable *male lovers*, the ocular demonstration of their infamy, to the young and beautiful wife of one of the monsters, must certainly have effected it', and get away with it, then Beckford's standing in the small, tight circle of England's élite had become difficult, though not absolutely untenable. By 10 December the *Public Intelligencer* was speculating as to how much money 'the Lady of Mr B' would receive for separate maintenance, now that her husband was going to Italy (the usual resort of 'outed' sodomites) while Sir William Hamilton in Naples received a letter from his nephew, Charles Greville, with a detailed account of what was widely believed to have happened at Powderham. William Courtenay's tutor had heard violent noises in his pupil's bedroom, looked through the keyhole of the locked door, seen 'goings on', and reported them the next morning. The story was not only disgraceful – much worse, it was funny.

Lady Margaret was perfectly prepared to stand by her husband; indeed, she recruited support from her aunt and, when her brother came down to Fonthill to remove her from the 'monster', refused to be removed. Already pregnant for the third time, she had no personal doubts about her husband's sexual identity. It is most unlikely that Beckford had ever attempted to hide his fondness for Courtenay from her. The boy was, in her eyes, a family friend: so what if there had been a little night-time horseplay. With her support, Beckford should have been able to win a libel case in court, even a counter-accusation of sodomy. The unknown factor is what actually went on in private negotiations between the Courtenay and Beckford families and their lawyers. How far was Lord Loughborough prepared to go? Was William Courtenay prepared to admit that he had been a partner in sodomitical intercourse for years? It is most unlikely that the Courtenay family would have been prepared to subject their heir to public ridicule and disgrace merely to put Beckford in prison – or have him hung, as the law still allowed. The telling factor must have been a whole heap of fatally emotional and loving letters written by Beckford over the years. Courtenay had kept them, and Lord Loughborough held them.

With exposure hanging over him, Beckford behaved like a guilty man – which he was, but it was an error of judgement. He fled to Dover, hesitated there a few days, then came back to Fonthill, ready to face the crisis out. But the lawyers got to work, and a little of the nature of the letters was revealed; Lord Thurlow was consulted and gave his advice, John Lettice was brought in and offered the same advice: a tactful retreat to the Continent until the incident was no longer newsworthy.

Pressure mounted, but still the husband and wife stood firm. On 9 April their daughter, Maria Margaret Elizabeth, was born. Beckford was able to forget his problems enough to engage with Henley in a lively correspondence over the text of *Vathek*: Henley pleaded that Nouronihar was relatively innocent, and therefore might perhaps be spared the pains of Eblis. If Henley felt he had a right to alter the plot, it suggests how closely the two men were involved in the book. Beckford held firm: vice must be punished.

With a daughter now as their solace, a retreat to the Continent and an escape from legal threats began to seem a better alternative than isolation at Fonthill, where they were shunned by even the local gentry. In July the Beckfords, father, mother and child, set out for Geneva. The long intermittent exile had begun.

CHAPTER NINE

No wife, no heir, and daughters lost

From the safe distance of more than two hundred years, it is easy to describe Beckford's retreat to the Continent in July 1785 as both weak and unintelligent, since there had never been any real danger of a prosecution for sodomy. A more sympathetic and kindly truth would be that it was the decision of a bisexual, torn by his complex nature, between two possible courses. He could stay on in England, defiantly weathering the social turmoil, or he could choose domestic happiness abroad in a setting of romantic beauty and with the company of his Franco-Swiss friends. He chose the latter, and by any conventional judgement made the right decision.

If life had gone on as he might reasonably have expected it to, he would have settled comfortably in Switzerland on his handsome income, with a loving wife producing a child a year, soon the father of a large family, with sons and heirs to give him stability and a sense of purpose. Trips into the Alps might have produced worthy flights of scenic analysis and there would have been music concerts on the terrace by the lake. An affair or two with sensitive local youths would have been almost inevitable, but his wife had already come to terms with that side of his nature. She could have coped. As he once wrote revealingly, speaking of himself in the third person, 'she pardoned with such a sweet endearing cheerfulness, his childish errors'. Male lovers would have been dismissed as easily as that – mere 'childish errors'.

It is true that the invading French armies would have prised him out of both Savoy and Switzerland in the 1790s, but he could have returned to England. By that time the corrupt practices of the Wildman brothers might have decimated the Beckford fortunes, but even their wreck would have been riches enough, and Splendens would have remained. There would, however, and this is where posterity would have lost out, have been no Fonthill. Happily married, Beckford would never have become a legend in his lifetime, or a significant figure in English architectural history. The death of his wife in May 1786, less than a year after the retreat from England, was to be the making of Beckford's character and of his later achievements. Alienation and embitterment brought out the defiant and positive side of his nature.

In one way, that flight across the Channel was a very conventional gesture, almost one of *noblesse oblige*. If Beckford had been advised intelligently by his solicitor Thomas Wildman, and if Mrs Beckford and the committee of dowagers had not been pressurising him to do the decent thing, he might have noticed that his own position in the scandal was a strong one, while Lord Loughborough's was remarkably weak. How could Viscount Courtenay have dragged his only son and heir through the courts when the boy, now seventeen and virtually a man, would have had to confess to immoral activities carried on over a period of several years with his own free and, from the tone of his letters to Beckford, eager and affectionate consent? Courtenay was plump and effeminate: a good defence lawyer would have cut him to pieces even if he had agreed to go through with the humiliating ordeal merely to satisfy his Uncle Loughborough. And how would Lady Loughborough – the victim's aunt – have emerged if that wildly revealing letter written to her by Beckford in 1781 appealing for her support had been read out in court? Might it be suggested that she had sacrificed her nephew's moral welfare in the hope that she might marry into the Beckford fortunes? Both she and her brother the Viscount would have appeared either as grossly negligent, or as having subsequently condoned an obviously unsuitable attachment plainly revealed in this melodramatic declaration of love for a twelve-year old boy.

Lord Loughborough, a shrewd lawyer, took the only possible course if it was he who fed the popular press with rumour and innuendo. Of course Beckford had been guilty of some kind of sexual relationship with the Courtenay boy for several years, but only the boy himself, and possibly close members of the family, could have proved it: Loughborough must have calculated that pressure from Beckford's female relatives would force him to follow the established code of his class when an implication of sodomy became public. The precedents were as well known in the eighteenth century as the Oscar Wilde case became in the early twentieth century. Only three years earlier Edward Onslow, a young man of Beckford's age and a son of Lord Onslow, had been the victim of a political sting aimed at his father's reputation: four Irish youths, one of whom, Dennis O'Brien, belonged to an opposing parliamentary faction, claimed that Edward Onslow had made an indecent advance to one of them, not once but three times, in the unlikely setting of a crowded public picture viewing at Somerset House. No one else witnessed this improbable sexual propositioning, but almost everyone observed the blow which one supposedly outraged Irishman landed upon Onslow at what it was claimed was his third attempt. Onslow made no stand at all against the accusations but simply left for exile in Paris. A Lord Tylney had been at the centre of another and earlier case of the same kind: on his Grand Tour Beckford made disaparaging comments on the camp style of the Tylney *ménage* in Florence but nevertheless accepted a dinner invitation from the notorious sinner a few days later, so he knew the form. That curious flight as far as Dover in October 1784 was Beckford's attempt to behave correctly. His wife's loyalty, combined with her pregnancy, gave him the confidence to return to Fonthill, outface the gossip for another nine months, and eventually retreat in good order to an extremely desirable refuge.

Those who think of Beckford and Lady Margaret's Swiss exile as an unhappy episode have never visited la Tour de Peilz and its Château de la Tour. The western and middle shores of Lake Geneva are beautiful enough, with modest hills, vineyards and small towns, each with its little port and guardian castle. But as the lake narrows towards the east, after Cully and St-Saphorin, the Alps close in, snowy mountains take over, and the scenery becomes positively Olympian. The château the Beckfords took as their new home commands this sublime cul-de-sac of the lake superbly, and across the water, only a short boat ride from la Tour de Peilz's neat harbour, was

Beckford's own enchanted riviera of Blonay and Meillerie, where he had already twice revelled in style.

The tower of the village's name belongs to the château, a very tall round tower at the west end of a handsome eighteenth-century wing that looks out from large windows across the terrace to the lake and the Savoyard shore. Behind that range of modest entertainment rooms is a sheltered courtyard within a circuit of medieval walls. It is a particularly delightful house, strikingly antique yet eminently commodious, secluded within its walls yet convenient for the bustling village and all the gentry residences of the north shore. Vevey, a substantial town with a lively bourgeois society, is only a mile away to the east, Lausanne with its cathedral and college about fifteen miles further. Beckford had travelled this end of the lake twice on trips with Jean-Daniel, and must have marked the château out as a possible future residence.

The nature of the Beckfords' new social life in Switzerland can be judged from a letter written from the Château de la Tour to a friend, Robert Pigott, in February 1786:

> Our Balls continue quite amusing – a fine shew of young innocent Tits in the first heyday of Spirits & tender Inclinations, prancing and curvetting & giggling & whisking from one room to another. No Papas, no Mamas, no Uncles. A long range of Appartments, animating Musick, flowing drapery, snug corners in the Windows – four feet deep! Rare work for young fellows you must allow & nice hotbeds for expanding the hearts of these lovely Blossomes.

It is all rather too blatantly heterosexual, one randy young fellow joshing another, to ring true; but Beckford had a reputation to re-establish, and obviously he was working hard at it. There is certainly no trace of agonised retirement from a hostile world.

As the day of Lady Margaret's next confinement drew near, John Lettice travelled from England to lend her husband moral support. Aunt Phemy (Lady Margaret's aunt, not Beckford's) was on her way too, bringing Evangelical comfort to her niece. Lettice arrived at the château on Thursday, 15 May. On the previous Sunday Susan Euphemia, Beckford's second surviving daughter, had been safely delivered. Lettice wrote rapturously that 'the prejudice which met him [Beckford] on his first arrival here is entirely overpowered by a thousand testimonies of the most flattering respect shown him by everybody of the least consideration in the capital [Lausanne] and all over the Canton [Vaud].' But on the 26th of the same month Aunt Phemy arrived to find her beloved niece desperately ill with puerperal fever, unable even to recognise her. Lady Margaret died that evening.

Beckford's reaction to his loss was eccentric, but then death had always horrified him: two days later he set off on a tour of northern Switzerland to distract himself from overwhelming grief. Lettice was his companion, as bland and complaisant as ever. The clergyman wrote home to England to explain: 'As he will yet listen to consolation from scarcely anybody but myself it is impossible for me to leave him till his affliction is somewhat abated.'

Aunt Phemy, though touched by Beckford's grief and personally in favour of forgiveness for the sinner, had indicated that the family might be against his return to England, even for his wife's burial service at Fonthill. She had therefore taken charge of the newborn Susan and year-old Maria Margaret, to return them to their grandmother's care at West End, the Beckfords' Hampstead dower house. This meant that Beckford was never able to pass through the harsh therapy of laying a lost loved one to rest in the earth: it had all to be imagined over and over again in his mind for years to come – profoundly disturbing for someone as obsessed with the tomb as he had always been. Nor had he even the positive distraction of trying to care for and bond with his two daughters. Yet at Moudon, his first stop on that macabre jaunt, Lettice noted how 'the singularity of the public walks and the company which thronged them seemed to steal my companion a few moments from his affliction'. At L'Isle de St-Pierre on 31 May, 'he confessed his grief was strangely soothed amidst the fascinating scenes which often stole him from himself', while from Zurich, on 11 June, Lettice was able to report that 'his first transports of grief having yielded to a more pensive sorrow, which is likely to last long upon him, he prepares to finish the tour in about eight days'. He would have had time to return to England for the interment of his wife's embalmed body, but his family was unrelenting. At Berne, on 16 June, came 'an express from England with letters that determined Mr Beckford to continue some time longer in Switzerland'.

He would not, however, continue at the château in la Tour de Peilz: 'Mr Beckford, with more imagination and livelier sensations than almost any other man', found that 'every object around him at Vevey reminds him of his irreparable misfortune'. He therefore took 'the resolution of quitting this hitherto charming residence and returning to it no more'. His duty done, Lettice slipped quietly back to England by way of Paris, to report in person to the dowagers and to prepare for his own marriage – which, given his relaxed and tolerant disposition, was to prove happy.

During these months another disaster had been in preparation for Beckford, one that he well deserved but which came at just the right time to distract him from sorrow and rouse him to a healthy fury. Ever since Christmas 1782 he had been prevaricating over the publication of *Vathek*. He intended to publish simultaneous English and French versions in London and Paris, but was uneasily conscious that his own French required careful editing by a native speaker. Playing for time with Samuel Henley, who had a large family to support and was desperate for money, Beckford insisted that *Vathek* needed a covey of four extra 'Episodes' to explain why the group of four princes and one princess were awaiting their doom in the antechamber of Eblis. Time and again over the ensuing three years he claimed to be making progress with his princes, while keeping poor Henley involved in a debate over stylistic and moral points in the main *Vathek* text and never allowing him to see the unfinished 'Episodes'.

Oddly, considering the generally excellent quality of his translation, Henley's stylistic suggestions were inept. At one point he proposed enriching the text with:

> The beam of the setting sun just breaking from the last cloud of the west lighted up the green bulges of the mountain with a golden verdure, and cast a ruddy glow over the sheep that grotesquely varied their sidelong shadows as they gambolled down its steeps.

Beckford dismissed that out of hand, and by some double alchemy, from his own unidiomatic French and Henley's heavyweight English, the light confection of *Vathek* emerged. Beckford took writing very seriously and considered himself not only a scholar in Persian and Arabic, but a full-time professional author. The 'Episodes' (two and a half were eventually published, in 1912), were only the tip of an iceberg of translations, re-tellings and original inventions, all in French, which poured out over these years. Many were up to three hundred pages long; only one, a part of 'Alraoui', was ever translated into English and published. Most are thoroughly third-rate, eighteenth-century fantasy fiction not unlike the twentieth-century *Conan the Barbarian* series. At this time Beckford was a compulsive rather than a reflective writer: all have fast-moving, improbable plots, cardboard characters, magical interventions – and instantaneous Oriental romance, as in '*Alors Ticlah tendit ses beaux bras à Chemnis qui s'y precipitat avec ardeur*', or '*Aladdin courut les bras ouverts à ses femmes, qui s'y precipiterent dans des extases de joye*'.

A list of their titles conveys the remarkable scale of his labours on these 'Contes Arabes': 'Histoire d'Alraoui contée à l'Emir du grand Caire', 'Suite de l'Histoire de'Alraoui', 'Histoire d'Elouard Felkanaman et d'Ansel Hougioud', 'Histoire de Mazin', 'Histoire d'Aladdin, Roi d'Yemen', 'Histoire du Prince Mahmed', 'Histoire d'Abou Niah, Roi de Moussel', 'Histoire de la Princesse Fatimah, Fille du Roi Ben Amer', 'Histoire du Prince Ahmed, Fils du Roi de Khotan et d'Ali ben Hassan de Bagdad', 'Histoire de Kebal, Roi de Demas contée par Mamabébé Nourrie de la Princesse Hajain'.

What is interesting is that out of all this Thousand and One Nights superficiality the one worthwhile book of *Vathek* should have emerged. While Beckford was writing it he was in the complex grip of real feeling – presentiments of personal damnation, sexual success and bereavement – and these emotions seeped through into his text, deepening it by literary osmosis.

Henley waited for the 'Episodes' with rising anger, and a devious plan: for some time he had been plotting to publish *Vathek*, pretending without actually printing a straight lie that it was a genuine Arabic text. To that end he had been correcting the scholarship, to allow it to pass scrutiny as an original literary discovery, and adding encyclopaedic footnotes to give it weight. On 1 June Beckford, still recuperating on his bereavement holiday, wrote to Henley:

I fear the dejection of mind into which I am plunged will prevent my finishing the other stories, and of course *Vathek* making his appearance in any language this winter. I would not have him upon any account come forth without his companions.

But Henley had already decided to act. On the same day that Beckford was insisting on a further postponement, Henley was entering the book at Stationer's Hall. It was published later that month in London, with no mention of Beckford's part in writing it, as 'An Arabian Tale from an Unpublished Manuscript with Notes Critical and Explanatory'. The first edition of 1786 is an impressive volume: any ordinary reader looking over the massive footnotes would naturally assume it to be of authentic Arab invention. Beckford, understandably, was mortified. But instead of bringing out a rival English edition under his own name and with an explanatory preface, he bought a copy of Henley's publication and paid a Lausanne scholar to translate it, badly, back into French. By the time this came out with his name on the title page, in late November 1787 in Lausanne, Beckford was away travelling in Iberia and so lost all the satisfaction of publication. To complicate matters further, he had subsequently engaged his new friend, the doctor and prominent Freemason François Verdeil, another citizen of Lausanne though educated in Paris, to write a much better translation back into French. This version was published in Paris in 1787, shortly after the Lausanne version, but anonymously, thus creating diverting problems for later bibliophiles to unravel.

Vathek's first critical reception in England must have been another disappointment. The *Gentleman's Magazine*, reviewing it in July 1786, described it as 'generally vivid and elegant' and offered two long excerpts from the moral climax of the book – but what really impressed the reviwer was Henley's footnotes. These generated letters to the editor discussing scholarly and entirely irrelevant points, such as parallels between Dante's *Inferno* and Eblis, and an erudite analysis of Virgil's knowledge of palm trees. One correspondent dismissed *Vathek* with the comment that 'it would seem it has been composed as a text, for the purpose of giving to the public the information contained in the notes': perhaps the most hurtful criticism that could be written.

Yet the book went through nine editions in Beckford's lifetime. It was Byron who popularised it most effectively: he added a note to his Turkish tale of 1813, *The Giaour*, admitting his debt to *Vathek*, 'the sublime tale', and adding, 'even Rasselas must bow before it; his "Happy Valley" will not bear a comparison with the "Hall of Eblis".' Beckford's publishers thereafter rubbed salt in his wounds by printing Byron's encomium in all future editions of *Vathek*. Beckford was convinced, correctly, that Byron had drawn characters for *The Giaour*, *The Siege of Corinth* and *The Bride of Abydos* from *Vathek*, knew that the poet had made lewd jokes about his relationship with Courtenay, and felt understandable chagrin at having to depend upon condescending praise from a man he heartily disliked.

Beckford's reputation in France suffered because of the inexplicable omission of his name from the improved Paris edition of *Vathek*; only the inferior Lausanne version was clearly attributable to him. It was not until ninety years later, when Prosper Mérimée had drawn Stéphane Mallarmé's attention to its merits, that the book captured critical reaction and praise. Either through shame or from an aristocratic reserve, Beckford seems to have been reluctant to claim full credit for such a morally ambivalent, nihilistic text.

To understand Beckford's fixation with his reputation in France, when he was not even a perfect French speaker, several factors have to be remembered. He was a snob, and Paris has always had a *cachet* for snobs; his equivalent to a university education had been delivered in Geneva, which was, culturally at least, a French city; and the French were infinitely more sophisticated Orientalists than the English. As a final factor in his disenchantment with his native country, the English newspapers, not content with branding him a sodomite, were suggesting that he had been indirectly responsible for his wife's death, the *Morning Chronicle* claiming that 'Poor Lady Margaret Beckford's illness, which brought so much merit and elegance to the grave, was a broken heart.' Alienated by all this and rejected by his closest relatives, Beckford willed himself for the next thirty years, throughout the long struggle with Napoleon, into being at least as much French in his loyalties as English. And France, as a result, has repaid him with shrewd and balanced criticism: easily the most scholarly study of Beckford's literary work to date is André

Parreaux's *William Beckford, auteur de Vathek* (1960), though even the French have not been able to penetrate the mystery of what exactly Beckford got up to during the French Revolution. The most genuinely adventurous episode in his life, one where there would have been no need for any Mozartian invention, was the one period which Beckford chose never to write about, and to discuss with Cyrus Redding only in the vaguest and most evasive terms.

Dr François Verdeil has been mentioned earlier in relation to Beckford's probable connection with circles of Swiss Freemasonry, and as a translator of *Vathek*. Now, as John Lettice enjoyed a well-earned break from shepherding Beckford through his troubles, Verdeil took his place as the tolerant older friend and adviser Beckford still seemed to need. When sections of the English press suggested that Beckford was responsible for his wife's death, twenty-eight of his Swiss friends were so outraged that they organised a testimonial to his virtues and to the calm of his married life. This they characterised as '*rempli des attentions les plus délicates et les plus soutenues, comme sa conduite en général a été celle d'un Homme d'honneur, bienfaisant et des Moeurs les plus honnêtes*'. Verdeil was not one of the signatories, but the document may well have been a gesture of Masonic solidarity.

At this point a brief digression into the complexities of Swiss politics is necessary in order to follow Verdeil's role in Beckford's life over the next ten years. Canton Vaud, of which Lausanne is the capital, was at that time under the semi-feudal political control of Berne, whose 76 patrician families disliked Freemasonry as much for its bourgeois connotations as for its libertarian tendencies, and banned it as early as 1745. Verdeil, a leading Freemason, Master of the local Lodge of St Jean, was not truly Swiss, though he had Swiss citizenship. His father, a political refugee, had fled Paris for Lausanne in 1765 when François, his eldest son, was already 24 and a qualified doctor. Both the north and the south shores of Lake Geneva were French-speaking, but the north shore was Canton Vaud, part of largely German Switzerland, and the south was Savoy, part of the Italian kingdom of Sardinia, so in a linguistic sense its political division was illogical. At this stage in his life Verdeil probably hoped to see the whole area become a part of France, whenever France itself should become a constitutional monarchy: he was therefore politically suspect in the eyes of Lausanne's ruling, Berne-appointed, Bailli. He had recently, at the age of 39, married a 34 year old wife, Sophie Dufey Joly de Frey, but as an undercover Masonic agitator – code name, 'Philaletophane' – he appears to have been quite eager to leave his new wife for a while and travel with Beckford as his personal physician.

The two men became close friends. Verdeil never concealed his religious agnosticism and radical political views. Although later, in 1788, Thomas Wildman contrived to create a rift between them over payments for the editing of the Paris edition of *Vathek*, they continued to correspond affectionately during the 1790s, when Beckford became dangerously involved in Swiss politics and French subversion.

For the last six months of 1786, apart from an excursion to Geneva, where old Jean Huber had lately died, Beckford settled at his favourite spa, Evian, across the lake from la Tour de Peilz. While there is no proof that Verdeil tried to influence his literary style, his years with Beckford coincide with Beckford's most relaxed and outward-looking writing, in which sunsets and mountainscapes begin to take second place to people and social observations. On that short Geneva trip, for instance, a return to the Salève, his magic mountain, the two letter-essays Beckford wrote focus not so much upon the landscape as upon an angry analysis of the theatre-going habits of Geneva's new upstart financial entrepreneurs.

Those wearisome 'Episodes' continued to occupy him, but the latest of the three, 'Princess Zulkais and the Prince Kalilah', written at this time, is the only one in which Beckford allowed himself to become personally involved, purging himself of an adolescent fantasy of incestuous love for his half-sister; it has also a fierce Aldermanic father, Abou Taher Achmed, who tells his son 'it is not in the lurking haunts of effeminacy that great characters are formed'. Alexander Cozens, another who died in that year of changes, featured as an ingratiating creature called 'the Palm Tree Climber', who has to be carried everywhere and loves to share the sexual confidences of disturbed young people. Beckford was beginning to analyse his past.

The two earlier 'Episodes', by contrast, written between the 1784 scandal and Lady Margaret's death, are mechanical exercises in unmotivated wickedness. The eponymous hero of 'Prince

Barkiarokh' achieves damnation through so many vices that the reader suspends belief. In 'Prince Alasi' Beckford might have written a homosexual parable, as the first version features two princes, Alasi and Firouz, who are in love with each other. But the Courtenay-figure, Firouz, is so unmitigated in his malice and spite – he finally disfigures his lover's wife with corrosive acid – that the 'Episode' cannot be accepted as a plausible version of Beckford and Courtenay's love affair. Much later Beckford rewrote the 'Episode' with Firouz as a woman, Firouzkah, to make the jealousy more credible and an English publisher more likely to be tempted.

As 1786 drew to a close, all manner of circumstances were conspiring to jolt Beckford back into creative originality. England and the high society he enjoyed had cast him out; his wife's death had rescued him from the blight of domestic happiness; his daughters had been taken from him, and with them any sense of emotional stability and focus. The three older people on whom he had relied for some direction – Lady Hamilton, Jean Huber and Alexander Cozens – were all dead; even the usually dependable Lettice was otherwise engaged emotionally. Verdeil was at hand, not only to administer the occasional literal purge but for straight talking when it was called for, the commentary of a shrewd, broad-minded radical and a man under no illusions about Beckford's complex sexual identity.

All that was needed now was a removal from the safe shores of Lake Geneva, and in the last month of the year, by a process which the Beckford Papers never satisfactorily explain, his mother and his solicitor effected exactly that. Somehow, and it seems by threats rather than persuasion, they induced Beckford to leave Evian and return to Fonthill. Problems with finance may or may not have been the excuse. Already in January of 1786 Wildman had cut Beckford's quarterly allowance, on the grounds of a succession of bad hurricane years in Jamaica which had reduced the sugar revenues. When Beckford came face to face with his mother, however, he was made to believe that Lord Loughborough and the Courtenays were likely to make public the damning letters he had written to his lover, and that the only way to escape further disgrace, perhaps a court case, was to cross the Atlantic to Jamaica, to attend to his sugar plantations.

Clearly there is a lack of logic here. Financial considerations aside, if he was to be an exile why could he not have been left contentedly at Evian, rather than sent to Jamaica where he would be subject to fever, earthquakes, hurricanes and colonial society? Mrs Beckford's motives are suspect. Now that she had granddaughters in her care, the Beckford estates would still be safe from the bastard Richard Beckford even if her son died. To a severe Evangelical Christian, even a dead son might possibly have seemed preferable to a live son who indulged in sodomitical practices. Whatever her state of mind, there seems to have been an interview at which Beckford gave way, pro-testing, to his mother at her most dragonish. He even accepted the humiliation of having the dour, self-righteous Scot Robert Drysdale, his first tutor, foisted upon him as companion and guardian of his morality. Concessions were made: as an inducement to brave the perils of the sea, one of Beckford's own ships, the *Julius Caesar*, was to have a cabin specially fitted up for him, with wallpapers, gerani-ums, books and furniture, and François Verdeil was to go as his per-sonal physician.

On 3 March 1787 Beckford arrived at Falmouth with an entour-age of servants to take ship for the Caribbean. He had to wait twelve days for a favourable wind and these he spent in a deliberate exercise of writing and self-expression, effectively a preparation for his time in Portugal, the only period in his life when he kept a frank and unguarded journal day by day. His papers for those twelve days, the transcripts and trial runs for letters, the jottings and observations, were all permitted to survive, as if he realised later that this had been a significant mental and literary turning point, a time when he was vulnerable to tedium and fear, and also exposed almost for the first time to a cross-section of ordinary society.

'My Dear Mother' received from Falmouth the kind of joking, grumbling letter an intelligent schoolboy might have written: 'The very sight of the waves gently heaving the vessels in the harbour makes me sick. However I am in for it – now – & cannot escape – unless I was to let myself down into a Mine & bid adieu to Daylight.' He found 'your dearly beloved Mr Drysdale most completely Hum drum – I think for singing a Babe asleep he need not turn his back to any old Woman in Christendom – & wd. be more useful in the Nursery at West End than on board the Julius Caesar.' Over the next eleven days Drysdale was to be eased out of the party, probably with a bribe. 'Alack aday,' Beckford continued playfully, 'the late damp mild weather has invited a number of COCKROACHES to creep out of their concealments', making him fear for the safety of his books. Two days later he wrote to Lettice, 'I would give a thousand negroes to be restored to the cascades of Meillerie.' An account in an American newspaper of natural disasters in Jamaica had determined him never to settle on the island, and he asked Lettice if 'proper re-commendations' could be procured to ensure that he would be well received if he moved on to the United States. Evidently Lettice replied with a negative, as Beckford's next scheme was to sail as far as Madeira, buy a villa on that island, eat oranges, make wine, and worship 'my beloved St Anthony'.

By 7 March he had dropped the wine-making idea and was writing to tell Thomas Wildman that 'the more I hear of Jamaica the more I dread the climate ... it will certainly give my constitution such a shock as I shall never recover ... you must excuse my going any further than Madeira – from Madeira I will return to Engd or to any other place you choose to appoint.' This was a clear admission that Wildman, though only his solicitor, was in a position to direct Beckford's movements, and that something between a confidence trick and moral blackmail had been engineered. Even so, he was now only prepared to stay away for six months.

The literary backdrop to these protests was remarkably cheerful. Like Harold Pinter, Beckford had noticed that if normal conversation was collected, word for word, its cumulative banality broke through a tedium-barrier and it became amusingly significant. Trapped in a Falmouth inn with his fellow passengers, he sat record-ing the idle chatter he heard around him:

> Pray, Sir, help me to a bit of crust ... Hoot ... le croute demi le croute ... The old Scotchman went for himself to Philadelphia all the time of the War ... got money and lost it ... I mean he was well off ... His friends gone ... he was a sufferer amongst the rest of the good people ... but got his passage home for nothing ... Here's a boat ... comes or goes from the South ... See Cap'n Gomme, Sir ... what says he to the wind ... J'aimerai mieux le pain tout croute ... A little more, Cap'n ... I see the *Diana* now ... could not see her before.

For Beckford to be in a position to collect such stuff was vulnerability indeed. No more travelling like a Holy Roman Emperor incognito; instead he was confronted with the boredom of real people, and subjected to the salutary discipline of having to cope with them, hour after hour, in smoke-filled rooms.

On another occasion he looked across Falmouth harbour to 'tall elms, several avenues ... a stone pryamid about 30 feet high, a low white house built in and out in a very capricious manner' and spied 'two young girls beautifully shaped and dressed with a sort of Romantic provincial elegance walking up and down the Grove'. This was a Virginia Woolf-like vein which he was to develop richly in Portugal. Fear even produced comic verse:

> Ah me, how doleful to support in vain
> The sickly heavings of a troubled main:
> To dance impetuous on a rocky shore,
> To taste the sweets of clouted cream no more:
> In Cabbins pent to hear the angry Gale
> And pour alternate from the head & tail.

For most of the letters which he sent at least two trial runs exist on scraps of notepaper: every emotion was hoarded up for later deployment. On one verso fragment is written, under the consciously literary heading 'Resolving in my mind. Clarence's Dream':

> I take a melancholy walk on the slippery groundwork of the hatches ... a shrill wind whistles in the shrouds so the storm is blocked in the north ... Sometimes folded up in myself I think over the sad consequences of last May when I lost all I doated upon. When my peace was destroyed forever & I beheld the object of all my tenderness in the last ghastly agonies. Never shall I forget those awful days of sunshine & spring without, death and gloom within, how fearfully did the pale light of a sick room contrast with the mild breeze & blue sky of May.

These are provisional jottings for what was intended to be heroic, introspective writing – alone on the storm-torn deck the tragic hero braves the elements. The reality proved rather different:

> Last night I went on board – No sooner had I set my foot on deck than my stomach turned, my head swam – I reeled like a drunkard.

The lights & verdure in my cabin had a pleasing effect – After struggling half an hour, returned to Falmouth.

When the wind changed at last and the *Julius Caesar* put to sea there was no 'melancholy walk on the slippery groundwork of the hatches', and not a single word of writing recorded as Beckford retched his stomach empty in a fumigated cabin, with geraniums and cockroaches for company. But his mind was made up before sea-sickness closed in. There might be convents of St Anthony on Madeira but in Lisbon, the ship's first port of call, there was St Anthony's own birthplace, a more worthy object of pilgrimage. In Portugal Beckford would begin the best English travel book of the eighteenth century, his own finest writing in his native language, and an account of a year in the life of a bisexual, written without any attempt to either dramatise or conceal his sexual nature. In its original form he would never publish it, but he did leave the text intact among his papers, carefully checked and censored though they were, with the hope or intention perhaps that in a more tolerant era it could reach a public, as in 1954, indeed, it did.

CHAPTER TEN

Lisbon and a pilgrim for St Anthony

> I really am inclined to believe I am on the threshold of great adventures ... It is amazing how I get into scrapes. To me a scrape is like a dram ... It is too hot for fairies in Portugal.

B eckford's first visit to Portugal was the most relaxed and human episode in his long, tense, hyperactive life. Of those nine months he left two accounts. One is a mannered, literary version in the form of thirty-four letters which he published under the title *Italy; with Sketches of Spain and Portugal* in 1834, forty-seven years after the events it claims to describe, when in his old age he had become anxious to project the image of a genial connoisseur of the Picturesque. The second text is his *Journal*, an almost day-by-day diary, preserved in the Beckford Papers and not published until 1954 when Boyd Alexander edited it with an introduction and scholarly notes. Lies, compressions, fantasies, erasures and second thoughts enrich both texts: they make fascinating reading, the *Journal* in particular as it is far less guarded, despite much rewriting, than Beckford usually chose to be. He must have intended it as an exercise in self-expression and relief from tension in a complex social situation.

Although Beckford landed in Portugal on 24 March, his published *Sketches* does not open until 31 May, while the *Journal* begins abruptly on 25 May, when he was already well established in Lisbon and predictably deep in deviousness. There are then 32 days to be accounted for by reasonable hindsight.

So, in the ninth day of a voyage which normally took seven (and which Lord Byron later managed in only four) Beckford came sailing up that gloriously open, sea-gate estuary of the Tagus. First, on his left, rose the dramatic wooded hills of Sintra, then Lisbon itself, the city of St Anthony, sprawling up a valley and two steep hillsides. Never the most distinguished of European capitals, Lisbon was a port with no deep-water quays, so Beckford's party would have gone ashore in small boats. The first thing to catch their attention would have been the town's one great set-piece, the Terreiro do Paço, the Palace or Market Square – three ranges of uniform arcaded buildings open on one side to the Tagus. Regularly grand but other-wise unremarkable, they were at the time painted bright yellow, 'which being more or less discoloured by the rain, produces a very bad effect'. Beckford would have had to be told that the north-west section housed not only Lisbon's town hall but a Royal palace – or, more accurately, a Royal apartment. It made an unimpressive intro-duction to the degree of state kept by the Royal House of Braganza-Aviz.

After the square came anticlimax: the Pombalist new town, a logical grid of cheap, soulless neo-Classical façades. A later English visitor analysed it shrewdly in 1790:

> This quarter is superb; but it produces a dull monotonous effect upon the mind of the spectator. Perhaps it would have a more agreeable aspect if it were ornamented with fine palaces, handsome hotels, elegant public buildings.... We cannot behold without regret the most beautiful part of Lisbon occupied by tradesmen, whose shops, low, dark, and destitute of ornament, have nothing of that showy, splendid appearance which they exhibit in most large cities.

Though superbly sited to face south across its great estuary, the city was not looking its best. The two hills beyond it were in Beckford's time still untidy with ruined churches and gutted palaces from the great earthquake that had struck the city on the morning of 1 November, All Saints' Day, 1755, as High Mass was being cele-brated in the hundred and twenty churches of the devout capital. The effects of the tidal wave which followed the 'quake have been exaggerated: it was the fire which burnt for eight days after the first shock that caused such ruin and distress. Beckford was not impressed, noting within days of his arrival:

> The more I am acquainted with Lisbon the more I dislike it. Its appearance announces neither the wealth nor dignity of a capital, but rather a succession of ugly villages awkwardly tacked together. The churches in general are contemptibly small and so deficient in point of architecture as to resemble certain imaginary views of Mexican temples to be found in a Dutch atlas. Most of these have turrets in the delectable taste of old-fashioned French clock cases.

Packs of howling dogs scavenged the streets at night. 'This town', another English traveller of the time noted disdainfully, 'was always remarkable, I believe, for being at once sumptuous and nasty.' The English residents, a numerous group of merchants, were generally disliked, and kept to themselves. For his new residence Beckford moved out along the coast road to the west, almost a mile from the centre, towards Belém. There he took a substantial wooden house – most of the new houses, including one Royal palace, were built of wood – behind the Necessidades Palace in the Rua Cova da Moura. It was large enough for his English staff of twenty, with a yard for two high-sprung English coaches. His banker and agent, Thomas Horne, 65 years old, fat, companionable and a dandy, had arranged everything for him, and was hoping soon to move him into a vacant Royal palace, the Quinta dos Bichos in Belém. Horne was a shipper of whale oil, though Portuguese subordinates handled all the business. His partner Mr Sill had two daughters, the elder of whom, Betty, Beckford praised for 'an excellent heart and a clear judgement'.

To keep up the myth of a moral pariah, biographers suggest that Beckford avoided his fellow countrymen in Lisbon, and it is true that he detested 'that malevolent cuckold', The Hon. Robert Walpole, British Envoy in Lisbon and nephew of the great Prime Minister, Sir Robert. But in reality he had immediately any number of English friends, with whom he regularly dined and took tea. There were the Sills, the Hornes, 'old Mr Collett', General Forbes, and Captains White and Macdonald. He often sought out English middle-class company and found it readily available. Until October Horne was Beckford's constant companion, friend and advisor, able to point out the political and social pitfalls – into which Beckford then deliberately proceeded to tread. 'An honest Englishman,' Beckford described him, 'he always rejoices when any little event takes place to disgust me with Portugal.' Horne provided a dry commentary on the country: 'We had a long conversation', Beckford wrote, 'upon the dirt, dullness and despotism of Portugal, and the little such a government had to offer worth my acceptance. Our opinions perfectly coincide.' Another valued English friend, General John Forbes-Skelater, kept him closely informed on the Marialvas' manoeuvres at Court and warned him 'that like the Land of Egypt this kingdom is a broken reed upon which if a man lean he shall pierce his side'. 'I must take care what I am about', Beckford noted, 'and beware of splinters . . . I am more and more convinced that some great scheme of rooting me in this country is in agitation.'

The warning was accurate, but might as well not have been delivered: Beckford enjoyed what he called 'scrapes' or social perils. From his first days in Portugal, more by religious accident than by design, he fell in with the right-wing, reactionary, anti-British opposition party in Lisbon, and it is that, rather than the Courtenay scandal and his reputation for sodomy, which accounts for Walpole's refusal to present Beckford officially to Queen Maria. Wealthy British deviants were common in Lisbon, but they were not expected to threaten to put enormous wealth on the side of aristocrats hostile to Britain's commercial interests.

Portugal was at that time in a delicate and unresolved political balance: a country taking its breath to recover from recent traumas, poised uneasily between the forces of reform and reaction, with pro-British, pro-Spanish and Portuguese 'enlightenment' factions all jostling for influence. Rather as France had often fostered first Scottish and then Irish independence as a check to English imperial ambitions, so Britain had consistently supported Portuguese nationalism to embarrass Spain. The price of that support had been the subjection of Portuguese commerce to British interests. By the second Methuen Treaty of 1703 Britain, in exchange for giving Portuguese wines preference over those of France, secured the unhindered sale of its textiles and industrial products to Portugal and its Atlantic colonies, a valuable market. But this automatically crippled

1. A statue of Alderman William Beckford in full flow of libertarian oratory. His son grew up in the shadow of a father remembered as a popular hero of the political left, a colonial with little time for kings or aristocracy

2. A sentimental posthumous portrait of 'our Mam' as châtelaine and musician. Beckford's mother was a firm, devout and conventionally minded Scot who mishandled her loving and obedient son at every crisis in his life

3. Fonthill Splendens as rebuilt after the fire of 1755. A second-rate City builder's notion of how a Whig grandee of the 1720s might have been housed in Palladian opulence

4. A chimneypiece carved by J. F. Moore for the new Fonthill Splendens suggests that the interior was one of unbridled sensuality

5. The Lakeside Grotto at Fonthill was built for the Alderman by Joseph Lane of Tisbury. In its prime it was not only encrusted with glittering crystal spar and sea-shells, but had heavily perfumed hot-house flowers set within its earth floor to look as if they were growing naturally

6. The Hermitage represents a second stage in the Alderman's creation of a Rococo garden. It still contains the vandalized reliefs of a river god and a hermit with a fireplace for Gothic picnics

7. Incorrectly described by John Britton in his guide as a 'Cromlech', this viewing tower is another example of the Alderman's taste in garden design as he moved from the 'Arcadian' to the 'Savage' Picturesque

8. An illustration from *The Adventures of Abdalla son of Hanif* of 1729, by William Hatchett, gives an impression of the magical oriental tales popular in the mid-century which could have inspired Alderman Beckford's 'Turkish Room' in Fonthill Splendens

9. William Courtenay, 3rd Viscount. Beckford's schoolboy lover has grown into the plump young man who would soon have to take refuge in France from the English judiciary and its obsessive pursuit of sexual deviants

10. Louisa Beckford acted as the eager go-between in Beckford's relationship with young Courtenay. She is here shown in a painting commissioned by Beckford from Sir Joshua Reynolds as Hebe, a disreputable figure who preceded Ganymede as cupbearer to Zeus

11. St Denis carries his own head – this frontispiece to the 1834 edition of *Biographical Memoirs of Extraordinary Painters* illustrates Beckford's wry sense of humour and a distinct vein of religious scepticism

12. The Château of Blonay stands on the southern shore of Lake Geneva within a stone's throw of the woodland clearing where, from 1777 onwards, Beckford celebrated a series of Arcadian revels in the style of the Swiss prose-poet, Gessner

13. Beckford settled down in July 1785 to live a notably respectable life with his wife and daughter in the Château of la Tour de Peilz on the northern shore of Lake Geneva. His wife died there in 1786

14. The abbey church and monastery of Batalha, Portugal, seen from the west and giving that impression of an entire medieval town which Beckford intended to repeat at his Fonthill estate

15. The vault of the octagon mausoleum of the Plantagenet princes in Batalha, one source of inspiration for the central Octagon at Fonthill

16. Beckford spent the summers of his last visits to Portugal in the Quinta of Montserrat. The cheerful Gothick profile as he knew it survives under a heavy later overlay of Moorish detail

17. The Quinta of Montserrat was not built by Beckford but he designed this, now overgrown and ruined, Gothic pavilion in the densely wooded valley below the house

18. The isolated block of servants' quarters at Montserrat was a clumsy attempt at the Lanes' 'rockifying' techniques using Portuguese labour

19. James Wyatt's tower design from Joseph Farington's *Diary* illustrates Beckford's original idea for a garden building – half viewing belvedere and half Arthurian dining pavilion with minimal sleeping accommodation

20. William Beckford in world-weary, careworn middle age by John Hoppner

21. Turner's 1797 view of Fonthill Abbey from the south-west includes the frail spirelet which blew down in a strong wind. In the foreground is the compact south-west wing where Beckford actually lived from about 1798 onwards. His double Yellow Drawing Room occupies the range of windows over the five arches

22. This 1823 view of the Abbey shows how gloriously disproportionate the East Transept was to the earlier main south–north axis of the house

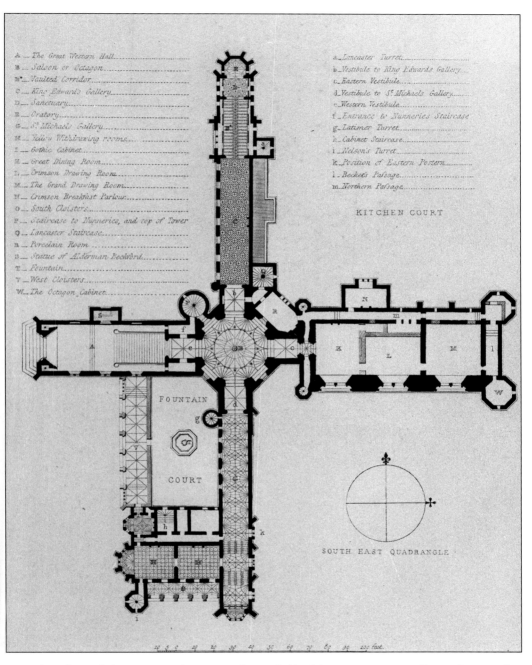

A — The Great Western Hall...............
B — Saloon or Octagon......................
B* — Vaulted Corridor.......................
C — King Edward's Gallery................
D — Sanctuary.................................
E — Oratory.....................................
G — St Michael's Gallery....................
H — Yellow Withdrawing rooms..........
I — Gothic Cabinet...........................
K — Great Dining Room....................
L — Crimson Drawing Room..............
M — The Grand Drawing Room...........
N — Crimson Breakfast Parlour..........
O — South Cloisters..........................
P — Staircase to Nunneries, and top of Tower
Q — Lancaster Staircase....................
R — Porcelain Room.........................
D — Statue of Alderman Beckford.......
T — Fountain..................................
V — West Cloisters...........................
VI — The Octagon Cabinet.................

a — Lancaster Turret........................
b — Vestibule to King Edward's Gallery
c — Eastern Vestibule.......................
d — Vestibule to St Michael's Gallery...
e — Western Vestibule......................
f — Entrance to Nunneries Staircase...
g — Latimer Turret...........................
h — Cabinet Staircase.......................
i — Nelson's Turret...........................
k — Position of Eastern Postern..........
l — Becket's Passage..........................
m — Northern Passage........................

KITCHEN COURT

FOUNTAIN

COURT

SOUTH EAST QUADRANGLE

23. The plan of the principal storey of Fonthill Abbey exposes an illogicality in the building's development. The ritual axis which Beckford imposed is a relatively narrow corridor running south–north to climax in the chapel of St Anthony. The broad west–east axis has no Christian significance and is interrupted by the change in levels between the west porch and the Octagon

24. St Michael's Gallery from Rutter's *Delineations*. It was here, before its northernmost bays were completed, that Beckford entertained Nelson and his party to an after-dinner dessert and concert of religious music

25. George Cattermole's splendidly exaggerated version of the Great Western Hall at Fonthill. The steps up to the central Octagon were an afterthought when Beckford realized that the space was not suitable for a dining-room

26. A jewel casket made for Beckford by Henri Auguste in the late 1790s when England and France were supposedly locked in mortal combat. In a perverse twentieth-century development the 'Beckford' provenance now sends prices soaring for these examples of questionable taste which destroyed the native English tradition of elegantly simple design

27. Beckford's design for a towered medieval mausoleum at Fonthill was drawn when he had discovered that his proposed burial chamber in the Abbey was subject to damp. This may also represent a preliminary version of the Lansdown Tower in Bath

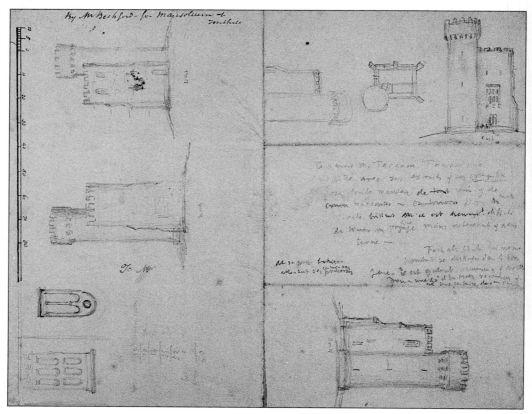

28. William Beckford portrayed in his Bath retirement by Charles Foote Tayler

29. This contemporary view of the Crimson Drawing Room in the Lansdown Tower shows how far Beckford had anticipated the heaviness of Victorian furnishings and the rich darkness of Victorian interiors

30. In his typical eighteenth-century obsession with privacy in garden design Beckford had this Grotto Tunnel dug under a public right-of-way which interrupted his scenic garden drive connecting Lansdown Crescent with the Lansdown Tower

31. This view of the Lansdown Tower captures the eclectic elegance of a building where the Italianate tower shaft and the Greek Revival lantern were improbably yet successfully united

Portugal's native industries and tilted the country's agriculture towards a vinous monoculture. Portugal's balance of payments problem was thereby temporarily solved, however, and the landed aristocracy gained some financial security. Thereafter the country dreamed its way through the pieties of João V's reign (1706–50). Its aristocracy was still virtually feudal, its peasants impoverished, and the English 'Factory' or colony of merchants in Lisbon was siphoning off the gold of Brazil at the rate of almost a million pounds a year to pay for English imports. Then, soon after the accession of José I to the throne, a double trauma rocked the state.

First came the earthquake of 1755; then the rise to power of Sebastião José de Carvalho e Melo, later 1st Marquês de Pombal. Taciturn, industrious and ruthless, in pursuit of a reformed administration and a more modern state he became the scourge of Portugal's church and aristocracy. On the pretext of a plot against the King's life in 1758, he had the Marquis of Tavora broken publicly on the wheel and his children executed in front of their mother. Two thousand opponents were flung into prison, most to remain there for the next twenty years. Riding on this wave of terror, Pombal expelled the Jesuits, freed black slaves in mainland Portugal, gave the Jews citizenship, and encouraged science, mathematics and native industry. The threat in 1762 of an invasion from Spain gave some new life to the Anglo-Portuguese alliance and with it the trade of the English Factory revived, but it was carried on now with rather less assurance, and an awareness of the need for tactful discretion.

During the years of his power Pombal had taken measures to ensure the permanence of his reform programme. The heir to the throne was a woman, Maria, a deeply religious princess of uncertain mental health who had, after the Ptolemaic custom of the Royal House of Braganza, married her uncle, Dom Pedro, equally devout and equally prone to melancholy. On this gloomy pair rested the hopes of the persecuted aristocracy, led by the three great houses of Marialva, Angeja and Ponte do Lima. To circumvent them, Pombal gave the Princess as her confessor Inacio de São Caetano, a relaxed and humane friar of humble birth, sympathetic to reform. São Caetano soon gained an absolute control over her frail wits. During the twenty Pombalist years the country's administrative system was taken over by efficient reformers, a new nobility of the robe, and by means of judicious favours and distribution of high office a number of the old aristocracy were won to the party of reform. Among them were the King's great-uncle, the Duke of Lafões, and Princess Maria's eldest son, Dom José, who had been educated by Pombalist tutors to become a brash and ardent reformist.

As a result, when King José died in 1777 and Pombal lost power, there was no radical alteration in political conditions. Imprisoned aristocrats were released, but not to power, or to vengeance. Dom José, now heir to the throne and Prince of Brazil, supported the established administration of Pombalist officials while the Court, mildly reactionary, moved towards a *rapprochement* with Spain, the old enemy. This obliged the administration to favour Britain and the English Factory, despite the growing rivalry between English and Portuguese merchants. As a consequence the long-standing British envoy Walpole, who held the office from 1772 to 1800, became an active and potent figure in Portuguese power politics; he would have seen any marital alliance between Beckford and the old aristocracy as a dangerous injection of wealth into a party hostile to England and potentially pro-Spanish. It is hard to tell whether Beckford would have had the political wit to appreciate these undercurrents. When he arrived in 1787 the King Consort, Dom Pedro, had lately died, leaving the Queen a vulnerable widow, nervously trying to balance conflicting forces. The Prime Minister, Martinho de Melo, was anti-clerical and pro-British; the Prince of Brazil was anti-clerical, but anti-British. Behind it all, and by his control of Queen Maria the real ruler of Portugal, was her confessor São Caetano, now also Archbishop and Inquistor-General, but more interested in maintaining the status quo and a quiet life than anything else.

Into this delicate equilibrium of forces Beckford stepped, self-centred and self-confident, intent upon impressing the natives with his theatrical but obsessively sincere devotion to Lisbon's patron saint. Because this reverence was so eccentric, often so flippantly expressed, it tends to be underrated. Beckford's choice of Lisbon as a refuge was religious in origin: his curious, intensely personal way of dealing with God was via St Anthony, patron of lost things, young brides and animals. The saint had been born in Lisbon in 1195; so there, when he was unhappy, rejected by his own relatives but in no way a broken man, Beckford had directed his own pilgrimage in his own flamboyant style.

Exactly how he conducted himself during those first eight Lisbon weeks, from 24 March 24 May, is not recorded. His more contrived and artificial *Italy; with Sketches of Spain and Portugal* includes a lavish set-piece, composed like a Delacroix painting, supposedly describing his first meeting with the two Marialva Marquises as they stepped out of a fifty-oar *scalera* in a blaze of flambeaux, 'attended by a swarm of musicians, poets, bullfighters, grooms, monks, dwarfs and children of both sexes, fantastically dressed'. But that was written to satisfy the aesthetic tastes of 1834: in 1787 Beckford still found such human chaos faintly distasteful. His *Journal* opens abruptly on 25 May, by which time he was already celebrated for his piety and the admired friend of Diogo, the 'young' or 5th Marquis Marialva who, with his aged but still hale and hearty father Pedro, the 4th Marquis (two men could, with Royal permission, hold the same title at the same time), was a pillar of the right-wing, anti-British opposition. Beckford did nothing by halves. He was lavish in his alms-giving, dowering several young girls who were anxious to take the veil; priests, monks and nuns clustered about him, offering little presents for large returns. Each Sunday he attended Mass in the elegantly austere Patriarchal church of São Vicente da Fora 'in state', beating his breast, crossing himself and gazing adoringly at the Host.

With those early days in Portugal a complete blank in the *Journal*, it is important to stand back for a moment and see the Englishman from the point of view of a Portuguese aristocrat. Beckford's annual income was roughly ten times that of the richest man in Portugal (the 2nd Marquis Pombal, who enjoyed 110,000 crowns a year). To the Portuguese, he must have seemed impossibly wealthy, and in unscrupulous hands money means power. In addition to wealth he was a good-looking widower, only 27 years old, sophisticated and, when it pleased him, charming. He had no son to succeed him, only two daughters, rich prizes to be married off. He had landed in his own ship with a large retinue, carriages and fine furniture. To all intents and purposes he was a devout Catholic, and he claimed to detest his native Britain. As eager to honour the Church as he was to meet the aristocracy, he must have seemed the catch of the century.

The Lisbon-based aristocracy moved in on Beckford fast, no one faster than Diogo José Vito de Menezes Coutinho, the 'young' 5th Marquis Marialva. Old Pedro, the 4th Marquis and still head of the family, was quietly supportive in the background. It seems clear that they caught their quarry through his church attendance, loosing upon him their chaplain, the 92 year old Abbé Xavier. Beckford took to him immediately, always referring to him as the 'Abbade'. A charming, garrulous old gentleman, the Abbade introduced him to the young Marquis, and soon he was seen not only as a Catholic convert but as a supporter of the reactionary party.

This was to prove fatal to Beckford's hopes of ever being presented at Court or allowed into the charmed circle of diplomatic entertainment. Presentation to the Queen could only be made by one's own national envoy, a man able to vouch for one's status at home. Now, as a result of these new connections and religious activities and with some justice, the envoy Walpole believed Beckford to be a potential threat to British interests: a Marialva cousin was the newly appointed Portuguese Ambassador in Madrid, and the two Iberian states were growing inopportunely close. The sooner Beckford was out of Portugal, the better. So there was to be no presentation.

Beckford was enraged but, confident that he could reverse the situation, he wrote asking his aunt Lady Effingham to send, or persuade someone else to send, a letter to Lisbon to vouch for his moral probity and put pressure on Walpole. It was typical of Beckford that he entertained no serious doubts that such a letter would be forthcoming: so the packet-boat which sailed in four times a month from Falmouth was eagerly expected.

And there the situation rested. By 25 May Beckford and his companion–friend Dr Verdeil had developed a pleasant evening ritual, driving out together west along the coast road to enjoy the sea breezes and dramatic sunsets. This took them past the Marialva palace, a twin-turreted seaside quinta, where almost invariably they would find the old Abbade waving to them from the long veranda. They would pick him up, listen to his gossip about the family, and drop him on the way back. That was how the Abbade had contrived to introduce Beckford to the 'young' Marquis – who was in fact 21 years Beckford's senior. The friendship had grown, and soon the bemused but flattered Englishman could write of Marialva's 'peculiar predilection' for him.

The Marialvas were one great family against whom Pombal had never dared to move. Natural courtiers and ingratiators, both the 4th and 5th Marquises held army rank as general, were Master of the Horse to Queen Maria, and Gentlemen of her Bedchamber. Both were deeply devout reactionaries, forever in and out of churches and fitfully plotting to undermine the Pombalists. In principle they disliked the English intensely, as cold and arrogant intruders; but, understandably, where Beckford was concerned they made an exception to this rule. The eldest of the 'young' Marquis's three pretty daughters, Henriqueta, 15 at this time, had become unofficially engaged, through royal pressure, to the 68 year old great-great-uncle of the Queen, the Duke of Lafões. Such a disparity in age was nothing in Portuguese society, but Lafões was of the other party, a Pombalist, and in William Beckford Marialva saw a heaven sent opportunity to escape an unwanted alliance with an aged Pombalist. There would be a young husband for Henriqueta, a huge accession of wealth to the old aristocracy, opportunities for political bribery on an undreamt-of scale – and, as a quid pro quo, a Portuguese title for William, to make up for the lost barony of Fonthill. Walpole's alarm at the prospect of such an injection of capital into a hostile party becomes understandable.

On 25 May Beckford drove out to the Marialva home for an unofficial glimpse of the possible bride, Dona Henriqueta. He reacted predictably: 'She appeared to me a lovely girl with eyes full of youthful gaiety and a turn of shape remarkably graceful.' Then nervous reservations took over: 'But of what do I talk? I only saw her as in a dream: perhaps her charms might vanish in open daylight.' Her mother being absent, he was only allowed to see the girl through 'the door of a dark apartment adjoining'. Henriqueta's brother, the 14 year old heir to the Marialvas, Dom Pedro, was, on the other hand, far more available. 'A young stripling not inelegantly made,' Beckford noted, 'he received me with great attention.' Was it the meeting with the girl or the boy that made the 25th a special date? For an extrovert bisexual, it may well have been both: a day when Portugal began to seem emotionally promising.

Beckford promptly sat down at the harpsichord 'to play and sing in a manner that surprised the whole herd of precentors, priests, musicians and fencing masters that were in waiting upon the heir of the Marialvas'. It was with such high-spirited displays that he was to charm and bewilder Portuguese high society for the remainder of his stay. Dom Pedro was impressed. 'Seeing in him a sort of unwilling-ness to quit me so soon, I pressed him to accompany us the rest of our drive, so he jumped into the coach.' (It was an article of faith with Beckford that all animals, birds in particular, and children found him irresistible.) The old Abbade must have thought the evening had gone well. But it was the first anniversary of the death of Beckford's wife Margaret, and he slept 'ill owing to the yowling and yelping of dogs and puppies. The sad idea of my sufferings this day twelve-month rushed into my mind and renewed all my agonies.' It is possible to see both the *Journal* and Beckford's seduc-tion by Portugal as in some way representing his recovery from that anguish.

Two days later, after a Sunday visit to the Patriarchal – 'two sublime motets of Jommelli, worth going two leagues in the sun to hear, I was exulted into heaven whilst they were executing' – the *Journal* becomes both a confessional and, typically, a concealment. This must have been the day when Beckford first met the boy who was to become his lifelong friend, lover and agent, Gregorio Franchi. 'Polycarpo', a first tenor in the Queen's Chapel who appears already to have got the measure of Beckford's proclivities, 'begged me to return tomorrow to hear one of the boys play, marvellously as he pre-tends. Well we shall see.' So according to the *Journal*, they had yet to meet. But there must that Sunday have already been at least an exchange of glances to explain the premonitory entry:

> I have half a mind to sleep in peace and coolness at Sintra but then the Patriarchal and Polycarpo's friend – I shall get into a scrape if I don't take care. How tired I am of keeping a mask on my counte-nance, How tight it sticks – it makes me sore. There's metaphor for you. I have all the fancies and levity of a child and would give an estate

or two to skip about the galleries of the Patriarchal with the *menino* unobserved. Dom Pedro is not child enough for me.

Yet in the same entry he comments on how all his English friends in Lisbon, Betty Sill in particular, 'think me rather inclined to fall in love with Donna Henriqueta', blandly concluding, 'so I am'.

Next day he met the '*menino*' Franchi officially, upstairs in the Patriarchal college during sermon time in the church, handling the meeting with predatory deliberation:

> The *menino* has surprising abilities and did ample justice to the glori-
> ous compositions of Haydn he played. I could have passed an hour
> agreeably in hearing of him and was in fact delighted; but rose up,
> after I had listened about a quarter of an hour, with dignity and
> apparent coldness.

Playing hard to get and to conceal his pleasure from the watchful Polycarpo, Beckford went 'back to my old station near the High Altar where I knelt out the remainder of the Mass with elevated eyes and hands crossed on my breast. I wish much to hear the *menino* again.' Polycarpo had hinted that Franchi would perform even better on Beckford's own pianoforte. 'I suppose he wants me to send for him' – Beckford had noted the musical pimping. 'All in good time.' He was to wait for a month.

Calculating as he may seem, it was nevertheless a day of regenera-tion for him. The year of official mourning for Lady Margaret was over. The old lusts and the old vivacity were stirring again. With his very private and proprietory religion, did he think that in St Anthony's city (Anthony had been born just up the hill, in a house near the Sé or cathedral) the saint had absolved him from past pain and given him some emotional green light to take his pleasures again, especially in holy surroundings? For Beckford, sex and religiosity worked oddly together. Next day he was at the Patriarchal mass again but made no venture upstairs: 'the fear of scandal kept me in prudent silence and gravity'.

Between them Dom Pedro and Gregorio Franchi had set Beckford's mind working. On that same day of 'prudent silence and gravity', he and Dr Verdeil rode out to visit 'the simple smiling friars' at the convent of São José de Ribamar. Beckford wandered out by himself into the wild garden.

> The underwood remains unclipped and intrudes wherever it pleases upon the alleys, which hang over the sea in a bold romantic manner. I looked down the steep on the smoothest beach imaginable. The waves, impelled by a cool wind, broke softly on the shore. How should I enjoy stretching myself on its sands by moonlight and owning all my frailties and wild imaginations to some love-sick languid youth reclined by my side and thrown by the dubious light and undecided murmurs into a soft delirium.

That night he slept badly again, wakened by 'a horrid cry of dogs':

> I wished them at hell for breaking my dreams which were very agreeable. Methought I was walking with William Courtenay on the declivity of green hills scattered over with orange trees in blossom. Our eyes were bathed in tears of affection and forgiveness, our hands were joined, and we seemed to have entirely forgotten the miseries we had occasioned each other.

Beckford could engineer dreams at will. Five days later he was reminiscing how 'three years ago I little dreamt of ever having a conference with friars in Portugal. I was then on the high road to fame and dignity, courted by Mr Pitt, fawned upon by all his adherants, worshipped and glorified by my Scotch kindred, and cajoled by that cowardly effeminate fool William Courtenay.' His lilting mood of purple prose could as easily be turned upon a young woman as a young boy. Two days after his wistful rapture in the friars' garden, 'Old Horne' – 'who has a colts tooth' – took him out to the private gardens of the Ajuda Palace to meet some *acafatas*, 'a species between a bed-chamber woman and a maid of honour'. There Beckford was smitten by 'a lovely blue-eyed Irish girl of fifteen . . . her hair of the loveliest auburn, her straight Grecian eyebrows and fair complexion form a striking contrast to the gypsy-coloured skins and jetty tresses of her companions. She looked like a visionary being skimming along the alleys and leaving the pot-bellied sopranos and dowdy *acafatas* far behind, wondering at her lightness.' She and Beckford 'coursed each other like children along the terrace and when tired reposed under a group of gigantic Brazilian aloes', until a priest came and ordered them apart.

A little later in June, after a good dose of Epsom salts administered by Dr Verdeil had relieved his melancholy (Beckford suffered badly from constipation), he was 'thrown into a langour' by the singing of a Signora Escarlate, and once again lapsed into an 'aesthetic' prose quite distinct from his usual crisp and even acid register:

> I am to meet her, thank Heaven, at Sintra in the wild shubberies which encircle her habitation, and we will sing like skylarks, and nobody shall hear us except a little sister of the nymph's with a fair complexion, blue eyes and long pencilled eyelashes. She may be allowed, I think, to languish away at these soft sounds at the foot of a branching citron, half lost amongst tufts of fern. I think I see her peeping from amongst them, and the old hairy Conservador in the shape of a satyr rousing her from her concealment and coursing her over the hills.

It is after reading gloriously self-indulgent fantasies like these that all the doubts of earlier biographers about Beckford's sex life can be appreciated. Was his real vice the writing of sexual prose rather than the performing of any sexual act? If those deadly letters to Courtenay which Lord Loughborough was holding over his head were as lustfully lulling as these passages which break out so often in his *Journal* when music or natural beauty stirs him, then all the scandal and the flight are comprehensible. Was Beckford's only real perversion poetic prose, and was all the rest only the dirty-mindedness of his contemporaries? Would he have simply lain beside that 'languid youth' on the sands of desire, and chattered away all night?

One other thing becomes clear, and explains Lady Margaret's love for her exotic husband: someone who could pour out this gushing, seductive language every time he made love was clearly a husband to treasure, and to stand by loyally when friends and even family urged her to abandon him. More than anyone, Lady Margaret could have believed that the supposed episodes of sodomy were only similar outpourings of words from a man intoxicated by pure emotion.

In his early Portuguese months those unwise letters to young Courtenay were still very present in Beckford's mind. For weeks he had been expecting the packet-boat from Falmouth to bring a letter from his aunt Effingham, or perhaps the Hamiltons, supporting his

claim to be presented at Court. On 18 June the packet sailed in: still
there was nothing from his relatives, 'so I must shift entirely for
myself in this kingdom'. His aunt and his mother had refused to
vouch for his probity in a distant country where their support could
have done little harm. It was a moment of truth which he bore with
remarkable stoicism.

There was one letter, from his lawyer, Wildman, concerning the
possibility of 'Lord Lilliput [Courtenay's father] consenting at length
to take certain dangerous papers [written no doubt in that impas-
sioned prose] out of the talons of Beelzebub' (Lord Loughborough).
But even that was a false hope. By the next packet-boat came the
bitter truth: 'I have just heard from Wildman that Lord Courtenay
has been once more overawed by old Beelzebub, and like a contempt-
ible coward suffers the most obnoxious papers to remain in old
Beelzebub's clutches. I cannot yet discover any decisive method of
smoothing my way home to England.'

All this while, the Marialvas were closing in upon him. Their most
potent weapon was not Beckford's 'zealous and affectionate friend'
Marialva, who usually bored him to tears, but yet another amiable
old cleric, Manuel de Noronha e Menezes, Grand Prior of Aviz.
Beckford, ever susceptible to old men, took to him at their first
meeting. 'His manner is full of mildness and dignity. I like him better
than any Portuguese I have seen, spiritual or temporal.' The Grand
Prior, an illegitimate uncle of Marialva, urbane, worldly-wise and
perceptive, was loosed upon Beckford when the Marialvas realised
that he was not a proper Catholic, and would need to be coaxed into
the arms of Mother Church. He became, along with the chattering
old Abbade, a constant companion of Beckford's evening rides with
Verdeil, and immediately perceived that Dom Pedro, not
Henriqueta, was the real focus of the rich Englishman's affections. In
no way deterred by this unpromising emotional factor, the Grand
Prior thereafter made a point of bringing the solemn young man with
him, as bait. Later developments suggest that he warned the boy's
mother to keep a wary eye on the relationship, but he probably left
the father, Marialva, in happy ignorance of the truth.

Beckford was at this time finding Dom Pedro hard going, a
reserved and serious boy, unlike his cousins, the Marquis of Tancos's

children. After a lively evening with these last, of which Beckford recorded that 'I could not help playing with the light brown hair of the eldest Tancos, a lovely boy of thirteen, nor could the poor little stripling help finding me more youthful and condescending than he expected', Dom Pedro called an abrupt halt to the goings-on and ordered the Marialva party home, cramped five in a coach. He sat silently, squashed between Beckford and the Grand Prior. 'Our excursion lasted till it was dark,' Beckford noted, and added savagely, 'D. Pedro is the proudest youth that ever sat by me, but I will humble him if St Anthony gives me health and spirits' – as interesting a pointer to the equivocal moral role and the pliancy of the Lisbon saint in Beckford's private pantheon as it is to Beckford's need for abject adoration from the young.

This he was to find from a safer direction. Gregorio Franchi, the 17 year old Italian student at the Patriarchal music academy, had been drawn to his attention as a promising musician back in May. At the time Franchi had made no secret of his eagerness for a closer relationship but Beckford, while noting the signals, had decided to play cautiously. Now that he was finding Dom Pedro unresponsive, he invited Franchi round to his house to play for him. While the *Journal* does not boast in so many words of a sexual conquest, the innuendos are strong. Franchi's eyes, Beckford claimed, had grown larger than ever, and the young man gave him such meaningful glances that he could not help blushing. He reported airily that: 'These Portuguese youths are composed of more inflamable materials than other mortals. I could keep them spellbound for hours at my side, listening to the childish notes of my voice, and dissolving like snow in sunshine.' Franchi's choirboy status at the Patriarchal will have enhanced his attractiveness.

In his own remarkable style, Beckford was having a wildly religious life in Lisbon. No one will quite understand his religiosity who has not experienced young students, typical ordinands of a High Church persuasion, preparing for the priesthood in their university years, before a church training college sobers them down. A bizarre levity of bells, smells and 'spikery' tends to seize them, and they react to the enormity of their faith with theatrical humour. Holy rituals and therefore the Godhead itself are controlled within a verbal game.

Implications too awesome are given human scale by little jokes. There is a chatter of chasubles and albs, pyxes and aumbries, of the strength of Communion wine. Hindus and some Zen Buddhists might empathise with this holy frivolity, but it is an essentially Protestant reaction as the Church of England sidles up to the Roman Church, filches its rituals and tries to outdo its pomp and its music, all the while sensing the un-Englishness of it.

William Beckford and Horace Walpole were both instinctive Anglo-Catholics before their time. With no High Church havens to sustain them in a uniformly Low Church century, they both created amateur sanctuaries. Horace had his little octagon of kitsch holiness next to his Gallery at Strawberry Hill. It was a 'Cabinet', 'Tribune' or 'Chapel', with an image of his mother, an altar, and candlesticks. Beckford eventually carried his off in hyperbolic scale at Fonthill Abbey, where his enduring obsession with the tower would be linked to an entire cruciform 'cathedral', its north–south axis leading to a sanctuary where Rossi's statue of St Anthony took the place of the conventional crucified Christ. Beckford could not cope with Jesus: St Anthony was handleable, a kindly human image, sometimes carrying the infant Jesus. He could be manipulated easily, avoiding any challenging concepts of salvation, redemption or resurrection. With St Anthony, Beckford's Christianity reached an adolescent stage from which, as his death-bed firmness showed, he never needed to move forward; indeed, towards the end of his life he possibly moved back to a kind of despair. But as the sheer scale of Fonthill and his self-mocking excess at Lisbon demonstrated, he was altogether more involved in religion than Walpole ever was, more aware of the problem of evil and nearer to Lord Byron's position.

A passage from the *Journal* for 20 June illustrates the complexity of his response to Portuguese pieties.

> I went broiling in the sun to the Antonine Convent at Campo de Santana and heard High Mass with edifying fervour. The Prior has spread a carpet for me within the rails of the High Altar and immediately under the image of St Anthony, where I remained kneeling above an hour. Several female devotees of quality attended by their pages crept in to observe my behaviour. Not a look did I vouchsafe them. My hands were clasped and my eyes riveted to the countenace

of my benign protector. Mass ended, the priests came forth in solemn procession with tapers blazing, and, kneeling before the image of St Anthony, acknowledged his great interest with the celestial powers and implored him to work out my salvation. A solemn hymn was chanted by a full choir accompanied by the organ. I filled my imagination with the mighty deeds and miracles of the saint, and appeared so rapt and sanctified that Mr Verdeil could not help staring. When all holy acts were finished, the fathers led me about their cloister, gardens and chapels, stuffed me with sweetmeats, and summoned their whole community to line the steps before the convent when I got into my carriage. Had I been Cardinal Legate they would not have paid me a higher compliment. I had some difficulty to stifle a laugh when I looked back on the group which was assembled in my honour, and saw so many boobies in hoods and cowls poking out their sturdy necks and aiming bows at me.

To interpret this episode as no more than cruel cynicism is to miss the elements of honest revelation of a man unsure of his own nature but still exercising a deplorable integrity of self-analysis. Was the raising of Fonthill Abbey anything more than a continuation of this exploration of what money could buy and how society could be fooled? Was it all a game, with a slight core of sincere reserve? Did Beckford leave Fonthill Abbey stifling his laughter, just as he left those 'boobies in hoods and cowls' at the Antonine Convent? After canvassing the opinions of those who had known him, Joseph Farington reported:

> Beckford is of a very unamiable disposition. Jealous of everybody who excells. – Parsons, his Music Master, He was jealous of on acct. of his personal knowledge. – He is an Actor, but no gentleman, said Fuseli. – He speaks many languages, – dances, – sings, mimicks, you see the Character is irregular by looking in his countenance, there is a twist in his look.

It is obvious from his narrative of this service in the Antonine church that the priests were not the only ones to be impressed by his performance. Even Dr Verdeil, his close companion and a shrewd free-thinker, the man who cut Beckford's corns and dosed him with Epsom salts, was at least half taken in. From the *Journal* it seems that Verdeil was, in so far as anyone could control and understand

Beckford, his real intimate and confidant in Portugal; and at this point, before the dangerous emotional developments at Sintra, Verdeil was still encouraging Beckford to settle in that Iberian Ruritania: 'He thinks me in the way to seize Fortune by those flowing locks she so invitingly holds forth to me at this moment, and make something of my peculiar position in Portugal. I might certainly climb up on the shoulders of the Marialvas to lofty dignities but I have not sufficient strength of nerves and spirits to run the risk of tumbles.'

Throughout June and July 'young' Marialva too was trying to persuade his new friend to settle in Lisbon. If he had been able to persuade the Queen and Melo the Prime Minister to defy diplomatic conventions and receive Beckford at Court, it is just conceivable that he might have succeeded; after all, to be the Marquis Beckford! Marialva assured him that all the grandees were on his side, and certainly a large number were, calling on him and receiving him into their houses – the Marquises of Penalva, Minas, Lavradio and Pombal, the Counts of Obidos, Assumar, Sarzedas and Vila Verde, troops of influential gentry. The Prince of Brazil was reported to be eager to meet him. Only dukes remained reserved: neither Lafões nor Cidaval was at home when Beckford called, nor was Mme Arriaga, the Queen's intimate friend.

Again and again Marialva bombarded Beckford with pleas, painting England and the English in the blackest colours: 'I see plainly', Beckford wrote apprehensively, 'he will never rest himself or allow me any quiet till he has rooted out the last fibres of attachment to my native country.' But Beckford still clung to the hope 'of re-establishing myself at home and enjoying in honour and tranquillity the lawns I have formed and the woods I have planted'. On another day he would recall 'the place of my nativity which I had rendered so eminently beautiful, the spot where my poor Margaret's remains were laid, my mother, my children!' Marialva urged, 'Would to heaven you would send for your children. I would answer for their forming the first alliances in Portugal.' That was a mistake, and when the old Abbade, primed no doubt, suggested that Beckford's eldest daughter might marry Dom Pedro, it struck at least two false chords. 'That would never do,' Beckford scribbled. 'The little spirited thing has too much of her father and mother's taste for beauty and elegance not to spurn away such a stiff, dismal, pigtailed sapling as Dom Pedro.'

Letters from Fonthill informed him that de Loutherbourg had painted two views of Wales for the Great Apartment, and that the sculptors Bacon and Banks were making new chimney-pieces. 'Alas!' he declaimed, 'when shall I enjoy these fair ornaments and improvements in tranquillity. When shall I cease acting the part of the Wandering Jew ... I should make a wretched courtier and should grumble myself into total disgrace the first evening I was forced to dangle after the Queen to a convent or sit down to a card table.'

When Marialva paid Beckford the ultimate compliment, inviting him to dine with his wife and daughters, Beckford panicked at being 'thus initiated in the very bosom of their family'. Obviously he was meant to begin courting a bewildered Henriqueta. Perversely, he only noticed that she was wearing 'one of those baby dresses of rose coloured silk that my lovely Margaret used to wear'. He claimed that 'the poor girl appeared in great confusion', and admitted that 'As God knows, I have no fixed plan concerning her, and should be miserable to disturb the peace of a family I so sincerely love and honour. My behaviour was not so attentive as might be expected ... I kept aloof and retired as often as I could contrive into the windows.' When dinner was served with feudal pomp, he observed sourly that 'the Portuguese had need have the stomach of ostriches to digest the loads of greasy victuals with which they cram themselves ... With such a diet and the continual swallowing of sweetmeats, I am not surprised at their complaining continually of headaches and vapours.' With the rain descending violently and all the windows shut, the dinner was not the success the Marialvas had intended. Their quinta is always described as a 'palace', but its courtyard was 'spread with dunghills, heaps of filth and harboured a swingeing sow and her numerous progeny'. Beckford particularly detested the 'shambling blear eyed domestics' who attended him at every step, and complained of being unable to make a joke 'without setting some hundreds of dirty teeth a-grinning, and being poisoned with a stream of garlic and bacalhao'.

It is not easy to judge how much sympathy Marialva deserved in all these manoeuvrings. Horne later claimed that he mishandled everything, and that if instead of rounding up the grandees and confronting the Prime Minister he had arranged for Beckford to go up to Caldas da Rainha when the Court was in residence and meet the Queen casually in a garden, there would have been no problem. But this very comment perhaps explains why the English were so generally disliked by the Portuguese for their crude, informal manners. Marialva himself admitted that he avoided strangers 'and particularly those of the English whose brutal fierceness and sullen insolence I abhor. But', he told Beckford, 'an unaccountable impulse drove me to you and inspires me with the same ardent wishes for your salvation and welfare as for my own.' Beckford listened to his protestations meekly, 'and we separated after embracing each other with devout tenderness'.

Clearly the two men were manipulating one another, the one angling for a fortune, the other hopeful, though not desperately hopeful, for status. But it would be an error to dismiss their relationship cynically. Marialva was 21 years Beckford's senior, and commentators are always quick to discount the possibility of there having been any sexual relationship between them. Yet when he was in high spirits or, as he described it, 'childlike', Beckford could be enchanting company, and there was certainly some body chemistry between him and Marialva.

One day, for instance, in late July, Beckford returned to his wooden house on the Rua Cova da Moura to find Verdeil and Franchi chatting animatedly in a mixture of Italian and Portuguese. 'I know not what demon inspired me,' he wrote, 'but I felt in a wild lively mood as if I could have danced on the slack rope or vaulted over three horses.' Franchi had brought 'a glorious aria by Cimarosa, but all my talents lay this night in my heels, and I kept cutting *entrechats à huit* and leaping over chairs and tables without intermission.' Then, suddenly, Marialva arrived from the Palace, 'stopped at the door a moment, cried "Bravo", and thought me bewitched. However, the same frenzy soon seized him', and he too began dancing, to his image in the long mirror. 'He has been an excellent dancer, firm and graceful in all his motions,' Beckford commented. There were to be other occasions for such high-spirited leaping and jumping as Marialva revived his youth with his new friend.

The incident offers a rare glimpse into that wooden town house. Beckford complained about its limitations, finding it 'close and confined', but its saloon was apparently large enough for dancing, and he often entertained quite large parties. Nevertheless, he criticised it because 'I have no suite of apartments to decorate, no galleries to stretch my legs in, no rural spots to resort to of an evening'. Beckford was never really happy if he could neither build, decorate nor garden. Even now, while he was exiled from Fonthill in Portugal, the architect John Soane was adding, with his usual spatial flair, a double-domed, Ionic-pilastered picture gallery to the attic floor of Fonthill Splendens and providing designs for chimney-pieces in the Tapestry Room and Parlour.

There were no trees around the Lisbon house, indeed no garden is ever mentioned. The house itself was 'tolerably neat and fair to the eye' and 'composed of planks and came ready made from America soon after the earthquake. If destiny impels me to spend many months longer in Portugal I must look out for a more substantial dwelling.' Apparently there was a brothel on the other side of the street, to which Beckford went one night, impelled more by curiosity than lust. It seems to have been a disappointing evening. His entry for that day, Thursday 2 August, is the briefest in the entire *Journal*: 'No paladin who drank at the fountains of Merlin was ever more suddenly disenchanted.' The fountain of Merlin in the magic forest of Ardenna, a favourite theme in Beckford's early writing, was supposed to turn to disgust the passion of love-sick knights who drank from it. This was Beckford's one and only Portuguese experiment in heterosexual intercourse. The next morning he noted that:

> One of the females over the way, who imagines no doubt from the tender compliments she probably received from me last night that I am sighing away my soul for her, had the goodness to let fall a flow of jetty ringlets over a panting bosom, to lean pensively on her arm, and to steal several looks at me full of pity and encouragement. She remained at this sport the whole morning.

It sounds as if he had been drunk the night before, and at least performed convincingly. However, the brothel employed a young lad whom Beckford seems to have preferred to the ladies. He christened him 'the sprite', spotted him in a church the next Sunday, and met him again a week later while strolling before supper in the fountain square near the Necessidades Palace. On that occasion the 'sprite . . . delivered me many kind messages from the signoras'. Beckford wrote wistfully that he 'could have fondled and caressed the sprite' but the severe presence of 'a black pig' (a clergyman, presumably) 'kept me within bounds of the strictest decorum'. He chatted instead to Gregorio Franchi's father and mother, who also happened to be out taking the evening air: an interesting pointer to the relaxed, even homely, nature of Lisbon's social life, and also to the openness of Beckford's relations with their 17 year old son.

Reading between the lines of the *Journal* there are hints that Franchi was becoming something of a social liability to Beckford's reputation. The Miss Sills of the English Factory had initially been Beckford's regular friends and close supporters, but when Franchi sidled in uninvited one afternoon 'looking silly and sheepish' the ladies, who were drinking tea, 'stared him completely out of countenance'. Beckford was sometimes sublimely unaware of, or perhaps simply indifferent to, the impression he made when in one of his more exalted moods. A sure sign of this phenomenon is the occasional consciously poetic haze which settles, mellifluous and flowing, over his usually crisp and disenchanted prose.

Once, when the Abbade was dining with him, the 'sprite' from the brothel began 'playing over its monkey tricks at the window'. In no way embarrassed by this, Beckford rhapsodised in his *Journal*: 'Oh that it were decent and proper for me to lay this spirit, not in the Red Sea, but on a bed of rose leaves, defended from mosquitoes by awnings of gauze, and cooled by an almost imperceptible rain of iced perfumed water.'

Another occasion which evoked this Firbankian style was an evening entertainment at the Rua Cova da Moura for the Marquis of Penalva's family and Dom Pedro. Present were the Grand Prior and the highly influential Conservador of the English Factory, Teles de Sousa, the judge appointed to guard English interests in Portugal. Beckford relates that instead of conducting himself soberly he reacted to the 'plaintive passionate modulations' of Portuguese piano-playing by 'gliding about the room and throwing myself into theatrical attitudes'. Dom Pedro, uncharacteristically, responded, 'and we danced together till the Marquis was tired of playing to us . . . languishing away in a minuet and never taking our eyes off each other'. The Conservador would have been well aware of the tales current in the English community about Beckford's past relations with an aristocratic boy, but the *Journal* naïvely notes that 'The sly old Conservador put on his sweetest smiles of admiration and launched forth into the warmest encomiums.'

Beckford then went on to write up the evening in exactly that enchanted, romanticising tone which he was to employ many years later in the famous passage evoking the atmosphere of his private coming-of-age party at Fonthill Splendens at Christmas 1781:

> No doubt every circumstance conspired to fascinate and inflame a youthful imagination – an apartment decorated with splendour and elegance; glasses rising from the ground, appearing like the portals of visionary chambers and reflecting light youthful figures swimming, the fragrance of roses, and the delightful music of Haydn, performed by Rumi, Palomino and two others, the first musicians in Lisbon and perhaps in Europe.

This, for William Beckford, was the peak of living, yet it was only an evening entertainment in a wooden house on a side street of a Lisbon suburb. It would be interesting to know whether the 'sly old' Conservador's imagination was equally fascinated and inflamed. It is more likely that influential figures in Lisbon society were beginning to lend more and more credence to the stories of paedophilia commonly repeated in the English Factory, and that Portuguese Court circles were becoming ever less inclined to risk the displeasure of the British Envoy by giving such an unguarded extrovert an official reception.

An interview which Marialva arranged with Melo, the Prime Minister, to discuss the matter of a Court presentation ended with Beckford storming out in a show of pretended rage. 'You have frightened Melo out of his senses,' Marialva reported. 'I have had my frolic' was Beckford's response. In his own mind he had abandoned the fight, while still humouring his friend's attempts to turn the situation.

Summer had come. The Court would soon be moving to the Royal palace at Sintra on the cool, wet, wooded slopes of those abrupt hills ten miles west of the capital. Everyone who was anyone in Lisbon society owned a country villa near Sintra. Beckford had recently been delighted by a reception at the Dutch consul Daniel Gildemeester's splendid new palace of Seteais. Mrs Gildemeester, with her raffish charm, dubious morality and open contempt for English merchants' wives, had caught his fancy. 'I am sick to death of sandy hills and leaden-coloured aloes', he wrote, 'and sigh after the waterfalls and verdure.' Sintra would supply both. He had hired a quinta for his own summer retreat, less than a mile away from the Marialvas'. There would be suites of apartments to redecorate, lemon groves to walk in, woodlands to explore and, once the Queen came into residence at Sintra, a whole troop of the best musicians in Lisbon, hired to delight his evenings, all for a fee of eight golden moidores a month. Portugal, putting aside that minor matter of a presentation, was beginning to feel a little more like Wiltshire.

CHAPTER ELEVEN

Sintra and the flight from friends

I have need of some young sweet-breathed animal to enliven my spirits, to run into the citron thickets and bring me flowery branches ... Did I consult the health of my mind I ought to dismiss these musicians ... Tomorrow! Tomorrow! He loves me. I have tasted the sweetness of his lips.

If the Salève was Geneva's 'magic mountain', then Sintra was Lisbon's. Beckford had noticed the abrupt range of miniature hills, forested and topped by a small monastery, on that first morning as the *Julius Caesar* sailed up the Tagus estuary. Indeed, if he had been able to stagger out on deck he could have seen them the previous day, for they are the Rock of Lisbon, a famous sea-mark, visible far out on the ocean. Quite early in his stay his agent Horne had driven him out there, ten miles from the capital, to visit the Quinta do Relogio, Horne's villa north of the hills. By its sheer physical drama Sintra had always been Lisbon's place of retreat, a refuge from the supposed but largely fictitious excesses of a genial maritime climate.

North of the capital the countryside is generally dispiriting, a dry, chalky landscape of few trees and scruffy villages, not improved by the presence of Mafra, the giant palace–convent complex which João V had built to rival Spain's Escorial, long after the spirit of the Counter-Reformation was exhausted. Beckford thought its domes looked 'like the palace of a giant, and the whole country around it as if the monster had eat it desolate'. But south of that dismal heap, above a narrow belt of orchard valleys and clear streams, Sintra's mountain rose up like some Grail vision from Parsifal, with Sintra village lying below its hanging woodlands, the Royal palace an architectural paradigm of Portugal's ramshackle monarchy. Two absurd conical kitchen chimneys dominated a wilfully asymmetrical cluster of Manoeline and Mudejar bits and pieces. There was no Royal park, but all along the lower hill slopes, half lost in dense vegetation, were the quintas of the élite. Inevitably, Beckford had to have a quinta of his own.

Uninformed about local weather patterns he had rented, without visiting it, the large quinta of Ramalhão, south of the hills on the Sintra–Estoril road, and sent his gardener on, ten weeks ahead of him, to plant the vegetables that were Beckford's staple diet. Much later, on 9 July, his friend Marialva drove him out to inspect his proposed summer residence. With four relays of fast mules they covered the ten miles in an hour and ten minutes.

Beckford soon realised why he had been able to rent the quinta so easily and why its owners, the Street Arriaga family, had celebrated the deal by inviting him to a banquet featuring sixty dishes, roast and stewed. The prevailing south-westerly winds swept in from the Atlantic, so Ramalhão was very exposed, and its only fireplace was in the kitchen. On that south side of Sintra's miniature mountain range the land was relatively bare, with long views over sea and promontories. Less than a mile away, and even more exposed, was the Marialvas' new and far more impressive Quinta São Pedro, its grand central pavilion decorated by the Frenchman Jean-Baptiste Pillement. This, in Beckford's envious description, had an interior like a foretaste of the Brighton Pavilion. The ceiling, he observed, 'represents a bower of fantastic trees mingling their branches, and discovering between them peeps of a summer sky. From the mouth of a flying dragon depends a magnificent lustre with fifty branches hung with festoons of brilliant cut-glass that twinkle like diamonds.' But its grounds, 'in the false taste of Portuguese gardening', with its 'statues and fountains, thick alleys of laurel, bay and laurustine, cascades, arbours, clipped box trees and every ornament', pleased less. Beckford preferred gardens with mature trees growing right up to the walls of a house.

After viewing both wind-blown quintas the two friends drove

round the corner of the hills to lunch at Sintra's village inn, a hostelry where years later Lord Byron began to write *Childe Harold*. There Beckford realised his error. The north side of the hills was a sheltered paradise of greenery with woods of an intense Douanier Rousseau luxuriance fit to harbour tigers to prowl the gardens of the elegant villas poised on steep lanes along the slopes. Mists and sunshine alternated in a mild relaxing climate. 'I thought myself in the orchards of Alcinous,' Beckford wrote wistfully. He could have rented a quinta there in a Lusitanian Arcady; instead, he had allowed himself to become settled in the eye of the winds. In future almost all his daily excursions would be taken in this favoured north, and it was on this northern slope, at Montserrat (Beckford's spelling; it is now known as Monserrate) that he would live on later visits to Portugal.

For the moment he expressed his irritation by insulting the welcoming owner of Quinta Mazzioti, who had invited them, 'with many bows and cringes', to view his garden. Instead of politely admiring the formal cascade of tritons and vomiting dolphins, Beckford retreated into the orchard and stuffed himself on the golden apples and purple plums 'rolling in such profusion about me'. Beckford had a passion for fruit, and was to suffer many an upset stomach that autumn.

As darkness fell he and Marialva drove back to Lisbon in a carriage loaded with jasmine and carnations; 'the pages riding full speed before us with flaming torches, and the wind driving back the sparks in volleys and smoke full in our faces, I was stunned and dazzled and felt like a novice in sorcery mounted for the first time behind a witch on a broomstick'. That was life seen in terms of self-conscious literary set-pieces; most such descriptions were written up deliberately from notes scribbled down on the day. Several times the *Journal* complains of whole days spent in writing without inspiration, but the subject is never revealed, so it was probably the *Journal* itself. It brims with human activity, as in this night ride, while those wearisome, mellifluous descriptions of landscape, prose versions of Alexander Cozens's blots, that make *Dreams, Waking Thoughts and Incidents* such boring reading, are rare. For just these few months in Portugal Beckford, despite his arrogance and his defence mechanisms, was vulnerable to real life, and excited by it. Where else would he have gone across the road, patronised the local brothel and then amusingly analysed the social consequences of the visit?

Beckford's time at Ramalhão, an autumn rather than a summer, never settled down to be an idyll. Even in July the house was very cold; for his first few nights he hardly closed his eyes for the fleas; head lice were a threat; the cook was a corrupt disaster and had to be dismissed; for most of August winds battered the house; and always he found the ability of his Portuguese friends to enjoy doing nothing quite incomprehensible. Yet the villa itself had possibilities: a whole suite of rooms opened onto a veranda, with a central 'lantern room' lit by eleven glazed doors or windows. Beckford, being a natural interior decorator rather than an architect, took the measure of the place, retreated to Lisbon to consult the upholsterers, and was soon hyperactively back again and 'tolerably comfortable'.

With no time to rival the Marialvas' oriental rococo pavilion, Beckford opted for a Chinese tent effect with touches of perspective, recalling his father's 'Turkish' room at Splendens, and of course lavish draperies. Before the month was out he was revelling sensuously in 'the metamophosis of my lantern room into a magnficent tent completed':

> The drapery falling in ample folds over the large sofas and glasses produces a great effect and forms the snuggest recesses imaginable. Four tripod stands of burnished gold, supporting lustres of brilliant glass half concealed by chintz curtains, add greatly to the richness of the scenery. The mat smoothly laid down and woven of the finest straw assumes by candlelight the softest and most agreeable colour, quite in harmony with the other objects. It looked so cool and glistening that I could not refrain from stretching myself upon it. There did I lie supine, contemplating the serene summer sky and the moon rising slowly from behind the brow of a shrubby hill.

With coverlets of chintz on every sofa, a Japan coffer or cabinet on every table and all the reception rooms papered, Ramalhão was almost a new house. He had set his mark on it. 'This is the first time since my arrival in this land', he wrote, 'that I begin to enjoy myself.' There was even a quality of aesthetic pleasure to be derived from tedium and melancholy in such surroundings: in the image of

Verdeil 'drinking a solitary dish of tea in the lantern to the piping of wintry breezes', or the sudden stimulating shock experienced as Beckford rushed out into the garden to enjoy 'the power of the wind and to observe the faint crescent of a new-born moon' while 'pears, apples and citrons shaken down by the fury of the blast rolled along the alleys'. And then came a welcome human relief, with 'retreat into the house, where I found Franchi just arrived, looking as pale as a phantom, shivering with cold and making sad complaints of the long time he had been on the road'.

The coachman had taken five and a half hours to cover the twelve miles from the Patriarchate. It sometimes appears that the Portuguese did not like Italian Franchi. He was bullied at his singing school because Beckford favoured his music, and a new Portuguese friend, João Bezerra, made a point of telling Beckford that Franchi had been seen parading the streets of Lisbon in a chaise emblazoned with the Beckford coat-of-arms, 'lolling at his ease and looking gay and triumphant'. Beckford noted stoically, 'I am in for a pound at present and must expect the circulation of many a pleasing story'.

As that unseasonal August closed in, a curious male domesticity settled upon the house: 'Franchi plays adagios of Haydn in the most mournful melancholy keys. Just before dinner we rambled into the citron orchards and gathered fantastic branches studded with buds of a reddish purple, but were driven home by cold blasts scattering leaves over the terrace.' Indoors, with his friends gathered around him, idle as ever, Beckford settled into his new tent and enjoyed his emotions.

> I sat snug amongst the folds of the drapery. The Marquis and Verdeil were tumbling over two folios of Hogarth and Franchi flourishing away with all his might on the pianoforte. Notwithstanding these loud musical sounds, and the murmur of M. Verdeil's explanation of Hogarth, the Abbade fell into a gentle slumber and I into a sort of doze. The recollections of dear old Cozens took possession of my fancy. I seemed to hear him commending the oriental scenery of my apartment and the lulling whispers of the winds. I seemed to behold him seated at my feet, examining the sprigs of citron I had gathered, and saying with a smile: 'Shall I give them to Lady Margaret?' I woke from my trance in tears, and to dissipate the impression it left upon me,

began dancing and coursing along the galleries. Marialva, who is never behind-hand in any sort of exercise, followed my example. We hopped upon one leg, I leaped over handkerchiefs held four feet from the floor, and amused ourselves like schoolboys with these fooleries. Franchi must have thought it rare sport to be playing about so familiarly with the Marquez Estribeiro-mor and the Fidalgo Rico. I often think what pleasure he will take in recounting our exploits at the Patriarchal.

Apart from the obvious comment that if Beckford could write with this Bloomsburyesque felicity it was a minor tragedy that he never wrote a serious novel, two other truths emerge. At all times through-out that evening, in depression and in exhibitionism, he was enjoy-ing himself. The other near certainty is that he did not love Franchi – he only used him. If there had been any deep affection he would never have been so pleased by his own social condescension: Franchi had been brought up to Ramalhão in the Beckford coach by express invitation. As the *Journal* explains: 'I have need of some young, sweet-breathed animal to enliven my spirits, to run into the citron thickets and bring me flowering branches.'

A few days later, that need satisfied, the coach returned Franchi to Lisbon. The giveaway phrase is 'sweet-breathed animal'. Setting aside the piano-playing and the excursions into the lemon orchards, Franchi's prime function was to be someone whom Beckford could hug, caper with, and kiss. His musical talents were both a bonus and a useful cover. At a guess, and it is only a guess, their relations were never sodomitical, only what Beckford calls 'childish' – bouts of heavy petting, to the accompaniment of a rapturous overflow of poetic phrases. In Beckford's personal vocabulary, 'childish' was applied not to children but to teenagers, and meant 'innocent', 'playful' and 'sub-missive'. Another coded word was 'stripling', meaning 'physically desirable'. Most weighted of all was the phrase 'to run with', which in Beckford's usage was virtually synonymous with 'to love'. Swift motion in company with a 'stripling' was, to Beckford, a kind of loving union, to be celebrated as an end in itself – racing through orchards, wet grass and wild woodland, sure-footed and untiring.

In that respect Franchi, the large eyed, over-ready-to-please musi-cian, was at a disadvantage, and Dom Pedro became the more attrac-tive and far more dangerous prize. Not only was the young

Portuguese a noble, he was athletic. Beckford was a sexual snob – the Courtenay affair proves that – and in an age when heterosexual unions were regularly based upon equality in rank and social class, it was inevitable that homosexual attractions tended to be similarly governed. Horace Walpole had never yearned after rough trade and working-class youth, only after the 9th Earl of Lincoln. Dom Pedro might be a reserved and inhibited young man (though Beckford had jealously noticed him with his arm very familiarly around a black servant), but he was the heir to one of Portugal's noblest houses. That he was also the son of Beckford's closest friend in Portugal seems to have been no great problem. After all the affair, as it developed that August in intervals between Franchi's visits, was conducted quite openly, in minuets danced together, in horse rides and races.

'The dismallest child I ever saw' soon improved: 'I never saw Dom Pedro appear to such advantage. He begins to grow childish and engaging.' Every alternate day Marialva and Beckford dined at each other's quintas, and Dom Pedro usually attended his father. On one expedition to the Cork Convent, so called for its floor and wall coverings, Dom Pedro and Beckford 'scampered' to the monastery, Nossa Senhora da Pena, on the topmost peak of Sintra, an impressive proof of physical fitness. On his visits to the Marialvas, Beckford usually 'gambolled' with Dom Pedro and the children. Dona Henriqueta was not included in these playtimes and Beckford noticed, with perhaps a touch of malicious satisfaction, that his potential bride, 'instead of turning out the lively girl I expected, appears to be the prey of a green and yellow melancholy, scarcely ever lifting up her eyes or opening her lips'.

Her mother, the Marchioness, features hardly at all in the *Journal.* She was fat, and physically very idle. Beckford noted once that 'the cascades were set a-playing and the Marchioness waddled forth to enjoy their murmurs'. But she would have noticed her guest's cold-shouldering of her pretty eldest daughter and, from her later firm control of Dom Pedro's activities, it is likely that she saw more of what was going on than did her complaisant husband, whose apparent blindness to his friend's tendencies is not easy to explain. The moral attitudes of an aristocrat in a foreign country two centuries ago are hard to define. His illegitimate brother the Grand Prior remarked to Beckford, after one return of the athletes from a run in the night-time garden, '*Vous aimez donc beaucoup le petit Don Pierre*' – so *he* had noticed. Beckford jotted the remark down in his notes, but did not include it in the finished *Journal.* The Portuguese probably considered homosexuality as common enough but rather second-rate, because it led neither to heirs nor to inheritance, the two things that really mattered in life. Choirboys, particularly foreign Italian choirboys, might be pursued – but not gentlemen.

These regular exchanges between Ramalhão and São Pedro were only the background to a lively social round with Beckford engaged at least as much with the English as with the Portuguese. He and Mrs Gildemeester were kindred spirits at dances, dinners and birthday parties. She glittered with diamonds (her husband held the monopoly contract for their export) and her conversation was sparkling to match: 'she is not of the merciful kind and spares nobody'. Both Mrs Gildemeester and Beckford found the English ladies comical, and so 'joined forces in cutting up the Factory'. Far from being ostracised by his fellow countrywomen, Beckford made a point of seeking out and persecuting the ones he disliked, by unravelling their little scandals and embarrassing them in public; one, whom he christened 'Mrs Fussock', suffered a string of loud insults; but far from ostracising him, the Miss Sills and Mrs Cotter remained his allies, and were often his guests. Apart from the Marialvas, João Bezerra and José de Mateus, both slightly older than Beckford, were his most regular Portuguese friends.

As the time of Queen Maria's residence in her Sintra palace approached, the old Duke of Lafões, Beckford's rival for the hand of Donna Henriqueta, arrived to inspect the preparations for the Royal reception. Beckford was dismayed, 'having been told that he was almost crippled with the gout', to find him spry for 68, able 'to turn on his heel and glide about with juvenile agility'. Disliking Lafões on sight, he criticised his rouge, his patches and his 'lisping French', describing him as 'the Duchess Dowager' and 'an old Lady of the Bedchamber'. The Duke in fact married Dona Henriqueta the next year, sired a new family and became Commander-in-Chief of the Portuguese army. So he can hardly have been either as effeminate or as decrepit as Beckford describes him.

A mood of Catholic triumphalism settled on Sintra. Not only did the Archbishop-Confessor become the new Prime Minister – an office that Beckford had confidently noted he would always reject – but an old English lady resident in Portugal was converted to the Mother Church literally minutes before her death. Beckford, seen as the next possible recruit, was pointedly coerced into leading her funeral procession, walking only paces ahead of her open coffin with 'the ghastly visage of the dead body'. Marialva was ecstatic with piety, crying out '*Elle se fout de nous touts à present*'. But Beckford reacted sourly to his friend's confidence that 'the Devil and all his imps could not prevent her marching straight to the gates of Paradise': he had been informed that the deceased had been the long-time mistress of 'a stout English merchant', and his inherited Calvinism did not take readily to the notion of redemption from sexual sin.

The visit that Marialva persuaded his friend to make, with Dom Pedro and Dr Verdeil, to the palace–convent of Mafra on 27 and 28 August, was intended not only to pressure Beckford into proposing to Dona Henriqueta, but also to set in motion an ill-conceived plot to win over the Archbishop and damage the heir to the throne. Like all Marialva's schemes it went hopelessly wrong, and in the event threw Beckford and Dom Pedro ever closer together socially in a strange environment.

The sheer size of Mafra and the quality of its marble interior impressed Beckford more than might be expected from someone of his Palladian upbringing. Far from yearning after the Gothic, he criticised Mafra's German baroque towers because 'their shape borders too much on a gothic, or what is still worse, a pagoda-ish style and wants solemnity'. Inside the church he took his usual pleasure in secondary visuals: 'black and yellow marble richly veined and so highly polished as to reflect objects like a mirror'. The Abbot had given the Marquis Marialva the full treatment of High Mass, Vespers and Matins, with a long tour of the palace and the monks' quarters. Beckford dismissed the palace apartments as 'the dullest and most comfortless I ever beheld', but enjoyed a race around the cloisters and the dormitories with Dom Pedro and a congenial young lay brother.

In the gardens next morning Marialva set to work on his friend more seriously than ever before, promising that 'The Queen, when she finds you married to perhaps the most distinguished lady of her Court, will employ all her power and influence to procure your re-establishment at home by soliciting your King to give you the peerage we know you were promised.' Trapped like this, Beckford could only splutter a few unconvincing excuses about long sea voyages and religious incompatibility. It was probably at this point that he agreed to humour his friend by becoming a key player in a ridiculous plot to discredit the Prince of Brazil. He was grateful that on the return home their springless carriage jolted so noisily that he could hear nothing Marialva said to him. In such circumstances it was safer to be deaf.

From that time onward Beckford began deliberately to unbalance his judgement by overindulgence in music. On 30 August he played to his dinner guests on the pianoforte all evening. 'I yielded up my soul to its influence', he wrote, 'and scarce moving my fingers over the keys, drew forth modulations so plaintive and pathetic that every person in the apartment was affected.' If they were all desperately bored, the pianist was happily unaware. Marialva 'sighed deeply', the Grand Prior 'hung his head', Monsignor Acciaoli 'had no spirits for joking'; best of all, Dom Pedro, 'leaning over my chair, breathed short with frequent sobbings'. The ego trip was complete.

That night there was a full moon and Beckford, the uninhibited aesthete, 'hastened out to inhale the perfumed evening air'. Dom Pedro dutifully followed him 'and, as we sat fondly leaning on each other, admiring the beauty of the scene, gave me a lesson of Portuguese. I shall soon acquire the genuine accent.'

The next evening, at the Marialvas', 'Dom Pedro and I took a run in the garden by our beloved moonlight'. Unluckily Pedro's little sister Joaquina ran after them, fell over and hurt herself, requiring the attentions of a doctor. The Marchioness was not pleased. In other ways the social pace was speeding up. That afternoon Queen Maria had come into residence at Sintra and Marialva came up with the obvious idea: Beckford should give a fête in the Queen's honour, hold a masked ball or stage a French play. The whole Court would be at Ramalhão. There would be lights, music, a half-mad Queen and social acceptance, at a stroke.

Incredibly, Beckford turned the suggestion down flat; he wrote: 'I have no great wish to have this honour. It will cost me a great sum and a vast deal of trouble into the bargain. Besides I am at a loss how to decorate the garden and terraces.'

Nothing that Beckford ever wrote, including his epitaph, can be taken on trust. But either this proposal is a complete fiction or he had decided, that morning in Mafra, to get out of Portugal. Otherwise how else could he have rejected the chance to entertain a Queen in his own house and garden? He must have realised that once he was accepted at Court there could be no excuse for rejecting the hand of Dona Henriqueta. 'Marialva knows not what he would be at,' Beckford wrote sulkily in his *Journal*, adding, 'nor I neither', which was nearer to the truth.

The following Sunday, 2 September, his ill mood intensified; everything to do with the Marialvas was a bore, and he began to write Dom Pedro out of his future:

> ... in the course of the evening Dom Pedro and I danced several
> minuets. We are growing much attached to each other. The scenery
> of my apartment, the music I select, the prints and books which lie
> scattered about it, have led his imagination into a new world of ideas,
> and if I am not mistaken he will long remember my stay in Portugal.

The message was clear: his stay was to be finite.

Dr Verdeil was deputed to make it clear to poor Marialva that a marriage was out of the question. Now that the Queen was in Sintra, Beckford could call up his six Royal musicians at any time and take refuge from reality. That night, he wrote, 'the violins and French horns played so enchantingly that I was inspired with musical ideas'. He favoured his guests with the *Serene tornate pupille vezzose* of Sacchini 'in its native key'.

For the first week of September he became, to escape from Marialva's distress, a melomaniac. 'Music', he explained in the *Journal*, 'has once more taken full possession of me.' Neither reading, writing nor conversing, he lolled about 'lulled by the plaintive harmony of the wind instruments, softened by distance', indulging in 'a thousand enervating and voluptuous ideas'. Both the Grand Prior and Bezerra were sent to try to change his mind. When he faltered in his resolution, as he soon did, Dr Verdeil, who was rapidly becoming a prime mover at Ramalhão, reminded him of Fonthill and England. The result was 'deep and chilling dejection' at the waste of his 'precious youthful hours'. 'Did I consult the health of my mind', he wrote with much truth, 'I ought to dismiss these musicians.' But they played on. Clouds settled around the hilltops. Shuddering at the gloomy aspect of the night, Beckford threw himself on a sofa. 'A whistling wind inspired me with sadness,' he wrote – 'but after all', he added, 'I believe it was the absence of Dom Pedro that rendered me so disconsolate.'

At this moment of self-indulgent escapism he had probably decided to aim for a seduction, an aristocratic scalp to add to his limited collection before cutting and running for Madrid. A more immediate problem was Marialva's plot against the Prince of Brazil, timed to a climax on Sunday, 9 September, with Beckford as its reluctant chief actor. 'What talents have I for Court intrigue?' he asked himself. 'None, I am too indolent, too listless to give myself any trouble.' All Saturday morning Bezerra, who was in the conspiracy, worked upon him, impressing the entirely false notion that the Archbishop, now Prime Minister, was 'strongly prepossessed' in Beckford's favour and needed only one light push to bring about his official presentation at Court.

The composer Jeronimo de Lima was in attendance at the quinta. That evening Beckford, with a keen relish for the dramatic, gave his guests 'the bitter cry of *Vendica i torti mei*' from Lima's opera *Aeneas in Thrace* with 'its full energy', and then 'was so possessed by these affecting sounds that I could hardly eat'. Instead, he and Dom Pedro ran out into the night 'hand in hand along the alleys, bounding like deer and leaping up to catch the azareiro blossoms which dangled over our heads'. He was still, he reassured himself, a youth: 'No child of thirteen ever felt a stronger impulse to race and gambol than I do. My limbs are as supple and elastic as those of a stripling, and it gives me no pain to turn and twist them into the most playful attitudes.'

The entry for the next day, Sunday, is the last in the *Journal* before an unprecedented eleven-day gap. It is a long entry, a carefully literary account of an excursion with the Marialvas to the Cork Convent on the far western side of the hills to witness the installation of a new Prior. It entirely omits, however, the true aim of the trip.

Waiting at the Convent was Luis de Miranda, Count Sandomil, Colonel of the Cascais Regiment and a close friend of Dom José, Prince of Brazil. In the *Journal* Miranda's presence is mentioned, without explanation, as a guest at a greasy repast of rice, four suckling pigs and an 'abundance of highly-flavoured cabbage stewed in the essence of ham and partridge'. The party returned home very late, long after dark, to be scolded by the Marchioness. But in another account of this visit to the Cork Convent, written up at length 47 years later for *Italy; with Sketches of Spain and Portugal,* Beckford relates (more or less) what really happened.

After the picnic lunch the Colonel-Count rode off with Beckford, on the excuse of showing him a notable viewpont. On the other side of the hills Dom José and his military escort were waiting under a striped awning that had been set up alongside a ruined cottage. The Prince's aim was to have half an hour's conversation with the very rich Englishman who, he had been led to believe by Marialva's agents, sympathised with the cause of Pombalist reform. 'Walk on as if you were collecting plants or taking sketches,' Miranda told a nervous Beckford, 'you will meet us as if by chance and without any form.'

Beckford described the Prince as 'a young man of rather a prepossessing figure', thus adding an instant sexual vibrancy to the plot. They talked in the half-Portuguese, half-Italian jargon of the Court, an authentic touch; but, and this is hard to believe, Beckford claimed that he said very little. He merely nodded, bowed, smiled and agreed as the Prince attacked the 'commercial greediness' of the English, the backwardness of his own country (the essence of its charm for Beckford), and set out persuasively his intentions of modernising Portugal by disestablishing the Church, shaking up the legal system and severing the alliance with England.

The monologue went on until sunset, when Beckford remounted his horse and rode back home with 'the most confirmed belief that *the church was in danger*'. At this point, his narrative in *Sketches* loses all credibility. He claimed to have sat down on his sofa, swallowed a cup of tea, then driven straight to the Palace to tell all to the Archbishop, whose reactions are not revealed. This is very understandable as the old priest, being himself a Pombalist reformer and supporter of the Prince, must have laughed genially at the excitable

Englishman when, not on the same day but at the same time in the following week, Beckford actually was given an audience. He would then have dismissed the whole business as further proof of the need to get Beckford out of Portugal and ensure that his wealth was removed as far from the aristocratic reactionaries as possible.

Marialva had been to blame. He was so helplessly devout and a child of the old style Church that he had been unable to credit that an Archbishop and one-time Grand Inquisitor could be of the reforming party, even though he knew perfectly well that it had been Pombal who originally appointed São Gaetano as Confessor to the future Queen. So Beckford had been propelled reluctantly into wrecking his own chances of presentation, which by that time may not have worried him overmuch. Nevertheless, the incident would have made him look a political bungler, which he was.

When the *Journal* recorded the real interview with the Archbishop, on 8 October, Beckford seems to have realised that he had been made to look a fool. He claimed to have found the old priest 'very hugging and kind, but I believe is heartily glad to get rid of me'. So he propped up his vanity with the idea that the Queen and her Archbishop believed him to be 'a very formidable personage' whose stay in their country 'might occasion them more trouble than profit'. The interview was brief and ended when 'the Archbishop went off to feed'.

In the *Sketches*, by contrast, all is transformed: Beckford the potent stateman is invited to dinner with the prelate. A gathering of envious aristocrats exclaims in stagey unison: 'Dine with him! Such an honour never befell any one of us, – how fortunate! How distinguished you are!' In addition, for the first time in his life Marialva is invited to the archiepiscopal table. The three men consume three roast pigs and finally the Archbishop makes Beckford a present of several pipes of the wine he has praised at the table. As a last convincing touch to the otherwise improbable narrative, Beckford complains at being let out by a lay brother 'with as little ceremony as he would have turned a goose adrift on a common'. The whole is a perfect instance of Beckford in his 'composing for Mozart' mood – life as it should have been if Beckford the European statesman had been given his due.

Sintra and the flight from friends

In reality, a few days earlier Beckford had recorded in his *Journal*, 'I continue firm in my resolution of leaving Portugal and have given orders to prepare for my journey'. What was happening was that he was settling down to enjoy the prolonged emotions of leaving rather more than he had ever enjoyed the difficulties of settling in. His most intense experiences, emotional and religious, lay ahead of him in these last two months as Marialva moved towards an emotional climax with Beckford, Beckford courted Dom Pedro, and Franchi courted Beckford.

Franchi had turned up again at Ramalhão with a rueful face and an unlikely story of having failed to secure an *aviso* for the new term at the Patriarchal Seminary. 'I felt no inclination to part with him,' Beckford reported, and the next day, after another round of futile interviews with Marialva and the Archbishop's chaplain, he returned hungry and tired to define very precisely his relationship with the young Italian: 'As I have renounced dogs this long while, I enjoyed being welcomed home by the gambols of Franchi, whom I have reason to think a very faithful animal strenuously attached to me.'

On the Mass of St Michael's day Beckford, in a characteristic but nevertheless significant gesture, identified himself more with Lucifer than with the Archangel who cast him down to Hell: 'Alas, we are both fallen angels!' Thoughts of his dead wife were beginning to haunt him again – 'The loss of Lady Margaret has harrowed up my feelings' – and that was often an excuse for some unwise episode. He followed Franchi back to Lisbon and between 10 and 16 October enjoyed a ballet, *The Magic Toy Shop*, at the Saltiri Theatre, Mass at the Antonine Convent, and Voltaire's *Merope* at the capital's second theatre in the Rua dos Condes. His command of Portuguese, negligible when he first arrived, was now almost complete, and in a typical mercurial response to urban pleasures he began to turn against Verdeil for persuading him to leave such a delightful country. Far more appealing than a long journey across Spain was the thought of a winter spent in 'some snug palace at Lisbon with a view of the Tagus and a garden well filled with early flowers and orange trees'. But a turgid novel by Mrs Frances Brooke, *The History of Lady Julia Mandeville*, upset him again, reminding him of 'the very being I ever truly loved', Lady Margaret. 'The swelling of my heart almost deprived me of respiration', he claimed, but he 'still kept on reading in spite of myself'. With true Gothic sensibility his imagination 'took its flight to Fonthill, and pictured to itself the pale image of my Margaret. This vision often recurs to me, and fills my soul with terror and bitterness.'

In that mood he drove back to Ramalhão, only to see, while watching a firework display, Margaret's image again in the young Countess of Lumiares: 'Her being with child too increased the resemblance, and as she sat in a corner of the window, discovered at intervals by the blue light of rockets bursting high in the air, I felt my blood thrill as if I beheld a phantom.' Anything Mrs Brooke could write, William Beckford could experience in real life.

It was natural in the isolation of the quinta for the evening routine of minuets and runs with Dom Pedro to revive. 'I believe Dom Pedro and I are never happy asunder,' he mused. 'To leave him will cost me many a pang.' Out riding with the inveterate gossip Bezerra he talked with a most unwise freedom, 'one moment exulting Dom Pedro to the skies and the next levelling all his merit with the ground. I could not help saying a thousand things which ought never to have been uttered.' There was a real danger here, as Bezerra had already assessed the nature of Beckford's relationship with Franchi. He had read *Vathek* appreciatively and had been given readings from 'part of this scrawl of a journal'. It was on this same ride that Bezerra suggested an excursion to the sea caves of Pedra de Alvidrar. Beckford's imagination took flight at the thought of caverns. 'I fancy', he enthused, 'it was beneath their craggy arches that the ancients imagined the tritons used to sleep and revel.' A triton hunt was arranged for the next day.

On Sunday 21 October they set off on an almost disastrous picnic: Beckford, Dom Pedro, Bezerra, the Abbade and the Grand Prior. At the cliff edge they were met by a party of young fishermen, all eager to demonstrate their rock climbing skills. Beckford had no head for heights, which is curious in someone so obsessed with towers, but 'the bloom of the atmosphere and the silvery light of the sea' caught him up into a Cozens-style rapture. He stood at the very edge to see the men go down, enjoying 'the cerulean prospect, the bloom of the atmosphere and the silvery light of the sea'.

Again that literary register was beginning to take over the *Journal*. Nothing in the rest of the entry can be trusted: it was all contrived at a later date. But something emotionally disturbing appears to have happened. The next day's entry claims that on that Sunday he had kissed Dom Pedro for the first and, as it turned out, the last time. 'He loves me,' he wrote. 'I have tasted the sweetness of his lips; his dear eyes have confessed the secret of his bosom.' This was the claim which determined Dr Verdeil to read the riot act to his highly strung patient. But did anything really happen the day before? If so, when and where? Was it another case of 'composing for Mozart'?

The party, it seems, had walked down a path into a place of 'cliffs and grottos', ideal territory for the heated imagination, 'a fantastic amphitheatre, the true abode of marine divinities'. But there the other four walked on, inexplicably leaving Beckford musing sombrely for an hour with no other company than the fishermen and a solitary cormorant. He thought he detected 'a wan and fatal paleness' in the young men's faces, as if 'they were destined on some future day to be dashed to pieces'. His friends returned, 'it was too cold for tritons' – and so, with no other diversions, they set off back to Ramalhão, where they dined at five 'and drank champagne and burgundy till Bezerra, after spinning round the room like a moth on the point of singeing itself, fell down dead drunk and was carried off to bed'.

That, perhaps, if they went for another run in the garden, was when Beckford had his kiss. He slept badly, woke early and rode past the Marialva quinta nervously, hoping that Dom Pedro had not tired himself. ''Tis certain I dote on him with too much fondness,' Beckford wrote. 'I tremble, and when I foresee events to interrupt our intercourse I feel cold at heart.' He tried to convert Verdeil to a longer stay in Portugal, but met with inflexible resistance.

That day Dom Pedro made no appearance. He had been obliged, ominously, to accompany his mother. Beckford was so overwrought that he kept rushing from one end of the house to the other. Tuesday dawned, and still no Dom Pedro. Apparently he had 'a headache and lassitudes'. Beckford went out for a carriage ride with the Grand Prior, talking all the while of his 'dear Pedrinho'. In the evening he learnt that the boy was not coming to dinner; he would be with his mother again. Alarm bells may have begun ringing in the Marialva quinta.

Certainly they were ringing in Dr Verdeil's head. That evening, walking in the garden, he took Beckford to task:

> More bent than ever upon uprooting me, he exerted his whole eloquence to display the folly and ignominy of my stay, and the danger which might arise from Dom Pedro conceiving for me too fond and unlimited an attachment. He has staggered me. I am lost in an ocean of perplexities.

That night Beckford sang 'over six or seven times that passionate aria of Sacchini, "Povere afettimiei", with such energy that [it] drew tears from the eyes of the Grand Prior'; it was a very Beckfordian reaction to a crisis: stylish, self-indulgent, defiant, and slightly absurd.

The most surprising thing is that he not only took Verdeil's severe rebuke, but recorded it as if it were just and merited. It was more the response of a child to a wise parent than that of an employer to an employee. The *Journal* records that he 'slept ill and woke in a feverish tremor. Read Theocritus': a flight from harsh reality to an idyllic ideal. At the Marialvas' in the morning he found 'Pedrinho' guarded in his manner, but begged his father's permission to take him on a long excursion the next day, Thursday, 25 October.

But on Thursday, whatever Beckford's romantic intentions may have been, there was to be no Theocritan conclusion of shepherd loves. He rode out to Colares with Pedro and the Grand Prior. There they left the priest in a chapel and rode off through the orchards of the Quinta do Vinagre to feast on arbutus berries. To his dismay Beckford learnt that, instead of the day-long togetherness which he had been planning, Dom Pedro would have to go home quite soon: Queen Maria was calling, and he would be expected to attend upon her. Suddenly the sight of the boy swallowing arbutus berries 'with avidity' disgusted Beckford. Enraged that the Queen's company should take precedence over his own, he leaped onto his horse and rode furiously away. 'I abhor from my soul', he wrote later, 'such passive character and will attempt at least tearing out by the roots my affection for Dom Pedro.'

That night, right on cue, as in some tragedy by Shakespeare, dreadful dreams assailed him: 'I fancied my dear mother was no more, and that a phantom, seizing me by the hair, was transporting me through the clouds to Fonthill, where I beheld her breathless body extended in a gloomy vault. I thought also that my eldest infant lay strangled on the steps.' He awoke with such a start – or so he claimed – that he ended on the floor, three paces from his bed.

The Marialvas behaved with perfect calm. The incident was never mentioned. The Marquis was his usual affectionate self, still full of schemes to have his friend accepted at Court. Catholic Portugal was not horrified, as Protestant England would have been, by a kiss between males: Dom Pedro was simply kept tactfully distant. When they were obliged to meet, Beckford 'shrank and hardly looked at him'. The entire episode is relevant to those unrecorded days at Powderham Castle back in October 1784, and offers a valuable commentary on the earlier time. If the incident with young Courtenay was similar in its emotional build-up and physical climax to the kiss with Dom Pedro, then it would explain why the Beckfords stayed on so long at Powderham after the Courtenays realised what was going on, and why the scandal was so slow to break and so ill-defined.

Being English, Beckford made far more of it all than did his Portuguese friends. He told his *Journal* that he would fall seriously ill: 'My bile is in a ferment, I squitter and feel the giddiness and nausea of sea-sickness', he claimed. When guests arrived he talked with febrile folly about 'the imbecility of the Portuguese Court', but was still sufficiently self-aware to be grateful for Verdeil's discreet handling of the situation he had created. After only a few days his composure returned, and he evolved an explanation for the whole affair: Dom Pedro had been lonely, his father was too severe with him and he had no friends. 'If he dared, could he but conquer the timidity which scares him, I fancy he would throw himself in my arms.' With honour satisfied and an emotional failure explained away, life could go on.

Back, permanently now, in Lisbon, religion replaced passion. Suddenly Beckford began to appreciate Marialva as 'the most affectionate friend Heaven ever bestowed upon me'. The two men fell into an orgy of nostalgia and church-going. 'My knees', Beckford reported with his usual teasing mixture of piety and self-mockery, 'are become horny with frequent kneelings. Verdeil thinks I shall end in a hermitage or go mad – perhaps both.' He might have added that if Marialva was the most affectionate, then Verdeil was the most intelligent friend Heaven had bestowed upon him, but one only retained by the payment of a salary and the promise of a pension of £100 a year.

One night when his two controllers, Marialva and Verdeil, were both absent, Beckford, who had just attended Mass in a church heavily decorated with skulls, determined to give the Marialva children a taste of the Calvinism his mother had doled out to him, in a dreadful hell-fire and damnation sermon:

> The most horrible denunciations of divine wrath which were ever sounded forth by ancient or modern writers of sermons and homilies recurred to my memory, and I dealt them about me with a vengeance. The last half hour of my discourse we were all in total darkness – nobody had thought of calling for candles; the children were huddled together, scarce venturing to move or breathe.

He went home, 'full of the ghastly images which I had conjured up'. He had been addressing the discourse to himself as much as to the children. Where Beckford's responses to religion are concerned, 'sincerity' is not a useful word to use. He simply enjoyed religion in so far as it offered intense emotion. A theme of the tomb, of dead bodies and a horrid afterlife had run through his dreams in Portugal. It seems fair to describe him as shallowly rather than deeply religious, yet deeply involved with shallow religious externals. For instance, he was returning with Verdeil from the quays one day with his mail and reading, precariously on horseback, a letter from his half-sister reporting the lies Walpole's friends were spreading about him in England. Suddenly he looked up, and saw the Blessed Sacrament being carried into the great monastic church of Belém. Without hesitation he leaped off his horse and followed 'the Bon Dieu' into that great and intensely Portuguese interior, 'vast, solemn and fantastic, like the prints of the Temple of Jerusalem in an old German Bible'. With 'the awful sound of the organ', choirs chanting, censers smoking and tapers lighted, the Host was returned to its place and Benediction delivered, 'which I received on my knees', Beckford wrote, 'with profound humility'. His devotion was spontaneous but he was still aware of Verdeil, standing out in the porch, distancing himself from 'these pompous rites' and 'scraping the dirt off his boots against the angular bend of a Gothic column'. For him to kneel in reverence yet still let his eye trail, as in some panning film shot, to pick up small significant visuals, was an instance of that odd shallow depth, a mark of the religious aesthete whose faith can never be wholly simple and sincere.

After one more glittering musical and devotional occasion, in the church of the Mártires up on the Barrio Alto, Beckford's time in Portugal, a time teeming with friends and enemies, warmth and irresolution, was nearly over. One last attempt to force Melo's hand had roused Walpole into giving an ultimatum: present that man, and you will lose all my support. Now even Marialva despaired. But that Mártires service had given Beckford an abiding ambition and a lasting image: to be transported 'not to a church but to a splendid theatre, glittering with lights and spangled friezes. Every altar on a blaze with tapers, every tribune festooned with curtains of the gaudiest Indian damask. A hundred singers and musicians executing the liveliest and most brilliant symphonies.' That was what he would aim to create for St Anthony at Fonthill. He had been disappointed by S. Antonio da Sé, the saint's Lisbon home. It was 'wretchedly proportioned', and had 'no constellations of golden lamps depending by glittering chains from a mysterious Gothic ceiling'. The intention of making amends to the saint on a Wiltshire hilltop was stirring already in his competitive mind.

On his last full day in Lisbon Beckford attended the Mártires again, this time for a Requiem. It closed with the '*Libera me, Domine, de morte aeternai* which thrilled every nerve in my frame and affected me so deeply that I burst into tears': again the shallow response to deep feeling. Alone with Marialva afterwards, the two friends talked together. Whatever may have sparked their friendship initially, there were now sincerities. 'He entreated me not to forget Portugal, to meditate upon the awful service I had been hearing, and to remember he should not die in peace unless I was present to close his eyes.'

Thrilled to have been able to inspire such emotions, Beckford 'execrated Verdeil and all those who had been instrumental in persuading me to abandon such a friend'. The truth was that at any time he could have been resolute and stayed; simply, it would not have been right for him; but he gave Marialva hope that 'in a year or two' he might return. Then he took a boat across the Tagus and set off, probably with some relief, for Madrid and a more familiar society.

CHAPTER TWELVE

Madrid – The winter of reacceptance

> The Duchess says I am wonderfully sobered and that there is now
> some chance of my going through the world without losing my senses
> by the way . . . Mme de Listenais runs in my head . . . Mohammed and
> I continued drinking in each other's looks.

For fifteen days of rain, mud and snail-paced travelling Beckford
retained his Portuguese persona, right up to the gates of the Spanish
capital. He was attentive to the tourist sights, politely interested in
the Spanish music and dancing – seguidillas and fandangos – laid on
for him by his hosts, he was even gracious to his cigarillo-smoking
muleteers, learning the names and dispositions of their mounts. He
was still vulnerable.

The route chosen from Lisbon to Madrid – Badajoz, Mérida,
Trujillo, Calzada and Santa Olalla – was no Spanish 'heritage trail',
but it was as carefully planned as any modern package tour, with no
rough nights in squalid towns. A gentleman had usually been prepared to offer hospitality; once Beckford stayed in an empty, echoing
palace. But always he played the competitive English traveller correcting errors in his guidebooks – Clarke's *Letters concerning the
Spanish Nation* (1763) and Major Dalrymple's 'dry, tiresome and splenetic' *Travels through Spain and Portugal* (1777).

If he had limited his reading to such publications, Beckford would
have been a happier traveller; but while staying the night with the
local magistrate at Almaraz, he happened to pick up 'a little old book
of my pious host's' which was to confirm him, for all his show of

mockery for its subject matter, in a lifelong obsession with the details of his funeral arrangements and the disposition of his body after death. The book, *Espeio de Cristal fino, y Antorcha que aviva el alma*, gave a graphic account of what it was like to be a corpse. Though dead the mind would still, so the book warned, be completely alert and active, conscious of 'the cold pestilential soil of a churchyard', of lost friends and dark isolation, the invasion of charnel worms and the dreadful processes of corruption. It was a very Spanish book, the kind of bedtime reading that painter of horrors José Ribera might have chosen.

Poor Beckford had been for some time obsessed with the graves of his dead wife, and even of his living and healthy mother. Now this book confirmed his worst fears. 'I read it', he wrote, 'till I was benumbed with horror' – a quotation not from the *Journal,* but from *Italy; with Sketches of Spain and Portugal*: 47 years later, he still remembered that fear. If anything, that hell-fire sermon he had delivered back in Lisbon to the Marialva children had underestimated the torments. Judgement Day was not the principal terror; it was Death itself that should be feared. Like some Egyptian pharaoh he would have to ensure himself a comfortable tomb, even perhaps one with a good view. Beckford often described himself as 'childish' and most of his biographers have picked up the word, but without always realising quite how apposite it was, how childishly direct, even simple-minded he could be in his actions and reactions, behind that arrogant, sophisticated façade.

His reaction to these horrors of piety explains a strange letter written much later in his life to his architect Henry Goodridge, which describes how a tomb chamber could be concealed in an upper storey of the Lansdown Tower in Bath to provide a centrally heated space well out of worms' reach. As the Fonthill Abbey chapters will reveal, this quest for a splendid but domestic grave on an upper storey was at one time a prime consideration in the design of his most celebrated architectural project. What his reaction also exposes is his sincere belief, at a crude level, in the Christian creed of the Resurrection of the Dead and Judgement Day, but with all the emphasis upon fear rather than upon mercy.

On the fifteenth day of travel, 12 December 1787, the slow caravan of coaches, baggage, servants and muleteers reached the straggling suburbs of Madrid, 'a confused jumble of steeples, domes and towers' appearing out of the fog and drizzle. Beckford took rooms in the 'Cruz de Malta', a good hotel on the main thoroughfare, the Calle de Alcalá. Then, in a quite remarkable personality transformation, either a new Beckford was born or there was a spontaneous revival of the old Beckford of Paris and London in those lost golden years before his marriage.

Few accounts of Beckford's life spend much time on his months in Madrid, from December 1787 to June 1788. This may be because he was extremely happy and active socially throughout that time. No one rejected him: old friends of high rank were delighted to welcome him back into their number. No Marialva figure appeared to involve him in the frustrations of being presented or not presented at Court. He fell lightly and liberally in love; that love was returned with flattering excess by both mature women and the young of both sexes. Every day there was 'high life' entertainment – gambling at faro, dancing on carpeted floors (Madrid did not run to sprung boards), carriage rides in the Prado, excursions on horseback into the bleak surrounding countryside, receptions and intrigues, hosts of new friends. After Lisbon, it was a return to the mainstream Europe of his first travels. Beckford responded in full measure, blossomed like the exotic flower he really was – and his *Journal* entries became, to be honest, increasingly dull. There were no more neurotic dreams, no visions of his dead wife, no long devotional sessions before the altars of saints. Within the space of one day he became again a wealthy young man-about-town.

The English tend, chauvinistically, to think of Spain as a country in perpetual decline from the defeat of the Spanish Armada in 1588 to the death of General Franco in 1977. But in reality Spain at the time of Beckford's arrival had been since 1759 under the bracing rule of the enlightened despot King Charles III. In a programme not unlike that of Pombal in Portugal, Charles and his bad-tempered chief minister, Count Aranda, had expelled the Jesuits, controlled the Inquisition and the religious orders, built roads and bridges and encouraged industry and commerce. Madrid could never be other than the least attractive of Europe's great capitals. It had been established in 1560 purely because of its central geographical position, rather as if Elizabeth I had abandoned London and made Nuneaton the capital of England. Nevertheless, in 1787 it was still the administrative centre of the most widespread empire on earth, and enlivened by the French manners of its Bourbon rulers.

On his first evening Beckford simply stood on the balcony of his hotel room, revelling in the pace and style of the city, the well-paved streets, the handsome carriages moving at breakneck speed down the Alcalá, the relief of having escaped from the provincialism, however picturesque, of pious, ravaged, inefficient Lisbon. First thing next day he went round to see an old friend of his Paris days, Caroline Augusta, the recently widowed and very rich Duchess of Berwick, at her town house, the Liria Palace. He absorbed the ambience gleefully: 'the best style of modern Parisian architecture – simple and graceful, no elaborate sculptures, cracked pediments and projecting cornices'. Shown up a majestic staircase of Corinthian columns he found the Austrian-born Duchess, 'a good natured indolent soul' but a daughter of Prince Liechtenstein, in an oval drawing room with semi-circular sofas and marble panelling. Pots of mignonette and rose trees were in full bloom and the Duchess seemed not to have moved from her chair since he had last seen her.

At tea-time he was round again, seated at the piano and, 'as I happened to be in voice', singing a nostalgic air especially composed for him – not by Mozart, but by John Burton, in 1780. It reminded him 'what a strange exotic animal I was in those days'. Rather worryingly, the Duchess found him 'wonderfully sobered', but he obviously determined to prove her wrong as quickly as possible.

Interestingly, it was not so much the Duchess who was to prove his key to Madrid society, though she did introduce him to the Marchioness of Santa Cruz, but rather a friend of Verdeil from his Lausanne University days, the Chevalier José de Rojas, a brother of the Marquis of Villanueva de Duero. M. de Rojas was a lively socialite full of plans for visits to theatres, museums and palaces with evening balls, assemblies and gaming salons. Beckford had a more precise objective. The two men rode out in a hired carriage to the Buen Retiro gardens and, though Beckford described it as chance, it can hardly have been mere serendipity that led them straight into the

Turkish Embassy. There, in an atmosphere perfumed heavily with aloes, the ambassador Ahmed Vassif Effendi was seated, surrounded by a motionless group of slaves. Beckford was instantly taken with this figure out of his own *Vathek*: fat, solemn, deliciously decadent, a bon viveur as fond of Italian opera as of the 'music like flutes and dulcimers, accompanied by a sort of tabor' with which he entertained Beckford on that first morning. Beckford quickly established his literary credentials with this distinguished Turkish scholar by quoting Persian and Turkish poetry to him. A friendship was sealed, and from that time onwards it was the Turk rather than Robert Liston, the British Minister in Madrid, who led Beckford by way of receptions and exotic picnics into the diplomatic society of the capital. While unable, out of loyalty to Walpole, his colleague in Lisbon, to present Beckford at Court, Liston for his part behaved in a thoroughly civilised way, enjoying Beckford's impromptus at the pianoforte and raising no objection to the attentions lavished upon him by the French, Venetian, Sardinian, Swedish and Tripolitanian ambassadors and their wives.

Beckford was far more interested in Madrid's bookshops than in its art collections. Hoping to ingratiate himself with the Admiralty in London, he tried to discover accounts of the latest Spanish explorations of Alaska and the north Pacific, but found them all impounded by a strict censorship. He did make one ritual tourist trip, to the Escorial, but whereas he had devoted nine pages of his *Journal* to Mafra, he became bored with writing up the vastly more impressive Escorial after a page and a half. Even the horrid stages of Royal entombment, the putrefaction room and the macabre rituals of death, failed to catch his interest. A feather from the wing of the Archangel Gabriel, three feet long, rose-coloured and preserved in ambergris, may have gone some way to subduing his religiosity.

Instead of attendance at long musical masses, a new pattern of pleasures set in. For masculine company, hilarious breakfasts and high-spirited gallops out into the countryside, there was the young 15 year old Duke of Infantado, the 14 year old Prince de Listenais, 'a smart stripling with wild hair and a low Grecian forehead', and his brother-in-law, the French ambassador's 19 year old son, Paul de Caussade, Prince de Carency. As in Portugal, Beckford found the combination of aristocratic youth, high speed and sporting good fellowship very attractive. The Prince de Listenais had a tutor, a M. d'Elmes; he, Beckford noted confidently, 'has conceived a strong pre-possession in my favour, which the young one, if I read him right, will take care to augment rather than diminish'.

In contrast to those three hearty young men, Beckford was extremely taken by 'little Mohammed', the 12 year old brother of the Tripolitanian envoy whom he had met through his ambassador friend, Ahmed Vassif. Little Mohammed, with 'a languid tenderness in his eyes' and a tone of voice that went to Beckford's soul, was as charmed by the English gentleman as Beckford was with him, press-ing his hands 'with inconceivable tenderness', Beckford wrote. 'I though myself in a dream – nay I still think myself so, and expect to wake. What is there in me to attract the affectations of these infidels at first sight, I cannot imagine.'

Beckford had succeeded in just over two weeks (he was writing on New Year's Day 1788), while only a plain, untitled Englishman recently arrived, in gaining the enthusiastic friendships of two young French princes and a Spanish duke, together with the warm affection of several eastern diplomats – all this, if he is to be believed, by means of his natural charm and persuasive manners, plus a regular supply of brioches baked by his French chef and sent each morning to Ahmed Vassif at the Buen Retiro. Another in the troop of Beckford's men friends was Carlo Ferrer-Fieschi, Prince Masserano, a Captain in the Royal Bodyguards, but he was a hunchback and Beckford was very aware of the deformity. To all of them the original key was José de Rojas and he, it will be recalled, was Verdeil's friend. Dr Verdeil's importance in all Beckford's Iberian adventures should never be underestimated. He gave his patient–friend both confidence and caution. If Beckford could have persuaded Verdeil to accompany him back to England, it is most unlikely that he would have retreated into social isolation.

These interestingly assorted male friends had their feminine equivalents, less easily handled and socially more dangerous. The Prince de Listenais had a wife, four years his senior, Marie Antoinette de Quelen de la Vauguyon, a daughter of the duc de La Vauguyon, French Ambassador to the Court of Spain. Meeting him at balls, at the opera and at entertainments, she became infatuated with Beckford, without, it appears, his doing much to gain her adolescent love. 'Upon the whole', he wrote, 'I like this family extremely and should be happy if they would like me.' That happiness was to be denied him. Verdeil, alert as ever to trouble, warned him that with three young members of their family, the two Listenais and Carency, all talking of very little else but this remarkable Englishman, the parents might make enquiries. This happened. They took fright, and hurried the two Listenais out of the country. But Beckford only saw it all as a compliment, as if a real Don Juan had come at last to Spain. His two older woman admirers were not to be disposed of so easily. Madame de Villamayor was never a serious threat; she represented no more than the kind of light flirtation Beckford liked to boast about. As he was arming her to a carriage one evening, she 'swayed and pressed significantly'. The Marchioness of Santa Cruz, on the other hand, was a very lovely and determined woman, only four years Beckford's senior, married to a much older man and desperate for a serious love affair. She was soon trying to persuade Beckford to elope with her to, of all places, Lisbon. Marialva's reactions if she had succeeded can be imagined, as he was at that time bombarding 'my Only Friend' with letters urging Beckford to come boar-hunting with him, or suggesting that the two men should live 'in a quiet corner of the world' together.

With all Madrid as his playground, Beckford had no interest in quiet corners of the world. Between routs at Mme Badaan's, sessions at the Duchess of Benevente's gambling hall, discussions on black magic with the sinister Saxon Count Leopold von Beust, and riding with his young men, not only his days were full but his nights also, and he was increasingly complaining about lack of sleep. Through de Rojas he had gained access to the exclusive apartments of Mme de Aranda, the young wife (a 'lily of the valley' stuck 'in Abraham's bosom') of Spain's elder statesman, the Count of Aranda. This lady's bed excited Beckford more than her person, as it was 'in a recess formed by ample curtains which are festooned with infinite elegance'. Beckford promised himself that 'the moment I have an opportunity I will set about making to myself a tabernacle and indulge myself in all the plaits and frills that can be thought of'. As a result he soon had the architect, John Soane, designing and building that staggering 'state bed', all scarlet and crimson draperies, with its Greek Revival canopy; the bed has not survived.

On 14 January, a month after their first meeting, Ahmed Vassif took Beckford and young Infantado 'a cavalcading', an expedition that illustrates perfectly the innocence, the charm and the harmless silliness of the *douceur de la vie* in Bourbon Madrid. The ambassador's 'favourites' rode Spanish horses 'almost hid by enormous Turkish trappings, glittering and clattering with thin plates of gold. Masserano on his beautiful parade horse curvetted on the left of the Ambassador.' At the Atocha Gate, Mme Santa Cruz, Mme Imperiali and the Venetian Ambassador joined the cavalcade. When they reached a canal, pages spread carpets fringed with gold over the grass, 'so down we all squatted … basking delightfully in the sunbeams'. Infantado and Beckford ran races with the Turks, 'Ahmed's messes were cooked by his own slaves' and 'a wild gaiety prevailed that completely intoxicated my imagination and set me a-talking nonsense to Mme Santa Cruz without intermission.' That nonsense may explain the enthusiastic tone of the love letters which Mme Santa Cruz was to write in pidgin French when Beckford had fled to France to escape her embarrassing importunities.

Then they all went home, Beckford 'to supper calmly with Infantado, whom I sent off sooner than he wished' – a typically vulgar innuendo that a great deal more could have gone on had Beckford bothered to encourage it. It has to be allowed that Beckford would not have been Beckford without a strong, even creative, streak of 'Jack-the-Lad' vulgarity.

His sober *Journal* lists on 29 December a reception by Pacheco, the Finance Minister, for 'the Sublime Ahmed Vassif'. It was not a great success. After some Turkish singing, 'a doleful ditty' that went on far too long, Beckford had a polite chat with the Archbishop of Toledo and then sat through an instrumental concert and some very inferior singing. Seated next to Ahmed Vassif, he was not able to escape until midnight. When he came to describe that evening in *Italy; with Sketches of Spain and Portugal*, everything was transformed. Here he recreated himself as he would have wished to be: a Beckford Münchhausen to dazzle all Madrid society into admiration and alarm. In this revised version Beckford had come dressed in full Spanish dancing costume, 'ties and tags, and trimmings and buttons, redicilla and all', only to sit through three-quarters of an hour of Turkish howling. Perceiving his disappointment, the Archbishop of Toledo persuaded Pacheco to bring on Spanish musicians – 'to my infinite joy' – whereupon, 'without a moment's further delay, I sprang forth in a bolera'. He, Beckford, showed the Spaniards how to dance their own native dances! The 'Billy Liar' invention is both entertaining and sad; because, of course, it is all a wish-dream, like so much else.

Impelled by his English high spirits, the docile Spaniards formed a circle, 'a host of guitars put in immediate requisition, and never did I hear such wild, extravagant, passionate modulations'. It all reads like a Hollywood musical of the 1930s. Ahmed Vassif began to chuckle and nod approval. The British and American Ministers were delighted. Only one Italian concert maestro protested angrily at the 'chromatic errors'. 'Is it possible', one Spanish 'fandango fancier' demanded, 'that a son of the cold north can have learnt all our rapturous flings and stampings?' Another observed that the French never could. Beckford, apparently still dancing, explained that he had been educated by Mozart, Sacchini, Vestris and Gardel in strict musical orthodoxy, but that no music could compare with the music of Spain. Finally, the Duchess of Ossuna intervened, told Beckford that he was making a fool of himself, a memory perhaps of a real incident on another occasion, then led him off to the Beneventes' to play faro. He lost.

In another even wilder fiction from *Sketches*, Beckford claimed to have been granted an audience in the Royal palace with the King's second son, Don Gabriel, and his Portuguese Infanta. The lady was so moved by their talk of the Ajuda Palace that, 'as we were making our retiring bows, I saw tears gathering in her eyes whilst she kept gracefully waving her hand to bid us a happy night'. Beckford's inventions are often more revealing than his honest narratives. There is always the desire to excel, to experience emotion, and to be accepted.

In the real life of his *Journal* the entries from Madrid do prove a genuine degree of acceptance. Away from England, guilt and ostracism, he was essentially still unchanged, unrepentant, exuberant, unwise. The French ambassador had sent his daughter and son-in-law out of the firing line but his son, the Prince Carency, was still writing to Beckford from Aranjuez – 'only Saint Anthony could tell you how much I love you ... I have not left room enough in this letter to say how much I love you, that is something you know, therefore farewell.' The *Journal* fades out, not in despair but in the sheer physical exhaustion of dance, gallop, gambling and gossip. Its last enigmatic entry, for 27 January 1788, still with four Madrid months ahead of him, reads: 'I have acquired a confirmed habit of going to Mass.' All that as late as 1788, such a short time before his retreat behind the physical barrier of a twelve-foot wall with spikes at Fonthill. The future Abbot was still a playboy, his spirit quite unbroken. Search must be made elsewhere for the cause of that retreat.

CHAPTER THIRTEEN

Beckford in transit, 1788–93

These should have been the most exciting and stimulating years in Beckford's long life. He became an obsessive traveller, witnessed France in the most turbulent years of its Revolution, and played a minor role as a Scarlet Pimpernel of the left in Switzerland. But in reality it was one of the most barren times of his life. His travels and his reactions were barely recorded and the details are obscure; his literary output was reduced to two rather silly novels, which are read now from duty rather than for pleasure. Spiritually, or mentally if the word is preferred, he had lost his way, and was attempting to move back into the high society world that he had enjoyed briefly in the early 1780s. Not only had that route been permanently closed to him by the Courtenay scandal, but the very fabric of the European society which had so delighted him was falling to pieces even while he hunted the Paris sales for bargains as the art treasures of émigré aristocrats were sold off.

One of those émigrés, Henri Meister, visited Beckford in 1791 at Fonthill, to be entertained lavishly in the house and in the garden grottoes. He found his host more interesting than the park, and left a sympathetic and penetrating study of him, published in 1799, which only steps back from his sexuality, the precise cause of Beckford's melancholy:

When he touches the harpsichord, you fancy you hear Piccini, Gluck, or Orpheus himself playing on it. If he expresses himself in our language, he does it with all the genius and glow of Diderot and the graces of Hamilton ... with all these endowments, with all that wealth is able to procure, I can assure you my enchanter is not a happy man. An air of melancholy and regret obscures the splendours which the graces of his person and the gaiety of his temper throw around him. I know well he has reason to complain of mankind, and I think he has cause of complaint against himself. With the best disposition and the most uncommon talents, spoiled by the gifts of nature and of fortune, his fancy must necessarily become early vitiated. Being endowed with great strength and activity of mind, objects were not easily found sufficiently interesting, and his most common notions became either terrific or whimsical, and were it not that his taste was just and refined, they would become more gloomy and fantastical.

In the course of the next few years 'gloomy and fantastical' was exactly what Beckford's 'common notions' were to become. For the time being he distracted himself by travel. Instability and uncertainty were the keynotes to this period of his life, and the immediate cause of that instability was Beckford's mother, working through Thomas Wildman, his plausible and unscrupulous solicitor. It is not always appreciated quite how ruthlessly she behaved to her only son or how abjectly he reacted in their confrontations. When he sailed from Falmouth in March 1787 he had been bargaining with Wildman for a six-month absence from England to satisfy Loughborough and the Courtenays, but there seems little doubt that Mrs Beckford thought she had seen the last of her ne'er-do-well. For women of her generation it was accepted that sodomites, when caught out, left for permanent exile. His return from Switzerland must have been an unpleasant shock to her in her affluent Hampstead widowhood, with two pretty grandchildren to bring up. A further irritation, when her son was dismissed a second time, was the way he gave the dour Scottish guardian of his morality, Robert Drysdale, the slip and then settled far too near to England, in Catholic Portugal.

Now he was in Paris, badgering Wildman again for an all-clear. At first he could be put off with the usual vague threats, but in December 1788 Lord Courtenay died; William, now the new Viscount, was in Paris, and Beckford became more pressing in his request for a permanent return. A remarkable letter from Wildman dated 14 April 1789, together with Beckford's furious marginal notes, makes it clear for the first time exactly what threat Loughborough was making to keep his enemy in exile.

Wildman's argument was that if Beckford returned now 'our enemies ... would have every justification from circumstances for interfering and as effectually as they might chuse'. Over this garbled legal humbug Beckford scribbled: 'The only method of interfering effectually would be to produce the wretched book in open daylight, and to such an exposition I am certain L. C. [William] would never consent.' This means that there had never been any serious threat of court action over sodomy, but that Loughborough did hold a 'book' or album of Beckford's highly embarrassing love letters to William – which would make a meal for the purple press. As Beckford rightly perceived, those letters were legally William's property: he appears to have contacted William, now living in the same city as himself, to get an assurance that the letters would not be used. 'Infernal rascal this Wildman', Beckford wrote on the back of the letter; but for all his righteous anger, he continued to employ Wildman until the rogue died in 1795.

He waited until September for permission to return; then, when he was back in England, with the astonishing meekness of a mother's boy he accepted the despised Drysdale once more as a moral nurse-maid. This vigilance was continued not only at Fonthill for the next year, but even in France when Beckford returned to Paris in October 1790. Drysdale was naturally triumphant, as he had a number of old scores to pay off. 'I have been enjoying the good things of life at Fonthill,' he wrote to his brother. 'I sleep in the very bed in which the late famous Alderman Beckford used to sleep.' Beckford, he reported, 'sleeps always in a small travelling bed like a child's bed'. He gave an interesting account of the dining arrangements: 'astonishingly extravagant – with very often three at table we have ten Men, at least nine men and a dwarf, behind the chairs to wait. Excellent wine at Will – good beer, and Bristol water.' The three diners must have been Drysdale, Beckford and Franchi – an ill-matched moral trio. The dwarf was a Savoyard, Pierre de Grailly, sometimes called Piero or Perro, whom Beckford had picked up in Madrid and employed for life, to the fascinated horror of ill-wishers; he reeked of body odour, but Beckford was devoted to him. Dwarves were a regular feature of noble households in Spain and Portugal, and Cosimo de Medici, one of Beckford's historical heroes, had had a celebrated dwarf, Pietro Barbino.

Even more surprising than his abject subservience to his mother in this humiliation by a Scottish male nanny was Beckford's relationship with his half-sister Elizabeth. He knew that she had tried to separate him from his wife when he was forced into Swiss exile, that she had been behind his mother and the terrible dowagers in prolonging his stay in Paris, and that she would never allow her young son to meet his half-uncle for fear of moral corruption. Yet he still corresponded with her, cheerfully and at length, sometimes as often as four letters a month, all full of amusing, spiteful gossip. She teased him archly about Franchi, 'the specimen of fine Portuguese eyes ... are these treasures still in your possession ... but I ask for no explanation'. In one particularly effusive letter she claimed, as he was about to leave the country, 'in losing you I shall lose one of the objects in the world most dear to me'. On the back of this letter Beckford wrote savagely, 'Instead of crossing the Kennet to do me service she wd. swim across 20 common sewers to complete my ruin.'

None of this makes emotional sense, which is why Beckford's biographers have all underplayed Elizabeth Hervey's role in Beckford's life. But love, hate, admiration and, above all, rivalry must have been bound together very intimately in their sibling relationship. Princess Zulkais and Prince Kalilah, in the third and liveliest of *Vathek's* 'Episodes', had an openly incestuous relationship, and as a long-shot guess it seems likely that Elizabeth was more responsible for Beckford's ambivalent sexual attitudes to women than was their mother.

The two refer to 'Our Mam' in their letters as a known trial and a mutually shared burden, but one shared willingly. Beckford remained trapped in affectionate fear of his mother until she died in 1798. Women rather than men were his principal correspondents and intimates at this period in his life: Elizabeth Hervey, Lady Craven, and Betty Sill. Elizabeth was certainly the reason why her half-brother wasted two years writing two light novels: *Modern Novel Writing or the Elegant Enthusiast* in 1796, *Azemia* in 1797. Their literary rivalry was strong yet supportive. Beckford was always lavish in his praise of his sister's *Louisa,* as well he might have been, for it is a thoroughly workmanlike romance of high society, much better than anything in the same genre which he wrote later. For her part, Elizabeth praised *Vathek,* reporting in 1789 that copies of it were hard to come by in London, and that the Duke and Duchess of Richmond (Elizabeth was an even more inveterate snob than Beckford) had been 'struck with the sublimity' of its concluding episode.

Beckford published both his novels under pseudonyms, as a joke. The first was intended to fool his half-sister. The second was to make a fool of his old acquaintance William Pitt, who as Prime Minister had just scornfully ignored an attempt by Beckford to make peace, on venal but not unfavourable terms, between England and France, hoping thereby to earn himself the barony he had lost through the Courtenay scandal. *Modern Novel Writing* is a mildly amusing soufflé of a book, a cross between Sterne, Thomas Love Peacock and Elizabeth Hervey. It is worth reading for its descriptions of Fonthill park. When she read it, Elizabeth is reported as saying with some puzzlement, 'Why, I vow and protest, here in my grotto' – and indeed it was hers; or, rather, the Alderman's. The novel's characters are without exception shallowly drawn and the book depends, like some Arabian story, on the plot moving fast to keep the reader's attention.

Azemia too has a lively plot – a lovely Turkish girl is captured at sea by the Royal Navy and exposed in England to a corrupt and lecherous society – but its desperately over-mannered style makes it hard reading. A typical literary apostrophe begins:

> Now once more, all ye Muses that sip the Castalian spring, or play on the biforked hill! Once more I invoke you – and you, ye graces! whether ye wanton amid the flaxen ringlets (postiche or otherwise) of Lady Seraphina, or beam from the eyes of the Countess of —— , whether ye wait on the Farren, or lurk in the arch smile of the Jordan – whether ye attend on ...

and actually continues in that tiresome vein for a full page and a half before allowing the narrative, a midshipman's honest love for Azemia, to stumble on for a paragraph. Beckford obviously enjoyed pretending to be two woman writers, the first Lady Harriet Marlow, the second, who dedicated her work to Lady Harriet, Jacquetta Agneta Mariana Jenks of Bellegrove Priory in Wales. J. A. M. Jenks insisted, in a preface to her second edition, that she really was a woman and, in a foretaste of Gore Vidal's *Myra Breckinridge*, advertised for 'some tender, yet sensible youth who could be content with rural felicity' to be her husband. If there is any truth in reincarnation, then Mr Vidal could easily be William Beckford born again to enjoy himself in a more tolerant age.

The one truly significant action by Beckford in these days of strict supervision by 'Our Mam' was his order for the construction of the great wall. This was given in the autumn of 1790. The architect James Wyatt was active in Salisbury at the time, pulling down the cathedral's porches, chantry chapels and bell tower, a 'restoration' project to which Beckford had subscribed handsomely. So Wyatt was invited to Fonthill to advise on the construction of a seven-mile wall topped with spikes. Beckford proposed to build this not around Splendens and the Alderman's rococo park, but around an extensive tract of wooded hill country to the west of the house. This was a project which he had nurtured for at least four years and not an impulsive gesture against a hostile society, although the notion of upsetting the local hunt undoubtedly filled him with self-righteous glee.

In 1786 he had read Madame de Lussan's *Histoire et Règne de Louis XI* and had come with typical perversity to identify himself with the most unsympathetic king in French history. The initial link was Louis' devotion to St Anthony: both King and Beckford wore a small silver image of the saint around their necks. Other links were the King's dislike of the nobility and of hunting, and his marriage to a Margaret by whom he sired two daughters. But what most caught Beckford's imagination was Louis' retreat to the great castle of Plessis-les-Tours where he lived, Beckford noted, 'a prey to remorse and the darkest superstitions. In his breast the worm that never dies seems to have taken up its residence.' The castle was surrounded by gloomy woodland and a massive barrier wall topped with a *chevaux-de-frise* – so for that reason it was called 'The Spider's Web', and Louis 'The Spider King'. This accorded perfectly with Beckford's mood, as he wrote to Lady Craven: 'In the process of time when my hills are completely blackened with fir, I shall retreat into the centre of this gloomy circle, like a spider into the midst of his web.' He was even proposing, probably as a joke, to set in among the trees 'hideous iron traps and spring-guns that snap legs off as neatly as Pinchbeck's patent snuffers snuff candles', because King Louis had favoured such devices against assassination.

This seven-mile, twelve-foot-high wall was to be three years in the building, but the decision to go ahead with it was defining. Once that wall was up, Beckford's reputation would rise with it, from that of an unpunished sex criminal to a British legend. It was a perverse master-stroke, for it delineated a secret country, a web of dark wooded hills soon to become even darker with Beckford's beloved but dreary conifers, and a web needs a centre. That centre was to be Fonthill Abbey; the wall predicated the Abbey, and it was the Abbey which would set the seal on Beckford's life and reputation. The wall was a symbol, not of spiritual defeat but of spiritual retreat, a tactic in an ultimately victorious battle with society.

In the meantime there was France and Switzerland, both interesting periods of residence, but neither of any real significance in the Beckford saga.

Verdeil had returned to Paris to practise as a doctor after the rift with his patron over payment for seeing *Vathek* through the presses. It was he who alerted Beckford to the bargains that could be picked up as frightened aristocrats realised their assets and fled the country. He wrote on 25 January 1790: 'There is a porcelain exhibition on at the Louvre – lovely stuff but I don't think there are many buyers. Everything is for sale and no one has any money. You ought to get here with a fat bank roll. The King seems well but not the Queen, she is a lot thinner, hardly recognisable; she's bored stiff.' Interestingly, Verdeil was passionate, and that is not too strong a word, to return to Beckford's friendship. 'I am drawn to you more than I can express and I seem to be all twisted up,' he wrote. 'Your spirit, your amiability, the sweetness and charm of your society, your general pattern of life, generosity and loyalty have more and more captivated my heart.' He was prepared to give up his wife and his practice: 'if my company can be in any way agreeable to you, give the order. We will expunge from our memories six months of separation.'

Not surprisingly, this was one letter which Beckford kept. 'I am yours, heart and soul,' Verdeil signed off. Beckford wrote back saying how bored he was in West End; his relatives were keeping a close control over him. '*Mes très dignes & très illustres parents me fait l'honneur*', he went on sarcastically, '*de me veiller de bien pres & et de me tener compagnie de la manuiere [sic] du monde la plus exacte & la plus exemplaire.*' That would be Drysdale! Musicians and artists, even Pacchierotti, had been banned. He was, however, allowed over to Paris in October 1790 – under guard. It would be fascinating to know what Verdeil made of the return of Robert Drysdale, whom he had met at Falmouth in 1787; but we have no record.

Beckford never gives the impression of being a physically brave man. During the Courtenay scandal he had allowed his brother-in-law, Lord Strathavon, to slap his face, without challenging him to a duel. He now fled from and returned to Paris with nervous irregularity as the mobs took to the streets or authority regained control. In November 1791 he wrote to Wildman that he was just back 'from dashing in the most invincible manner the sloughs of the Bois de Boulogne attended by half a dozen Captains and Lieutenants of the Garde Nationale'. So he was indulging in his usual pleasures of speed and the company of young men. In a notably shallow letter of December 1791 to Sir William Hamilton, he boasted airily that 'Two or three Deputies are chattering at one end of my room and swilling tea and observing that since the introduction of this English beverage, *on pense plus librement*, etc. etc. – a deal of French stuff.' He was taking a mischievous delight in Paris in convincing Girondist deputies and fierce *sans-culottes* alike of his left-wing, libertarian sentiments.

Verdeil was committed to the Revolution in a more practical way. He was of the Gironde, a relative moderate, and sensing the way extremists were taking over in Paris, he left the city. After a brief time in Nice he returned to Switzerland, to Hermanches, a château in the Vaud, which he made his base for some modest agitation against the Swiss authorities, following the regular French pattern of subversion by means of the 'Banquet'. No food was consumed at these revolutionary banquets, or at least only at the top table. The diet was words, inflammatory rhetoric for liberty, equality, fraternity, and down with the forces of feudal repression; so they were very middle-class affairs. It seems that the aim of the banquets staged at Lausanne and Rolle was to start up a groundswell of opinion which would eventually detach the *baillage* from the control of Berne and hand it over to the French. Verdeil had promised Beckford, in a letter of 14 May 1790, that with the British censors so active he would write nothing that would compromise him, '*soit directe, soit indirecte*'. His letters were therefore phrased cautiously. Nevertheless, writing from Hermanches on St Bartholomew's Day 1791 he passed on much information about the current season of 'banquets', in which, according to Verdeil's biographer, Verdeil himself was playing a very active part.

He told Beckford that heads were becoming more and more heated, and '*les gens de Morges*', a town outside Lausanne where Verdeil had a house, '*se sont rendus avec le drapeau de la liberté à la fête des vignerons de Vevey*'. So the agitations had extended to a country festival in Beckford's own old stamping ground. Inevitably, the conservative Bailli at Lausanne took firm repressive action and two ringleaders, Muller de la Mothe and Ferdinand Rosset, were sentenced to an exemplary twenty years in the Château d'Aarbourg.

None of this punitive action was mentioned in Verdeil's letter, which had to be circumspect, but he was obviously assuming that Beckford, possibly a fellow Freemason, would be sympathetic. Beckford was by this time in Paris again, having shaken off Drysdale at last, and was buying the celebrated Stanislaus bureau, a masterpiece of French over-elaboration and technical virtuosity. But in June 1792, claiming that Paris was a little too vibrant, he left for a summer season of nostalgia in Evian, across the lake from Lausanne.

Verdeil had prepared the way for Beckford by asking the Baron d'Erlach, Bailli of Lausanne, if he considered the political situation across the lake in Savoy to be stable. D'Erlach had been confident that Turin would deal firmly with any potential revolutionary trouble-makers. 'You'll be received like a god in Evian. You are adored there!' Verdeil assured him. 'I guarantee that if there is an insurrection it won't be in Evian.' Fortunately for Verdeil, he took no bets on this prophecy.

It was to be a last lavish season at the spa before the revolutionary wars closed in and the French invaded Savoy. Beckford, as usual, was exuding wealth, with thirty horses, four carriages, and a yacht on the lake. This was the time when the Irish adventurer Buck Whaley, who had known Beckford in Paris, sailed across with a party of Russian nobility to be entertained by Beckford at his Château de Neuvicelle in Evian. They were given the full treatment of piano recitals and hidden music in the woods while the revellers danced among scented flowers. 'I do not think', Whaley wrote in his memoirs, 'that I ever saw a man of more captivating exterior.'

But he, like all Beckford's acquaintance, was conscious of the 'crime' alleged against their host – 'of a nature so horrible', Whaley continued, 'that I wish to draw a veil over it, scarcely believing it possible that a man so amiable in every respect could ever have been so depraved.' One of the party, Prince Camille Apraxian, had boldly quizzed Beckford on the subject of the Courtenay scandal, whereupon 'Mr B—— solemnly declared that it was nothing but mere suspicion, and that he would not exist an hour under a consciousness of having wilfully given cause for such a suspicion, and hoped that time would manifest to the world a much clearer proof of his innocence than ever was adduced of his guilt.' While this is only reported speech, the vestigial tortuosity of the syntax indicates Beckford's defensive embarrassment when asked a straight question on such a delicate subject.

Great wealth can counterweigh a deal of suspicion. That Evian season has lived on in folk memory. Even now the Beckford legend and the Beckford tall stories are repeated in current guide books, which talk of a 'duc de Becfort' who made the season peculiarly brilliant. On a visit to the spa Karl Spizier grumbled at not being able to find a bed and described '*les tables gemissant sous les poids de mets succulents et des boissons, desquels toute personne bien mise pouvent se servir a volanté*.' All thanks to Beckford. Recent analyses of his fortune by Boyd Alexander and Martin Jack have tended to dwell on his later financial crises, and there is a danger of forgetting just how wildly wealthy Beckford still was. He claimed, correctly, that he travelled with a retinue of sixty-eight persons, an assemblage superior to that of any prince in Europe. In 1802 the people of Evian were still talking about '*l'extravagance de lord Beckford*', and praising his modesty in refusing to be called 'du' Beckford – only, apparently, the simple and retiring 'Duke Becfort'.

High above the lake down a side road from Maxilly to Maxilly Petite Rive, a wooden signpost still points the way to 'Le Bois du Bal'. A short distance down the path is the terrace, now a small public pleasure ground, where Beckford held his pastoral revelries over a sixteen-year period, from 1777 to 1792. The place has been ingeniously desecrated. Concrete picnic tables and benches punctuate its length; a busy main road runs below it on the lake shore. As a final profanation, a semi-active broad-gauge railway line rusts the entire way along the terrace. Only the woods where he concealed his twenty-four musicians, the royal band of the King of France, remain unspoilt, and two snow peaks look down through the trees. The nearby Château de Blonay is now an English condominium.

In September 1792 the French armies poured into Savoy. Evian's season was definitely at an end. Beckford, very much the parlour pink, had no fondness for revolutionary soldiers and sailed across the lake in his yacht to Lausanne, where he took a house for three months. That first evening, however, word came from d'Erlach that he was not welcome, as he had assisted in the escape of two dangerous troublemakers from the fortress of Aarbourg. If he was still in Lausanne at seven the following morning, he would be arrested.

Beckford fled in the night with all his retinue and, arriving at Lake Neuchâtel, promptly bought another yacht. With such revolutionary panache on show it is easy to understand why there is still a flourishing Beckford Society in London with a membership covering twelve nations. Also, perhaps, to appreciate why young Lord Cloncurry's parents wrote from England to forbid their son, who had been consorting with Beckford at Neuchâtel, to make any further pleasure voyages on the lake with that dangerous English radical.

On his return to Paris Beckford found that his affairs had taken yet another ugly turn. As a play-acting Jacobin he probably witnessed the execution of Louis XVI on 21 January 1793. If the hints he was to drop much later in conversation with Redding are any guide, Beckford was the man on horseback drawn in the foreground of several illustrations of that morbid scene. But on 1 February Britain declared war on France. Worse still, Lord Loughborough had become Lord Chancellor at last; he immediately engineered the passage of the Traitorous Correspondence Act, which could have meant Beckford being hung, drawn and quartered as a traitor for aiding the enemy and, even worse from Mrs Beckford's point of view, the forfeiture of all his wealth and possessions. While Loughborough was hardly activated by personal spite, the Act did put Beckford in a uniquely dangerous position and he had, with Wildman's help, to put up a smoke screen of rumours to cover himself. His bookseller Auguste Chardin was supposed to have disguised him as a clerk at his shop for weeks while the secret police hunted for him, and he claimed that appalling bureaucratic difficulties delayed his passport.

The truth was that Santerre, who commanded the Garde Nationale regiment which brought the King to the guillotine, was a friend of Beckford, and Destournelles, one of the six ministers in the Conseil Executif governing France at that turbulent time, had actually given Beckford the symbolic fraternal kiss. A committee investigating Chardin's association with Beckford cleared the bookseller because '*cet Anglais était généralement estimé pour ses principes révolutionnaires*'. Inspired, they found, by the love of Liberty, Beckford had wanted to buy an estate and settle permanently in France; but his dream had been frustrated '*par une fatalité de circonstances*', details unstated.

This explains an extraordinary, undated draft letter to Wildman, written sometime between 1789 and 1793. In this Beckford states that 'Mary Portugal' (Queen Maria) was ready to make him a marquis in return for some unstated benefit, probably financial. 'The creation is to take place immediately & will be notified in the Gazette in due form. No change of Religion is to be insisted upon – St Anthony answering for any interior piety. Mary Port', he continued confidently, 'must sign seal and deliver before I consent to pay her a visit.' As an insurance policy, however, he was in close contact with the French (and, more obscurely, the Russian) authorities, and 'supposing Mary Portugal should hesitate – I shall accept the propositions of the National Assembly and fix myself in France.' A report on Beckford's suitability for French citizenship exists among the Beckford Papers, and it is clear from the language that the French were completely in favour of its grant to someone whose immediate ancestor had been '*le plus rich particulier de l'Europe*'. Beckford's suspect moral reputation was dismissed in the report as mere calumny and political persecution.

This explains why the investigative committee concluded that Beckford left '*accompagné des regrets des sans-culottes* [the extremists of the Revolution] *et de l'estime des autorités constitués de Paris*'. It was no wonder that Beckford had to claim loudly that two of his horses had been confiscated by the French army as he made his way back to Dover. He would still have had fifty-eight steeds. Even now he left an English agent behind in Paris to look after his interests, and a whole suite of inlaid furniture, in the style that delights dowagers and museum curators, was being manufactured for him in the French capital.

He was back at Fonthill in May but, ever resilient, Beckford decided to re-establish himself with an allied country of iron-hard reactionary credentials. In November he sailed from Falmouth again for Portugal, to bolster the cause of Anglo-Portuguese friendship until such time as the English authorities had forgotten that his passport, when he left France, had been tactlessly endorsed: '*Étranger que Paris voit partir avec regret.*'

CHAPTER FOURTEEN

Portugal as a prelude to the Abbey

In a worldly sense, this second and longest visit to Portugal was much more successful than the first. By the spring of 1795 Beckford had wheedled a semi-official reception by the Prince Regent João, built himself a fine Lisbon town house on the site of his previous wooden residence, and for his summer seat secured the sheltered quinta of Montserrat in place of wind-smitten Ramalhao. But whereas his first stay in the country had produced the most human and engaging of all his writings, a *Journal* which with its attractive deviations from truth is virtually an English novel of bisexual life in all its subtle ambidexterities, this second visit produced only a literary silence.

In 1793, unlike 1787, Beckford had a diplomatic purpose, in which he more than half succeeded. Even with his airily inept grasp of politics he had realised that those Jacobin games in France had seriously endangered any chance of a peerage. The good times were over; Britain was in for a long pan-European war and his first task was to establish himself in Portugal as a true reactionary and therefore, in the eyes of the British Factory, a patriot. Since his last visit the Prince of Brazil, whom he had tried to betray to the Archbishop-Confessor for his radicalism, had been medically assassinated, by the simple device of dissuading him from having a smallpox inoculation. Grief at his death had completely overturned Queen Maria's frail wits and João, younger brother of the dead Prince, was the Regent. Dom Pedro, who had so nearly fallen into Beckford's arms in 1787, was now conducting an affair with Prince João's ugly wife. Ruritania was in full swing, and Beckford settled down to impress the Portuguese by spending money.

His retinue rose to 87 servants, and the new house he designed for himself on the Rua da Cova Moura gives a clear indication that it was he, not James Wyatt, who was responsible in the future for the broad outlines, if not the details, of Fonthill Abbey. This Lisbon house was very long in proportion to its width. As a visitor entered at the Gothic front door the Sanctuary of St Anthony, its altar backed by an apse, was immediately visible at the far end of a suite of reception rooms: Ante-Room, Dining Room, Octagon and Turkish Room (this last a borrowing from his father's Splendens) led up to the Saint's chapel, and there was a fountain in a court to the left.

This was virtually a foreshadowing of the central axis of Fonthill Abbey, though on a much smaller scale. It is significant that Fonthill's eventual cross arms, or transepts, were never properly integrated into that central axis. The west transept was a grand porch rarely used because it did not lead into the private apartments, the east transept a huge afterthought, out of scale with the other wings and never completed.

Beckford sent his plan for the Lisbon house rather apologetically to Wyatt with a revealing and important letter dated 10 April 1794: 'My projects here are very confined. I want a mere oratory, a sort of tabernacle with curtains & lamps, two candlabrums & six altar candle sticks.' Wyatt was only required to 'settle the proportions', but there would be more rewarding tasks ahead:

> My appetite for honouring St Anthony you see is still so keen that I cannot live without a little tid bit of a sanctuary to stay my stomach till the moment arrives when by the permission of providence & Mr Wildman I may carry yr magnificent plan for the chapel upon Stops Beacon into execution.

The letter continued reassuringly: 'We may still live to erect the buildings both Grecian and Gothic you designed for Fonthill.' This explains the apparently illogical scale of the great Barrier Wall which was already going up around a vacant wooded hilltop. Not only was it to include a Gothic chapel on Stop Beacon, a Wyatt design for which has survived, but at the other end of the hill, probably where

Fonthill Abbey was eventually sited, there was to be a classical house, the design for which has been lost. This house would have been a summer residence where Beckford could escape from the damps of the valley, which were ravaging his sinuses, and enjoy the views of his chapel – a place for study and solitary writing.

In this scheme, as in so many others, Beckford was following his father's lead. The Alderman had brought Witham House, Somerset in 1762, a dilapidated structure, part Classical of 1717 but retaining extensive ranges of a Carthusian monastery founded in 1188. Instead of repairing the old house the Alderman had left it as a romantic ruin, a key feature in the park of a palatial new house which he began building a short distance away, to Robert Adam's designs. This, if it had ever been completed, would have created the same Grecian and Gothic dualism which Beckford was proposing in 1794 for Fonthill.

His stay in Portugal caused Beckford to revise his ideas completely. He was struck by how closely the Tower of Belém, a late fifteenth-century fortified palace on Lisbon's waterfront, accorded with that visionary 'Tower dedicated to meditation' which had been a focus of his adolescent reveries. He either described or sketched his vision of a tower for Wyatt in a lost letter, and Wyatt then 'shewed' Joseph Farington 'the Plan & Elevation of a Tower, which He [Wyatt] is going to build for Mr Beckford. It is to be situated on a Hill, about 3 miles from Fonthill.' This palace–tower was to have been 175 feet high with a double-height 'principal room' around which were to be ridiculously cramped bedrooms, dressing rooms and a gallery. At the top was to be a 'lanthorn', in which Beckford 'would direct that He would be buried'. Farington recorded this in July 1796, but stated that the scheme had been proposed 'some four years since'. So already Beckford was giving up the notion of a Grecian summer residence in favour of a palace-tower with a mausoleum on the top: a patron of basically Grecian tastes was moving into that Gothic phase which was to make him famous. This was to last only until 1823 and his removal to Bath, by which time he would be expressing amazement at any deviation from 'the lovely Ionic so prevalent in Greece, the Doric grandeur of the Parthenon, and the Corinthian magnificence of Balbec and Palmyra'.

If it was Portugal which initiated Beckford's Gothic period, it is unfortunate that his only full record of this conversion was not written until 1835, and must be read with caution as he was prone to shameless retrospective readjustment. His *Recollections of an Excursion to the Monasteries of Alcobaça and Batalha* is a charming, heavily humorous concoction, based on diary notes made in 1794 on a journey during which he did not visit Batalha at all, only Alcobaça. This latter monastery had an early Gothic church which he disliked, describing it as a 'spacious, massive and somewhat Saxon-looking' building. This comment is valuable as it reveals Beckford's surprising lack of sophistication in stylistic dating, long after Thomas Rickman had published an accurate chronological sequence of medieval styles in 1817.

In the *Recollections* Beckford claims to have visited Batalha twice while staying at Alcobaça. However inaccurate this account may be, he certainly toured Batalha's sprawling and overwhelmingly beautiful monastic complex at some time during this Portuguese stay and was inspired to a totally new concept of what, with his wealth, he could raise within the Barrier Wall: this was to be not a Classical summer-house, a tower, a ruined convent or even an abbey church, but an entire monastic complex which would appear more like a Gothic city:

> I could hardly believe so considerable and striking a group of richly parapeted walls, roofs and towers, detached chapels and insulated [*sic*] spires, formed parts of one and the same edifice: in appearance it was not merely a church or a palace I was looking at, but some fair city of romance, such as an imagination glowing with the fancies of Ariosto might have pictured to itself under the illusion of a dream.

It was this impression of an entire city of the Middle Ages which Beckford commissioned Wyatt to recreate. The only way to grasp the achievement, now that Fonthill has fallen, is to visit Wyatt's largest surviving Gothic evocation, Ashridge in Hertfordshire, begun for the Earl of Bridgwater in 1808. There, almost a quarter of a mile of towers, spires and halls are strung out irregularly on a hill slope, presenting an astonishing variety of perspectives and silhouettes as a visitor approaches or walks around the building. A second visit, this time to Batalha, ignoring the coach parks, arterial road and tourist shops, will reveal how closely Wyatt came to the prototype he never studied in person but knew only from J. C. Murphy's *Plans, Elevations, Sections & Views of the Church of Batalha* of 1795 – and, of course, from his patron's enthusiastic descriptions.

Inside the monastic church two features caught Beckford's eye. The first was the sheer exhilarating and uncluttered height of the nave arcade:

> The valves of a huge oaken door were thrown open, and we entered the nave, which reminded me of Winchester in form of arches and mouldings, and of Amiens in loftiness ... No tapestry, however rich – no painting however vivid, could equal the gorgeousness of tint, the splendour of the golden and ruby light which streamed forth from the long series of stained glass windows.

The second impact was that of the lower octagonal tomb chapel of King João I and the Lancastrian princes – distant relatives, by flexible genealogical standards, of Beckford himself. João's wife, Queen Philippa, was the daughter of John of Gaunt and the granddaughter of King Edward III, from whom Beckford claimed descent by way of his Hamilton mother. Batalha could therefore, despite the prodigal Iberian richness of its decoration, be considered a half-English memorial, the burial place of Portugal's most famous, half-English princes. Putting together the height of the nave and the ground plan of the octagon, Beckford arrived at the soaring central space of Fonthill Abbey, the one feature which stunned all visitors and distracted criticism from the surrounding ranges. By Batalha's standards, Fonthill was neither too large nor too complex.

The seal was set upon Batalha's influence by its attendant flocks of young boys clad in white. At High Mass the austerity of the grave and simple chanting was 'mitigated in some parts by the treble of very young choristers. These sweet and innocent sounds found their way to my heart – they recalled to my memory our own beautiful cathedral service, and – I wept.' No such reaction was ever produced by the services at Alcobaça. Beckford's taste was for Batalha's late fourteenth-century work: 'fretted and pinnacled and crocketed in the best style of Gothic at its best period'. He described its chapter house (now the guarded resting place of Portugal's Unknown Soldier) as 'the most strikingly beautiful apartment I ever beheld': a fair judgement.

Montserrat, the quinta which he leased from its English builder Gerard De Visme, may, with its ground plan of a central octagon on a long symmetrical axis, have had another significant influence on the later design of Fonthill Abbey. The Abbey was eventually to have a central octagon on a far longer symmetrical axis, a south wing and a north wing, each 127 feet long. For some reason Beckford's biographers always write as though the quinta he inhabited so happily has been pulled down: it is in fact intact, and relatively unchanged from the central Gothic tower between two balancing round towers with pointed caps that De Visme built in 1789. Sir Francis Cook, who lived there in the late nineteenth century, merely added an overlay of Moorish and Italian detail to the main structure. Beckford loved the place. 'Not once have I left this enchanted circle,' he wrote to Betty Sill; 'here I remain spellbound.' He gave the park a symmetrical Gothic pavilion of three bays, a sober Early English affair. This was intended to centre the views down from the quinta on its hilltop, but the near-tropical growth of the Sintra hills has entirely concealed it. The double cascade which he constructed out of rough stonework above the Valley of Ferns was the result of his 'tracing rills & runnels to their source and examining every recess of these lovely environs'. Beckford was also responsible for a very peculiar Gothic servants' block built of huge unworked boulders. This strange building was a conscious attempt on his part to fuse the Gothic with the contemporary taste for the Savage Picturesque in landscape gardening.

The sheer profusion of the vegetable growth at Montserrat may have encouraged Beckford in his later taste for landscaping the new western park at Fonthill into a huge natural-seeming arboretum, where the trees were allowed to speak for themselves and the only park buildings were of wood, and unobtrusive. Certainly it was after his return from this second Portuguese stay in April 1796 that his interest in grottoes dwindled, and the Alderman's pleasure grounds on the east side of the lake were left to Dr Lettice and Beckford's two daughters to plant and alter as they pleased.

He was growing a little bored with his 'garden of the Hesperides' at Sintra and the provincial charms of Lisbon. With Marialva's assistance he had scraped up sufficient acquaintance with the Regent to extract from him a vague message relating to Portugal's uneasy balance of interests between Spain and Britain. This he was to take back to London and pass on, via the government, to George III. It seems to have been little more than a nervous declaration of friendship and would be treated with predictable disdain by Pitt, but to carry it was to take a step back on the road to respectability.

Before he could deliver it, however, Beckford was to experience the instability of the world at first hand. He set out in a Danish vessel from Lisbon to sail to Naples, where he could appear to take diplomatic advice from his cousin, Sir William Hamilton, still Britain's envoy at that court. A stay with such a respected diplomat could do him nothing but good when publicised in England. It was not to be. The voyage after Gibraltar was stormy, then off the Spanish coast a Barbary pirate ship sighted and pursued them. By Beckford's account, only a sudden change in the wind saved them from capture and incarceration in a dungeon which would have left him wholly disenchanted with Muslim civilisation. Quite how a change of wind direction could have been advantageous to Beckford's ship but not to the pirate went unexplained. When his ship put in at Alicante Beckford disembarked in a nervous panic, gave up the idea of Naples, and made an ignominious retreat by land to Lisbon again, visiting the Spanish Royal palace of Aranjuez on the way to write a short travel essay.

In the spring of 1796 he was safe in England again, to be greeted ceremonially as usual by the brass band of the Fonthill yeomanry, marching up and down on the lawns in front of Splendens to express delight at the return of their Prodigal Squire. Such local warmth and uncritical support tends to be forgotten, and Beckford's cold-shouldering by a section of the Wiltshire gentry (probably the fox-hunters) highlighted in order to make his disgrace appear dramatically darker than it really was. His entry, for instance, to attend an annual dinner in Salisbury in 1797, where he sat at the Mayor's left hand, was greeted respectfully by the assembled citizenry, and when his health was drunk 'the company rioted with Joy'. Later, members of the city Corporation accompanied him to his Salisbury town house to take a dessert. For all his lack of a title, he was one of the two most important landowners in Wiltshire. Yet what Farington chose to emphasise was that the Earl of Radnor, on the Mayor's right hand, had 'a cold manner' throughout the meal. In the same way, Pitt's indifference to the friendly message Beckford brought from Portugal tends to be interpreted as a brush-off delivered to an unforgiven sinner. The encouraging reality was that in July Beckford was received courteously in Whitehall by the Home Secretary, the Duke of Portland, to discuss the implications of the document. Beckford was on the way back to a national fame, as the grand seigneur of the best-guarded and most frequently discussed country house in Britain. Instead of trying vainly to re-enter Society's circles, he would make a reputation by appearing to bar Society from entering the dramatic walled circle which he had drawn around himself.

CHAPTER FIFTEEN

'Veil'd Melancholy has her sovran shrine' – the Abbey

Where Fonthill Abbey is concerned, the legend is more important than the building. It did, after all, fall down three times in its short life of thirty years from the laying of foundations in the winter of 1796 (if, in fact, proper foundations were ever laid) to its final quiet collapse on 21 December 1825. The way to approach the Abbey is to admire it as a glorious confusion of performance art and public relations, with secondary functions as a gesture of thanks to St Anthony and the intended place of Beckford's burial, three storeys up, safely out of reach of 'coffin-worms'.

This last point will appear frivolous; but Beckford's imagination was not commonplace – it was commanding. He built what he dreamed, and over his 84 years he dreamed his way with a flexible sensibility across the whole range of Romantic feeling, usually several years in advance of the great Romantic poets. Only Thomas Gray, with his amateur medievalism and self-conscious melancholy, anticipated Beckford in his adolescent Gothic-grotto period of writing. The others came to their distinctive poetic attitudes long after Beckford. He was delighting in lakes, mountains and expeditions into the hills in 1778, when Wordsworth was only eight years old. *Vathek*, with its evocation of the exotic East, was published two years before Byron was born, but Byron grew up to admire and imitate both the book and its author's arrogant posturing. In his last years at Bath, with his Italianate tower and lush flower gardens on Lansdown, Beckford presaged the gardenesque images and horticultural mood of Tennyson's 'Heavily hangs the hollyhock/Heavily hangs the tigerlily': an old man's poetry. In his teens Beckford had even toyed with the Arthurian legend; 60 years before Tennyson's *Morte d'Arthur* was written, that tower he projected was to be the retreat of a Lady, and knights were to feast in its banqueting hall – if, of course, those Arthurian reveries really were written in his teens, and were not retrospective forgeries of the 1840s. With Beckford it is wise to be wary, and they are in a secretary's hand.

There was one other parallel with the English Romantic poets far more impressive than these. Between Beckford's phases of the Byronic and the Tennysonian came Fonthill Abbey, and the Abbey was, visually, pure John Keats, a setting for *The Eve of St Agnes* before that poem was written in 1818. Keats, as Professor Ricks perceived, wrote on the edge of embarrassment, the almost Cockney vulgar. Recite 'Thou wast not born for death, immortal Bird!' with a Cockney whine and glottal stops on 'immortal' and that is how Keats would have voiced it, but with the addition of a deeply moving vulnerability to wonder and emotion. Keats, the full-blown, all but over-blown Romantic, was the antique dealer's poet. His poems are scattered with images that are rich but ill-connected:

> And lucent syrops, tinct with cinnamon
> Manna and dates, in argosy transferr'd
> From Fez.

The prize specimens in major antique fairs express in their inlaid intricacies and bejewelled baubles this same discordant display of flashy technique. Keats was, like Beckford, a joyful eclectic, a sensualist. He wrote of moonlight shining through casements 'high and triple-arch'd' with 'panes of quaint device', to cast colours splendid 'as are the tiger-moth's deep-damask'd wings' upon 'carved angels, ever eager-eyed . . . with hair blown back, and wings put cross-wise on their breasts'. Such angels, according to John Rutter's and John Britton's rapturous accounts, lined the corbel tables of Fonthill Abbey. Keats imagined a 'virgin-choir to make delicious moan/Upon the midnight hours'. Beckford actually heard a virgin choir, at morning High Mass in Batalha Abbey in 'the splendour of the golden and ruby light which streamed forth from the long series of stained windows' and, with true Keatsian spontaneity of emotion, 'wept'. But Beckford did more than weep. At Fonthill he recreated Batalha's long windows of stained glass with 'thousand heraldries, and twilight saints, and dim emblazonings' in an octagon higher than Batalha's nave, and planned, so James Wyatt told Joseph Farington in November 1798, 'the Abbey to be endowed, & Cathedral Service to be performed in the most splendid manner that the Protestant religion would admit'.

What Keats wrote with infinitely superior artistry, Beckford built and managed briefly to keep in vertical suspension. It is quite extraordinary how Keats, at the end of *The Eve of St Agnes*, a long poem of consistent nocturnal beauty, suddenly switches to Beckford's own obsession with the horror of the dead:

> That night the Baron dreamt of many a woe,
> And all his warrior-guests, with shade and form
> Of witch, and demon, and large coffin-worm,
> Were long be-nightmar'd. Angela the old
> Died palsy-twitch'd, with meagre face deform;
> The Beadsman, after thousand aves told,
> For aye unsought-for slept among his ashes cold.

One of the many half creative, half destructive contradictions behind Beckford's Abbey was that it was not simply a cross in its ground plan, but also a cross in its directions. For south to north it was a suite of reception rooms, crammed with treasures of European art and camp artifice but focused upon a Catholic shrine to Portugal's St Anthony: a vision realised, and a debt repaid. From west to east it was a failure. Projected as an English monastic church with nave, crossing and choir, all its levels went astray. Only the crossing, a Batalha octagon, was ever achieved. The nave began as a refectory-dining hall and was turned into a mere entrance porch; the choir was abandoned for a modish baronial hall to assert a dubious ancestral pedigree, but ended up a badly-proportioned set of reception rooms under unfinished bedrooms. If only it could have been built just a little more securely, to become a perpetual burden on the National Trust, Fonthill Abbey would stand as a perfect anticipation and allegory of that complex reaching towards Faith which gave England those riches and betrayals of the Oxford Movement that still bewilder the Anglican church.

First and foremost in Beckford's mind as he began his Abbey in 1796–7 was the drive to recover that peerage, 'Baron Beckford of Fonthill', which had been so nearly his in the autumn of 1784. 'Citoyen Becfort' had lost its charm, and somewhere along a series of bungled relationships he had mislaid that Portuguese marquisate, probably by not putting down enough money. England was now his best hope, but two men had to be won over if that barony was to be achieved: King George III and William Pitt, the Prime Minister. With soaring ambition he set out to win the first by employing James Wyatt, the Royal architect at Windsor Castle, to build the Abbey on a scale to equal and even surpass Windsor; to impress Pitt he began his own private negotiations to arrange a peace treaty between Britain and France. What he should have anticipated was that the King would soon be permanently mad, and that the last person Pitt, a notably unmarried man, would want to be indebted to in matters of State was a notorious sodomite to whom he had been affectionately related in his schooldays.

The peace deal got nowhere. Pitt blocked it with a curt note to Captain Nicholas Williams, Beckford's agent in Paris: 'Mr Pitt presents his compliments to Mr Williams. He has received his Note inclosing a letter from Mr Beckford, but as he does not think any advantage likely to arise from the Communication proposed, he will not give Mr Williams the trouble of calling on him; and begs the favour of him to convey the Contents of this Note to Mr Beckford.' When peace between the two countries (brief though it proved) was eventually signed at Amiens in 1802, the terms were marginally less favourable to Britain than those which Beckford, through Williams, had arranged with his friends in the venal Directory that ruled France in 1797. Britain would have kept the Cape of Good Hope, which in 1802 had to be given back to the Batavian Republic, a French pawn.

The trouble with Beckford's treaty was that he had arranged it, and though probably the most scandalous figure in the country he would have had to be rewarded with a viscount's title at the very least. Also, it smelt of money. Beckford had personally promised to fee certain French officials with an advance of £6,000, and to stand surety for a humiliating present, or Danegeld, of one million pounds to the Directory. It is difficult to calculate how many lives lost in the next five years of war might have been saved if Beckford's sane if self-seeking initiative had been followed up. Napoleon is unlikely ever to have become First Consul, or Nelson to have died at Trafalgar.

One interesting sidelight upon this Revolutionary War, supposedly the first really international conflict, is that Beckford, being hyper-rich, was given permission in 1793 by the Home Secretary, the Duke of Portland, to travel with his suite to Paris. He did not take up this option, but asked again in 1801 to travel to France for the sake of his health. Permission was given and this time he did cross the Channel, without adverse comment. The caution with which this apparently disgraced figure was treated by the highest in the land offers some support to the theory that the whole Courtenay scandal was engineered to neuter the possible left-leaning political influence of his huge fortune of ready money. His wealth had been seen as a threat to political stability in Portugal, and if cleverly directed it could still have been a potent influence in England.

As his diplomatic initiative nose-dived, so Beckford's Abbey rose – too fast for its future stability. James Wyatt and William Beckford, two brilliant monsters of egocentricity, richly deserved one another. They had been acquainted since before the Courtenay affair blew up, so had few illusions about each other. Wyatt was a handsome charmer; Beckford rationed his charm, but was highly susceptible to flattery from presentable males. Also, he needed an architect who had the King's ear and a proven record in hit-or-miss Gothic, so Wyatt was the only possible choice to design for him a cathedral of contradictions or palace of paradox.

Fonthill Abbey should never be seen as unique in its scale or its medieval mockery, only in its eventual cathedral profile. British landowners were growing more nationally conscious, more dissatisfied with the confining symmetries and predictabilities of Classicism. Robert Adam himself had been littering Scotland with unconvincing but mildly dramatic castles from 1771 until his death in 1792. In 1791 Charles Howard, 11th Duke of Norfolk, had begun a virtual reconstruction of Arundel Castle in Sussex, to his own unscholarly but imposing designs. The façades were given a rich sculptural iconography to convey England's debt to her aristocracy for the Liberties she enjoyed, and a new Barons' Hall was built as the setting for a medieval-style banquet to commemorate the anniversary of the sealing of Magna Carta. James Wyatt had shown a casual mastery of token Gothic at Lee Priory in Kent between 1782 and 1790; but more importantly for Beckford's purposes, he had converted King George. 'I never thought I should have adopted Gothic instead of Grecian architecture,' the King wrote to his daughter, the Duchess of Württemburg. 'I have taken to the former from thinking Wyatt perfect in that style.' As a result, throughout the 1790s Wyatt was conducting a sweeping Gothicisation of Windsor, with double cloisters, Gothic grand stairs, a Gothic tomb house (very relevant to Beckford's plans for a secure afterlife), and a Gothic grand entrance. In 1800 Wyatt was to begin a Gothic castle-palace on the Thames at Kew for the old King that would equal Fonthill Abbey in size and very nearly (27 years) in life-span. So James Wyatt it had to be. The King liked him enormously; he would design anything and in any style, and he was considered a genius.

Beckford must, unless he was quite isolated from social chatter, have had some initial warning of Wyatt's negative side: he was unpredictable, unreliable and overworked; he drank heavily; and he womanised whenever the occasion offered, hence Beckford's half-admiring, half-contemptuous nickname for him – 'Bagasse', or whoremonger. In 1796, when Wyatt began work at Fonthill, he also became Surveyor-General and Comptroller of the Office of Works. Inigo Jones and Christopher Wren had occupied that post with distinction, but Wyatt left it in such chaos and arrears that after his death in a carriage accident in 1813, the post and title were abolished as the only possible way to clear up the confusion. He had visited his office in Whitehall so infrequently that one of the cleaning women had used it for a kindergarten, sweeping the children out of sight when Wyatt made one of his rare appearances.

When an architect so able to soothe yet so lacking in scruples became linked to Beckford – rich, impressionable, impetuous and desperate for quick results – the pair could only produce disasters, but very memorable, even legendary, disasters. Within the wide limits of his profession, James Wyatt was perhaps as much a Romantic as Keats, equally torn between Grecian urns and barons' castles.

The pace of the first building work on the Abbey site in the autumn of 1796 was so frenetic that most of the later troubles must date from that period. Beckford had returned from Portugal in June; by October he was writing to Williams in Paris that 'Wyatt has been doing wonders according to custom, and he has given the great Hall another push 20 feet or so'; in November that he had 'extended the front of the Abbey in the Woods from the dimensions you saw us working upon, to near two hundred feet, and a good part of the building has already reached the first floor'.

To celebrate the progress, encourage the builders and demonstrate his influence as the richest landowner in the county, Beckford staged a Twelfth Night festival on 6 January 1797. Because its bucolic success did not accord well with that image of himself as a sexual martyr and social isolate which he came to prefer, he never wrote up the day's revelry and banquetings for posterity. But with many of the local gentry his guests and an astonishing eleven thousand of the peasantry enjoying his bounty, he was obviously hugely popular and respected. The *Bath Journal*'s account of the proceedings in its 23 January issue needs to be set against all those laments in subsequent biographies about his evil reputation and pariah status. Some part at least of that reputation Beckford masochistically created for himself in order to pose as a Romantic outsider.

Two huge bonfires were lit on the lawns in front of Splendens and kept burning all day and well into the small hours. Between the fires and the house a large Turkish tent was set up for Beckford and the gentry. On either side of the fires was a half-moon of tables for the children's lunch; beyond the fires was a large marquee with seven long tables, each seating a hundred people. This was for local tenants and villagers who came by ticketed invitation. To feed them all, an ox and ten sheep were roasted on eleven barbecues, and in addition,

> bread and strong beer were provided for ten thousand of the multitude of strangers who were admitted into the park... Many Gentlemen of Salisbury, having signified their intentions to pay their respects to Mr Beckford on this occasion, the Mayor and several of the Corporation were received at the grand entrance and were joined in the most handsome manner by many Gentlemen of the county. They were met on the lawn by Mr Beckford who expressed his great satisfaction at their presence.

It is easy to imagine what power someone who could entertain on such a scale could also exercise in a general election. Pitt's nervousness as Beckford attempted to move at the same time into peace negotiations with France is understandable.

After lunch there was wrestling, races and single-stick contests. Then a game of football 'afforded admirable diversion. This engaged not only the two parties concerned in the match but put ten thousand spectators, chiefly consisting of the peasantry, in motion, all in high glee at the different turns of the game, and yet without riot or any other disorder than a lively and continual change of place.' After dark the crowds remained around the fires to join in the singing and cheering from within the house. There the gentry were dining on roast beef washed down with thirty gallons of punch, 'the British nectar', and excellent wines. 'The true hospitality and polite attention shewn by Mr Beckford ... made it a day to be remembered with the greatest pleasure.'

Fourteen toasts were drunk, most of them to an appropriate chorus. The Mayor of Salisbury gave: 'Mr Beckford, and may his noble benevolence be as generally known and imitated by the world, as it is cordially felt by thousands this day at Fonthill.' Wyatt toasted 'the great works', and finally, in a superb display of patriotic cynicism, Beckford, the recent toast of Revolutionary France, gave 'Christmas, Twelfth Day, Old Times and Old Names for ever, and may the ears of John Bull never be insulted by the gypsy jargon of France.'

'This sentiment was received with that burst of applause which clearly evinced that a more loyal, or more happy, company were never assembled on any occasion.' The *Bath Journal* added that Mr Beckford had also distributed 'two hundred warm blankets' among the poor families of both the Fonthills, with a load of fuel to each of them, 'besides a considerable sum of money to the indigent'.

Impelled by all this goodwill, the building works advanced briskly. In a letter to Sir William Hamilton the next month Beckford was describing his 'little pleasure-building in the shape of an abbey' as 'already half finished. It contains apartments in the most gorgeous Gothic style with windows of painted glass, a chapel for blessed St Anthony (66 ft diameter and 72 ft high), a gallery 185 ft in length, and a tower 145 ft high.' His quoting its diameter but not its length proves that the original chapel was in the Octagon.

At this point Farington's diary becomes a useful commentary on the Wyatt–Beckford interrelation. Farington is a hostile witness, pruriently curious about Beckford's sexual past, forever poking about to find out his failings, his temper, his meanness, and what really went on at Powderham in 1784. But what his hastily written snatches do reveal is the social transformation which Wyatt had effected upon his patron's life in a matter of a few months. Suddenly Beckford had become the artists' friend and the generous patron of modern British art, with Fonthill a little Academy to which painters and sculptors hurried for good food and rich commissions. Wyatt had talked Beckford into a new concept of himself: no longer a mere collector of Old Masters, Flemish and Italian, but a modern Maecenas.

The wonder is that Beckford had not thought of it before. The hunting set disliked him and the country gentry bored him. He no longer saw himself as the squire of dames, the demonstration dancer; so artists, with their amusing conversation and their talent for seeking out a good dinner, were his natural circle. The artist De Cort and Wyatt both spent the Christmas of 1796 at Splendens, and Robert Smirke was soon on the scene with designs for 'Sapho' and 'Phaon'. The American history painter Benjamin West, who had succeeded Sir Joshua Reynolds as President of the Royal Academy in 1792, was first introduced to Beckford by Wyatt. By 16 May 1797 West had received an advance of £1,000 on an order worth £3,000 for paintings, and Beckford had put it about that he was ready to spend £60,000 'in purchasing Modern Art'. Not surprisingly, West was soon using his influence upon Richard Westall and Thomas Lawrence 'to obtain an invitation to the Academy dinner for Beckford', but it was refused. Even the lure of £60,000 could not buy Beckford back into the rituals of the artistic Establishment.

On Sunday 6 August 1797 Farington recorded that Beckford's Abbey had reached one of its episodic pauses in construction: 'The *Tower* is not proceeding with at present but in his will Beckford has directed it shall be finished shd. He die before.' The emphasis now was to be on furnishings: 'four Cabinets of £500 value each – all in a Gothic taste – four Gothic statues to be executed by Nollekens,

Flaxman, Rossi & Westmacot.' There is a danger in following Farington too closely after this time. He never visited the rising structure himself, and often misinterpreted casually expressed intentions as actual commitments, minor refacings as catastrophic collapses.

What had happened, as Wyatt gained his initial ascendancy over him, was that Beckford's two pet projects – a half-ruined convent with chapel and study, and a three-storey tower with a mausoleum on the top – had become confused with his excited memories, and possibly his sketches, of Batalha and its 'insulated spires'. Wyatt, taking all this easily on board, persuaded his patron to adopt a somewhat enlarged version of his own old designs for Lee Priory: a central octagon fronted by a transept, with the residential sectors of the house in picturesque but considered groupings around it. For Beckford Wyatt heightened the octagon, topped it with a lantern stage supported on flying buttresses (a close copy of the lantern on King João's tomb chapel at Batalha), and then took it one jaunty but disastrous step further: to humour Beckford's memory of that 'insulated spire' over Batalha's north transept, he struck an approximation to it on top of the João lantern, in a candle-snuffer effect, and gave it a flagstaff. That was the chapel completed.

Beckford had wanted a monastic refectory for grand occasions. Lazily, Wyatt took the crudely Gothick chapel design he had prepared earlier for the ruined convent, scaled it up with a ridiculously large door – which had the visual effect of scaling it down – and set it at the west side of the Octagon. Sited at a level twenty feet lower than the floor of the Octagon and with no rational link, inside or outside, between the two structures, the refectory was an error in composition from which the Abbey never completely recovered.

From the south side of the Octagon Wyatt ran out a gallery 127 feet long, perfectly adequate in height to compliment the Octagon but very narrow, a mere 17 feet wide. This disproportion would only have been evident from a balloon, or from a study of the ground plan. Referred to initially as the 'Library', this was to become St Michael's Gallery, fan-vaulted in plaster for most of its length and, after the Octagon, the most impressive architectural interior in the Abbey. At the south end of this gallery Wyatt provided his patron with what amounted to a self-contained gentleman's country residence, a handsome villa, Perpendicular Gothic in detail and therefore wholly English in feeling, not Portuguese. Its basic disciplines were symmetrical, with two octagonal turrets at its west side and two balancing square towers on its east façade. In one of these last, above the fine Gothic oriel of St Michael's Gallery, was the unpleasant, badly lit and unheated chamber in which Beckford would with self-denying and saintly austerity set up his narrow truckle bed. On the ground floor between these two sets of small towers was the Oak Parlour or dining room, darkened by a cloister front, and above it was the Yellow Drawing Room, flooded with light from south and west.

This completed and virtually detached villa, linked to the unfinished show rooms of the Abbey – the Octagon and the Refectory or 'Great Western Hall' – only by one range of an open cloister and St Michael's Gallery, explains why Beckford already could be proposing to demolish Splendens and move up the hill into his Abbey. Farington recorded the intention on 6 November 1797: 'Beckford yesterday told Wyatt that he had an intention of taking down *Fonthill House,* which is badly situated – and in that case enlarge the Gothic Building now erecting to be his Mansion House.' When Wyatt warned him that he would be criticised for demolishing such a fine Classical house Beckford replied, like the actor he was, with noble hauteur: 'You are older than I am, yet I have lived long enough not to mind what the world says' – a notable half-truth.

What had happened, after just one year of building and exposure to Wyatt's influence, was that Beckford had been seduced by the potential charms of gentry living. This may seem a bizarre claim to make for proposed residence in a Gothic folly, but at the south end of the new complex was that attractive and easily maintained Gothic villa. It commanded splendid views; it was lively in outline, elegant in detail; above all, it was compact. The accounts of the long march food had to make from the Abbey's kitchen to its dining room date from after 1816, when the kitchens and servants' halls had been moved out to the East Transept. For someone accustomed to Splendens with its quadrant arms and side pavilions, this new south wing must have appeared temptingly habitable.

Following the example of Horace Walpole at Strawberry Hill,

Wyatt had conceived the Abbey as two houses: one to live in, and one to amaze the visitors – the only problem with his rational solution was that the second house was not, by Beckford's exacting standards, amazing enough.

That first and short-lived Fonthill Abbey was recorded in a watercolour which J. M. W. Turner, one of the new group of artists whom Beckford gathered around him, made for his patron before Beckford left on a third visit to Portugal, in 1798. The charm of the complex is obvious. From the south-west it composes finely with the south wing in the foreground, and Beckford's future bedroom is just visible on the extreme right, over the oriel to St Michael's Gallery. When Turner came sketching again in 1799 that long sloping roof had been replaced by an attic storey to accommodate the 'Board of Works'. This was to be Beckford's study-school and reference library for his artists, architects and craftsmen. Beyond the Gothic villa stands an engaging oddity, an approximation of King João's octagonal tomb chapel, reduced in size but none the less a memorable 145-foot souvenir of Batalha. Composed of brick and compo-cement (Wyatt's disastrously unsuitable new building material) laid against a timber frame, the Octagon rises no more than one step above the roof-line of the monastic Refectory, the thirty-five-foot-high door to which Turner has decently veiled in a wash of light. There are no gardens or outbuildings; the Abbey lies idyllically isolated, as if in some forest clearing. One feature only is missing: it has no Tower.

As early as 1796 both the London and the local papers had been eagerly looking forward to the raising of a 280-foot tower, so ambitious in scale, the *Salisbury and Winchester Journal* claimed, 'that a coach & six may be driven with ease and safety from the base to the top and down again. This stupendous work will probably employ hundreds of the neighbouring poor for near ten years': here instead was a saucy little dunce's cap a mere 145 feet high. Beckford had failed his readers, and he was conscious of the failure. The Abbey's desperate problems in the future arose from his determination to astonish, to raise that 280-foot tower. It should have been built on solid foundations at Stop Beacon; instead it was to be heaped upon the feeble base of what had begun as 'a little pleasure building' at the other end of the ridge, below the summit of Hinkley Hill. The Tower would rise eventually to 276 feet, and be clearly visible twenty miles away on the far side of Salisbury. But Wyatt's concession to his client's vaulting ambition would have to be propped up not by buttresses but by bedrooms, a crazy supporting ziggurat of bachelor rooms, the so-called Nunneries, 'the highest bedrooms in Europe', with servants' quarters stacked up even higher on top of them. His drawings in the RIBA indicate that the ziggurat was only intended initially to support a short, stumpy spire: that 276-foot Tower was a client's afterthought.

Denied a role as a major European statesman, Beckford had instead become addicted to building operations. At a polite level there were architects for him to wine and dine, and to argue with as a well-informed gentleman amateur. Wyatt had two sons following in his profession, Philip and Benjamin, and both were involved with the Abbey; later there would be his nephew Jeffry Wyatt. Charles Wild, George Cattermole, J. F. Porden, J. C. Buckler and John Le Keux all made drawings of the prodigious works. Cattermole in particular exaggerated the scale of the already ambitious arches so convincingly that the Abbey fallen lived on more impressively in his illustrations than it had been when it was intact. Porden's Eaton Hall in Cheshire, another lost Gothic palace, was to be the true child of Fonthill, almost as impressive as its parent. In this way Beckford's 'Board of Works' was a real academy where food, drink, conversation and a rich reference library combined to advance the whole course of the Gothic Revival, a movement that was to reach its climax in an institutional response to Fonthill's tremendous vistas – the Palace of Westminster.

In addition to these scholarly refinements, there was also an exciting masculine world of labourers – a whole army, more than a hundred, sometimes as many as five hundred men and boys, sweating, swearing and roistering in a tented 'town' up on the hill. Beckford could patronise these men as the grandee from the palace down by the lake, direct and spur them on in the long intervals when Wyatt was absent, and set them particular objectives to reach with a reward of guineas for drink if they worked fast enough. It was even popularity of a kind.

After that Twelfth Night fête and football match Beckford wrote to his mother: 'I need not tell you that I have the satisfaction of giving constant Employment to some hundreds of People in one way or another. If this is doing any good or Service with my Fortune [he continued in his most priggish register] and that you know is my meaning in most of these occupations, I may, I suppose, content myself with my own interior approbation.'

Jamaica was the one cloud on his contentment at the end of a first year of building. The sugar revenues were dwindling alarmingly as other tropical countries were developed to compete in the trade. By 1797 'England's wealthiest son', as Byron was to describe him in *Childe Harold*, was overdrawn and paying more than 5 per cent interest on a loan from Wildman, his unscrupulous lawyer. This initial debt was a mere £742, but by 1800 it would be £89,976 and rising.

Mrs Beckford's response to that self-righteous letter from her spendthrift son is not recorded. He destroyed all her letters, which indicates that they made unflattering reading. On 25 July 1798 she died at her house, West End, in Hampstead. She was 74 and her death was not unexpected. For some time her son had been cultivating his old tutor again with a view to Dr Lettice taking charge of the two daughters, Maria Margaret and Susan Euphemia, when their grandmother died; Lettice had been tutoring them in London, but not as a full-time task. Beckford had always kept up a friendly contact with the girls, indeed they had recently come with Mrs Beckford to stay at Splendens, but his interest in them was detached rather than warm; he referred to Maria, the elder girl, as 'the stupid egoist' and to Susan, his favourite, as 'the hysteric'. For their part they were devoted to him as the glamorous, enchanting father who, on the rare occasions of their meetings, was all charm, high-spirited games and generosity. After Mrs Beckford's death they continued to live in the Hampstead house in winter and spring, enjoying the pleasures of the capital and the social season; for the summer and autumn, they would now migrate to Wiltshire and occupy Berwick House, the original dower house for the Fonthill estate, half-way between Fonthill Bishop and Hindon. Living there they could call on their father every day. A cousin, Lady Ann Hamilton, acted as guardian and chaperone.

As for his mother, it would have been remarkable if Beckford had been stricken by her death. She was a conventional Christian of her time and class, rigid, moral and disapproving. He had been a disappointment to her, a circumstance she had made no attempt to hide. At her grand funeral in Fonthill Gifford church the Association band of local yeomanry, 30 strong, gave her corpse the Dead March from *Saul.* Burials were an obsession with Beckford, but not one he enjoyed. In November, partly for relief, partly to do a favour to Gregorio Franchi, he set off on his last visit to Portugal, taking Wyatt with him as far as Falmouth in order to instruct him on the next building stage.

There was to be a Tower, it was to be substantial, of cathedral size, and it was to go up fast. Wyatt was eager, even excited. He had exhibited a design in the Royal Academy that summer, and this exhilarating panorama of towers, spire and lordly galleries explains why Beckford retained Wyatt's services despite his distressing irregularities. He had planned a north wing even longer than the existing south wing, with a large chapel at the end. Farington noted on 16 November:

> Beckford gone to Lisbon for 2 years. Unwilling at last to depart –
> Wyatt went with him to Falmouth – New building to be called
> Fonthill Abbey – the Spire to be 17 feet higher than the top of St
> Peters at Rome. . . . A gallery leading from the top of the Church to
> be decorated with paintings the works of English Artists – Beckford's
> own tomb to be placed at the end of this gallery, – as having been an
> encourager of Art. Society of artists, He says, He prefers to all other.

Beckford's tomb was to be housed in a 'Revelation Chamber', so called for the terrifying paintings which Benjamin West was to provide, illustrating the opening of the six seals at the Day of Judgement, as described in the sixth chapter of the Book of Revelations:

> And I beheld when he had opened the sixth seal, and, lo, there was a
> great earthquake; and the sun became black as sackcloth of hair, and
> the moon became as blood.

It was a tremendous concept, and if only West had been a second Michelangelo and Beckford another Pope Julius, it could have been a Sistine Chapel of doom-laden Calvinism. On 22 December

Farington had gleaned all the details from Wyatt. The north gallery was to be 125 feet long and 12 wide (much as it was built) and wainscotted in ebony (oak was the final compromise).

> The Revelation Chamber is to have walls 5 feet thick in which are to be recesses to admit coffins. Beckford's Coffin is to be placed opposite the door. The room is not to be entered by strangers, to be viewed through wire gratings. The floor is to be of Jasper. This Gallery and room are to be over the Chapel.

So Beckford's corpse was to lie safely three storeys above ground level, out of worm's reach, in case, like the Pre-Adamite Sultans, he might be dead but still conscious. That frightening book read on his winter journey to Madrid had prophesied a similar undead condition; he was taking no chances.

Projecting above and dominating like a finger-post to Heaven all other ranges of the design was Wyatt's superb octagonal tower and spire, richly detailed and buttressed yet propped on an unrelated huddle of bedrooms. To describe it all as a prodigy would be an understatement, and in two years the exterior shell of the Tower, though not the spire, would be complete.

Beckford set sail for Lisbon, reasonably confident not only of an immortality but of a tomb with a view. His mission in Portugal was discreditable yet also magnanimous, a typically perverse mixture. Prince João, the Regent, had offered him some unspecified honour in thanks for his diplomatic efforts on Portugal's behalf. Beckford had declined anything for himself, but asked instead that Franchi be made a member of the Order of Christ, which would give him the title of Chevalier. The Portuguese, Marialva included, were both embarrassed and angry. They considered Franchi to be no more than an Italian catamite, quite unworthy of a chivalrous distinction. When Beckford persisted the Regent gave way, but only on condition that Beckford come over to receive the order in person and then hand it on to the new Chevalier. It was not a happy conclusion to the Portuguese episodes. Beckford fell ill during his stay, and hankered after a return home. He was so anxious about the progress of his Tower that in May 1799 he wrote commissioning Turner to make a second visit to sketch the building operations at the Abbey.

He would be back himself in July, but by then the damage had been done; he had been away too long, and at exactly the worst possible time. When one building scheme, that with the dunce's cap spirelet, was being cannibalised within another, that of a full-sized octagonal tower, and relieving arches on deep foundations should have been laid for the total reconstruction of the Octagon to carry the enormous weight of the Tower, he had been in Lisbon and Wyatt at Windsor. Wyatt's clerk of works George Hayter was left unsupervised, and the relieving arches were not built. The negligence was gross, probably criminal, but whose was the criminality? It is hard to believe that in July 1799, when Wyatt came hurrying up from London to greet his client, neither he, an experienced architect, nor Beckford, the critical amateur, noticed that there were no relieving arches. No plaster was to be laid over the brickwork for another nine years, so the construction should still have been clearly visible.

Years later the fairy story would be put about that on his death-bed George Hayter sent a desperate message for Beckford to visit him. Beckford, who so loathed death-bed scenes that he even left Franchi, his lover, business adviser and friend, to die alone, is supposed to have done so, and to have heard a feeble, whispered confession that the foundations to the Tower had never been laid. Beckford in his turn is said to have gone dutifully to old John Farquhar, who had bought the Abbey from him for a staggering £300,000, to warn him of an impending collapse: Farquhar took this news philosophically, saying that it would last out his lifetime. As is well known, it did not. The whole story sounds suspiciously like another composition for Mozart. Beckford knew perfectly well from his years in residence that the Tower was unstable. It swayed so violently in high winds that on one occasion the dwarf Piero left his bed in a panic and hid in a downstairs rubbish tip. At night Beckford often lay awake listening to the whole structure creaking and groaning. He was to manipulate the sale of his Altieri Claude paintings quite unscrupulously, hinting at rival bids that had not been made, so he would have felt no qualms at concealing vital facts about the building when he sold the Abbey.

That cheerful little spire on the first version of the Octagon had blown down in the wind merely as a result of the stresses exerted on it by Beckford's house-flag, flying from the mast. Turner's new sketches showed a frightening grey ghost of a tower rearing up to the 200-foot mark, but built only of timber and cement, webbed in with scaffolding – a disaster waiting to happen.

Beckford is reported by Cyrus Redding to have celebrated his return from Lisbon with an epic tantrum. The high galleries of the new Octagon had been given plain safety-balustrades of stone instead of Gothic balustrades with central shields, but the Saloon below was already furnished with sofas and curtains, proof that the lantern had been closed to the weather:

> One day Mr Beckford mounted to the gallery in disgust, and placing his back against the interior wall, and his feet against the edge of the stone balustrades, kicking with all his force, he disjoined them and tumbled them in ruin upon the stone pavement a hundred feet below, which was shattered by the fall, and the furniture crushed or covered with rubbish.

One interesting feature of this revealing anecdote is that Beckford seems to have supplied it proudly, against himself. He could have spared his efforts because in May 1800 there was a catastrophic collapse of the Tower into the Octagon – a year's work wasted.

A brave face was put on the incident; Beckford's willpower is never in question. But when the enthusiastic account of the Nelson visit of 21 December that year is examined carefully, it can be seen as a cover-up. The one great entertainment, when Fonthill Abbey was used to the full, with stately processions of the great and the good up titanic staircases beneath rocket-soaring arches, never happened. It was, however, a delightful occasion when three thoroughly embarrassing people – Beckford, Nelson and Emma, Lady Hamilton – came together under the muted direction of the gentlemanly and long suffering Sir William Hamilton in what amounted to a charade to celebrate their celebrity, a foreshadowing of a modern publicity event.

With his Abbey still largely unbuilt or in ruins, Beckford kept his guests securely penned into Splendens for the first two days, playing cards. It was helpful that the weather was bad, and that Beckford had drawn on his credit with Benjamin West to persuade him to be one of the party. Looking around at the others – Beckford's Alsatian doctor Ehrhart, whose favourite topic was 'tumours I have operated on', the Chevalier Franchi, Wyatt, who was drinking heavily, the comic verse writer John Walcot, the Abbé Macquin, a gossipy old hanger-on, and Madame Banti, a Neapolitan opera singer expert in coloratura passages – Nelson must have wondered what exactly he had let himself in for in becoming a national hero. On the last evening of the visit, 23 December, he found out.

Up to that point the visitors had not been allowed even a glimpse of the wrecked Abbey. Beckford had taken Nelson out for a ride one damp afternoon in his four-horse phaeton but Nelson, unstable with only one arm for support and balance, had been frightened by the pace of Beckford's driving and demanded to be put down, crying out that 'this is too much for me'. The two had walked the horses back to Splendens with Nelson more silent than usual and Beckford exuding insensitive triumph. For Nelson's last treat the carriage procession set out as soon as it was dark and the Abbey could be stage managed. The short journey up the hill, less than a mile, took three-quarters of an hour as the carriages followed a devious route punctuated by music, drum-rolls, gunfire to make the Admiral feel at home, and murky tableaux of hooded figures half-concealed in the leafless woods. The stated intention was to give the effect of an approach to a medieval abbey.

Arrived eventually beneath half-revealed walls, the party entered, not by the giant 35-foot doors opened by a grotesquely leering dwarf but by the regular north-west postern gate, a small door on the near-windowless east flank of St Michael's Gallery. The entire entertainment was restricted to the villa in the south wing. A medieval banquet was served in the Oak Dining Room, the food 'unmingled with any of the refinements of the modern culinary art'. Then the guests climbed the winding stairs of a turret, subsequently named after Nelson. At each turn stood a hooded monkish figure with a burning torch. They passed through the Yellow Drawing Room to the sound of 'silver snarling trumpets' from an orchestra concealed behind a scarlet curtain in the half-finished St Michael's Gallery. This, though with only 60 of its final 127-foot length of fan-vaulting in place, was impressive enough. Emma Hamilton slipped out to prepare her 'Attitudes', and a dessert was served in baskets of golden wire. As music played the guests nibbled spiceries, drank wine, and took in a religious display of candles, reliquaries and devotional statues. Nelson, moved at last to make some comment, observed that the whole was 'a representation of the religious worship of Sicily which he had seen there' – in a word, 'Papish'. He was the son of a Norfolk clergyman.

Returning to the Yellow Drawing Room the party was seated and as a wonderful climax of peculiar taste Emma entered, clothed in a chemise of white muslin which displayed her buxom figure to the full. She was eight months pregnant at the time, but like a regular old trouper was concealing the fact from the world and continuing to put on her act. An 'Attitude', 'Agrippina mourning the death of Germanicus, poisoned by Tiberius', took place in dead silence, which must have required rigid self-control in any watcher with a tendency to giggle. She carried Germanicus's ashes in a golden urn and indicated emotion by slight tilts of her head and slight readjustments of her head scarf. Apparently the performance was made moving by her own total commitment. Before her transient art is dismissed, how is a reader in the twenty-second century likely to react to the texts of plays by Harold Pinter and Samuel Beckett, or a viewer to a video sequence of a young woman lying asleep in a glass case in an exhibition? Some art dates quickly, but is none the worse for being strictly contemporary in relevance.

Beckford, for all his fantasy of an elevated tomb chapel, seems from the very beginning to have looked on his Abbey as a public relations exercise, an entertainment for a bemused audience, performance art in fact, the compo-cement equivalent to Emma Hamilton's Attitudes. Visitors were only excluded as a device to make them want to pass the Barrier Wall. When the poet Shelley came in company with Foxhall, the furnisher, hoping to be allowed to view, he was told politely that visitors were not permitted until the buildings were complete. The fact that outsiders were to look at Beckford's tomb through a grille, as Farington noted, is another indication that like most of the great houses of England at that time, the Abbey was eventually to be open to casual visitors when the family was not in residence.

As the Nelson party drove back to Splendens from the largely unseen Abbey that winter night, they are reported to have felt 'as if all that had been taking place, before passing the Barrier Wall, was the awakening from a dream, or the reversal of some magical spell which had enchanted all present'. It was true. They had taken part in a sanitised episode from a Gothic novel, no closer to horror or to the real Middle Ages than Jane Austen's *Northanger Abbey*. Under the pressure of a prolonged war and that collapse of normal emotional and imaginative restraints which is what the Romantic movement really represented, Beckford's self-indulgence could be shared as a comfortable, patriotic fantasy. There was, however, an implicit danger in Edmund Burke's vision of the nation as a great tree, whose branches might be pruned but never lopped too severely. If politicians came to revere the roots rather than the branches, there was the risk that in times of aesthetic and philosophical uncertainty they might take refuge in traditional forms and practices instead of facing up to the future with new solutions. When an obsessive like Beckford could stand in that southern oriel and see, up the long axis of his Abbey, the sanctuary of his saint dimly illuminated at the far north end, it may seem to have been a harmless fixation realised. But when, not so very much later, the palace of a nation's legislators was to be set out on precisely the same lines, so that the Speaker seated in state in the House of Commons could, if all the intervening doors were opened, see the monarch seated on a throne in the House of Lords, there is something disturbing in the parallel. Ought an obsessive's short-lived Abbey to have been a model for the halls of a living democracy? Was historicism in the architecture of a public building the wise way forward?

Jane Austen thought it important to mock. Her *Northanger Abbey* was written during the late 1790s, and on her many journeys between Bath and Hampshire that octagonal tower on its hilltop would have been familiar to her. She was so conscious of the shallowness of Beckford's illusions and taste that it is almost as though she had been smuggled in for a preview. Her verdict is delivered through Catherine Morland's disappointed reflections on first entering Northanger Abbey, General Tilney's house:

An abbey! – yes, it was delightful to be really in an abbey! – but she doubted, as she looked round the room, whether any thing within her observation, would have given her the consciousness. The furniture was in all the profusion and elegance of modern taste. The fireplace, where she had expected the ample width and ponderous carving of former times, was contracted to a Rumford, with slabs of plain though handsome marble, and ornaments over it of the prettiest English china.

She might be describing the Yellow Drawing Room. A Rumford was a recent invention, a grate with a sloping back that projected heat forward and a hood which drew the smoke in. Beckford, who lived in terror of chills, had himself installed Rumfords in the Abbey (except, perversely, in his own bedroom), and supplied them with scuttles of scented coal to feed their flames.

None of this is to Beckford's discredit. Society had caught him out and was unforgiving. He fought back imaginatively, and caught Society out in its weakness for nostalgia, mystery and medieval play-acting. The paradox is that such a frail and short-lived house should have been remembered for so long. The nation revels in sensationalism. In the 1820s Penrhyn Castle was built for the Welsh slate magnate G. H. Dawkins Pennant to the inspired designs of Thomas Hopper. Penrhyn Castle is still with us, intact within and without. It is as enormous as Fonthill Abbey and, more splendid in its composition, it stands like a noble medieval city on a headland above the sea and the Menai Straits, with all Snowdonia as its Salvator Rosa-style backdrop. Yet who ever talks about it? The National Trust was uneasy at taking it over, and has to work hard to keep up the flow of visitors. The castle has never become the legend it deserves to be, because it never fell down in its building stages and because Dawkins Pennant was a good, quiet man who kept what must have been a colossal ego gently hidden. If he had been a suspected sodomite, or run the castle as a brothel notorious from Caernarvon to Colwyn Bay with dungeons for flagellation, would anyone now spare any more thought for Fonthill Abbey than for Bayons in Lincolnshire or Alfred Waterhouse's Eaton Hall, two great Gothic palaces that were demolished without protest as recently as the 1960s? William Beckford himself is the legend of Fonthill, and if a nation chooses its myths on a standard of prurient curiosity and scandal, then these are the gods it deserves.

Beckford's Fonthill Abbey perverted the nation's taste in architecture, making it backward-looking and foolishly grandiose. The opposite viewpoint can be argued, of course — the Abbey proved that medieval forms could be revived and applied on the grandest scale, reminding the country, whenever Parliament sat or the Law Courts functioned, of its glorious traditions and its historic past.

CHAPTER SIXTEEN

A Gothic villain for a Gothic abbey

The problem with this penultimate episode of Beckford's life, his time at Fonthill Abbey between 1800 and 1822, is that for these years of epic achievement in building works we suddenly, from 1807 onwards, know too much about him to support the near-heroic stature he seems to deserve. The only intimate and relatively uncensored record of Beckford's real emotional life before 1807 is of that eleven-month interlude in 1787–8 covered by the Portuguese *Journal*, and even that has been edited by the author. For all his other years, biographers have to depend upon what Beckford chose to allow posterity to know about him: a selection of true letters heavily censored in brown ink and a large number of faked letters which he felt, in manipulative retrospect, he ought to have written in an ideal past.

Horace Walpole was Beckford's rival in the posterity stakes, but he never actually forged his past, though he was equally ruthless about the letters he allowed to survive. Satisfyingly, however, both men failed in one major instance. Walpole never recovered the twenty-six love letters he wrote to Lord Lincoln, and without them it would not have been known that he was once passionately and very movingly in love with another man. Beckford's slip-up was more spectacular.

As his old lover Gregorio Franchi aged, their sexual relationship had wilted away. Indeed, Franchi had married a Portuguese wife and sired a daughter, but his strongest attachment remained to Beckford. Leaving his wife in Lisbon, he had settled in London to act as Beckford's agent and art dealer while running his own business as a shipper of contraband goods through the various blockades imposed by the warring powers. Beckford still depended upon Franchi absolutely for advice, affection and moral support. With him he needed to conceal nothing of his true nature. So close was his relationship with Franchi that almost every day, and occasionally twice a day, when they were apart, he wrote Franchi a relaxed and revealing letter, pouring out his unguarded emotions and concerns of the moment. Literally thousands of these letters were retrieved and destroyed after Franchi's death in 1825, but over a thousand escaped. These, covering erratically the period from 1807 onwards, were bought back from potential blackmailers by Beckford's devoted daughter, the Duchess of Hamilton, and for the most part kept, though she would naturally have burnt the more revealing.

Written in that ugly, hasty hand and in Italian, with a spattering of Portuguese and French expressions, these letters were not readily accessible until in 1957 Boyd Alexander, the most perceptive and tolerant of Beckford's British scholars, had a generous selection of the letters translated and published, under the title *Life at Fonthill, 1807–1822*. The working papers for his Beckford studies are now in the Bodleian Library, and those for *Life at Fonthill* constitute an interesting record of his growing embarrassment. At first he seems to have been very happy with the revelations contained in the letters, and prepared to write an amusing study of interacting characters. He began by introducing his comic cast, all labelled by Beckford in his usual mocking style: 'Cowpat' for Betty Bezerra, 'the Macaw' for Lady Ann Hamilton, who had a beaky nose, 'the Great Dolt' for his steward, J. C. Still, 'the Shepherd', an inoffensive title for his favourite cousin and future son-in-law, the Marquis of Douglas, 'Rancissima' (the smelliest) for Lady Craven, and so on. But then reality seems to have intruded, and Alexander's vision of jolly Dickensian goings-on at the big house to have faded. As a biographer he missed nothing and never deluded himself; only occasionally he soft-pedalled on unpleasantness. The idea of a domestic interlude was dropped; instead, Alexander simply printed a selection of the letters in chronological sequence, a year or two years to a chapter, prefacing each with a summary of related current events, adding invaluable scholarly footnotes, but coming to no awful conclusions.

It is not easy, when translating from an Englishman's bad Italian, to decide what his original English tone might have been. Boyd Alexander's translator settled for fluent, lively narrative with more than a touch of old-fashioned 'camp' comedian – Frankie Howerd in the television series 'Up Pompeii', or Kenneth Williams in a 'Carry On' film – which may well be a fair representation of Beckford's register as he aged into his fifties. A few 'scabrous' passages were cut out, but from my own study of the texts with the help of a translator I have found that, if anything, Boyd Alexander tended to select the most revealing and sexually explicit passages for his book. By 1957 readers were becoming broad-minded, and the permissive Sixties were only a step away.

So, quite abruptly at this stage in his life, it is possible to read Beckford in all his lively, earthly complexity: a warts and all portrait presented at exactly the time when he was behaving most heroically in financial adversity. What does emerge is the completeness of his own self-knowledge. He was under absolutely no illusions about himself and, writing to an intimate, paraded his weaknesses with a comical confidence as 'Barzaba', a horrid, slobbering, ineffectual old boy-fancier, an alter ego to be mocked and enjoyed. No one but Gregorio Franchi was ever supposed to read these revelations, and there has to be some reservation in making too much of them. Beckford was, however, so ruthless in the editing of the rest of his life's record that it is hard to feel any sympathy over the revelations that escaped him. Franchi's massive replies, and he was in real trouble if he failed to write back by return, were in Portuguese and they too survive but, having been censored by Beckford, only as a respectable and business-like account of his transactions in the art world.

The six years from 1801 to 1806, those immediately before this light floods in upon Beckford's motivations and scheming, are not only unusually unrecorded and obscure but particularly puzzling in the scanty records. There are signs that Beckford was beginning to behave like one of the more outrageous villains in the contemporary Gothic novels of the Minerva Press: a sinister aristocratic father from one of Mrs Radcliffe's books. Then, when the flow of the Franchi letters begins in 1807, it becomes evident that while he was indeed occasionally Gothic in his rages, he had a leavening sense of wicked humour.

Since their events have been so well concealed it is necessary to move quickly over these dark six years, even though they covered a significant period in Beckford's life. Apart from the fact that it allowed him to exact a return visit to the Admiral at his house in Merton, Surrey, the Nelson visit had been an infuriating missed opportunity. With the eyes of the nation upon him and the chance for a perfect public relations coup, Fonthill had failed its creator. A year earlier Nelson could have climbed a 200-foot Tower, taken a cold collation in a Refectory 56 feet high, with minstrels playing in a gallery at one end and the Gospels being read from a pulpit at the other. Finally, he could have marvelled at the Octagon – unfinished, but 126 feet high to its 35-foot diameter. But the collapse of the Tower in May 1800 had ruined everything, and such an opportunity would never occur again.

Beckford was bored with low, damp, Classical Splendens. In order to rebuild the Tower using stone instead of compo-cement he directed in 1801 that one of the two pavilions at Splendens should be demolished (it was as large as a sizeable house) and its freestone used for the Abbey. This work went ahead slowly over the next five years. In May of the same year, while Britain was still at war with France, he set off, for health reasons so he claimed, for Paris. Not only did he intend to settle in the capital of the enemy, but he took with him as his companion for the first few months James Wyatt, 'Bagasse', the supposedly scorned and even detested 'Whore-Monger' (Boyd Alexander translated an alternative form, 'Bagassona', as 'the Bugger'). Wyatt will have relished the opportunity to study the artistic loot which Napoleon had collected in the Louvre, but that Beckford should have chosen him of all people for the privilege casts doubts on whether any of Beckford's recorded reactions can be taken at face value.

Wyatt went back to London and after a quick visit to Lausanne Beckford returned to Paris, where he rented in December the very grand hôtel Kinsky in the Faubourg-St-Germain. He behaved as if he was meaning to live there permanently, employing the architect Larsonneur to alter the interiors and improve the garden. He had sold some of the fittings of Splendens in 1801 when the pavilion was demolished, and in February and March of 1802 there was a major sale of any important paintings and furniture that would be inappropriate to a Gothic abbey. Farington reported on 4 July 1801 that 'Beckford has ordered the Colonnade, & wings of Fonthill to be pulled down. The body of the House is to remain & to be the residence of his daughters, who are to have an establishment of £10,000 a year.'

In Paris Beckford found, as usual, that he fitted far more easily into the French Establishment than he ever had into the English. In August 1802, by which time peace had briefly broken out with the Treaty of Amiens, Beckford took part in the procession to celebrate Napoleon's birthday and his acceptance of the title 'First Consul for Life'. The fact that Beckford nicknamed Napoleon 'the Cuckoo Philosopher' means nothing. Nicknames were Beckford's way of scaling people down to manageable size. He was very impressed by Napoleon. In that procession Beckford must have felt he was in the last days of Republican Rome, with a new Caesar or Augustus rising to shape Europe. He remained in the hôtel Kinsky, collecting bargains in his predictable style – Japanese lacquer, paintings and furniture – only returning to London reluctantly some months after hostilities broke out again. At the back of his mind now was the probability that France would launch a successful invasion of England, and win the war. Napoleon was his man of destiny and he was living in expectation of a great reshaping of Europe.

It is not easy to appreciate Beckford's apocalyptic times. We tend to see the long wars that raged after the French Revolution in terms of jolly Jack Tars victorious at sea, the Scottish squares standing firm at Waterloo and the Prince Regent gorging in the Brighton Pavilion. Beckford lived in the thick of it, hostile to a British ruling class which had scorned him, and untroubled by the possibility or even the probability of defeat. He was as much an eclectic in his religiosity as in his stylistic preferences; and one Calvinistic side of his essentially superstitious nature had latched on to the fifth chapter of Revelation that foretells the end of the world in terms of the opening of seven seals on a book 'written within and on the backside' and held by 'him that sat upon the throne' set in Heaven. The opening of the sixth seal would herald Doomsday, but Beckford seems to have interpreted Napoleon as the rider foretold by the opening of the first seal:

And I saw, and behold a white horse: and he that sat on him had a
bow; and a crown was given unto him: and he went forth conquer-
ing, and to conquer.

This explains Beckford's dutiful presence in that procession on
Napoleon's birthday. Having decided that Napoleon was going eventually to win the war, he proposed to be on the winning French side
since the British had so little time for him. Before mocking his
gullibility and lack of patriotism, it has to be remembered that if a
society rejects some members on the grounds of their sexual identity,
those members tend to accept the rejection and behave accordingly.
Also, great wars do stir up apocalyptic terrors: at the height of the
1939–45 conflict a whisper went around Britain that 'the number of
the beast' mentioned as 666 in Revelation (chapter 13, verse 18) could
be equated to 'Hitler' if A in the alphabet counted as one hundred,
B as 101, and so on. Such revelatory expectations would also account
for Beckford's appreciation and patronage of the wilder ranges of art
– the paintings of John Martin and Francis Danby, Benjamin West's
haunting *Death on a Pale Horse* (the opening of the fourth seal) and
his commissioning of West to decorate the unexecuted 'Revelation
Chamber' with paintings of the opening of the first six seals.
Beckford's return from Paris to England in 1803 was reluctant, and
those surviving letters to Franchi throw some light on his peculiar
behaviour over the next few years.

Ever since 1802 there had been suggestions in the air that
Beckford's favourite younger and plainer daughter, Susan Euphemia,
might marry his cousin the Marquis of Douglas. But Douglas,
twenty years older than Susan and only seven years younger than
Beckford, held out for a huge marriage settlement as the price of
making Susan the prospective Duchess of Hamilton. In 1804, having
rejected the rich banker Thomas Hope as a son-in-law Beckford, in
the role of tyrannical father from a Gothic novel, put very strong
pressure on Susan to marry Casimir Pignatelli, Count Fuentes and
Egmont. Pignatelli was the 19th Count of his line, so he would have
brought innumerable heraldic quarterings into Beckford's collection;
but he was also a well-known homosexual, and Susan firmly rejected
his advances. Beckford flew into one of his famous rages, declaring

that she would bring her old father to a premature grave, but Susan brought two Hamilton relatives – Lady Ann, her guardian, and Lord Aboyne – to support her, and the Count was turned away. The only excuse for Beckford's behaviour, unless he was a moral monster, which is always possible, is to see it as a devious manoeuvre to provoke Douglas into rivalry. If so, it was ineffective, as Douglas delayed his proposal until 1810, when a generous marriage settlement had been agreed.

In another surprising move Beckford, who had always expressed contempt for the political complexities of Parliament and resigned his own seat in 1795, became an MP again in 1806, standing for one of the two seats in the rotten borough of Hindon. At the same time he declared his intention of demolishing the central block of Splendens. This provoked an agonised protest from the Marquis of Douglas, who may have been looking forward to inheriting the great Classical house eventually. Beckford could have snubbed him for unwarranted interference, but Douglas's prospective dukedom was not his only attraction as a son-in-law: he was an even more ardent Bonapartist, a fellow admirer of the man of destiny in Europe. Beckford therefore wrote reassuringly to his cousin that when he saw the Abbey, whose Tower and Octagon were in July 1807 still unfinished, he would soon forget Splendens, that 'old palace of tertian fevers with all its false Greek and fake Egyptian'.

It is from this time that the surviving Franchi letters date, and immediately our perspective on Beckford widens. Beckford the builder, the collector, the would-be diplomat and the angry father, stands back a pace, and there instead is a cheerful, giggling Beckford pretending to be half-crazy with love for a young male tight-rope walker called Saunders, threatening to seize hold of his rope and telling Franchi that '*un marmo istesso non e piu duro ch'una certa porzione della mia personna diventera* (a chunk of marble is not as hard as a certain part of my anatomy will become).' Whether this is all a middle-aged lecher's frustrated fantasy – as Brian Fothergill, the only Beckford biographer to have taken Boyd Alexander's material on board, piously hoped – is open to question in view of Beckford's past history. Certainly the fantasies are precise, and Franchi is their apparently willing focus. Beckford was planning another visit to

Portugal – the 'Paradise of D. Fagundes', as he called that country – and hoped to take a number of likely lads with him, Saunders for one. Franchi was to visit the Saunders house in Duke Street, ingratiate himself with the parents and 'find out what you can about the site of the Earthly Paradise'.

Amid a wonderful jumble of war news, comments on the sublime galleries of Westminster Abbey ('Its height about the same as St Denis but cannot compare with Amiens') and cautions to Franchi on his illegal export trade of contraband to the Continent, Beckford found time to propose that Saunders, 'Montsu' (*Mon çu* or 'my bum'), be asked if he 'would be agreeable to an engagement abroad'. This, one suspects, was the real Beckford all along, as excited by a triforium as by an adolescent's bottom. Nine days later, on 8 September 1807, he wrote as 'the miserable carcass of poor, love-sick, drooling, sorrowing Barzaba', telling Franchi that he would be failing 'in all the duties of friendship and Christian charity' if he could not stop Saunders leaving for a circus tour of Ireland. 'Go to his house,' he ordered, 'where I live, where I breathe – for elsewhere I do not exist.' The letter ends 'Ah! Ah! Ah!', and Saunders seems not to have left for Ireland.

By 12 October, Beckford/Barzaba could hardly control his excitement. He saw Franchi as Charon, the boatman who would row him across dark rivers to the Underworld of Desire:

> I am ashamed to hold this pen – I really write such a load of balls, so many Barzabarisms. Oh Day! Oh Hour! Oh ultimate moment! Oh stars that plot to make me a poor man! Oh my impoverished purse! Ah! Ah! Ah! The day dawns at last – I am trembling, burning with desire – freezing with it! I can't rest. Oh my beloved Charon. I must write to you in the most impassioned language. If only he comes! If only he allows himself to fall in with your desires. Ah!

– and for the remaining months of 1807 there is much more of the same. Franchi certainly visited the house in Duke Street of the 'Leg' family, as Beckford nicknamed the Saunderses. One idea was that on his next London visit Beckford, though he still rented a town house, should lodge with 'Father Leg'. If so, 'what splendid economies might be effected'. Then, with supreme illogicality, Beckford got down to the more serious matter of a lawsuit against the rector of

Fonthill Gifford, who had publicly and with 'stupid brainless malignity' cast aspersions on Franchi's moral probity.

At such times Beckford's hypocrisy is bewildering. Boys preyed on his mind and the obsession could break through any letter without warning. At one moment he would be writing cheerfully about 'the happy wedding of my Caroline and my adored Nephew', two favourite spaniels who had been mated; the next, his own sexual frustration would erupt:

> ... at least the weather is not too bad so I can go bathing. But what's the use of bathing, taking exercise, sleeping, eating, running or horse riding, merely to prolong my miserable existence? No use at all – we must come to an agreement – if I am to avoid the last resort of despair – I must – I must – I must at least catch a glimpse – only a glimpse – of this person you happened to mention in that last letter to poor suffering Barzaba.

That his political morality was equally flexible became apparent during 1808. The French had seized Spain and Portugal, so Beckford was more than ever confident that 'as absolute master of the fleets of Cadiz, Carthagena, Ferrol etc' Bonaparte would win the war. This determined him on a return to Lisbon now that Marshal Junot, recently-created Grand Duke of Abrantes, was the Governor, and the Portuguese Royal family, Beckford's old friends, had fled to exile in Brazil. Franchi was to scout out the land. On 3 June Beckford wrote confidently, 'I'm sure you'll find friends. I'm certain that the Grand Duke will receive you with open arms, especially when he begins to hear our song against the cursèd isle.' The 'song' is not specified – but Beckford was a Member of Parliament when he scribbled this casual treason. Three days later he assured a probably nervous Franchi that 'Junot will not fail to show you favour, and with his favour and that of a friendly Commissariat, one might lead a pleasant life in a thousand ways, and perhaps make some nice profit as well.' Franchi was busily employed breaking the British blockade. Now Beckford, drooling over the art bargains he could pick up in those war-torn countries, saw how he could take advantage of his agent's expertise: 'Ah if only I could go there to gather these beautiful things, they would fall into our nets cheap.'

Convinced that Napoleon was plotting a decisive invasion of Britain ('each hour his power takes a firmer root'), Beckford was still desperate, as late as 7 June, to leave 'these insular mists' for Portugal. Two of his most celebrated paintings, the Altieri Claudes, were about to be sold for 10,000 guineas to provide ready cash for the trip. But then news reached London of patriotic risings against the French all over Spain, those struggles immortalised by Goya in his *Third of May* paintings. Immediately the turncoat Beckford changed his tune: 'These events in Spain are going to be splendid and terrible,' he told Franchi confidently on 12 June. 'They do not surprise me: my notions of Castilian and Portuguese energy have always squared with what is going on now.' Suddenly he had decided that 'Junot is not on a bed of roses'.

The Claudes, however, were sold; he was in funds, and now that the idea of sailing a boatload of boys to the 'Paradise of D. Fagundes' had become unattractive he turned about, swore an oath by St Anthony – the only sort of oath that bound him, or had bound King Louis XI – and strove like a superman to have the Octagon stuccoed and complete by 30 September. Predictably, 'Bagasse' was busy elsewhere, so Beckford took control himself, climbing up and down the scaffolding, urging, threatening, bribing, and revelling in the chaos. Often his army of several hundred labourers, some lured away from the King's works at Windsor, toiled in shifts all night, by torchlight.

Beckford was intensely happy. He once told Franchi that 'Some people drink to forget their unhappiness. I do not drink, I build', and lied, as usual. He built to surround himself with men and boys whom he could command. The brick columns were plastered over, the rose in the central vault was in place, and at last the stained glass in geometric patterns was fixed within the three long 'Batalha' windows. His letters end 'the Octagon calls me', or 'I am sinking myself in the Octagon'. On 18 September he wrote that memorable rapture of power, equating himself with Lucifer at the raising of Pandemonium in Milton's *Paradise Lost*:

> It is really tremendous, the spectacle here at night – the host of men at work, the boys lighting them up; innumerable torches suspended everywhere in the vast unbounded spaces with the drop below; above

is the vast spider's web of scaffolding. When I stand under the count-less completed arches of the tribunes I hear the echoing voices in the stillness of the night, and see huge buckets of plaster and water swing-ing up, as if drawn from the depths of a mine, and from deep below the curses of hell itself and the hymns of Pandemonium or the Synagogue.

Like some figure outside natural law, certainly outside British law, he had turned in mere days from treacherous flight, greed and self-advantage, to spend those Altieri Claude guineas on a structure beyond reasonable expectation. The dimensions of Amiens and Rheims were to be concentrated onto a rich man's saloon, a space only 35 feet across but soaring 125 feet up, the extreme narrowness of the eight supporting arches making their height seem even greater. When George Cattermole came to draw them in 1823 to illustrate Rutter's *Delineations*, he added almost a third again to the actual elevation, making the impact sublime indeed; and so the legend of Fonthill was launched, two years before it all fell down, part brief reality, part artist's licence.

Out at Beckford's beloved Sintra the British, landed by the Royal Navy at Lisbon, had agreed a convention with the French, and Beckford raged angrily at their semi-success, declaring they would scatter Portugal, 'poor Portugal', with blood-soaked ashes. And still his workers toiled on, glazing the eight topmost circular windows, five of which, by virtue of Wyatt's hastily improvised constructional solution, only let indirect light from the Nunnery bedrooms into the Octagon. By 30 September the exercise had been completed, and the oath to St Anthony fulfilled.

With Portugal now out of the question and a 'General Damn-my-eyes' bivouacked in Montserrat, Beckford was taking his Abbey seri-ously again. In the course of 1809 and 1810 the Refectory in the west transept was turned into an entrance hall and linked to the Octagon, by a flight of steps that filled half its length. The north wing was extended, and by 1810 was being carpeted and decorated. That Revelation Chamber intended for an airy burial was forgotten. Beckford had discovered the precious Japanese lacquer displayed up there in the Lancaster Gallery to be 'all covered with lichen and sta-lactites like Fingal's cave', the gilt work 'ash-colour like the first day of Lent'. The idea of a damp tomb with his own corpse sprouting the same kind of mould dissuaded him from the project. Susan Beckford had landed her Marquis of Douglas at last, and Beckford now had his eye on another kind of posterity. It is not easy to believe, but the Franchi letters prove that at this stage he was deluding himself with the possibility that, given a successful invasion by the French, his daughter might sit on the throne of the United Kingdom. His basis for that truly apocalyptic conclusion was the fact that the Dukes of Hamilton, like several other lines of the Scottish aristocracy, had a reasonable claim to the lost throne of the Stuarts. As Douglas was a fervent if secret Bonapartist, Beckford could imagine a time when Napoleon, having sent the mad King George off packing to Canada as the Portuguese Royals had fled to Brazil, would set a Hamilton as a Pretender monarch on the Coronation Chair in Westminster Abbey. It followed that there would be a Queen Susan seated beside him. Quite what title Beckford himself might take he never suggested, but as he had convinced himself that he was descended from twelve crowned kings, the sky was the limit.

'I was personally aware', he told Franchi in a moment of astrological insight, 'of the importance of this alliance [with Douglas], looking into the future and seeing among clouds and constellations the great shadow of the Cuckoo Philosopher. God knows what portents may show themselves on the horizon.' It was this manic grasp on the world that gave him the psychic strength to press on and raise a rival to Salisbury Cathedral on an exposed Wiltshire hilltop, then live in it when the whole fabric groaned and shook in autumn gales. While never mad, neither was Beckford entirely sane in the accepted sense of that word. If he had been sane, no one would remember him now. His apartness from reality, shaped by his sexual identity, allowed him to embrace both treason and the Gothic Revival.

It did not, unfortunately, allow him to accept his elder daughter's wish to marry for love, though that in itself was a very Gothic episode. One May morning in 1811 Margaret simply left her guardian, Lady Ann Hamilton, a letter announcing that she was marrying Colonel James Orde, a decent Northumbrian gentleman, the son of a clergyman, who had been shown the door when he asked Beckford for his daughter's hand in the normal fashion. Now

Beckford reacted precisely as the Wicked Father in a romantic novel was supposed to react: he cut Margaret off without a penny, and ignored her, until a month before her death in 1818, at which point he staged a reconciliation. Once she was dead he became quite friendly with her widowed husband and their two children. This could be seen as Beckford acting out a last, correctly penitent chapter in a romantic novel.

The Octagon was not the end of Beckford's obsession with his Abbey. In 1812 he was actively assisting James Storer in the production of a handsome illustrated volume, *A Description of Fonthill Abbey, Wiltshire*, which was to blazon the fame of his creation over the whole country. Storer, describing the bare east side of the Abbey as it then stood, mentioned that 'it is the intention of Mr Beckford to build a superb chapel directly opposite the great hall'. In a letter of 16 August that year Beckford, still concerned to keep the news of his extravagance from 'Rottier' (Richard White, the lawyer who had replaced Wildman), told Franchi that the giant East Transept (out of scale with everything else in the Abbey, even the Tower) had been begun. Detached and self-aware as ever, he commented that if only 'the wretched Rottier would pimp me a little, I would save a great deal': in other words, a supply of young, willing boys would have distracted him from building. He intended the walls of the new transept to be 90 feet high by November, and they were achieved, hunched up hugely, with two octagonal turrets rising even higher.

Sex and building were inextricably linked in his mind at this time. Some affair with a youth on Hounslow Heath, a gipsy camping-place, was in the offing. 'I have as many daggers in my heart as the image of Our Lady of Sorrows!' he exulted. 'Where is the balm for these wounds? Where is the medicine for such torments?.... I know – I know – I'm going to say it – it is at – Hounslow.' Even as he was lavishing more money than he possessed on the transept, which he intended should house a hall commemorating his baronial ancestors who had signed Magna Carta (an idea stolen from the Duke of Norfolk's Arundel), he was fantasising on life in a Hounslow cottage, where 'I'd finish my days in the lap of Platonism and devotion, educating the little rogue!'

Was there perhaps rather more in that line than the usual self-mockery of an ageing lecher? Probably not; English bisexuals have, understandably, taken a long time to recover from Edward II's attempt to live out the love-style of Provençal Troubadours seriously. Beckford cut out from a newspaper the account of a married Londoner who was hanged for sodomy with a stable boy and tried on the scaffold to implicate a whole list of fellow 'criminals'. If there had ever been any chance of Beckford relating affectionately to a man with style and constancy, it had passed when Gregorio Franchi became his pimp, plying the streets of London for willing youths. Yet his letters to Franchi often end with the warmest endearments: 'I embrace you affectionately, my dear Gregory', 'come to your true and affectionate Protector', 'I embrace you with all the strength of my heart'. But if he loved Franchi, why did he eventually leave him to die alone and uncomforted in London, denying sentimentalists the ending they require?

Nothing in Beckford is ever quite constant. As he awaited Rottier's furious reaction to the extravagance of his improbable new transept, he had already repented of the work – 'would God they could be stopped'. But he had taken another of his oaths by St Anthony, to finish the transept, so finished it had to be. Paradoxically, however, as early as 1812 he was already considering leaving the Abbey for ever: 'Then I will become grossly, enormously, formidably rich and will escape to some agreeable site with the retinue I desire.' This was even before the transept had been roofed.

Sugar prices rose to an all-time high in 1813 and continued so for two years, quite long enough to lift Beckford's depression. For a short time he was a very rich man again. By 1815 the elaborate carving of the transept's new turrets and parapet had been completed. He wrote:

> What battlements! Grace, elegance and just proportions. Enchanting! Marvellous! A work like this will bring to his knees, even in mud and ice, anyone who can recognise and feel the triumph of architecture (in this style at least).

As he finished the letter he could hear the noise of chopping, carts passing and men running to empty them. His Abbey, against all the odds, was virtually complete: 'What sweet music! What joyful harmony!'

He deserved that moment of triumph. Up there on his windy hilltop he had obliged James Wyatt to design, and sometimes to supervise, two quite separate buildings which met each other only at the cross-roads of the Octagon. So distinct were they that anyone drawn to them unawares by that toppling Tower could be excused for thinking them the work of two different architects, designing on two different scales to fulfil two opposing functions.

From south to north was a narrow enfilade of reception rooms running from the attractive, almost detached villa at the south-west angle, disappearing into the unwieldy jumble of the Octagon and Tower to emerge unchanged on the other side and run an equal distance to the Sanctuary of St Anthony. The scale of this essentially domestic unit can be assessed accurately today because the whole Sanctuary, the Lancaster Tower and the site of the Lancaster State Bedroom survive, gutted within and converted into a pleasant house. There are no staggering excitements; it is very ordinary in size and Gothic in detail – a few Perpendicular windows and some Early English lancets, the mouldings rather thin, the ashlar grey-green. The illogicality of that south-to-north range was that although it was the 'holy' part of the Abbey, focused upon Rossi's statue of St Anthony which stood immediately below those lancet windows, yet it was far more domestic in feeling than the second building which ran west-to-east across it. Beckford changed his mind so often that the most overwhelmingly vast section of the final complex, the East Transept, rose above a basement kitchen, some badly-proportioned reception rooms, and little else.

The west-to-east half of the Abbey began with the Great Western Hall, intended as a Refectory but impractical from the start because of its 35-foot-high entrance door. The Hall ran supportively into the structure of bedrooms propping up the Tower. These buttressing bedrooms gave the exterior of the Abbey an unexpected and frivolous profile of diminishing stages, with their pedimented roof-lines and those strange circular windows lighting rooms which in their turn then lit the interior of the Octagon, by way of a second set of circular windows. Without its long Batalha windows the Octagon would have been almost pitch dark. Telescoping rather than soaring out of this jumble of roofs was the Tower, probably 276 feet high though accounts vary. Originally intended to be topped by a spire, it ended as an octagonal compromise between tower and spire forms, unresolved as to its image, receding a little at each stage and not great enough in its width to justify its height. All these faults combined to make a wonderfully dramatic and characterful whole that from the first seemed to suggest its own impending collapse. The artists who flocked to paint the Abbey usually responded to it, Turner in particular, by exaggerating its appealing disproportion and over-dramatising – as Beckford complained – the surrounding rather ordinary landscape. It was a perverse triumph, and deserved better structural foundations.

The East Transept, Beckford's last gesture of defiance against forces unknown, was one part of the building which could never be described as lacking in drama or disproportion. As Wyatt originally designed it there should have been four corner turrets, not two; but most of it was completed after Wyatt's death in 1813, when 'Coxone' – George Hayter, the clerk of works – was in control and acting under Beckford's close supervision. The transept had originally been conceived because the north, west and south limbs of the Abbey were all more or less inadequate in profile alongside the Tower. If anything, this new transept was now almost too bulky for its tall neighbour. Easily the most exhilarating and disturbing views of the building were those taken from the south-east. From that angle the Transept rose threateningly over the long, largely windowless south range. However it may have functioned internally, this was a great and memorable design, and those twin octagonal turrets, so much taller than the pair on the gateway at Canterbury Cathedral on which they were modelled, gave the Abbey that complex of city-like towers which Beckford had so admired at Batalha. All the other turrets – Nelson, Latimer, Lancaster and the rest – were too small to compose well. Once again Beckford, his own best critic, acknowledged their failure in the composition. Another fault was that only on the south-western villa and on the roof-line of the East Transept were the mouldings of the arches, windows and parapets cut with sufficient depth to cast shadows and lend a third dimension. The Abbey remained, nevertheless, breathtaking, and the nation held its breath.

Predictably, Beckford grumbled about the Abbey from the start. He wrote to Franchi in 1815, 'this place makes your flesh creep as soon as night falls. Yesterday I thought that everything was coming down.' A little later: 'Really this habitation is deathly in the stormy season ... I didn't sleep a half hour in succession – I thought I heard sobs and lamentations, cannon shots, bomb explosions, and all the delights of the battles of Borodeno or Waterloo.' He had noticed the inadequate scale of the south-north axis: 'the miserable Fonthill sanctuary does not satisfy me. In vain they tell me, and think that it is fine – I don't believe a word of it – pitiable.' He was right; even a small Lisbon town church like São Antonio da Sé could put it to shame in the matter of vaulting and altar display. It was only gorgeous by the standards of Protestant England. By 1818 he was yearning for Rome, 'if I could live there cheaply in the way I like without seeing English people, playing at being devout, churchifying, strolling about the ruins'. Beckford's religious faith caused much unresolved speculation. The *Morning Herald*'s gossip columnist claimed in September 1823 that on his first visit to Portugal, Beckford had become

> a member of the monastic order of St Anthony. The Chevalier was also an extern associate of that order and initiated with Mr Beckford in its mysteries. Both always wore the cross of the order as a distinguishing character in their breasts & like Louis XI of France, Mr B always carried about him a small silver image of the Saint.

It is safe to say that Beckford would have been happier, spiritually at least, if he had been born in 1860 instead of 1760, and become an Anglo-Catholic with a house in North Oxford and a villa outside Florence.

Consideration of the interior decoration of the Abbey will be reserved for the next chapter, on Beckford as an interior designer and collector, or more accurately on Franchi as the collector by proxy for Beckford. The Franchi letters are most enlightening. Franchi collected in London and abroad while Beckford built, or escaped boredom as best he could with the limited company at the Abbey. The companions – 'friends' would not be the right word – who appear to have sustained Beckford in his isolation were the Abbé Denis Macquin, his librarian and specialist on heraldry, 'Warwick'

Smith, a second-rate landscape artist, and the dwarf Piero. Macquin was a 'spoilt priest', a lapsed Catholic who at the Revolution had fled from Meaux, where he had been Professor of Rhetoric. As a learned, corrupt and cynical companion, he was someone to whom Beckford could always feel generally superior: 'He laughs and talks, roisters, eats and drinks ... he swallows everything ... if he does not die, if he does not become a fountain of diseases then he must have special favour, not from the Pope but from God himself.' But Beckford ends a list of criticisms unexpectedly, with: 'in spite of all this and his spiritual defects, I love him with my whole heart and hold him in some esteem.' Garrulous cheerfulness would appear to have been the Abbé's real recommendation; with him around, Beckford could forget 'foreboding whisperings at midnight and lamentations as of devil-possessed cats in the gutters'. After dark the Abbey must have been an intensely melancholy and haunted place.

The dwarf acted the role of Beckford's oracle. He spoke rarely and what he said appears banal in Beckford's repetition, but it was taken as a kind of earth-wisdom, and valued as such. Told that the Abbé was going blind, the dwarf asked whether he would be returning to the Abbey if he did lose his sight. 'No,' Beckford told him. 'Good, let him go blind then,' was the dwarf's reply. It was this ruthless cynicism which his master relished. Only Duchess Susan pleased the dwarf and she, so he believed, loved him 'like the best bon-bon in the universe'. Beckford was very sensitive to perfumes, cedar-wood closets, honeysuckle and jasmine flowers, but the dwarf's body odour, which he commented on with amusement, did not trouble him. Some Regency gentlemen customarily rode out with a Dalmatian as a smart accoutrement; Beckford rode out with the dwarf on a pony beside him.

One very old homosexual friend once told me wistfully that the great age of sodomy passed away when domestic servants became unfashionable. Beckford kept a whole army of menservants about the Abbey. According to that ill-natured account in the *Morning Herald*,

'the lazy vermin of the hall those trappings of folly' swarmed at Fonthill. Mr Beckford never moved but with a circle of them in attendance. They formed an appendage of his invincible pride; there was not a bell throughout the Abbey but he needed no summons to command attendance. The liveried retainers stood in numerous succession, watchful sentinels at his door & at fixed periods anticipated their proud master's wants.

Normally his dinner table was waited upon with elaborate formality, and even at Bath, where Beckford's establishment was much reduced, Venn Lansdown was impressed by the retinue of mounted servants who accompanied him respectfully on rides. It is plain from hints dropped here and there that Beckford sometimes, though not often, found them sexually convenient. He kept a keenly assessing eye open upon his stable-boys, which could explain his alarm at that newspaper report on the London sodomite hanged for an affair with a stable lad. Like most men with particular sexual appetites, he could tell at a glance whether the latest employee was a 'patapouf' – the contemporary term for homosexual – or what Beckford called 'nice', meaning desirable but unavailable. This is probably what Beckford meant when he claimed he could look into a man's eyes and read him like a book.

Such of his domestics as interested him physically were given nicknames like 'The Ghoul', 'Countess Pox' or 'Mme Bion'. This last was his valet Richardson, whose 'certain kind of frigidity and insipidity' irritated Beckford: 'the devil take you, you blond beast!' he complained in one letter. But after one expensive and unsatisfactory assignation (or 'flash', to use his code word) in a Paris hotel, Beckford had to admit that 'Bion always counts for something', despite being apparently 'insipid, monotonous and frigid'.

Ali Dru, a young Albanian boy, was Beckford's favourite among the Abbey's domestic staff. He called him 'the Turk', possibly because he was a 'Mahometan', and when Beckford was in one of his 'poor Barzaba' moods, 'every now and then certain lightning flashes' from Ali Dru would cheer him up, 'and in less than the beating of a heart, all becomes sunny and blue'. In the reverse of modern custom, Beckford used to swim in the Bitham Lake in the woods below the Abbey not when the sun shone but when it was raining. On 27 June 1817 he wrote that he had 'profited by the lack of sun to bathe with the Turk, who is what Naïs would give all his bronzes to be'. Naïs was a male spirit of fountains in Classical legend, represented as very young and slim. Beckford became seriously upset when Ali Dru began to shave, and put on weight. By that time, too, the relationship had become mercenary and, as can happen when a servant also acts the part of lover, the Turk was tending to exercise a little too much authority, suggesting when Beckford posted 25 guineas to Franchi that it was 'A Pity to send them away'. It is interesting that Beckford, in his role as puppet master, should have wanted Franchi to know this, playing one lover off against a jealous ex-lover.

There is nothing in the letters to suggest that Beckford indulged in the riotous sex life at the Abbey rumour claimed. He was far too fastidious, and always complaining to Franchi of frustration and disappointment. When he stayed at his rented London house he had an occasional sexual routine which he relates with the weary elegance that could so easily have made him a fine, realistic novelist, or the poet of Sodom:

> Late last night, coming out of Jacquier's, I went in search of a little amusement in an accustomed quarter. I knock. They've gone away. 'Past one o'clock, Past one o'clock'; I recognise the voice – it is an old acquaintance, such a good fellow. I give him the commission of finding out, and he has done so. 'Excuse me if I write down the address.'

With his experience and his style, Beckford could so easily have become the English Gide and written about deviant life as it really was. It would have been a relief from the condescending cartoon version of people and relationships that Dickens offered and the old maid's refinements of Jane Austen. If it is not too pretentious, it is possible to see the entire structure of Fonthill Abbey as a symbolic protest against repression and concealment – one that only a multi-millionaire could afford. But when that multi-millionaire was also an accomplished writer, the Abbey appears to be effort misdirected and a dead-end of demonstration, an English preference for a Gothic folly rather than sexual realism.

When he was not directing his builders or disdainfully eyeing up his footmen, Beckford was an open-air man. He grizzled about his nervous fevers, constipation and piles, but actually enjoyed superb health, rising early, eating and drinking exquisite food and fine wines with Spartan moderation He rode out in the grounds all day, supervising tree felling and tree planting along the rides he had prepared through the woods.

Beckford's record as a landscape gardener was one of response to changing fashion, an inconstancy that by the time he left the Abbey in 1822 had resulted in one landscape on the east side of his estate in decay, and another entirely different on the west, immature and dependent upon an army of gardeners to keep an entirely artificial state of 'natural woodland' in impermanent suspension. From his father he had inherited the conventional and very attractive Arcadia, already described, with temples, grottoes and a hermitage set about the woods and green spaces around the long artificial lake or 'river'. Until he travelled widely on the Continent, Beckford had been very satisfied with this. As late as 1784 he had employed the Lanes to continue 'rockifying' the existing grottoes, enriching them with spar, shells and concealed flower vases, his natural feeling for internal decoration inclining him to treat such outdoor artefacts as indoor rooms. Henri Meister recorded in 1792 and the Beckford novel of 1796 describes the trick of sinking pots of flowering plants and shrubs into the earthern floors of the grottoes, removing them as soon as the flowers had blown and replacing them with new plants from the estate's greenhouses.

While very charming in a precious way, this is not real landscaping, more like municipal gardening as now practised on city roundabouts. As he became converted to the wilder and more natural-seeming landscapes of the Picturesque movement Beckford was never able to free himself from this culture of greenhouses. As a result the new western park which he began to create as a setting for the Abbey was a compromise. In fairness, he had few natural advantages of the sort enjoyed by Richard Payne Knight at Downton Castle or Uvedale Price at Foxley. It was unwise of Beckford to move away from the 'river', his one good natural feature, to the mild hillslopes of Stop Beacon and Hinkley Hill: these offered good viewpoints, but no rugged cliffs or sudden ravines. Some accounts describe the Bitham Lake as a Beckford creation, designed to look like the crater of an extinct volcano in imitation of Lake Nemi in

Italy. The truth is that the Bitham Lake was a fishpond dug by the Cottingtons in 1639. It was originally called 'Bottom Lake', but as Beckford had a sense of the absurd and bathed regularly there, he preferred the more obscure spelling. All that he ever did was to repair the dam and plant obscuring trees and bushes around it. From the south-facing windows of the Abbey, notably the oriel in St Michael's Gallery, the lake would have been visible beyond the colourful azaleas of the American Garden, so-called from the flowering bushes native to the Appalachian mountains which had been introduced from the American colonies.

When Beckford realised that with his sugar revenues in permanent decline he would have to sell the Abbey before he could ever hope to open it and the grounds to a discerning public, he encouraged the publication of no fewer than three superbly illustrated books on Fonthill in the space of two years: two by John Rutter and one by John Britton. If the text of Rutter's *Delineations* was not actually dictated by Beckford, it certainly represents his views very closely, and where the park is concerned it virtually admits failure. On the subject of the grounds, Rutter accepted that 'we must at once premise that we almost despair of producing any very distinct impression upon the mind of the reader ... they contain very few objects that will admit of individual expression'. Naturally Rutter then tried to write himself out of this sorry confession, but as it was no more than the strict truth he had to keep admitting in his various set tours to a walk 'without any great variety of scenery', one path 'planted without order', another 'path without any particular beauty', and 'the comparative recent creation of these walks'.

The trouble was that Beckford had attempted a Picturesque landscape with no really picturesque features to support it. Realising its insipidity he had crammed it with the flowering bushes and even the flower beds of what was by that date the modish nineteenth-century almost-suburban 'Gardenesque'. He could have built his way out of this compromise, but that might have drawn attention away from the Abbey, which he wished to be seen in '*l'architecto pittore*', at the centre of a natural forest. To that end he avoided gravel drives and straight lines; the Western Avenue was simply a 'wide green path', its edges 'planted without order', its grass scythed at night so that there should be no taint of ordinary humanity to disturb Beckford's rides in the daytime. Sensitive souls were intended to enjoy the contrast of foliage, yellow, green and dark green. But at the time of Beckford's departure most of the planting was still immature and for instant effect he had had to rely everywhere on bushes of hawthorn and quick-growing larch, so that appreciation depended more upon goodwill than fine grouping.

Beckford, if Rutter is any guide, had been following the literary lead of Milton's Eden in *Paradise Lost*, where

> Flowers worthy of Paradise, which not nice Art
> In Beds and curious Knots, but Nature boon
> Poured forth profuse on Hill and Dale and Plain ...

So the new grounds were intended to combine 'the wildest and most ornamental scenery, the picturesque and the beautiful in close society'. Rutter praised the way 'the furze and the lily blossom in equal comradeship' and 'the rose and rhododendron bloom beneath the larch and hawthorn'. For a year or two they might well do that, but without an army of gardeners replanting each year and pruning, the lily and the rose would soon be defeated and the rhododendron would create a wasteland under its spreading branches.

On his ideal route within the confines of the Barrier Wall, Rutter had little to offer his readers until they reached the American Garden near the end. All he could do was halt them at certain points and direct them, in the accepted Picturesque mode, to look back at set angles – usually to the Abbey, which all the planting was supposed to frame. Yet he admitted that the building only composed well with moonlight 'breaking down all its minute parts into one broad and majestic mass'. Viewers were to think of it as a medieval building before which 'the belated peasant would have prostrated himself in holy awe when the dying sounds of the Evening Hymn were borne upon his ear by the fitful breeze'.

This new western sector of the park never made a clear visual impact except where the chemical yellows and carmine of flowering bushes stood out in the American Garden above Bitham Lake. Otherwise it was no more than a series of woodland walks; and unless a visitor was interested in birds, rabbits and insects, or garden flowers struggling with adversity, it can have offered very little. There were no mature groves, no temples – only one 'Norwegian' log hut. The planting along Beacon Terrace was almost entirely of small trees – laburnums, acacias, birch, thorn, firs – so it was virtually a shrubbery, apart from a few oaks. From some angles the Abbey must have towered up out of a wilderness of bushes. Rutter tried hard on one featureless stretch to interest the reader in the moss, and there was actually a 'moss house' on the route. Twenty years after Beckford had sold Fonthill, Venn Lansdown was impressed by the decaying beauty of the place. By that time most of the planting would have had about fifty years to mature. Beckford's garden-park was a little, but only a little, better armoured against time than was his Abbey.

CHAPTER SEVENTEEN

'I adore Buhl' – Beckford as collector and interior decorator

The Abbey was an act of creative irresponsibility, and nothing was more creative or more irresponsible than Beckford's leaving of it: not the last but certainly the greatest of all his many 'compositions for Mozart'. It was wonderfully staged. Beckford had learnt in the art market all the tricks of boosting a price by puffs, bluffs and outright lies. When it came to selling the Abbey in 1822 with the structure visibly crumbling and the press well informed of its instability, he drew upon all the accumulated credit of mystery and inaccessibility, bloodhounds, mantraps and rejected intruders that had been gathering over the past twenty years and threw the place wide open for public inspection and the sale of the century – which never happened. This was his ultimate revenge for nearly forty years of imagined ostracism by Society.

The auctioneers Christie's were his innocent accomplices. They prepared a catalogue of all the Abbey's treasures, irresistible to any fine arts connoisseur, even at a guinea a copy together with a ticket for entry and inspection. (Modern equivalents are difficult to calculate, but a probable underestimation of a twenty-fold increase would make £21 at the very least as the price of admission: much more than for Buckingham Palace today.) Yet the crowds flocked in, as many as 700 a day, travelling in their coaches to that remote rural area. There had never before been a country-house mania to equal it, and with that price tag it had to be an upper- and middle-class phenomenon. Beckford drew in exactly the people he wanted to impress, the people who he felt had treated him as a dangerous pervert. There was one

Royal duke – Gloucester – in the visiting throng, also the Duke of Beaufort and the Duke of Somerset, who was seriously interested in buying the place and quitting his dim little seat at Maiden Newton. The great Duke of Wellington, the ultimate sightseer, came and was impressed; and there were marquesses, earls, viscounts and baronets in the most satisfying numbers. In all, 7,200 catalogues and tickets were sold.

Beckford had begun to commission furniture on a grand scale only when the French Revolution had reduced Henri Auguste's prices. Indeed, though he had enjoyed the competitive atmosphere of great sales much earlier, Beckford's career as a serious collector dates from the period when war had begun to limit his wanderings on the Continent. By that time he was building an Abbey which could contain his wholesale squirrellings in dramatic spaces.

Consequently all these 1822 visitors, unlike those tourists who were to come over the next three years, saw the Abbey in its Beckfordian prime, with all its art treasures and exotic furnishings intact and unsold. Franchi was the impresario, staging the event in a manner remarkably similar to the way stately home owners and the National Trust arrange visits today. There must even, with 700 visitors in one day, have been a special coach park. Ticket holders had to approach via the Western Avenue and enter through the 35-foot doors of the Great Western Hall, so that the most sensational part of the house, the Octagon, hit them first. Piero the dwarf was not on hand to open the great doors by a mere touch; he was kept in reserve as a later attraction. When the ticket holders had toured the house, with a servant guarding every room, Franchi was at hand to organise coach rides around the grounds for garden enthusiasts; or, if the visitors preferred, they could walk down towards Bitham Lake to inspect the shrubs in the American Garden. On the way they passed the dwarf's herb garden with Piero presiding to welcome the curious and show them around. Refreshments were available back at the Abbey, from the huge new kitchens under the East Transept. Beckford, the creator of it all, remained aloof. In similar circumstances at Strawberry Hill, Horace Walpole would occasionally emerge from his private rooms to impress an important visitor. But the master of Fonthill was busy in those summer months of 1822, before the advertised sale date of 19 September, arranging the real sale of what he had contrived to present as the most prestigious and desirable gentleman's property in Britain – one worthy of a duke, no less.

The Abbey was visually generous to those first visitors. In time Rutter was to devise a more grudging visit, one that began at the mean south-eastern postern with the relatively small rooms of the villa, leaving the set-pieces as the climax of the tour. In 1822 the intention, exactly as in a great Gothic cathedral, was to bring people to their knees at the first moment of entry. Nothing else in the Abbey was as vast and vertical as that initial *coup d'oeil* of the stairs rising up into the Octagon. There had been no need for Cattermole to exaggerate it. After broad daylight, the effect was one of infinite spaces half-perceived and instant dimness – gloom, even – infiltrated (if the sun was shining, and the Abbey depended upon sunshine) by the near-abstract light of the heraldic Batalha windows, purple, scarlet and gold. All the wall surfaces of these two linked spaces – the Great Western Hall and the Octagon – were of rough pale pink plaster; very little stone was visible except on the galleries of the Tribune.

At Ashridge, Wyatt's comparable Gothic complex, the detail of the stone carving in its central reception space is refined; at Fonthill such carving was heavy and heraldic. But while Ashridge offers only one vista, back towards the entrance, Fonthill had five, all presented simultaneously once a visitor had climbed the stairs, examined four groups of allegorical statuary cast in cement, and marvelled at the vault – 120 feet 8 inches, although accounts of the exact height differ.

First there was the vista looking back into the Great Western Hall and out through open doors to the green length of the Western Avenue. Then, in contrast, came the immediate complexity of the stairs. These were tucked into the Octagon's north-western bay, circling up between gilded balustrades around a central core with all the coming and going of servants and visitors to be seen, like a huge peep-show, through a soaring arch of the Octagon. Next, due north, was the long, low, numinous vista of the King Edward III Gallery, phasing into darkness and concluding in an altar, with lit candles and Rossi's statue of St Anthony, half blessing, half preaching. If the visitor swung round to look in the opposite direction, due south, there was a fourth vista of the same length, 127 feet, but quite different in impact. Here, after the gilded lattice of the Tribune screen, was the pale pink and creamy yellow length of St Michael's Gallery, fan-vaulted in stone-coloured plaster, its carpet crimson and starred with white cinquefoils, all brightly lit by a large oriel window at the far end. The fifth vista, due east, was the most immediate and overbearing, Beckford's last major work of the interior. Over a tall Gothic arch leading to three other portals was the Music Gallery and above that the Organ Screen: three stages of stone trefoils, quatrefoils and cinquefoils designed by Beckford himself, the panels lined with scarlet damask and trimmed with brass.

John Constable, one of the two greatest living English artists but one never patronised by Beckford, wrote a bemused and probably typical reaction after his visit:

> Imagine the inside of the Cathedral at Salisbury, or indeed any beautiful Gothick building, magnificently fitted up with crimson and gold, antient pictures, in almost every niche statues, large massive gold boxes for relics etc. etc. beautiful and rich carpets, curtains and glasses, all this makes it on the whole a strange, ideal, romantic place, quite fairy land.

That 'etc. etc.' and 'on the whole' are the give-away phrases. Constable found it hard to focus on or to recollect clearly anything except those Papist reliquaries, which would have seemed more appropriate to a museum than to a gentleman's house. He was nevertheless impressed, although 'fairy land' suggests he saw it as a one-off exotic rather than an example to follow.

Denied the standard Classical decorative motifs of urns, guilloche scrolls, anthemions, metopes and triglyphs by his choice of Abbey Gothic, Beckford had fallen back upon the heraldic devices of his supposed ancestry. In the Great Western Hall alone there were thirty-nine Scottish coats-of-arms brightly painted along the frieze beneath the dark, open wooden roof. The King Edward III Gallery flaunted an even wider display. Only St Michael's Gallery had a correctly ecclesiastical array of angels supporting its fan vaulting.

Beckford's next preference in decorative schemes was for upholsterers rather than carvers or *stuccodores*. Ever since his brief stay at Ramalhão in 1787 his first instinct when presented with a suite of rooms had been to apply soft folds and festoons of rich material to the walls and around windows. Regency England, influenced by the French, was becoming a curtain country, so here Beckford was in tune with his times. Most of the large reception rooms in the Prince Regent's Carlton House were swathed from cornice to skirting in crimson or rose-pink, their windows flounced, pelmeted, betasselled and pinned into swags and loops with contrasting folds of gold material interposed. Some of the reception rooms in Buckingham Palace, though a little later in period, still give an impression of those rich, airless, over-upholstered interiors, suggesting life lived out within a giant set of lavish silk ladies' underwear. Beckford's personal preference was for straw-coloured or yellow silk hangings to reflect the light and flatter displays of small bejewelled treasures; the Yellow Drawing Rooms at Fonthill were the heart of his living quarters. For that main south–north axis at the Abbey, however, with its relatively coarse detail and tunnel-like proportions, he relied upon much darker colours – scarlet and purple curtains, with some gold relief in their fringes to hint at his royal ancestry and to control the light flooding through the windows.

These rich fabrics presented a problem because he loved the visual release of plate glass, still at that time an innovative luxury. To compromise he usually confined Francis and Raphael Eginton's crude stained-glass saints and elders to the upper panes, and then both enriched and subdued the direct light with double draperies at every window, an inner purple and an outer scarlet curtain, bordered with the 'regal tressure' of the Kings of Scotland in white and gold. The effect must have been vaguely sumptuous and served to distract the eye from the repetitive plaster units of fan vaulting, identical in spirit and close in design to the vault of Walpole's Gallery at Strawberry Hill.

The effect of the northern sector of this axis was openly manipulated, more than elsewhere relying upon concealment because it had a flat, undramatised and non-Gothic ceiling. Its first stage, the King Edward III Gallery, was multi-crimson in its carpeting and walls, had the same double crimson–purple curtains on one side, and featured a solemn procession of portraits of Beckford's putative ancestors on its windowless east wall. Then came a deliberate piece of theatre, with the curious insertion of the claustrophobic 'Vaulted Corridor'. This had dark wooden walls and vaulting, the only light filtering through gilded trellis-work from the crimson-curtained windows of two flanking passages. Subdued by this gloom the visitor arrived suitably chastened at the Sanctuary and the Oratory, grateful for a little more light from candles on the Classical altar and for the delicate golden fan vaulting above it. Beckford was never satisfied with this area, and darkened the approach because the scale was so sadly domestic: 17 feet wide by only 18 feet in height. After the astonishing 50-foot draperies that hid some blank walls of the Octagon, this shrine of St Anthony was something of an anti-climax.

Wisely, Beckford lived in the rooms of the south-western villa. These could be easily heated (except, of course, for his bedroom) and must have been charming, lavish yet functional. With them, it is no longer possible to avoid some inevitably subjective discussion of Beckford's taste in fine art and objects of virtu. Obviously judgements here are bound to be personal, but in the late twentieth century it is now acceptable to make certain broad generalisations about homosexual and bisexual taste in and influence upon the arts. For instance, no one any longer conceals the fact that homosexual designers all but dominate the world of fashion, as they probably always have; and that many fine arts connoisseurs tend to the same sexual proclivities. There are undoubtedly some homosexuals with the most austere and refined decorative tastes, but generally theatrical excess predominates.

This is all a roundabout and tentative way of approaching Beckford's taste as a collector and suggesting that it often verged upon the self-indulgent and the indiscriminate. Before becoming lost in the usual list of the Old Masters he collected (and frequently sold at a profit, as he was a shameless dealer) and his various tazzas, nautilus cups, hookahs, sceptres, tankards and lacquer chests, it may concentrate the mind to analyse a typical piece, with a sound Beckford provenance, that came on the market in the summer of 1997. This was a jewel casket commissioned by Beckford in the early 1790s and ready for collection before 1802, by his favourite Parisian goldsmith and craftsman Henri Auguste after designs by Jean-

Guillaume Moitte, the cabinet-work probably by Weisweiler and the panels painted by Sauvage. Auguste's working drawings are inscribed 'for M. Beckford', and it is known that Beckford's agent Captain Williams stayed on in Paris over this dangerous period with the express purpose of overseeing commissions given to Auguste.

On the panels of the casket white cherubs fight the battles of Love on a blue-gold marbled ground. They are enclosed within delicate flower wreaths of gilded metal, and further oval wreaths of the same hang down at each corner of the casket, which is a sizeable object (45 by 26.5 by 20.5 inches) in honey-brown wood. It has an anthemion cornice of the same gilded metal and stands on a broad plinth of the same, with a Vitruvian scroll enclosing medallions, vases, tripods, altars and naked boys. That might seem enough craftsmanship for one piece, but there is more to come. The casket is raised to inspection level on four ebony legs, each topped with golden-winged seraphim and bound by wreaths of miraculously delicate metalwork; there is a tray half-way down, and each black leg ends in a knobbly gryphon's foot of the usual gilt metal, with stockings of golden leaves.

The casket and its incongruous but delightful legs epitomise Beckford's eclectic taste, hovering between the neo-Classical and the French Empire styles. It is visually diverting, but is it admirable? Does its beauty derive from the exquisite intricacy of its craftsmanship, or from the arresting mixture of its stylistic motifs? Is it, indeed, beautiful at all in the conventional sense? Would it have influenced contemporary taste? Is it of any significance to us now, apart from the superb workmanship of the Royal craftsmen who made it?

One crude answer to these questions is the fact that the casket must still be valued highly by collectors because in the sale it easily exceeded its pre-sale estimate of £400,000–£500,000. So the casket has more than kept its value; Beckford's taste and the cachet of his ownership have proved to be enduring. But was it 'good' taste, or merely one that art dealers and museum curators have perpetuated? A walk around the furniture in, for instance, the Wallace Collection, which is largely French, is an awesome experience, as a visit to Fonthill Abbey in its prime must have been; but is it positive or inspirational? Does it advance a visitor's understanding and appreciation of design and beauty?

Fonthill – the building, its decoration and its collections – obviously made such an advance. It was relevant to the whole confused and highly debatable area of nineteenth-century taste in this country, to a taste which tended to equate craftsmanship and sheer complexity with beauty. Beckford's jewel casket on its long black legs indicates that we have still not escaped from those values, despite the intervening periods of Art Nouveau, Art Deco and Bauhaus Modernism.

Was France the corrupter, the seducer, or the inspirer? Beckford and France were inseparable. He was ardently, uncritically Francophile. 'I adore Buhl,' he wrote, and the influence of André Charles Boulle (1642–1732, a dangerously long lifetime) is inescapable in French art of the eighteenth century. No one would question the fact that France's craftsmen, nearly all in fact Germans or Flemish, were far superior in skills to their English equivalents who, confusingly, were again often foreigners. The French could inlay anything with anything: gold, silver, brass, pewter, tortoiseshell, mother-of-pearl, ivory – name it, and the French could penetrate every kind of wood with every reasonable material in complex impressive patterns and make believe that it was high art. Buhl furniture was an aesthetic drug, and the single greatest European state was high on it. Beckford was completely smitten. There was buhl in almost every room of the Abbey, the two most celebrated pieces being the Aumont Armoire ('cupboard' seems too humble a term) and the secretaire of King Stanislaus, actually made by Reisner for the *arriviste* comte d'Orsay.

The Auguste jewel casket was not buhl, but it was a late representative of that overwrought, over-decorative tradition of design which Gérard, Boudin, Foullet, the Oeben brothers, Garnier, Baumhauer and Joubert had been pouring out for a century of over-sophisticated aristocrats. Beckford and the Prince Regent were equally guilty of depraving English taste by their indiscriminate Francophilia. In architecture they were both patriots and positive; in the fine arts they were negative or corrupt.

It is only a personal view of Beckford's influence, but one offered for consideration, that English design in furniture and silverware had, over the eighteenth century, evolved an elegance of form that was simple compared with French equivalents, but in no way inferior; and that by 1820 this tradition of design was in danger. Rich collectors like Beckford and his competitors in the auction rooms were flooding England with alien French design. The impact of all that alien if impressive craftsmanship in buhl, ormolu, glass, semi-precious stone and overwrought metal was to be disastrous. The country's taste broadened, and lost its way. French artefacts opened the door to the confused internationalism of the Great Exhibition of 1851. Antique dealer's art and Victorian taste are not far from being synonymous. It may appear a 'Little England' affectation to regret that rampant eclecticism, but it can be argued that it was a poor bargain to give up the rich variety of national styles, all evolving separately, for a mere international modishness directed by media appreciation and rock-bottom prices. Beckford's taste was informed, but it was still indiscriminate. The Prince Regent was less of an aesthetic menace. Like a magpie, he too collected everything from France that glittered or was gilded. Visitors today walking around the museum-like rooms of Windsor Castle can appreciate the way in which their rich contents are stylistically unrelated. But at least the Royal Family have kept their disparate acquisitions within their own palace walls. They have not, like Beckford, thrown them all out onto the open market to 'broaden' taste and give the buying public an appetite, not only for the overwrought, but for the aesthetic irrelevance of provenance.

For a salutary reminder of the native tradition which Beckford helped to destroy, it is only necessary to visit Stourhead, the Wiltshire house of his near-neighbour Richard Colt Hoare. In the Library, contemporary with Fonthill, a wonderful economy of line and colour informs every detail of the great writing table and the portfolio table, the set of armchairs, the library steps, and the simple green-and-ochre carpet. This is Regency taste at an effortless peak of restrained English understatement.

In absolute contrast, the St Michael Gallery was lined with expensive complexities like the Auguste jewel casket. Beckford imposed some aesthetic unity by introducing a black element into almost every piece of display. At that time the underpaid craftsmen of the Far East, Ceylon, Goa and Indonesia were providing cheap ebony furniture with ivory or mother-of-pearl inlay, and Beckford could pass this off as Tudor work, attributing some of it to Cardinal Wolsey's palaces. Faced with the same need to add a note of unity to an eclectic collection of bits and pieces at Strawberry Hill (the house Beckford claimed to despise, as a Gothic mousetrap), Horace Walpole made precisely the same use of black furniture in the rooms that needed authority most.

In his King Edward III Gallery, Beckford did something rather more original and much more influential: he persuaded English craftsmen to imitate several pieces of the most clumsily bulbous and fretted Jacobean furniture (this is, again, a subjective description of what could equally be described as a great period of native English design). He put those gouty sideboards one either side of the central chimney-piece in the Gallery; but instead of giving them their correct back legs, he had them set flush to large mirrors, so that all the objects of virtue laid on their shelves were reflected and doubled for easy examination. Between the windows on the other side of the gallery was a set of matching tables with candlesticks in the same neo-Jacobean style.

These pieces were commissioned between 1810 and 1818. The Victorian craze for things Jacobethan would not take hold until the 1830s, pioneered by George and Mary Lucy who began re-edifying their house, Charlecote in Warwickshire, in 1829 with a number of pieces originating from Fonthill Abbey. These included an ebony bed made from an East Indian settee, in which Nelson is said to have slept during his visit to Fonthill in 1801, and a sixteenth-century Italian *pietra dura* slab with a Jacobethan oak base designed for it by Jeffry Wyatville. Here we have Beckford, not importing an alien French example but reviving a native style, perhaps the most ornately challenging he could have fixed upon. Here he was, in a real, factual sense, a proto-Victorian for the better or for the worse: a founding father of the most eclectic period in British taste. There is no logical, connecting thread to link an Edward III gallery in a fake Gothic abbey with the style of Elizabeth and James I, though Horace Walpole had described the architecture and style of those periods as 'Good King James's Gothick'. It was the Abbey itself that steered Beckford into this twenty-year phase of hit-or-miss historicism.

Between 1798 and 1820 he and Franchi went through a period of designing often quite riotously historicist silverware together. As early as 1800 Beckford had commissioned Paul Storr to work grotesque details from Holbein onto some candlesticks, and Vulliamy was persuaded to do the same with a silver-gilt pair. Even Auguste supplied candlesticks of 'a Gothick pattern'. Later, in the teens of the new century, smallworkers and jewellers such as William Burwash, John Robins and Samuel Whitford were commissioned to set pieces of ivory and porcelain in silver mounts of the style of about 1600. Burwash and Whitford also produced salvers and dishes heavily decorated in a Venetian–Saracenic patterning which Franchi particularly favoured. Nothing to equal it would be designed again in English silverware until the 1840s. Yet as soon as Beckford moved to Lansdown Crescent in Bath in 1822, this phase ended and he reverted to Classical design. The Abbey itself appears to have cast a short, stylistic enchantment over him; he never became deeply committed to medieval design, unlike Pugin in the next decade.

Beckford's feeling for Gothic was always more theatrical than scholarly. William Hamilton designed a few competent-enough saints for the Egintons, father and son, to transpose, but those near-abstract effects of heraldic glass in the Octagon, with their Hamilton and Latimer devices, were Beckford's pride. The Lord Mayor's Chapel in Bristol has 28 lights of German and French Renaissance glass in its windows, all bought in the 1823 Fonthill sale, yet only a monochrome window of St Thomas à Becket designed by Benjamin West, now in the north aisle, ever featured in the Abbey: the Renaissance glass, once bought, was merely stored at Fonthill, despite its fine quality.

Intricacy and subtle craftsmanship in everything, not just in furniture, was irresistible to Beckford. Aware as always of his own weaknesses, he sometimes railed against his addiction, recognising that serious collectors are monomaniacs:

> I do not know where to turn – tempted here, robbed there, moaning and desperate to buy at one moment and then when I've bought something – ! It is the most intoxicating, feverish sensation you can think of.

It was better to be dead, he complained, than caught up in 'this fatal, expensive, ruinous, treacherous, cursèd activity'. At that time, the winter of 1814, he had just bought a disastrously expensive painting, one which seems from a late twentieth-century perspective foolishly overvalued, simply because it was elaborately detailed and finished: the lure of mere craftsmanship again. This was Gérard Dou's *The Poulterer's Shop*, now hanging in the National Gallery for anyone interested in comparing their taste with Beckford's. Dou was a pupil of Rembrandt. When Beckford discovered the painting in Paris he hailed it as work by 'the famous, stupendous and purest Gerard Dou ... this most rare and costly master'. He was tempted, bought it, and then tried to persuade the Prince Regent, with whom he was on distant but affable terms as a fellow connoisseur of the intricate, to buy it. The Prince declined.

Beckford lived between two periods of taste in art. He had been brought up by Alexander Cozens to value the 'Ideal', so in his first published book, *Biographical Memoirs*, he mocked the style which he instinctively preferred: detailed studies of carefully observed real life, as in sixteenth-century Flemish painting. When Venn Lansdown met him in 1838, Beckford was still paying lip service to 'the heavenly resignation, the very beau ideal' of his *St Catherine* by Raphael, though he sold the painting soon after to the National Gallery for a 4,000-guinea profit. He could appreciate the power of Velázquez' *Pope Innocent X*, but not really like the work: 'stupendous, but without that harmony which bids me buy imprudently'. Increasing age, however, converted him into a near-pre-Raphaelite. He owned a brilliant Cimabue altar-piece, and from the Strange Collection he bought a Cima da Conegliano, a Civetta and a Mazzolino di Ferrara, all originally in the possession of the Nuncio di Verona. The red, blue and gold colouring of early Italian primitives, as well as their careful detail, attracted him. What is not in doubt is his dealer's eye for quality, regardless of a painting's style or date.

In the Christie's catalogue of 1822, among quantities of eggshell china, Japan tea caddies powdered in gold and ivory carvings by 'great artists', there was a range of paintings which could have stocked a respectable national gallery. There were works by both the Poussins, Murillo, Bronzino, Bassano, Cranach, Van Eyck, the elder Breughel;

two Leonardos, an *Infant Saviour* and a *Laughing Boy*; Rembrandt's *Portrait of a Rabbi*; a Salvator Rosa of *Job and his Friends*, 'the pathos of his story greatly enhanced by the solemnity of the Colouring'; a Mantegna of *Christ in the Garden*; and two typical Wests – *St Michael with Falling Angels* and Abraham about to sacrifice Isaac. Tucked away among these masters, to represent Beckford in another mood, was a Fragonard of 'a lady in a red corset and satin dress, standing by her female attendant who is kneeling and chastening a favourite spaniel. Treated in the delicate and high-finished manner of the Dutch school.'

In December 1814, when his stay in Paris was driving Beckford into a frenzy of desire for art and boys, he was desperate to buy a Lorenzo Lotto, 'an onyx for its colour, an evangeliary for its purity of preservation', and was also attracted by a Leonardo da Vinci, 'for the grace and sweetness of its boys'. These descriptions are as revealing of Beckford as of the paintings: he was morbidly suspicious of restorations. But it was *The Poulterer's Shop*, a clever piece of genre painting, nothing more, which he bought and carried home in triumph.

As a patron of contemporary British art, Beckford was an enthusiastic failure. In 1817 he had to sell for £120 a history painting by Benjamin West that had cost him £600 thirty years earlier. Apart from J. R. Cozens, with whom he quarrelled bitterly, it is hard to find a British painter of worth whom he consistently encouraged; he sold most of his Turners because they were topographically inaccurate, and never bought a Constable. Apart from Old Masters, for which he had a good eye, his taste was directed to water-colour landscapes and doom-laden apocalyptic canvases by painters like Francis Danby. He bought Turner's *The Fifth Plague* because it illustrated a dreadful thunderstorm raging over a city of pyramids: a satisfying reflection of the famous Beckford rages, just as the water-colours responded to that other side of his nature, the pastoral and the Arcadian.

Where objects of virtue were concerned, he was on more confident ground. During that same trip to France he exclaimed in mock despair:

Alas, I was seduced by certain little Saxon tazza, sea-green bottles incredibly decorated with bronze, gilded in hell-fire – so bright and clear their colours. Two words breathed in my ear would have made me buy two fantastic Buhl armoire-like cabinets, magnificent, of a Salomonic richness, 400 livres the pair.

He did, in the event, buy the lot. Once back in Fonthill he was rhapsodising over the tazza: 'The two most sublime sea-green bottles with vine twigs etcetera, transparent, luminous and perfect, of a colour to rest and enchant the eyes.' They were for his private sanctum, the Yellow Drawing Rooms, where 'their divine, calm and cheerful splendour' made 'the most harmonious effect possible'.

Lust for art and desire for boys worked closely together in Beckford's mind, and between these descriptions of the tazza he reminisced to Franchi about the old days when he used to stay at the hôtel d'Empire and 'the nocturnal visits of the staff almost gave me a consumption'. How much better, he declared, to exhaust yourself sexually than to live chaste and frustrated as he was now: 'but I'm still alive,' he boasted, 'fit to troll the streets, fresh as a daisy and stiff as a Carmelite' – Carmelite friars, according to French folk-lore, were sexually hyperactive.

In such a mood he would complain to Franchi 'I cannot exist on agates, china and crystal; I need nourishment as a human being', but it was not true. The quivering emotion with which he brooded over his beloved tazza prizes proves that subtle swirls of abstract colour in glass, china and above all in semi-precious stones, could sustain him very well. Boys at his age were a fantasy indulgence: he had lost all his teeth, and never bought false ones; his nose and his chin were on a collision course, and someone of his pride and fastidious self-awareness could no longer take sex seriously; 'agates, china and crystal' endured, boys were ephemeral. He had cups of mammillated chalcedony, striated agate, white agate and riband agate, and their softly confused patterns of colour drew him irresistibly. 'Those lovely agates, alabasters and cornelians, mingled with the glittering mother of pearl' were his ideal.

The perfect Beckford purchase would combine the semi-precious – 'the largest known block of Hungarian topaz' – with a dramatic provenance – 'the undoubted execution of Benvenuto Cellini made as a marriage present for Catherine Cornaro, dragon handle in gold, tripod of three small dragons in green and blue enamel'. Add to those a personal association – Catarina Cornaro, briefly Queen of Cyprus, was a distant ancestress of his large-eyed lover in Venice in 1780 – and the artefact would deserve a place in his private rooms. There it could stand alongside boudoir curiosities like the 'coffer of Japan incrusted with animals of solid gold and silver formerly the property of Cardinal Mazarin', 'black and gold Japan salvers with Fuang Huang and foliage from the collection of the Duc de Bouillon' and 'a gold Japan cabinet with the arms of the Japanese Empire, storks and trees. This very curious article presented by the States of Holland to Lord Chancellor Clarendon' – always there was this need for provenance to eke out art. The true exposition of Beckford's taste in late middle age lay not in the Abbey's Gothic parts but in that double Yellow Drawing Room.

Rutter disliked the rooms intensely: 'the light from whose windows, already too numerous, is repeated by mirrors in every pier, and reflected from the gold and crystal and precious stones of a thousand articles of virtue which fill the armoires or cover the marbles of the room'. It was an antique dealer's paradise, all glitter: an oval cup of rock crystal 'from the Royal collection of France', a shrine from St Denys 'brought by St Louis from Palestine', and next to that a jewel casket which would acquire an almost equally resonant provenance for antique dealers of the future just because it was 'designed by Mr Beckford'. Then, to give some note of authority to that camp boudoir, 'an ebony armoire eight feet high'.

Although John Rutter, a Quaker by religion, was all but writing to Beckford's direction, he manages at this point to cringe a little at the Gothic disproportion of the room. John Britton, whose *Graphical and Literary Illustrations of Fonthill Abbey* came out in the same year, 1823, as Rutter's *A Description*, betrays the same stylistic unease at Beckford's daring, even though the book is written in a general tone not far short of hero-worship. It was those Jacobethan sideboards in the King Edward Gallery that Britton found hardest to digest, furnishings 'in which singularity if not beauty of design is as conspicuous as extreme labour and excellence of execution'. Rutter and Britton were men of eighteenth-century upbringing and stylistic reservations. Beckford, though older than either of them, shocked both by his eclectic daring. Born in 1760, he was still capable of edging a younger generation nervously forward into the wilderness of nineteenth-century stylistic experiment.

That was in art. In personal presentation Beckford was missing his moment. Those months of open house at Fonthill in the summer and autumn of 1822 could have been his chance to take the stage again. Society was coming to him, 7,200 of the great and the good. The Powderham scandal was forty years in the past; even the English can forget. The world had changed with Napoleon. He had shaken Europe like some horror-hero out of the German *Sturm und Drang*. Society by now had grasped the literary notion that heroes are not all perfect, can indeed be rendered more seductively heroic by their very imperfections. Women authors writing for women readers in the Minerva Press had popularised the idea of the sexually threatening Gothic villain–hero. In 1842 Heathcliff would capture the imagination of the reading public. More immediately there was Lord Byron, mad, bad and dangerous to know, promiscuous, even incestuous, whose death in Greece in 1824 would throw not just Britain but all intellectual Europe into mourning, young Tennyson and old Goethe alike; 1822 could have been the time for Beckford, once 'Vathek', now 'the Abbot', to posture magnificently. That organ in the Octagon could have presented the opportunity – solemn fugues resounding in those perfect acoustics, the visitors sitting entranced and then, stepping down modestly from the organ loft, the organist in person, the mysterious Mr Beckford, neatly dressed and all courtesy, dispensing a word here and a greeting there. He could have become acquainted with half the British aristocracy, on his own terms.

Instead he was busily scheming behind Christie's back with the auctioneer Harry Phillips, coaxing the almost senile gunpowder millionaire John Farquhar to believe that he 'ought to have a property of importance to elevate him', and that Fonthill Abbey with its park and some of its accumulated art treasures and junk was the property most likely to do so. Franchi was left to do the honours instead, but 'the Portuguese orange', crippled now with gout, was merely a reminder of old insinuations and a lost reputation. The organ, so far as any visitor has recorded, remained mute; Beckford had been snubbed too often by the hunting fraternity of Wiltshire to wish to retake English society by theatrical presentation. Either he had not noticed that Europe's concept of the hero had changed, or he had come to enjoy the role of a supposed monster.

Money was the distraction. Beckford had been 22 years in debt. Each bloodstone and silver tazza and every Flemish genre painting had cost him a grove of trees. The park creator had been forced to become a timber merchant. Sugar revenues from Jamaica had fallen each year, apart from that brief boom of 1813–14 which financed the East Transept. The price of male black slaves had gone through the roof. Lawsuits and elections had cost small fortunes; ships, uninsured, had been lost at sea; agents had cheated Beckford shamelessly, and on an epic scale. An appeal to his son-in-law, now the Duke of Hamilton, for a rescue package had been politely rejected.

Against all this depressing background Beckford, the magnificent obsessive, still wanted to build and so still needed to be rich. In his papers for these last two years at the Abbey are four careful sketches with a floor plan and details of windows. These illustrate a three-storey, 50-foot high Norman-Italianate tower and are captioned 'By Mr Beckford – for Mausoleum at Fonthill'. They represent a union of two enduring fixations: that adolescent fantasy of an Arthurian pavilion–tower with a first-floor dining room, and that morbid nightmare of a corpse still conscious after death. The damps and fungus of the Lancaster Gallery had obliged him to give up any idea of a high tomb in the Revelation Chamber of an Abbey which he was well aware was poised to fall. At 62 and scornfully indifferent to the fashionable host that had come driving up to his doors, he was still gloriously eager to begin again and achieve that tower at last, that safe resting place under a slab of clouded pink jasper.

As Harry Phillips played old Farquhar like a foolish fish, Beckford played for time. Without warning, the date of the sale was delayed by two weeks. On 27 September Mr Farquhar went down to view the property and then, on 8 October, when the great sale should have begun, the agreement was signed: £275,000 for the Abbey and the estate, £25,000 for the art treasures (or some of them) and the furnishings: a remarkable £300,000 in all. Beckford was rich again. 'I am rid of the Holy Sepulchre', he wrote to a Swiss friend, 'which no longer interested me since its profanation ... For twenty years I have not found myself so rich, so independent or so tranquil.'

'Rich'? Yes. 'Independent'? Yes. 'Tranquil'? Never. Only a year before he had written pathetically to his son-in-law about the prospect of losing his 'Holy Sepulchre': 'The purpose which (like so many other) I have most at heart is to save and inhabit this incomparable residence, which is more precious to me from this point of view than any other.' If he had to leave the Abbey, he said, he believed he would be like that man who had been a prisoner in the Bastille for 30 years and who, on being released, wanted to be imprisoned again. 'Therefore', he concluded abjectly, 'to retain a pied à terre such as this I am willing to sacrifice what has to be sacrificed with a joyful heart, and will adapt myself to the smallest income.'

No one called his bluff by enforcing these proposed economies, but it was not a likely tale. One of the many fascinating things about Beckford is that for every positive statement he makes, its negative contrariety can be quoted. On 20 December 1818 he had written despairingly to Franchi: 'in cold weather the Octagon is a horror, an inferno of draughts, and has an atmosphere of ice: without £3,000 or £4,000 to the Marquis de Chabannes [an inventor of a type of gas central heating] it will never be possible to live in it or even to walk across it for seven months of the year. Since I got back from Bath I have not gone any further than St Michael's Gallery.' He knew, from 26 years' experience, that the Abbey was functionally and structurally a failure. As a legend, however, it was incomparably a success.

An item in the *Gentleman's Magazine* for October 1822, the month of Mr Farquhar's purchase and the Christie's sale that never happened, seems to prove that the eyes of the nation, or at least those of the Gentlemen of the nation, were not only fixed upon Fonthill but misting over with nostalgia at the thought of Abbot Beckford's imminent departure:

> The pleasing vision is now past, and the noise of the Auctioneer's Hammer will not be heard – silence pervades the long drawn aisles – the lofty portal is closed – and the Abbot is returned to his Cloysters, with thanks to his Patron saint, St Anthony, for the numerous Pilgrims who have been attracted to his Shrine.

As usual with William Beckford, however, matters were not quite as they appeared. These reverential lines were not a mark of nationwide sorrow; they were written under the *nom de plume* of 'Viator', and 'Viator' was no other than Beckford himself, slyly covering up the deceit he had just practised and trying to make the whole confidence trick he had played sound elegaic, even devout.

The Abbot was not returning to his Cloysters: they belonged now to the gunpowder merchant. The time was right for a change. Beckford was too old and, against expectation, too English now to live abroad: 'I'm frightened by the far awayness of Italy,' he wrote; 'as a place to travel in, well and good, but to live there continuously – God save me from it!' Bath was a familiar place, a city he had often visited for its shops. Its newspapers had always given him a good press; it was elegant architecturally, full of old people more decrepit than himself, and it had doctors by the dozen for a rich hypochondriac to bully. He would settle there and build, after so many false starts, that Tower.

CHAPTER EIGHTEEN

Bath – the Tower, and the Disraeli factor

B eckford chose to settle in Bath at an intriguing time, when the city built for fashion had become deeply unfashionable. Instead of new terraces to house rich and modish visitors, its current major building project was Partis College, an almshouse for distressed gentlewomen. The regular Classical housing which had been Bath's pride was now considered an offence for its insistent horizontality, a wasted opportunity in a grand natural setting. Connoisseurs of the Picturesque like Uvedale Price had written disparagingly about the place and even Jane Austen's heroine Catherine Morland, in *Northanger Abbey*, was ready to reject 'the whole city of Bath, as unworthy to make part of a landscape'. The city, it was agreed, needed more trees and more points of vertical emphasis. So when the rumour went around that Beckford, author of the supremely vertical Fonthill Abbey, had bought land on Lansdown 'with a view to erecting a house in the same', the *Bath Chronicle* hailed the project: 'We may anticipate a model of architectural beauty.'

As late as 1817 Beckford had described Bath as 'incredibly dingy and wretched', full of predatory old woman and 'infamous old men'. But his great-uncle Charles Hamilton had retired there very happily and it does seem possible that he had for some time had his eye on young Henry Edmund Goodridge as an efficient, biddable architect, the absolute antithesis of James Wyatt. Goodridge was only 25 in 1822, but he was a Freemason and had been articled to John Lowder, a local architect who may have worked at Fonthill. Goodridge had enlarged a chapel in Bathwick in 1821, but it was only when Beckford began commissioning him in 1823 that his architectural career took off.

Initially disoriented by his descent from a Wiltshire hilltop into suburbia, Beckford faltered. He bought two-end-of-terrace houses separated by a wide mews road on Lansdown Crescent, and had Goodridge design a bridge with a gallery room to link them at first-floor level. The complex so rashly created failed to work, and he had to sell the smaller of the houses, only retaining the gallery–bridge to add an extension with an interior mini-vista to the pretentiously named Duchess of Hamilton State Apartment on the first floor of Number 20. This single house, he now accepted, would have to be his new, limited base. Though wealthy, he was no longer rich in the way he had once been; but he was still determined to live in style, and with the help of his gardener Vincent and of Henry Goodridge, he evolved an ingenious suburban 'sublime'.

First, he bought several small farms to gain control of all the fields between the back of his crescent and the top of Lansdown. Instead of turning them into a small park, which would have been the obvious reaction for someone of his generation, he kept the fields hedged and rural in aspect, actually sowing them with wild meadow flowers. Through them to the top of Lansdown he drove a linear park, no more than a bridle track for horse-riding, often only a few yards wide, but packed with picturesque incidents for the whole of its five-eighths of a mile length. On Lansdown, as a destination for his morning rides, Vincent was to create a garden and Goodridge a tower.

In the Beckford Papers at the Bodleian Library there are several careful drawings by Goodridge dated September 1823, versions of those sketches for a mausoleum tower which Beckford had intended to build at Fonthill; others are in Bath Reference Library and in the Hornby Library in Liverpool. In all the tower is heavily machicolated and fortress-like in aspect; one is Saxo-Norman, another is medieval Italian. By November 1826 the Lansdown Tower as we know it had taken shape. There is a sketch of that date in the Bodleian of a quite different building, with a plain shaft of smooth ashlar rising up to a wide Tuscan eaves cornice and above that a belvedere stage with three round-arched windows on each face. This is close in design to an

Italianate viewing tower which Thomas Hope, one of the rejected suitors for the hand of Susan Beckford, had built onto The Deepdene, his house in Surrey. What was to transform it into a tower which defies normal stylistic definition was the next stage: a free version, largely in cast iron, of the Choragic Monument of Lysicrates. By adding this purely neo-Classical feature to a plain Italianate viewing tower, the two designers had achieved a striking vertical emphasis for the Avon valley skyline. Both men had used the Choragic Monument before, Goodridge in an unexecuted design for a monument to Queen Charlotte, who had visited Bath in 1817, and Beckford for the canopy of a state bed for Splendens, so they would have been in agreement over using it as a crowning feature.

The Lansdown Tower was built, fitted up and complete by 1828, with its suite of rooms for study and leisure contained in a two-storey block next to the Tower. One step down from this on the other side was a single-storey block for a kitchen and basement. Almost by accident the Goodridge–Beckford duo had achieved the prototype of a middle-class villa, picturesque in outline and functional in its asymmetrical layout. The reception rooms were placed where they were needed, not where the confines of symmetry dictated. Goodridge was quick to realise the potential of this model. By 1828 he was building Montebello, a similarly picturesque Italianate villa for himself and his family, on the steep hillside of Bathwick, across the valley. Fiesole, La Casetta and Casa Bianca followed, to compose a mildly charming Tuscan suburb. These, with their irregular belvederes and small towers, were the relief Bath's monotonous horizontals required.

In his Lansdown Crescent complex Beckford had surrounded himself with the superior furnishings and paintings he had salvaged from Fonthill, buying them in when his old accomplice Harry Phillips held the sale in 1823 which Christie's had hoped to hold in 1822. Many extra items were smuggled in by Phillips to gain a Beckford provenance, which explains the frequent appearance at auction in the twentieth century of such bogus pieces. The Lansdown Tower had its own allocation of Old Masters, lacquer and porcelain, but for its furnishings and display cabinets Beckford made a complete break with his eighteenth-century past. He commis-

sioned Goodridge to design cupboards and sideboards with a unify-
ing motif of round arches carved with a coarse heavy moulding.
Strictly speaking these should be described as 'Williamane', as they
were evolved in the brief seven-year reign of the Sailor King, William
IV. However, surrounded by the usual heavy draperies, scarlet and
purple in one drawing room, crimson and purple in another, they
prefigure, in colour illustrations of the interior by Willes Maddox,
the decorative style of the Victorians. Once again Beckford was
ahead of his time.

The same is true of his linear park, up which, it will be recalled,
Venn Lansdown was conducted by a servant on his second visit to
'the great Vathek'. In its prime this precursor of the modern nature
trail or heritage route must have offered a delightful variety of visual
surprises. Immediately outside Number 20, in its back yard in fact,
was a pretty onion-domed Moorish kiosk, topped with a crescent.
This served as a miniature garden house in a small formal layout with
a pool, a quartz-pebble path, beds of flowers and – a Gardenesque
touch – vegetables. Above this, on the other side of the mews up a
steep terraced hillside, was the authoritative note of a large Norman-
style gateway, unscholarly in detail and heraldically spurious.

This gateway led to the true linear route, a steep climb up the
flowery meadows by plantations of young trees with ever-expanding
views opening out behind the visitor. At one point an original farm
was Tuscanised with round arches to create an effect more Claudean
than native English. Near the top the path sank into an old quarry.
There Vincent the gardener took advantage of the shelter to plant
flowers and shrubs: very much the tricks he had been required to
deploy in the woods at Fonthill, but far more appropriate up here
where flowers could grow without fighting a losing battle with tree
roots. This area merged into the Dyke Garden, still within the
quarry, a sunken way under mature apple trees which Vincent, an
expert in such transplanting, persuaded to flower though not to bear
fruit. A right of way across the path had been turned to advantage:
the route plunged down by a pool and a dripping wall of ferns into
a long grotto underneath the public lane. The grotto surfaced
dramatically into an arboretum of exotic foreign conifers, more
examples of Vincent's persuasive way with roots. There was a fir from

Larissa, a rose tree from Peking, Himalayan, Siberian, Scotch and Irish specimens, all planted around with the scented herbs Beckford relished. Out of this fragrant, entirely artificial wilderness rose the Tower, with books, art treasures and refreshments all to hand within a rosy, optimistic glow of controlled light. Beckford, blessed with eagle-sharp eyesight, climbed every morning into the belvedere room (or 'belvidere', as Goodridge insisted on spelling it) to survey through the twelve plate-glass windows how the world was faring.

Secure in the easy ritual of that morning ride attended by respectful grooms which so moved the reverential Venn Lansdown, Beckford's life should have been sinking to a mellow Tennysonian close. He had two small palaces of art, linked by a perfumed way. All he needed to do was annotate his books, add to his collections, and occasionally visit 'Cesspool House' – 127 Park Place, London, which he leased as a base for visits to the opera and for arguments with dealers and auctioneers. But the problems with its drains were never solved, and there was no sign that he was declining into a contented old age.

In August 1826, after elaborate preparations, Beckford set off for Rome, became painfully sunburnt before reaching Marlborough, and cancelled the whole trip in a fit of screaming rage when he arrived in London. Two years later Gregorio Franchi, the faithful – even, it might be assumed, the beloved – servant was dying in his London home, lonely, heavily in debt and guilt-ridden over the wife in Portugal and the daughter whom he had abandoned in order to serve Beckford. He was desperate for comfort. With unforgivable coldness his master–friend ignored all pleas for a last meeting and even absented himself from the funeral at Marylebone Cemetery. It was Duchess Susan who paid for a tombstone.

General Orde, Margaret's widower and the father of two of Beckford's grandchildren, both girls, was also short of money. Beckford was only prepared to help him if Orde would use his influence at Court to revive that 'lost' Beckford peerage – an impossible cause. A negative mood of splenetic rages seemed to have settled permanently over Lansdown. When a rival collector died, Beckford wished 'his well-spiced, port soaken carcass to be placed on the top of a Martinish-looking pile composed of his entire collections, brought forth from all their filthy sinks and dirty corners'. In his copy of Shelley's *Queen Mab* he scribbled:

> the very sort of production ... supposed to have come forth on the eve of the avenging Deluge ... when the original milk of human kindness had stiffened into a poisonous curd, and the abominable human animal, drunk with crime and with arrogance ... pillaged, tortured and violated without restraint, spat in the face of Nature, and denied his God.

Byron he described as 'running a furious muck with Serpents (which turned out to be stuffed eels) and pretending to whip himself into madness'. He had some excuse for laying into Byron, a fellow bisexual who had himself been passionately in love with a choir boy when he was up at Trinity but who still made lewd jokes about Beckford and Courtenay and wrote priggish and grossly hypocritical verses addressing Beckford as a man '... smitten with th' unhallow'd thirst Of Crime unnamed, and thy sad noon must close In scorn and solitude unsought, the worst of woes.' Beckford had every right to be glad that he had refused all Byron's pleas to be allowed to read the 'Episodes' of *Vathek*. But what had Shelley done to raise such spite?

Only two thoroughly deplorable literary ventures half surfaced in these dead, negative years between 1822 and 1832. One was a proposal to publish a collection of those venomous notes he had written in other men's books; the title was to be 'Flowers'. Nothing came of it, so we will never know, fortunately perhaps, Beckford's verdict on Keats's *Endymion*. The other was a malicious and sour-grape-ridden analysis of the present condition of the British peerage, listing all the misalliances and links with tradespeople that Beckford, himself descended from cobblers, was able to gather together. This was eventually published as *Liber Veritatis* in 1930, a graceless tribute to Beckford's memory.

This seemed to be the end: an angry, frustrated and unworthy twilight to a life of some real achievement. Beckford had built his Tower on Lansdown, a delightful toy and locally influential – yet against the successful construction of that tower must be set the ruin, long anticipated, of another. On the morning of 21 December 1825 the cracks and internal rumblings of Fonthill Abbey's central Octagon had become so alarming that John Farquhar and the servants gathered on the lawn outside. Mr Farquhar seems to have had, for a gunpowder merchant, an inappropriately calm and optimistic disposition, and he soon retired indoors for lunch and his afternoon nap. It was during his sleep that the Tower, an amalgam of decaying compo-cement, stone facings and timber bracing, collapsed quite quietly, pulling the central Octagon and the Great Western Hall down with it, raising a great cloud of dust and projecting one servant 30 feet along a corridor in a blast of compressed air – but not waking Farquhar.

Beckford had already covered himself with that tale of a contractor's death-bed confession of faulty workmanship; even so, Farquhar could probably have won a lawsuit against him, had he been so minded. Beckford's great building work was now a national joke. He too pretended to be amused by the collapse of the Abbey, but it cannot have been a boost to his morale. All he now had to look back on with pride was *Vathek*.

Then, in 1832, Beckford received an unsolicited present in the post: the latest novel by young Benjamin Disraeli. Its author had originally intended to give it the title 'A Psychological Romance'. But John Murray, its publisher, insisted that it should be called *Contarini Fleming: A Psychological Autobiography*.

At this point in Beckford's life any judgement has to be left to the reader. There is some evidence that Disraeli's novel, the third of the eleven he eventually published, transformed Beckford, roused him from a period of negative complaint and inactivity into one of renewed literary ambition. Nothing can be proven and without a personal reading of *Contarini Fleming* no judgement will be of much value, but the book is probably the key to Beckford's next ten years.

Disraeli's first and highly successful novel, *Vivian Grey*, was widely interpreted as being based on a number of living figures, and Byron's character is often suggested as the key to Contarini Fleming. But Beckford, usually so sour and hypercritical in response to other men's writings, appears to have taken the book as a personal compliment. He responded to Disraeli's gift, not with approval but with rapture.

In his letter of thanks to the author he declared: 'How wildly original! How full of intense thought! How awakening! How delightful!' The important exclamation in that response was 'How awakening!' To understand why Beckford was then tempted back into authorship, publishing *Italy; with Sketches of Spain and Portugal* (1834) and *Recollections of an Excursion to the Monasteries of Alcobaça and Batalha* (1835), two very well reviewed and admired works which established his reputation as an acceptable Victorian writer, it is essential to analyse the plot and style of *Contarini Fleming*.

The book has a flashy briliance, a glib profundity which makes it difficult to assess. Vulgar melodrama and descriptive passages of breath-taking immediacy alternate in a fast-moving narrative that makes for extremely easy reading. The sheer accessibility of the book and the mind of its creator alike rouse grudging suspicions. Can a great but eccentric nineteenth-century Prime Minister have also been a great and eccentric novelist? Can the lightning bolt of fame strike twice on the same individual? It has to be possible; certainly Beckford was bowled over by the writing and shamed into activity by the example of its hero. He *was* Contarini Fleming; therefore he must in his old age continue, like Contarini, to aspire, to write prose poetry.

The early chapters of the book must have achieved Beckford's seduction. It is narrated in the first person by Contarini himself. His Italian mother is dead and his father, 'the only person before whom I ever quailed', is a Swedish baron, a diplomat too busy at Court to pay much attention to his son. Contarini, like the young Beckford, wanders alone in a park with 'cool grots' and 'a mossy hermitage'. Like Beckford, he is an avid reader but finds his tutor's teaching 'a museum of verbiage'. As Beckford had his private devotion to St Anthony, so Contarini secretly worships Mary Magdalene. Sent to school he meets his Courtenay and the romance is described with such uninhibited gusto that Disraeli must have had bisexual empathies if not actual experiences:

There was a boy and his name was Musaeus ... it seemed to me that I never beheld so lovely and so pensive a countenance ... rich brown curls clustered in hyacinthine grace upon the delicate rose of his downy cheek ... I beheld him ... I loved him. My friendship was a passion ... he looked upon me with interest, and this feeling soon matured into fondness. Oh! days of rare and pure felicity when Musaeus and myself with our arms around each other's necks wandered together amid the meads ... I lavished upon him all the fanciful love that I had long stored up: and the mighty passions that yet lay dormant in my obscure soul ... I forced him to assure me, in a voice of agitation, that he loved me alone.

Beckford cannot have failed to identify with this: this was the love he had never dared to declare, here openly expressed. Contarini falls into a nervous fit, grows bored with Musaeus and presses on, arrogantly confident, entirely aristocratic and self-centred. A wandering artist called Winter becomes a philosophical influence over him, even though Contarini cannot draw well – the parellel with Beckford and Alexander Cozens is obvious. There are thoughts of suicide. In uncontrollable rage Contarini fights a bully and flings the battered 'half animate body' onto a dunghill – the famous Beckford fury, Vathek's terrible eye. A lovely older woman, a Louisa figure, comes and goes at unpredictable points in his career; he learns to dance exquisitely and speak fluent French, writes a ridiculous tragedy. Then, when his authorship of a brilliant novel titled *Manstein* (like *Vathek*, published anonymously) is made known, he decides abruptly to quit a promising political career and travel to find his true self.

At one level Contarini is still Disraeli; but being only 27 years old, the author seems to have looked around for the model of a controversial older man and picked from Beckford's life the incidents he needed to enrich his own. The ostensible aim of the book was to explain how incidents and influences combine to produce a surge of poetic inspiration. Ingeniously, Disraeli contrived his analysis to prove that poems were not needed to confirm a true poet. In a series of easy generalisations – and writing with brazen impudence in the time of Tennyson and Browning – his Contarini declares that poetry which depends on metre and rhyme is dead. 'Now at least, it was full time that we should have emancipated ourselves for ever from sterile metre ... Ah! Contarini, beware of your imagination.' Beckford, aware of his own lame verses, must have responded eagerly to this, and the passionate dedication could not fail to shame him into activity: 'I swore by the Nature that I adore, that in spite of all opposition, I would be an author, ay, the greatest of authors!'

Journeying with a faithful servant, Lausanne, Contarini visits Switzerland, his headquarters 'usually Geneva' by 'the fair and gentle Leman whose shores have ever been the favourite haunt of genius' – Beckford's place of education, and his honeymoon home. He goes on solitary rambles – 'there is something magical in the mountain air ... I dissolve into a delirious reverie' – as Beckford had, on the Salève. There follows the excitement of Italy, after a violent and staccato account of an Alpine crossing. Then, in Venice, 'this Aphrodite of cities', Contarini meets and courts his cousin Alcesté. In a deplorable scene Disraeli, obviously quite inexperienced in such matters, brings the courtship to a climax in a Venetian chapel: '"I come", I said, "to claim my bride." She screamed; she leaped upon the altar and clung to the great ebony cross ... I carried her fainting out of the chapel ... "I am yours, Contarini."'

Now married, Contarini and Alcesté take ship to Crete where their days pass in idyllic happiness, as did the Beckfords at la Tour de Peilz, but then Alcesté dies giving birth to a still-born son. Contarini again contemplates suicide, but Lausanne restores him to sanity. From that point onwards the book, having played a subtle fugue around certain events in Beckford's life, becomes no more than an interesting travelogue of Disraeli's own recent journeyings: Italy, Spain, Albania, Turkey, Syria and Egypt. Nevertheless, this section of the book must have been all the more influential once Beckford had identified himself with the fated bisexual hero of the first part. If Disraeli could write up his travels in Italy and Spain so engagingly, what was to prevent Beckford from doing the same? He could canibalise the book his family had censored, *Dreams, Waking Thoughts and Incidents*, and use his Portuguese notebooks to evoke that lost enchanted Ruritanian Lisbon of pre-revolutionary days.

In the end Contarini decides to live nobly. In Disraeli's wonderful 'Brewer's' English he declaims:

If I am to be remembered, let me be remembered as one who, in a sad night of gloomy ignorance and savage bigotry [i.e., the Reform

Bill of 1832], was prescient of the flaming morning-break of bright philosophy

Beckford's Lansdown Tower had recently been burgled by local colliers from Kingswood, so he may have identified with that outcry. He was obsessed with an old man's fears of change, riot and a rebellious under-class. (Venn Lansdown made the error of contradicting him regarding that craven fear.)

Contarini settled outside Naples, where he 'resolved to create a Paradise', and planned a tower, 'which shall rise at least one hundred and fifty feet'. Was it pure coincidence that the Lansdown Tower had risen 145 feet? 'This tower I shall dedicate to the Future and I intend that it shall be my tomb.' As he read that sentence, Beckford must have been shaken. It was what he had long intended, but had still not achieved. 'Here', Contarini–Disraeli concluded in pure Beckford mood, 'let me pass my life in the study and the creation of the Beautiful.'

Beckford could not have put it better himself. Could one book written in broad brush strokes of passion by a swashbuckling fellow author have whipped an idle, spiteful, old decadent into idealistic new life? Almost certainly it could, and did. Contarini had observed that 'after writing a book, my mind always makes a great spring ... I thought no more of criticism ... I want no false fame! ... But if I possess the organisation of a poet, no one can prevent me from exercising my faculty, any more than he can rob the courser of his fleetness, or the nightingale of her song!' Beckford could still think of himself as that courser and that nightingale. He eventually met Disraeli at the opera one evening, and they talked for three hours. George Clarke, Beckford's pet bookseller, had prepared him for the worst: Disraeli smoked like a chimney (a habit Beckford effetely loathed), he had greasy curls, a yellow complexion, and dressed like the high camp dandy he was. Disraeli's motives in orchestrating the relationship, as he undoubtedly did, are obscure. He was pleased with the old gentleman: 'he amused me very much ... I have had three interviews of late with three remarkable men – O'Connell, Beckford, and Lord Durham. The first is a man of the greatest genius; the second of the greatest taste; and the third of the greatest ambition.'

Beckford continued to correspond with his literary hero for five years, so he cannot have been entirely disenchanted; he had a fellow feeling for arrogance and for life as theatre, but not a trace of anti-Semitism. He may have seen Jews as romantic outsiders like himself and Disraeli's style, 'the loveliest and most superior I ever met with', as a flattering reflection of his own writing. Disraeli's next novel, *Alroy*, was, he believed, 'strongly imbued with *Vathek* ... partaking of the same awful and dire solemnity' – by which he meant the same aureate picaresque. His contact with Disraeli stimulated Beckford into putting the much delayed 'Episodes' from *Vathek* on the market again.

A more positive and enduring example of the inspiration of *Contarini Fleming* lies in the two books which Beckford not so much wrote as compiled, from scraps and leavings of the past together with half-memories and half-inventions. *Sketches* was a considerable critical success, with English, French and American editions. The *Quarterly Review* for June 1834 stated confidently: 'We risk nothing in predicting that Mr Beckford's travels will henceforth be classed among the most elegant productions of modern literature: they will be forthwith translated into every language of the Continent – and will keep his name alive, centuries after all the brass and marble he ever piled together.'

It was a verdict which must have gratified him, but not one with which it is possible to agree. His *Sketches* was cautiously edited to remove the youthful spontaneity of *Dreams* and his Portuguese journal. It ended up as a book which is self-satisfied, arch and consciously 'olde worlde' in its evocation of the *ancien régime*, inspiring nothing but regret for lost vulnerability and authenticity. The author of *Dreams* was a tremendous prig, but he was a real adolescent, posing as confident but unsure at heart. The author of the Portuguese journal did not condescend to the Portuguese as the re-vamper of *Sketches* did; he experienced them as equals. He was mistrusted, furtively lustful and socially often unsuccessful, but he felt no need to spin pompous lies about interviews with princes and Infantas which never took place.

As in art and architecture Beckford had the ability to move on, but where literature was concerned this moving on was from eighteenth-century directness to nineteenth-century artifice. Foreigners have become comical inferiors, good for a laugh with their quaint ways and picturesque customs – an ineffable Victorian superiority has settled upon the text. Yet it was not only as the 'great Vathek' but as 'the author of *Italy*' that Venn Lansdown revered Beckford before he ever met him. The book made Beckford's reputation and worked exactly as he intended it to work. Time had made him cautious.

His second venture towards Contarini's ideal – 'Create. Man is made to create, from the poet to the potter' – was the Alcobaça–Batalha book. As previously noted, this was a compression of a number of Portuguese journeys into one happy twelve-day excursion in the company of two old clergymen. To give it an air of authority Beckford pretended that they accompanied him by the express order of the Portuguese Prince Regent, and for the end of the trip he invented a sensational interview with Prince João in person at the Royal palace of Queluz. Some biographers rate this short piece as his finest writing, and it is indeed a delightful evocation of a lost world, authentic in detail even if contrived in construction. Beckford had some thin, pencilled notes to work on, and for the rest, his memory served him genially; he remembered only the shining hours of a pastoral country, and kindly, half-feudal clergy. The one episode in the book which lingers most hauntingly, the sound of the mad Queen Maria wailing in the darkness of a palace night, is probably based on nothing more than gossip and hearsay. His supposed *tête-à-tête* with the Regent is interrupted when 'the Queen herself, whose apartment was only two rooms off from the chamber in which we were sitting, uttered those dreadful sounds: '"Ai Jesous! Ai Jesous!" did she exclaim again and again in the bitterness of agony.' It is one of those events which, if they never happened, should have.

The Münchhausen streak in Beckford's nature must never be underestimated. Lies and imaginative inventions are inevitably confused in a man who could write *Vathek* at the age of 21 to express a parallel personal conflict. His tales of entering the lions' den in the zoo at Paris and that sinister Freemasonic subterranean temple with the magic vases can merge, imperceptibly in biographical material, into the Christmas revelry of 1781, a sexual foursome in Venice in 1780, a passionate relationship with Louisa, a cottage breakfast with

Alexander Cozens. Which were real events and which were the wish dreams of an old man reconstructing his past life to make it one of which Contarini in his tower would have been proud? If we recall Beckford's relationship with the King of Spain, Charles III, everything slips into perspective. As his daughter related the story, her father got on so well with the King (whom he never in fact set eyes upon) that he declared, as Beckford was leaving Madrid, 'Ask me a favour and it will be granted.' Ever the questing connoisseur, Beckford asked to be allowed to view the embalmed face of the Holy Roman Emperor Charles V, to check whether Titian had painted him faithfully. Done! said the King, and off went Beckford to the Royal vaults beneath the Escorial, where masons prised open the marble tomb and Beckford was able to gaze in satisfaction upon imperial mortality.

It is a tremendous story; and in that spirit, with some ten years on his hands and always a secretary to take dictation, Beckford set about the great revision. His life, purged and perfected, was going to be his best gift to posterity, a poet's life with none of that outdated nonsense of metre and rhyme. It is a rewarding experience, working through the long chain of biographies, studies and lectures which Beckford has inspired, to see how writers have taken his bait. Redding, the first, was so heavily censored by the Duchess and so stuffed with false reminiscences by Beckford himself that only the original Redding manuscript in the Bodleian is of much value. Subsequent biographers have tended to take their quotations on trust from one another. Melville, their prime source, quoted page after page of letters, actually written in a disarmingly legible secretary's hand, as true Beckford material written on the date when it claims to have been written. Chapman was more open than any in his suspicions that a confidence trick was being played: for instance, that all Beckford's witty and poised letters to Louisa with their implications of a long-standing romance were not what they claimed to be. Then there was all the elegant 'juvenilia' about an ideal tower, and any number of transcripts, often half-finished but in Beckford's handwriting, that may or may not have been accurate versions of letters really sent to his sister from Geneva. Where are the original letters? The Beckford Papers present an entirely different situation from that of Horace Walpole's vast correspondence. This was retrieved after Walpole had gone around himself, nagging and persuading to have years or even decades of letters returned and preserved.

Obviously there are some broad outlines of truth behind what Beckford has allowed later researchers to believe, but it was all contrived by a man with much to hide and a gloriously verbose literary model, *Contarini Fleming*, which he aimed to excel. It must have been the inspiration of Contarini's tomb-tower which caused Beckford, late in 1834, to commission Goodridge to devise a tomb in the upper corridor of the reception rooms at Lansdown Tower. There is no question about this at least, as Yale's Beinecke Library has Beckford's authentic letters to Goodridge in his own hand giving instructions: 'Form a marble panel in the centre of the present florr – conceal this pavemt. under a rich carpet – and keep the Tomb in a packing case till wanted.' At the same time, Goodridge was designing a tomb for Beckford's ailing spaniel. 'Do you still propose', Beckford queried, 'modelling the heads "d'apres nature"?' Death, from being something of a terror in his youth, was now becoming an enjoyable hobby. That corridor tomb may never have got very far, because there is a drawing in the Bodleian dated 28 May 1837 for a domed mausoleum, intended presumably to stand alongside the Tower. But this idea too was soon abandoned, for in a letter to Goodridge of 7 July he wrote: 'I have made up my mind, dear Sir, not to disturb the imposing solitude of L. Tower by the erection of a rival edifice.' The mausoleum appeared again in June 1843, the obsession still working in his mind a year before his death, when he already owned a perfectly adequate pink granite sarcophagus. Now the mausoleum was to be an extension to a gabled villa he had designed for his property at Milford, on the east side of Salisbury. A sketch in the Bodleian shows the domed building with urns at each corner and alcoves for at least eight coffins; neither the villa nor the mausoleum was built.

It was typical of Beckford's inattention to practical detail that he never noticed that legally he could only be buried on consecrated ground. As a result, when he did die, all his careful schemes to be laid to rest next to his dog up on Lansdown had to be deferred until his daughter had presented a plot of land there to Walcot parish and had it blessed; then Beckford's body in its above-ground pink granite sarcophagus had to be brought back up the hill from its first resting place in Lyncombe Cemetery, on the other side of the valley, and re-sited.

All the undignified posthumous travelling followed somewhat ironically upon the stately deliberation and artifice with which Beckford had approached his end. On 28 January 1844, to set his daughter on the wrong track, he wrote an enthusiastic account of a Roman Catholic funeral procession he had lately seen crossing Belgrave Square in London, with all the pomp of vestments, crucifix and a choir chanting the De Profundis: '*On se croyant à Rome: c'était ravissant. La populace, à ce qu'il paraît, l'a trouve tel – car elle s'est conduit avec un respect sans example.*' One of the endearing little affectations of the Hamilton–Beckford trio was that all three pretended to understand each other better in French than in their native language.

Then, as a 'final' communication, Beckford composed an elegiac farewell to his son-in-law the Duke, keeping two copies of it, one in French and one in English, for the record. It ended with the lines which every authority quotes, as everyone was intended to quote them. Spring was making its presence felt all the way up the linear park –

> Gia riede primavera
> Now spring returns, but not to me return.
> Those thrilling joys my vernal years have known.
> In the midst of this sweet renewal, and of this
>   pastoral charm,
> I remain – alas – sad and sickly – I am not tired of life,
>   but life is tired of me.

An unwise excursion up the hill in an east wind fulfilled this prophecy. Beckford lay coughing on his truckle bed, complaining about doctors but still mean-minded enough to have his dog's sleeping blanket burnt. It would be instructive to know what actually happened to the poor dog: was there to be a suttee ceremony? Then he wrote emotionally to his daughter, demanding the comfort of her presence, as Gregorio Franchi had asked in vain for his presence in the same circumstances: '*O abrégez la distance! – O abrégez la! –* fatal distance.' As a loving daughter she came and offered, with a woman's instinctive tact, to bring in a Catholic priest to give her father the last rites which he appeared to crave. He refused them. The less romantic services of a Church of England parson were suggested next; these too he stoically refused.

Finally, Henry Goodridge had his revenge for all the years he had endured of anecdotes repeated, advice rejected and rages blandly absorbed. Now that the old tyrant was immobile and silent, he took his chance:

> I suggested to her Grace that she should ask Dr B. to draw his attention to the near approach of death, which she did; – and he very kindly undertook to do so. Dr B. informed me, that when speaking to him on our common depravity – that we had no merits of our own – but must all come as guilty sinners to a crucified Saviour, whose atonement alone was sufficient for a penitent, he listened with much calmness and attention, clasping his hands with evident approval and acquiescence.

Or was it, more probably, with suppressed fury at such impertinence? Had St Anthony still got matters under control?

That was on 1 May 1844. Beckford died the next day, secure in the confidence that his legend was launched, and so peacefully that the exact time of his passing went unremarked. For his tomb he had prepared two inscriptions, both surprisingly optimistic. At one end:

> "ETERNAL POWER!
> GRANT ME THROUGH OBVIOUS CLOUDS ONE TRANSIENT GLEAM
> OF THY BRIGHT ESSENCE IN MY DYING HOUR."

Why 'obvious', one wonders? But Beckford was always a mediocre versifier. At the other end was inscribed a deliberate denial of the doom of Vathek. The Caliph and Nouronihar 'lost the most precious of the gifts of Heaven – Hope'. William Beckford lay there,

> "ENJOYING HUMBLY THE MOST PRECIOUS GIFT OF HEAVEN – HOPE".

Manuscript Sources

In a biography like this, intended for the informed, intelligent reader, I believe that footnotes are entirely out of place. So many people write doctoral theses in our hyper-educated times that the tiresome but necessary impedimenta of scholarship have slipped insidiously into several biographies. These should, in my view, be written in clear, inclusive English; if a detail is important, then it should find its place in the text, not in a gutter at the foot of the page or in a far more interruptive section at the end of the book. I have prepared a list of sources for anyone who may wish to follow up my reading. The majority of my quotations, roughly seven-eighths of the total, were taken directly from the Beckford Papers in the Bodleian Library, Oxford. These have been professionally catalogued and are all perfectly accessible. My advice to a scholar following up any Beckford study is to read these and trust no quotation from any printed source.

Bodleian Library, Oxford
The Papers of William Beckford (1760–1844); catalogue compiled by
    T. D. Rogers, 1987. The following is a list of those sources which
    have been useful in the preparation of this biography:

	Correspondence
MSS. Beckford c.1–11	Beckford to Franchi in Italian (1807–28).
MSS. Beckford e. 1	The 'Red' copy book, supposedly to Cozens, most in a secretarial hand.

MSS. Beckford c. 15	Falmouth letters, and letters to Pitt.
MSS. Beckford c. 17	From Louisa, and drafts from Beckford to Louisa.
MSS. Beckford d. 1	As c. 17.
MSS. Beckford c. 18	Origin of the Halls of Eblis, Lady Craven's 'Pastoral'.
MSS. Beckford c. 28	Drafts to Cozens.
MSS. Beckford c. 31	From Sir William and Lady Hamilton.
MSS. Beckford c. 32	Drafts to his half-sister; letters from Henley.
MSS. Beckford c. 33	To and from Lettice; drafts concerning puppets at Eton.
MSS. Beckford c. 36	From Verdeil.

Journals and Travels

MSS. Beckford e. 2	'Little green notebook': travels in Switzerland.
MSS. Beckford d. 3	English tour of 1780.
MSS. Beckford c. 43	Portuguese *Journal.*
MSS. Beckford d. 7	Notes and drafts for *Alcobaça and Batalha.*

Literary Papers

MSS. Beckford e. 3	Juvenilia.
MSS. Beckford d. 10	Fonthill foreshadowed.
MSS. Beckford c. 47	'Satyr's Range' and 'Fountain of Merlin'.
MSS. Beckford c. 11	'L'Esplendente'.
MSS. Beckford c. 12	'Histoire de Darianoc, Jeune Homme du Pays de Gou-gou'.
MSS. Beckford c. 48	Fragments of Nouronihar.
MSS. Beckford d. 13	'Histoire des deux princes'.

Miscellaneous Papers

MSS. Beckford c. 84	Vevey testimonial; French report; Pitt's petition; Milford Villa drawings.
MSS. Beckford b. 8	Soane state bed for Splendens.
MSS. Beckford c. 85–6	Draft of 'Memoirs of William Beckford Esqr.' By Cyrus Redding.

*

Manuscript Sources

MSS. Eng. lett. c. 687–95 — Boyd Alexander Papers: Working notes relating to Alexander's published works on Beckford.

MS. Beckford c. 27, fols. 9–49 — John Britton–Beckford Correspondence

Bath Public Library
Letters from Beckford to Clarke and Franchi.
Scrapbook entitled 'Fonthill Abbey' presented by Captain Frederick Henry Huth.
Design for the Lansdown Tower by Henry Edmund Goodridge.

Victoria Art Gallery, Bath
Drawings and paintings by Goodridge and Henry Venn Lansdown.

Beinecke Library, Yale University, New Haven, Connecticut
William Beckford Collection (Gen. MSS. 102).

British Library, London
Watercolours by J. M. W. Turner and drawings by James Wyatt of Fonthill Abbey.

Brown, Picton and Hornby Libraries, Liverpool
Designs for the Lansdown Tower by Henry Edmund Goodridge.

Library of the Wiltshire Archaeological & Natural History Society, Devizes Museum
John Britton archive relating to Fonthill.
Drawings by Beckford for Mausoleum at Fonthill.
John Buckler drawings of Fonthill.

Fonthill Estate Office, Fonthill Bishop, Salisbury
Material relating to the landscaping at Fonthill and several reports commissioned from the Debois Landscape Survey Group

Print Room, Victoria and Albert Museum, London
Design for a monument to Queen Caroline by Henry Edmund Goodridge.

Manuscript Sources

Royal Institute of British Architects Drawings Collection, London
Drawings by James Wyatt for Fonthill.

Sir John Soane's Museum, London
Bills relating to the Picture Gallery, State Bed and chimney-pieces for
  Fonthill Splendens.

Royal Collection, Windsor
Manuscript of Joseph Farington's Diary.

Select Bibliography

Books by William Beckford

Biographical Memoirs of Extraordinary Painters, 1780
Dreams, Waking Thoughts, and Incidents, 1783
Vathek, 1786
Popular Tales of the Germans, 1791
Modern Novel Writing, 1796
Azemia, 1797
Italy; with Sketches of Spain and Portugal, 1834
Recollections of an Excursion to the Monasteries of Alcobaça and Batalha, 1835
The Episodes of Vathek, 1912
The Vision and Liber Veritatis, 1930

Secondary Sources

Alexander, Boyd (ed.), *The Journal of William Beckford in Portugal and Spain: 1787–1788* (Rupert Hart Davies, London, 1954)
——(ed.), *Life at Fonthill: 1807–1822* (Rupert Hart Davis, London, 1957)
——, *England's Wealthiest Son* (Centaur Press, London, 1962)
Ballantyne, Andrew, *Architecture, landscape and liberty: Richard Payne Knight and the picturesque* (Cambridge University Press, 1997)
Beard, Geoffrey, *Upholsterers and Interior Furnishing in*

England 1530–1840 (Yale University Press, New Haven & London, 1997)

William Beckford Exhibition 1976, Tisbury, Wiltshire (Catalogue)

William Beckford and Portugal, exhibition catalogue entitled 'A Viagem de uma paixao', Palácio de Queluz, 1987

Bower, C.R., *The Portuguese Seaborne Empire 1415–1825* (Hutchinson, London, 1969)

Britton, John, *Graphical and Literary Illustrations of Fonthill Abbey* (London, 1823)

Brockman, H.A.N., *The Caliph of Fonthill* (Werner Laurie, London, 1956)

Chapman, Guy, *Beckford* (Jonathan Cape, London, 1937)

Clark, Kenneth, *The Gothic Revival: An Essay in the History of Taste* (John Murray, 3rd edn, London, 1962)

Costa, Francisco, *Beckford en Sintra no verao de 1787* (Camara Municipal de Sintra, 1988)

Crook, J. Mordaunt, *The Greek Revival: Neo-Classical Attitudes in British Architecture 1760–1870* (John Murray, London, 1972)

——, *The Dilemma of Style: Architectural Ideas from the Picturesque to the Post-Modern* (John Murray, London, 1987)

Dale, Antony, *James Wyatt, Architect: 1748–1813* (Basil Blackwell, Oxford, 1936)

Davis, Terence, *The Gothick Taste* (David & Charles, Newton Abbot, 1974)

De Sandisson, Mr *The Adventures of Abdalla, son of Hanif* (translated by William Hatchett) (London, 1729)

Disraeli, Benjamin, *Contarini Fleming: A Psychological Romance* (Peter Davies, London, 1927)

Effra, Helmut von & Staley, Allen, *The Paintings of Benjamin West* (Yale University Press, New Haven & London, 1986)

The Diary of Joseph Farington, Kenneth Garlick, Angus Macintyre and Kathryn Cave (eds), 16 vols (Yale University Press, New Haven & London, 1978–1984)

Fisher, Stephen (ed.), *Lisbon as a Port Town, the British Seaman and other Maritime Themes* (University of Exeter, 1988)

Fitzpatrick, William john, *The Life, Times and Contemporaries of Lord Cloncurry* (Dublin, 1855)

Fothergill, Brian, *Beckford of Fonthill* (Faber, London, 1979)

Magnificent Effects at Fonthill Abbey, Wilts., Christie's Auction Catalogue, 1–10 October, 1822

Gemmett, Robert J., *William Beckford* (Boston, 1977)

Girod, Louis, *Evian et le Chablais* (Cabedita, Evian, 1993)

Grey, Zachary, *A farther Account of Memorable Earthquakes* (J. Bentham, Cambridge, 1756)

Hibbert, Christopher, *The Grand Tour* (Methuen, London, 1987)

Jack, Malcolm (ed.), *Vathek and Other Stories: A William Beckford Reader* (William Pickering, London, 1993)

——, *William Beckford: An English Fidalgo* (AMS Press, New York, 1996)

Jackson, Neil, *Nineteenth Century Bath: Architects and Architecture* (Ashgrove Press, Bath, 1991)

Jacques, David, *Georgian Gardens: The Reign of Nature* (Batsford, London, 1983)

Jenkins, Ian & Sloan, Kim, *Vases and Volcanoes: Sir William Hamilton and his Collections* (British Museum Press, London, 1996)

Jomini, Edmund, *Dr François Verdeil, un grand Vaudois: 1741–1832* (Imprimerie Jordan Fils, Lausanne, 1950)

Kendall, Paul Murray, *Louis XI* (George Allen & Unwin, London, 1971)

Lansdown, Henry Venn, *Recollections of the Late William Beckford* (1893: Kingsmead Reprints, Bath, 1969)

Views of Lansdown Tower, from drawings by Willes Maddox (Edmund English, Bath, 1844)

Lees-Milne, James, *William Beckford* (Compton Russell, Tisbury, Wiltshire, 1976)

Philippe Jacques de Loutherbourg, RA, GLC exhibition catalogue, London, 1973

Mahmoud, F. Moussa (ed.), *William Beckford of Fonthill 1760–1844* (Cairo, 1960)

Masefield, Muriel, *Peacocks and Primroses: A Survey of Disraeli's Novels* (Geoffrey Bles, London, 1953)

Mathew, David, *Catholicism in England* (Eyre & Spottiswood, London, 1936)

Select Bibliography

Meister, Henri, *Letters Written During a Residence in England* (1799)

Melville, Lewis, *Life and Letters of William Beckford* (Heinemann, London, 1910)

Millington, Jon (ed.), *Souvenirs of Fonthill Abbey: An exhibition to commemorate the 150th anniversary of the death of William Beckford* (Bath Preservation Trust, 1994)

Mitchell, John, *Conjectures Concerning the Cause and Observations upon the Phaenomena of Earthquakes* (London, 1760)

Mowl, Timothy, *Horace Walpole: The Great Outsider* (John Murray, London, 1996)

Neale, J.P., *Graphical Illustrations of Fonthill Abbey, the Seat of John Farquhar* (Sherwood Jones, London, 1824)

Oliver, J.W., *The Life of William Beckford* (Oxford University Press, London, 1932)

Oppé, Adolf P., *Alexander and Robert Cozens* (Charles Black, London, 1952)

Parissien, Steven, *Regency Style* (Phaidon, London, 1992)

Parreaux, André, *Beckford et le Portugal en 1787* (Livraria Bertrand, Paris, 1955)

——, *William Beckford, auteur de Vathek* (Nizet, Paris, 1960)

Pevsner, Nikolaus & Cherry, Bridget, *The Buildings of England: Wiltshire* (Penguin, Harmondsworth, Middx., revised edn, 1975)

The Travels Through England of Dr Richard Pococke, J.J. Cartwright (ed.) (Camden Society, New Series, vol. 44, 1889)

Pradère, Alexandre, *French Furniture Makers: The Art of the Ébéniste from Louis XIV to the Revolution* (Sotheby's, London, 1989)

Quest-Ritson, Charles, *The English Garden Abroad* (Viking, London, 1992)

Ralph, Elizabeth & Evans, Henley, *St Mark's, The Lord Mayor's Chapel, Bristol* (City of Bristol, 1979)

Redding, Cyrus, *Memoirs of William Beckford of Fonthill, Author of Vathek*, 2 vols. (Charles J. Skeet, London, 1859)

Robinson, J.M., *The Wyatts: An Architectural Dynasty* (Oxford University Press, 1979)

Rutter, John, *A Description of Fonthill Abbey and Demesne* (Shaftesbury, 1822)

——, *Delineations of Fonthill and its Abbey* (Shaftesbury & London, 1823)

Sloan, Kim, *Alexander and John Robert Cozens: The Poetry of Landscape* (Yale University Press, New Haven & London, 1986)

Storer, James, *A Description of Fonthill Abbey, Wiltshire, Illustrated by Views* (London, 1812)

Stroud, Dorothy, *Sir John Soane, Architect* (Faber, London, 1984)

Sulivan, Richard Joseph, *A Tour Through Parts of England, Scotland and Wales in 1778* (1785)

Summers, Peter & Bishop, Philippa, *William Beckford – some notes on his life in Bath: 1822–44* (Bath, 1966)

Tonioli, Girolamo, *Il Tributo: A Pastoral Cantata* (Collins & Johnson, Salisbury, 1781)

Victoria County History: Wiltshire, vol. 13 (1987)

Wainwright, Clive, *The Romantic Interior: The British Collector at Home 1750–1850* (Yale University Press, New Haven & London, 1989)

Warner, Revd Richard, *Excursions from Bath* (1801)

Waterfield, Giles (ed.), *Soane and Death* (Dulwich Picture Gallery, 1996)

Watkin, David, *Thomas Hope 1769–1831 and the Neo-Classical Idea* (John Murray, London, 1968)

——, *The English Vision: The Picturesque in Architecture, Landscape & Garden Design* (John Murray, London, 1982)

——, *The Buildings of Britain: Regency* (Barrie & Jenkins, London, 1982)

Whinney, Margaret, *Sculpture in Britain 1530–1830* (Pelican, Harmondsworth, 1964)

White, Roger & Lightburn, Caroline, *Late Georgian Classicism: Papers given at the Georgian Group Symposium 1987* (Georgian Group, London, 1988)

Williams, J. Anthony, *Catholic Recusancy in Wiltshire: 1660–1791* (Catholic Record Society, London, 1968)

Williamson, Barry, *Lord Arundell's Park at Wardour* (Barry Williamson, Bristol, 1997)

Wilton, Andrew & Bignamini, Ilaria, *Grand Tour: The Lure of Italy in the Eighteenth Century* (Tate Gallery, London, 1996)

Select Bibliography

Articles

Alexander, Boyd, 'William Beckford as Patron', *Apollo*, July 1962
——, 'Fonthill, Wiltshire, II and III: The Abbey and its Creator', *Country Life*, 1 and 8 December 1966
The Beckford Journal, edited by Jon Millington, Spring 1995 (volume 1) onwards
Bishop, Philippa, 'Beckford in Bath', *Bath History*, vol. 2, 1988
Brockman, H.A.N., 'Fonthill Abbey', *Architectural Review*, June 1944
Crallan, Hugh, 'Beckford's Houses in Bath', *Architectural Review*, March 1968
De Beer, Gavin, 'Anglais au Pays de Vaud', *Review Historique Vaudois*, 1951
Harris, John, 'Fonthill, Wiltshire – I: Alderman Beckford's Houses', *Country Life*, 24 November 1966
Hauptman, William, 'Beckford, Brandoin and the "Rajah"', *Apollo*, May 1996
Kann, Roger, 'Marquise de Santa Cruz: Lettres d'amour à William Beckford', in *Studies on Voltaire and the eighteenth century* (Voltaire Foundation, Oxford, 1986)
Lees-Milne, James, 'Beckford in Bath', *Country Life*, 29 April 1976
Mowl, Timothy, 'The Williamane – Architecture for the Sailor King', in *Late Georgian Classicism* (Georgian Group Symposium, 1987)
——, 'A Taste for Towers', *Country Life*, 1 October 1987
Rowan, Alistair, 'Wardour Chapel', *Country Life*, 10 October 1968
Townshend-Mayer, Mrs G., 'The Sultan of Lansdown Tower', *Temple Bar*, vol. 120 (May–August, 1900)
Wainwright, Clive, 'Some Objects from William Beckford's Collection now in the Victoria and Albert Museum', *Burlington Magazine*, May 1971
Wilton-Ely, John, 'The Genesis and Evolution of Fonthill Abbey', *Architectural History*, vol. 23, 1980
——, 'A Model for Fonthill Abbey', in *The Country Seat* (Allen Lane, London, 1970)
Wilson-North, Robert, 'Witham: From Carthusian monastery to Country House', *Current Archaeology*, no. 148 (June 1996)

Index

NOTE: Works by Beckford appear directly under title; works by others appear under authors' names

Index

Beckford, Maria (*cont.*)
with William, 102; and WB's paedophilia, 107–8; writes words for Rauzzini's *Il Tributo*, 108; alarm at WB's moral reputation, 123; nurses Margaret in Paris, 125; and WB's exile abroad, 130; arranges WB's return from exile in Switzerland, 140–1; and WB's return from abroad, 202; WB's relations with, 203–6; death and funeral, 235–6; WB writes of building work to, 235

Beckford, Peter (WB's cousin), 87

Beckford, Peter (WB's grandfather), 25–6

Beckford, Peter (WB's uncle), 26

Beckford, Richard (Alderman Beckford's illegitimate son): independent life, 19; closeness to father, 26; in father's will, 37–8, 75; litigation over Jamaica property, 97–8, 140

Beckford, Richard (WB's uncle), 26–7

Beckford, William: biographical sources, 1–3, 245–7, 251, 301–2; twenty-first birthday celebrations (1781), 1, 103–6, 109–10, 113, 167; appearance and manner, 9, 42, 282; art collection, 9–14, 270–1, 274–84; death and burial, 18–19, 302–4; political views, 18; generosity to poor, 21–2, 60, 229; sexual life and interests, 23, 31, 70, 74, 77–8, 87–8, 90–1, 93–4, 100, 104, 157, 165–6, 174–5, 193, 252–3, 257–8, 263–4, 281–2; achievements, 24; background and family, 25–6; birth, 30; upbringing and education, 30–2, 38–40; artistic endeavours, 39–41, 44–6, 75; juvenile writings, 39, 41–3, 45–6, 60; lacks boyhood friends, 40; and Roman Catholic church, 43–4, 56, 65, 73, 92, 151–2, 155, 158–66, 177–8, 187–8, 200, 261; Freemasonry, 44, 56, 60, 64, 125–6, 138, 209, 300; stays in Switzerland, 45, 47–9, 53, 55–6, 59–60, 64, 66–8, 74–8; as art critic, 47–8, passion for music and singing, 51, 89, 92, 94–5, 98, 154, 178–80, 186, 194, 201; superstitiousness, 56; idealises simple life, 57–8, 60, 64, 68, 77; writing style, 65–7, 92–3, 114, 120–1, 142–4, 174, 185, 300; and the Gothic, 69–70, 80, 104, 177, 184, 222, 232, 234, 242, 247, 256, 279; pilgrimage to Grande Chartreuse, 72–4, 81; semi-vegetarianism, 73, 121, 170; physical activities and sports, 75; declines political career, 79–80; poetic instincts and writings, 80–4, 222–3; on Grand Tour, 81, 84, 89, 90–101; Romanticism, 83–4; infatuation with William Courtenay, 84–7, 90–1, 96, 100–2, 107–9, 111, 116, 123, 125–6, 156, 157, 187; tour of England (1779), 84–6; as animal-lover, 87, 121–2, 154; presented at Court, 89; pantheism, 96; Jamaican

financial problems, 97–8, 119, 130, 140; open-air childhood, 97; hypochondria, 99, 264, 287; rewrites letters, 103, 107; active paedophilia, 104, 107, 109; marriage to Lady Margaret, 111, 123–4; moderation and fastidiousness, 111, 264; social performances and dancing, 116–17, 119, 164, 166–7, 174, 199; illness in Naples, 119–20; influence over parliamentary boroughs, 119; knowledge and use of French, 120, 134, 303; and Margaret's miscarriages, 125–6; parliamentary career, 126, 251, 253; seeks barony, 126; public scandal over relations with Courtenay, 127, 130–1, 201, 210; birth of daughters, 128, 132; exile abroad, 128, 129–34; and wife's death, 130, 133, 138, 140, 154–5, 183–4; and English publication of *Vathek*, 136; returns from exile to Fonthill, 140, 202–3; sails for Jamaica, 140–4; first visit to Portugal (1787), 144–90; and children, 154; moves to Ramalhão (Sintra), 168, 169–71; knowledge of Portuguese language, 183; responses to religion, 188–9; leaves Portugal for Madrid, 190, 191–3; obsession with death and burial, 192, 222, 236–7, 285, 302; life in Madrid, 193–200; Meister describes, 201–2; travels, 201–2; melancholy, 202; pseudonyms, 205–6; in Paris during Revolution, 208–9; in Switzerland during French revolutionary wars, 209–11; wealth, 210, 226, 258, 285–6; proposed French citizenship, 212–13; revisits Portugal (1793), 213, 214–20; near-capture by Barbary pirates, 220; reception in England on return from Portugal, 220; fails to acquire peerage, 225, 292; seeks peace deal with France, 225–6, 229; entertaining, 228–9, 239; as art patron, 230, 233, 281; financial difficulties and debts, 235, 285; final visit to Portugal (1798), 236–7; use of nicknames, 246, 249, 263; self-knowledge, 247; wartime stay in Paris (1801–3), 248–50; mental state, 256; manservants, 262–4; good health, 264–5; open-air activities, 264–5; landscape gardening, 265–8, 289, 291–2; sells and leaves Fonthill, 269–71, 284–7; Francophilia, 276; designs silverware, 279; moves to Bath, 287–9; rages, 292–3; inspired by Disraeli's *Contarini Fleming*, 294–302; fear of change and rebellion, 298; lies and imaginative inventions, 300–2

Beckford, Alderman William (WB's father): speech to George III, 11, 30, 89; portrait, 18; career, 26, 30; illegitimate children, 26, 33; inheritance, 26; buys and develops Fonthill House and Park, 27–8, 32–3, 35–7, 44, 49, 96, 265; marriage, 29; death and will, 30,

Index

Index

Hoare (London builder), 29
Hoare, Henry, 1st Baron, 38
Hoare, Richard Colt, 277
Holland (Netherlands), 90
Holland, Henry, 81
Hooper, William: translates Gessner, 81
Hope, Thomas, 250, 290
Hopper, Thomas, 243
Horne, Thomas, 147–8, 156, 163, 169
Howard, Sir George, 89
Huber, François, 59
Huber, Isabella (*née* Ludovisi), 60
Huber, Jean, 59–60, 93; death, 139–40
Huber, Jean-Daniel: friendship with WB, 59–60, 68, 74–8, 124, 132; art, 60, 75; lost illustrations for *Vathek*, 122
Huber, Pierre, 59

Imperiali, Mme, 198
Infantado, Duke of, 195, 198
Italy, 91–8, 115, 119–20
Italy; with Sketches of Spain and Portugal (WB): as source, 1; Venn Lansdown quotes from, 13; Chartreuse in, 73, 192; published, 92, 145, 295; and WB's stay in Lisbon, 145, 151; on meeting with Prince of Brazil, 181; and WB's meeting with Archbishop São Gaetano, 182; on life in Madrid, 198–9; reception, 299–300; writing, 299

Jack, Martin, 210
Jamaica: WB's family in, 25–6; WB's legal dispute in, 97–8, 119, 130, 140–1; WB sent to, 141–3; decline in sugar revenues, 235, 285
João I, King of Portugal, 218, 231, 233
João V, King of Portugal, 149, 169
João, Prince Regent of Portugal, 214, 220, 237, 300
Jones, Inigo, 28
José I, King of Portugal, 149–50
José, Dom, Prince of Brazil, 150, 162, 178, 180–1; death, 214
Joseph II, Emperor of Austria, 119
Journal (WB): as source, 1, 245; and WB's life in Portugal, 141, 145, 151, 154, 159–61, 165–7, 171, 174, 176, 179–83, 185–7, 214; on life in Madrid, 193, 195, 198, 200; spontaneity, 299
Julius Caesar (ship), 141, 144, 169
Junot, Marshal Andache, Grand Duke of Abrantes, 253–4

Keats, John, 4, 80, 83, 223–4, 227; *Endymion*, 293
Knight, Richard Payne, 114, 265

Lafões, 2nd Duke of, 150, 153, 162, 176
Lafões, Dona Henriqueta, Duchess of (*née* Marialva): relations with WB, 5, 153, 155, 158, 163, 175, 179; marriage to Lafões, 176
La Mothe, Muller de, 209
Lane, Joseph, 33–6, 61–2, 265
Lane, Josiah, 33–5, 265
Lansdown Crescent, Bath, 7, 14, 222, 279, 287–92; tower, 289–90, 293, 298, 302
Lansdown, Henry Venn: visits WB, 6–18, 280, 291–2, 298; writes WB's obituary, 16; visits and tours Fonthill after WB's death, 19–23, 52, 60, 268; on WB's influence, 24; on WB's fitness, 75; on WB's servants, 263; admires WB's *Italy*, 300; *Recollections of the Late William Beckford*, 5
Larsonneur (French architect), 248
Lausanne, 138–9, 209, 211, 248
La Vauguyon, General Antoine Paul Jacques de Quelen de Caussade, duc de, 196
Lawrence, Thomas, 230
Le Coultre, Abraham, 69
Ledoux, Claude Nicolas, 125
Lee Priory, Kent, 227, 231
Lees-Milne, James: *William Beckford*, 3
Le Keux, John, 234
Lettice, Revd John: tutors WB, 38–40, 47, 49, 80; accompanies WB to Switzerland, 55, 59, 70, 72–3; tours England with WB, 84; on Grand Tour with WB, 89, 91–2, 100; Henley displaces, 114; accompanies WB on second trip to Italy, 119–20; translates *Vathek* into English, 120; advises WB over Courtenay scandal, 128; joins WB in Switzerland, 132–4; marriage, 134, 140; letters from WB proposing settling in America, 142; plants Fonthill Park pleasure grounds, 219; and WB's daughters, 219, 235
Liber Veritatis (WB), 293
Life at Fonthill 1807–1822 (WB; letters), 146
Lima, Jeronimo de, 180
Lincoln, Henry Fiennes Clinton, 9th Earl of, 175, 245
Lisbon: Belém tower, 52–3; WB visits, 144, 146–8, 150–67, 171–2, 219; WB builds town house in, 214–15; WB's final visit to, 237; *see also* Portugal
Listenais, Marie Antoinette Quelen de la Vauguyon, Princesse de, 191, 196–7
Listenais, Prince de, 195–7
Liston, (Sir) Robert, 195
London Magazine, 12
Long Story, The (WB) *see* 'Centrical History, The'
Loughborough, Alexander Wedderburn, 1st Baron (*later* 1st Earl of Rosslyn): marriage, 101, 107; and scandal over young Courtenay,

Index

Index

Index

Rousseau, Jean-Jacques, 60, 91
Ruskin, John, 92–3
Rutter, John, 34, 223, 271, 283; *Delineations*, 255, 266–8; *A Description of Fonthill Abbey and Demesne*, 283

Salève (mountain, Switzerland), 64–5, 76, 139
Salisbury and Winchester Journal, 233
Sandomil, Luis de Miranda, Count, 181
Santa Cruz, Marchioness of, 194, 197–8
Santerre, Antoine Joseph, 212
São Caetano, Fr Inacio, Archbishop, 149–50, 176, 180–2, 214
'Satyr's Range' (prose-poem; WB), 81–4
Saunders (tight-rope walker), 251–2
Sauvage, J.P., 275
Savoy: France invades, 210–11
Selwyn, George, 117, 119
Seymour, Georgina, 100, 104, 117
Shelley, Percy Bysshe, 241; *Queen Mab*, 293
Sill, Betty *see* Bezerra, Betty
Sill, Mr (of Lisbon), 147
Sintra, Portugal, 168, 169–79, 219, 255
Smirke, Robert, 230
Smith, 'Warwick', 261–2
Soane, Sir John, 50, 165, 198
Somerset, Edward Adolphus Seymour, 11th Duke of, 270
Sousa, Teles de (Lisbon Conservador), 166–7
Spain: relations with Portugal, 148–50; WB visits, 191–6; conditions, 193–4; France occupies, 253; risings against France, 254
Spizier, Karl, 210
Sterne, Laurence, 66
Stewart, Lady Euphemia, 50, 56, 123–4, 132–3
Still, J.C., 246
Storer, James: *A Description of Fonthill Abbey, Wiltshire*, 257
Storr, Paul, 279
Stourhead, Wiltshire, 277
Strathavon, Alexander, Lord (*later* 5th Marquis of Huntly; WB's brother-in-law), 45, 208
Strawberry Hill, 160, 232, 270, 273, 278
Street Arriaga family, 170
Stuart, James ('Athenian'), 81
Swedenborg, Emmanuel, 63–4
Switzerland: WB in, 45, 47–9, 53, 55–78, 128–9, 131–4, 207–11; politics, 138–9; and French Revolution, 208–9; in Disraeli's *Contarini Fleming*, 297

Tancos, Marquis de, 158–9
Tavora, Marquis of, 149
Taylor (Courtenay's tutor), 126
Tenducci, Giusto, 108
Tennyson, Alfred, 1st Baron, 222–3, 284, 296

Thorpe, Father John, 44
Thurlow, Edward, 1st Baron, 50, 74, 105, 118–19, 123, 126, 128
Toledo, Archbishop of, 198–9
Tonioli, Girolamo, 108
Traitorous Correspondence Act (1793), 212
Travolta, John, 116
Turner, J.M.W., 233, 237, 239, 260, 281; *The Fifth Plague* (painting), 281
Twelfth Night festival (1797), 228–9, 234
Tylney, John, 2nd Earl of, 131

Valadier, Luigi, 44
Vardy, John, 28, 34
Vathek (WB): children sacrificed in, 2, 115, 118; qualities, 3–4, 71, 112, 135; English version, 13, 120, 122, 134–5; French version, 15, 120, 134, 136–7; writing of, 49, 103–4, 111, 115, 119–20, 122, 128, 135, 300; inspired by Fonthill Splendens tower, 51; youthfulness in, 62; early drafts, 70; Louisa Beckford portrayed in, 88; Caliph's power in, 91; casual violence in, 93; themes, 104, 109, 115–16, 122; and WB's social performances, 117–18; Huber's lost illustrations for, 122; publication, 123, 134–6; reception and reviews, 136–7; Elizabeth Hervey praises, 205, and Disraeli's *Alroy*, 299; *see also* 'Episodes of Vathek'
Velázquez, Diego: *Pope Innocent X* (painting), 280
Venice, 93–4, 98, 297
Verdeil, Dr François: relations with WB, 40, 136, 138, 140, 161, 188, 196, 207–8; Freemasonry, 61, 138–9, 209; retranslates *Vathek* into French, 136, 138; background, 138–9; accompanies WB abroad, 141; in Portugal with WB, 152, 155, 157–8, 161–2, 164, 173, 177, 179, 183, 185–9; in Spain, 196–7; practises in Paris, 207; and Drysdale, 208; and French Revolution, 208–9; in Switzerland, 208–9
Verdeil, François, junior, 138
Verdeil, Sophie Dufey (*née* Joly de Frey), 139
Vidal, Gore: *Myra Breckinridge*, 206
Villamayor, Madame de, 197
Villaneuva de Duero, Marquis de, 194
Vincent (WB's gardener) 14, 289, 291
Virgil, 95
Vision, The (WB) *see* 'Centrical History, The'
Voltaire, François Marie Arouet de, 59, 65, 91
Vulliamy, Benjamin Lewis, 279

Walcot, John, 240
Walmesley, Charles, Roman Catholic Bishop of Rama, 43